Emotional monasticism

Manchester University Press

artes liberales

Series Editors

Carrie E. Beneš, T. J. H. McCarthy, Stephen Mossman and Jochen Schenk

Artes Liberales aims to promote the study of the Middle Ages – broadly defined in geography and chronology – from a perspective that transcends modern disciplinary divisions. It seeks to publish scholarship of the highest quality that is interdisciplinary in topic or approach, integrating elements such as history, art history, musicology, literature, religion, political thought, philosophy and science. The series particularly seeks to support research based on the study of original manuscripts and archival sources, and to provide a recognised venue for increased exposure for scholars at all career stages around the world.

Previously published
Writing the Welsh borderlands in Anglo-Saxon England
Lindy Brady

Justice and mercy: Moral theology and the exercise of law in twelfth-century England
Philippa Byrne

Emotional monasticism

Affective piety in the eleventh-century monastery of John of Fécamp

Lauren Mancia

Manchester University Press

Copyright © Lauren Mancia 2019

The right of Lauren Mancia to be identified as the author of this work has been asserted by her in accordance with the Copyright, Designs and Patents Act 1988.

Published by Manchester University Press
Altrincham Street, Manchester M1 7JA
www.manchesteruniversitypress.co.uk

British Library Cataloguing-in-Publication Data
A catalogue record for this book is available from the British Library

ISBN 978 1 5261 4020 3 hardback

First published 2019

The publisher has no responsibility for the persistence or accuracy of URLs for any external or third-party internet websites referred to in this book, and does not guarantee that any content on such websites is, or will remain, accurate or appropriate.

Typeset by Newgen Publishing UK
Printed in Great Britain
by TJ International Ltd, Padstow

To the CUNY students who strive, fight, and sacrifice: none of my grandparents had a college education. My parents were first-generation college students, too; my father at CUNY. This book, and the opportunities that I have had, are the fruits of their labour. Your perseverance will be worth it, too.

And to my female mentors and teachers, past and present, of all ages and professions: thank you for your advice, your encouragement, and (especially) your example.

Contents

List of figures and maps	page *viii*
Acknowledgements	*x*
Note on translations and editions	*xv*
List of abbreviations	*xvi*
Maps	*xviii*
Introduction	1
1 Reforming the reader's interior: defining emotional reform and affectivity in John of Fécamp's *Confessio theologica*	18
2 *Dicta mea sunt dicta patrum?*: tradition and innovation in John's *Confessio theologica*	46
3 Reforming the monastic community: the uses of John's devotional method within the walls of Fécamp	83
4 Reforming monks in the temporal world: John's devotional principles cultivated in the secular landscape	116
5 John's medieval legacy: the monastic roots of affective piety	154
Conclusion	191
Bibliography	*197*
Index	*259*

Figures and maps

Figures

1. An initial with the three Marys at the tomb (thirteenth century). Rouen, Bibliothèque municipale, ms. 245 (A190), fol. 120v. — *page* 88
2. Augustine triumphing over Faustus the Manichean (eleventh century). Paris, Bibliothèque nationale de France, ms. lat. 2079, fol. 1v. — 98
3. Athanasius triumphing over Arius (eleventh century). Paris, Bibliothèque nationale de France, ms. lat. 1684, fol. 1r. — 99
4. Apsidal vault mosaic from Sant'Apollinare in Classe, Ravenna (sixth century). Photo: Art Resource/SCALA. — 120
5. Sacrifices of Abel, Melchisedech, and Abraham mosaic from Sant'Apollinare in Classe, Ravenna (sixth century). Photo: Art Resource/SCALA. — 121
6. Tonsured monk before an enthroned Christ in a twelfth-century *Confessio theologica*. Barcelona, Archivo de la Corona de Aragón, Ripoll ms. 214, fol. 6v. — 171
7. Opening leaves of a twelfth-century *Confessio theologica*, with crucifix dating from twelfth century on the right and fourteenth-century Passion meditations on the left. Zwettl, Stiftsbibliothek, ms. lat. 164, fols 0v–1r. — 173
8. Christ wounded by the Sponsa in the fourteenth-century Rothschild Canticles, fols 18v–19r. Beinecke Rare Book and Manuscript Library, Yale University. — 175

9 Bernard and Augustine with Christ's 'darts of love' (thirteenth century). Paris, Bibliothèque nationale de France, ms. fr. 17115, fol. 156r. 178

Maps

1 John of Fécamp's life, network, and influence. xviii
2 A plan of the precinct of the monastery of Fécamp (including the ducal palace) as drawn in 1711. Rouen, Archives départementales de la Seine-Maritime, 7H49. xix

Acknowledgements

I first came across John of Fécamp's name in a footnote in the summer of 2009; since then, I have benefited from a tremendous amount of support for this project. Margot Fassler, Denys Turner, and Anders Winroth were there for the initial discovery, and helped me when this project was in its infancy. Susan Boynton, Fiona Griffiths, and particularly Paul Freedman provided essential advice as this project grew from adolescence into adulthood. Alongside Susan, several early mentors have rooted for me from the sidelines: I thank Carmela Franklin, Joel Kaye, Patricia Dailey, Consuelo Dutschke, Nancy Wu, Jennifer Harris, and Isabelle Cochelin for their encouragement and continued interest and investment in my scholarly growth.

I spent large parts of 2010, 2012, and 2013 performing research in Europe with the support of a Fulbright grant to France; an Etienne Gilson Dissertation Grant from the Medieval Academy of America; a John B. and Theta H. Wolf Travel Grant from the Society for French Historical Studies; an Elizabeth Ann Bogert Fund for the Study and Practice of Christian Mysticism, and travel grants from *Medium Aevum*, the National Organization for Italian American Women, the Yale MacMillan Center, and the PSC-CUNY Research Fund. I would like to thank the librarians and archivists at the Archives départementales in Rouen and Calvados, the Institut de recherche et d'histoire des textes in Paris, the Médiathèque de Metz, the Biblioteca Apostolica Vaticana, the Stiftsbibliothek Zwettl, the Staatsbibliothek in Berlin, the Burgerbibliothek in Bern, the Bibliothèque universitaire de médecine in Montpellier, the Österreichische Nationalbibliothek in Vienna, the Cathedral Library in Salisbury, the Bayerische Staatsbibliothek in Munich, the Cambridge University Library, the Fitzwilliam Museum Library, and the Walters Art Gallery in Baltimore,

Acknowledgements

MD. Extra-special thanks to the librarians at the Bibliothèque nationale de France (especially Charlotte Denoël) and the Bibliothèque municipale de Rouen (especially Brigitte Quignard and Claudine Brabetz), where I spent most of my days; and to Sébastien Roncin, archivist at the Palais Bénédictine in Fécamp. Florence Leclerc and especially Azélina Jaboulet-Vercherre helped me with the uniquely formal style of correspondence required to communicate with foreign libraries and scholars. Back home, Sue Roberts, Emily Honing, and Lidia Uziel at the Yale University Library and Michael Carter at The Cloisters Library purchased books or microfilms that I requested, and the Interlibrary Loan Department at the Brooklyn College Library procured articles and books that I needed in record time and in great quantities. Last, but by no means least, I'd like to thank the series editors of *Artes Liberales*; the team at Manchester University Press; the anonymous readers of my manuscript; my copy editor Christopher Feeney; Zeba Talkhani for spearheading the book's production; and Emma Brennan, Thomas McCarthy, Alun Richards, and Meredith Carroll for shepherding this project to its conclusion. An extra-special thanks to Thomas, who went above and beyond the role of series editor and drew Map 1. Parts of Chapter 3 appeared as an article, 'John of Fécamp and Affective Reform in Eleventh-Century Normandy', in *Anglo-Norman Studies* 37 (June 2015): 161–79, here reprinted by permission of Boydell & Brewer.

Over the years, my work on Fécamp has benefited from the sound advice and expertise of many interlocutors. Many thanks for the questions and comments that I received from scholarly audiences at invited lectures, seminars, conferences, and colloquia at venues ranging from New York to Kalamazoo, Montréal to Ghent, Baltimore to Caen. Particular gratitude goes to Jonathan J. G. Alexander, François Avril, David Bates, Michaël Bloche, Katrin Brockhaus, Greg Bryda, Katie Bugyis, Sarah Ifft Decker, François Dolbeau, Cédric Giraud, Alexis Grélois, Catherine Letouzey, Jacques Le Maho, Carolyn Marino Malone, Clare Monagle, Laurent Morelle, Karl Morrison, Michel Parisse, Peter Potter, Cassandra Potts, Diane Reilly, Greg Roberts, Edward Schoolman, Ourdia Siab, Tjamke Snijders, David Spear, Patricia Stirnemann, Lucile Tran-Duc, Steven Vanderputten, Anne Wagner, and Teresa Webber, who all pointed me towards sources, helped me work out ideas, and made necessary introductions. Marie-Thérèse Gousset visited me weekly in the Salle des Manuscrits at the Richelieu site of the Bibliothèque nationale in 2012 – without her substantial aid, encouragement, and advice, this book would not have been possible. Marcus Elder looked over my Latin translations and provided learned tweaks and sage advice. Monique Peyrafort and especially Stéphane Lecouteux spent hours

Acknowledgements

and hours with me gleefully making connections between the library of Fécamp, the network of Norman monasteries, and the ideas of John – our conversations have taught me what scholarly community can be. Jean-François Cottier, Véronique Gazeau, Fiona Griffiths, Liesbeth van Houts, Barbara Rosenwein, and especially Piroska Nagy have been beyond generous with their time, energy, enthusiasm, and support for the project and my career: I thank each of them with all my heart.

For the last six years, I have been fortunate enough to call Brooklyn College (CUNY) my home. New Faculty Release Time, several PSC-CUNY Research Fund Awards, Mini-Grants from the School of Humanities and Social Sciences, a Whiting Award for Teaching Excellence, and stipends from the Department of History have given me the time, research assistance, and subvention funds needed to complete this book manuscript. But more than these, the debts of gratitude that I owe to my colleagues at Brooklyn College is tremendous. First thanks go to my department chairs over the years, David Troyansky, Christopher Ebert, and Gunja SenGupta, whose advice, shelter, and support has been unflagging. Anne Ciarlo and Lorraine Greenfield have been supportive and resourceful beyond imagining. The collegiality of my fellow historians at Brooklyn College, and that of Brigid O'Keeffe, Karen Stern, and Jocelyn Wills in particular, has nourished me on a regular basis: to them all I am deeply appreciative. An extra-special thanks goes to the incredible faculty in the Late Antique-Medieval-Early Modern (LAMEM) reading group at Brooklyn College, especially Andrew Arlig, Jennifer Ball, David Brodsky, Bilal Ibrahim, Nicola Masciandaro, Andy Meyer, and Karl Steel, whose company I am so honoured to be keeping. To my colleagues, mentors, and academic friends around (or once around) NYC, especially Susan Boynton, Peggy Brown, Bob Davis, Meredith Fluke Davis, Jay Diehl, Thomas Dodman, Julia Fawcett, Arnold Franklin, Fiona Griffiths, Sara Lipton, Sara McDougall, Christia Mercer, Sarah Novacich, Janine Peterson, Ellen Rentz, Christine Sciacca, Neslihan Şenocak, Andrew Romig, and Abigail Zitin: thank you so much for your time, truth, encouragement, humour, and advocacy. A Kurz Research Assistantship for my student Laurence Bond helped me to complete the research required for Chapter 4, and Laurence's enthusiasm for things medieval reminded me why I got into all of this in the first place. Finally, the brilliance and wonder of my Brooklyn College students has brought me a joy that I never thought I'd find in the halls of academia; their commitment to learning fills my soul, grants me perspective, and keeps me going daily: this book, in part, is for them.

This book was born with a tremendous amount of personal, intellectual, emotional, and practical support. I am privileged to have been able

Acknowledgements

to have Laura Avelar, Valentina 'Titi' Ramos, John 'Papa' Gidwitz, Linda 'Gaga' Boyd, and especially Guadalupe 'O-O' Montiel, among others, to care for my daughter so that my husband and I could work. Inge Bloom and especially Lisa Weiser helped me wrestle with thoughts that got in the way of my progress. Treasured non-medievalist friends and family travelled with me to monasteries, tolerated my visits to museums and discussions of religious arcana, forced me to see the glass as half-full when I could not, and helped me in general to take myself less seriously: special shout-outs go to Nicole Bryant, Julia Kelly and Phil Coakley, Brandon Woolf and Tina Petereit, Zachary and Pai Pai Gidwitz, Bill Fertik, and Julian Mancia; and extra-special hugs are for Raquel Otheguy and John Pierpont. The model of M. Danielle Savasta (the first college degree – from CUNY – and the first PhD in my Italian immigrant family), and the love of Leela Savasta, Rose and Joe Savasta, Leonard and Lucille Mancia and my extended family has guided me through this process, both in presence and in spirit. Patricia Lewy's determined support, playful spirit, intellectual engagement, grandmothering, and editing prowess has been essential. John and Linda Mancia planted the academic seedlings that bore fruit in my career, and their model, their teaching, and their love has provided the grounding and support that has been key to my success: it is only now that I am a parent that I can truly appreciate all they have given to me. Ellie Rose's arrival transformed my life and gave this project fuel in unexpected ways, allowing me to grow in confidence and to learn to enjoy the writing process; I look forward to the day when I can share 'stories' of the medieval world with her, and hear what she has to say about them.

A huge debt of gratitude is due to my husband, Adam Gidwitz. I met Adam in Paul Strohm's Chaucer seminar at Columbia in fall 2003. I had anticipated taking the course for a whole year in advance, and had gotten there early on the first day to get a seat right up front; Adam stumbled into the classroom late and on a whim, looking to fulfil his English major's medieval requirement. Our relationship endured his getting an A+ in that class (while I got an A-), and the medieval world has made us partners in unexpected ways for the last fifteen years. With him as my travel companion, I have made historical discoveries, braved historical archives, journeyed to far-flung places, and gone on medieval scavenger hunts. With the help of his brilliance, interlocution, listening, and editing, I have grown as a writer, a thinker, and a person. His belief in this project, and in me, has allowed me to get this far – I am so profoundly thankful for him.

I have been lucky enough to have had the support and inspiration of so many wonderful teachers and mentors over the years. But, at the end of

Acknowledgements

the day, it was the presence of women – mentors, teachers, idols, friends, colleagues – that gave me the strength I needed to keep going with my larger academic project. In their generosity, experience, and encouragement, they spoke my language and genuinely nurtured the confidence I needed to find myself as a scholar. I am thankful for their time, their stories, their advocacy, their path-breaking, and their reassurance, and I look forward to fighting alongside them to make our future world as filled with the voices of women as it possibly can be.

Lauren Mancia
Brooklyn, New York
September 2018

Note on translations and editions

The English translations contained herein are my own unless otherwise noted. My translations of the chief work examined here, John of Fécamp's *Confessio theologica*, are taken from the Latin edition of the *CT* cited in the list of abbreviations, below, unless otherwise indicated. All biblical quotations in English are taken from the Douay-Rheims translation of the Bible; biblical quotations in Latin are taken from the Vulgate edition of the Bible; and the Psalm numbering system used in this book is that of the Vulgate. All quotations from Augustine's *Confessions* are taken from the edition and translation by Henry Chadwick (New York: Oxford University Press, 1991); all quotations from Anselm of Canterbury's *Prayers and Meditations* are taken from the edition and translation by Benedicta Ward (New York: Penguin, 1973).

Abbreviations

Anselm	Anselm of Canterbury, *The Prayers and Meditations of Saint Anselm with the Proslogion*, trans. Benedicta Ward (New York: Penguin, 1973)
BHL	*Bibliotheca hagiographica latina antiquae et mediae aetatis*, 2 vols (Brussels, 1898–1901), with supplements in 1911 and 1986
BM	Bibliothèque municipale
BnF	Bibliothèque nationale de France
Chadd	David Chadd (ed.), *The Ordinal of the Abbey of the Holy Trinity Fécamp (Fécamp, Musée de la Bénédictine, Ms 186)*, 2 vols (London: Henry Bradshaw Society, 1999); edited from Fécamp, Musée Bénédictine, ms. 186
CT	*Confessio theologica* text from Jean Leclercq and Jean-Paul Bonnes (eds), *Un maître de la vie spirituelle au XIe siècle: Jean de Fécamp* (Paris: Vrin, 1946)
Faur	Marie Fauroux, *Recueil des actes des ducs de Normandie (911–1066)* (Caen: Société d'Impressions CARON, 1961)
Gazeau	Véronique Gazeau, *Normannia monastica: Prosopographie des abbés bénédictines* (Caen: CRAHM, 2007)
Glaber	Rodulfus Glaber, *Rodulfi Glabri opera*, trans. John France and Paul Reynolds (Oxford: Clarendon Press, 1989)
MGH	*Monumenta Germaniae Historica* (Hanover, 1826–)
Mor	Gregory the Great's *Moralia in Job*

List of abbreviations

Nortier	Geneviève Nortier, *Les bibliothèques médiévales des abbayes bénédictines de Normandie* (Paris: Paul Lethielleux, 1971)
Paris	Paris, Bibliothèque nationale de France, ms. lat.
PG	*Patrologia cursus completus, series graeca*, ed. Jacques-Paul Migne, 161 vols (Paris, 1857–66)
PL	*Patrologia cursus completus, series latina*, ed. Jacques-Paul Migne, 221 vols (Paris, 1844–88)
RB	Benedict of Nursia, *Rule of St. Benedict*, trans. Bruce Venarde (Cambridge, MA: Harvard University Press, 2011)
Scriptura	François Dolbeau, 'Passion et résurrection du Christ, selon Gerbert, abbé de Saint-Wandrille (d. 1089)', in Michael W. Herren, C.J. McDonough and Ross G. Arthur (eds), *Latin Culture in the Eleventh Century* (Turnhout: Brepols, 2002), pp. 223–49.
Zwettl	Zwettl, Stiftsbibliothek, Cod.

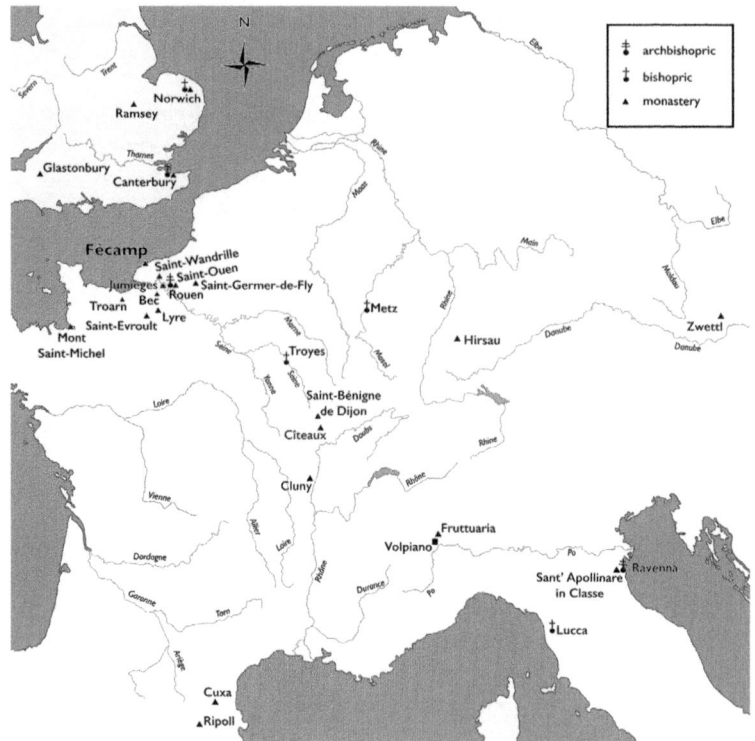

Map 1: John of Fécamp's life, network, and influence

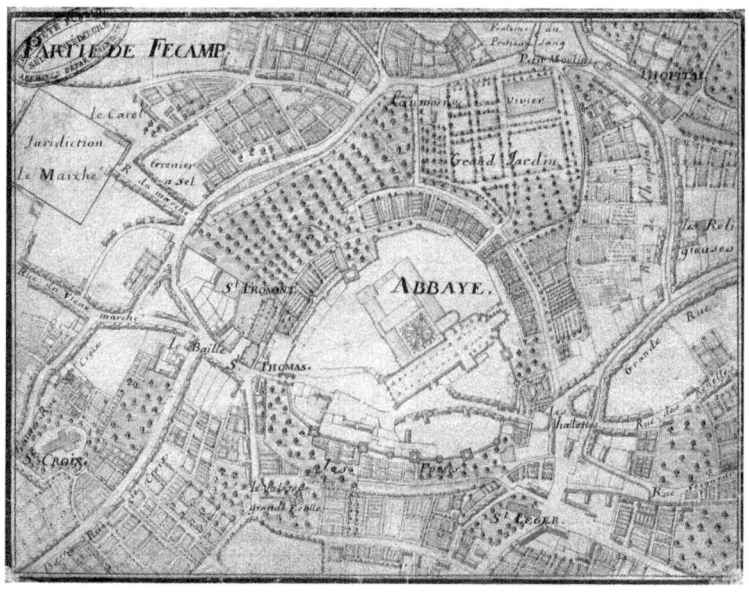

Map 2: A plan of the precinct of the monastery of Fécamp (including the ducal palace) as drawn in 1711

Introduction

Through those saving wounds which you suffered on the cross for our salvation and from which flowed precious and vivifying blood ... wound this sinful soul of mine for which you were willing even to die; wound it with the fiery and powerful dart of your excessive compassion. You are the living Word of God, efficacious and more piercing than every sharpest sword. You, double-edged sword, cleave my hardness of heart and wound this sinful soul, and pierce more deeply into the inmost parts with your powerful virtue. Give me an abundant source of water and pour into my eyes a true font of tears running day and night out of excessive feeling and desire for the vision of your beauty, so that I may grieve constantly all the days of my life, taking no consolation in the present life, until I merit to see you, my God and my Lord, as a beloved and beautiful spouse in your heavenly chamber.[1]

For many years, scholars believed that this prayer excerpt was written in the fourteenth century.[2] The misattribution is understandable. First, the prayer was transmitted with the Pseudo-Augustinian collection of the *Meditations of St Augustine*, which enjoyed a formidable circulation in the Late Middle Ages.[3] Second, the prayer approaches God in a way commonly associated with late medieval devotion to the crucified Christ: a more human God, suffering on the cross, body wounded and bloody.[4] The dramatic presentation of the crucified body was typical of late medieval Christian prayer, as was the tearful compassion prescribed.[5] As a result, this prayer has been regularly used to uphold the narrative that a so-called 'affective' approach to God was an artefact of the post-twelfth-century, post-Anselm of Canterbury period, that is, of the Cistercian, Franciscan, lay, and female devotional contexts of the High and Late Middle Ages.[6]

In the 1930s, however, André Wilmart identified this prayer as the work of John of Fécamp, the second abbot of the newly reformed Norman monastery of Fécamp, who lived between c. 990 and 1078.[7] In fact, Wilmart attributed four prayers from the *Meditations of St Augustine* to John, noting that they were part of a much larger treatise, posthumously called John's *Confessio theologica* (Theological Confession), which was likely written between 1023 and 1028, fifty years before Anselm of Canterbury's more famous affective prayers.[8] Since Wilmart's reattribution, several scholars have characterised John as the earliest medieval writer prescribing 'affective' devotion.[9] And so while John's interest in the graphic, suffering body of Christ in his *Confessio theologica*, and his commitment to drawing parallels between the sufferings of the sinner and his God, resonated tremendously with the late medieval audience (an audience hungry for the affective writings of Anselm, Aelred of Rievaulx, Francis, Thomas à Kempis, and Ludolphus of Saxony), John did not compose his prayers with that late medieval audience in mind. He instead wrote his treatise for an audience of traditional, eleventh-century monks, whose use for such affective piety remains heretofore unexplored.[10]

This book examines the role of affective devotion in the eleventh-century male monastic context through the lens of John of Fécamp and the devotional culture of his monastery. It also works to understand John's ideas, his ingenuity, his reception among his peers, and the use, application, and legacy of his kind of emotional devotion. It will fill four lacunae in the scholarship. First, John of Fécamp was an important eleventh-century abbot – it was from his monastery that William the Conqueror launched his ships in 1066 – and yet this will be the first book since the *Confessio theologica*'s 1946 edition to systematically examine his work, and the only full-length study ever to situate his writings in a wider devotional and historical context. Second, John is part of a lineage of famous tenth- and eleventh-century reform abbots, including several from the Ravenna, Cluniac, and Gorze reform movements. Yet few scholars have reflected on the reform aspects of John's agenda, and none have discussed the contemplative, affective, interior components of these eleventh-century monastic reform movements; this study will reveal how, alongside regulating observance, customs, and liturgy, eleventh-century monastic reformers attempted to transform the inner emotional lives of their brethren. Third, on a broader level, this book will offer one of the only in-depth expositions of the affective devotional lives of traditional, often called 'Benedictine',[11] monks, known more for their presumed adherence to unfeeling, blind, communal ritual than for their emphasis on an individual, affective relationship with God. And finally, on its broadest

Introduction

level, as a study of the earliest manifestations of affective piety, this book will recalibrate our understanding of the roots of later medieval spirituality.

John and his monastery of Fécamp

The monastery of Fécamp had been originally established in 658, but was refounded as the Holy Trinity Abbey of Fécamp (*Abbaye de la Trinité de Fécamp* or *Monasterium Sanctae Trinitatis Fiscannensis*) in 1001 by an Italian reforming abbot named William of Volpiano at the behest of Duke Richard II of Normandy.[12] John of Fécamp was born between 990 and 995 in Ravenna, Italy, and lived there until he followed his teacher, William of Volpiano, to the Burgundian monastery of Saint-Bénigne de Dijon (where John was a monk under William) and then to the newly reformed monastery of Fécamp (where John was prior under William).[13] While prior at Fécamp, John wrote his *Confessio theologica* sometime between 1023 and 1028. Once he became abbot at Fécamp in 1028, John revised this treatise two times: once, by 1030, creating the *Libellus de scripturis et verbis patrum collectus ad eorum presertim utilitatem qui contemplativae vitae sunt amatores* (Little Book of Extracts from the Scriptures and Words of the Fathers, Especially Useful for Those Who are Lovers of Contemplation) recension, and once, around 1050, creating the so-called *Confessio fidei* (Confession of Faith) recension. Thus, instead of writing diverse works over the course of his life (like his Norman colleague Anselm of Canterbury), John created a single major life's work, the *Confessio theologica*, and revisited it over the course of his abbacy. During his time as abbot, John built up the library of Fécamp by eighty volumes or more; he travelled to Rome around 1050, perhaps as legate to Pope Leo IX; he served as abbot of Saint-Bénigne de Dijon from 1052 to 1044 simultaneously with his abbacy at Fécamp; he visited Fécamp's possessions in England in 1054, likely bringing his brand of piety to that region;[14] he allowed Fécamp to serve as the launch site for William the Conqueror's ships in 1066;[15] and he substantially increased the economic prosperity of his monastery and its ties to the noble families around Normandy.[16] John died on 22 February 1078, having served as Fécamp's prior and abbot for fifty-five combined years, and having left behind substantial evidence of the life of his monastery under his leadership.

John of Fécamp provides us with an unparalleled case study of the earliest moments of affective devotion in the eleventh-century monastic context. Along with three recensions of John's *Confessio theologica* and additional fragments of writings from John, there survive from his fifty-five years as prior and abbot of the monastery of Fécamp library lists, charters, letters, liturgical texts, and over eighty other manuscripts. The Fécamp charters have been compiled;[17] the monastery's proposed exemption has been interrogated;[18] its manuscripts have been identified;[19] their palaeography has been studied;[20] the liturgical texts have been partially edited;[21] the Fécamp relics, archaeology, and church space have been examined;[22] and John's *Confessio theologica* has been analysed.[23] But this study is the first to use the wealth of the Fécamp sources to create a holistic picture of the production, the reception, the use, and the immediate legacy of John of Fécamp's landmark work, the *Confessio theologica*.[24]

Fécamp as evidence of emotional monasticism

A study of John of Fécamp's *Confessio theologica* and its place in his monastery's devotional culture provides information about the oft-forgotten emotional, interior aspects of monastic reform in traditional monastic houses in the central medieval period. Historically, scholarship on monastic reform in the central Middle Ages (sometimes called the 'Gregorian Reform' or 'Benedictine Reform') has characterised reform as stemming from an *externally* regulating spirit: a desire to reform economic organisation, liturgical readings, ecclesiastical organisation, legislation, monastic customs and routine, and the monastery's dealings with property and relationship with its patrons.[25] In the last few years, scholars have rightly been reconsidering what we mean by 'reform'.[26] But this reassessment has yet to question the internal character of eleventh-century 'Benedictine' monastic reform. Reform to these scholars remains an external process, while the internal and spiritual dimensions of these reforms remain unexplored.[27]

While John, like William, enforced orthodox external practices and combated unorthodox behaviours in the Norman monastic world, he also elaborated on these ideas of orthodoxy by extending his attentions into the inner workings of a monk's mind and soul.[28] His was an emotional, spiritual reform. The characterisation of John as an *emotional* reformer thus works to erode the lingering idea that a 'crisis of coenobitism' overtook the medieval monastic landscape in the eleventh century, in need of an affective dimension.[29] While this idea has long been refuted, the residue of that past remains.[30] Scholarship on Bernard of Clairvaux, for instance, continues to emphasise the revolutionary nature of Bernard's reforms, distinguishing him from the monks who came before by highlighting the 'originality' of his regard for the inner heart and emotion.[31] Even studies of traditional monasticism in the earlier Middle Ages largely neglect focusing on monks as contemplatives interested in interior investigations,[32] more interested in

Introduction

the monks' lay and religious networks, or in their concerns for their lay patron's soul, than in the devotional practices of the monastic worshippers themselves.[33] Scholars persist in characterising charismatic monks who fostered a direct connection with God as *violators* of monastic ritual behaviour, implying that traditional monastic life was antithetical to such an affective connection.[34] This book will banish this old idea of traditional monastic devotion as mechanised and communal as opposed to heart-felt and interior; it will instead argue that even ritual repetition at the monastery served to cultivate an embodied disposition (a *habitus*) that attempted to engender more sincere feeling.[35] John of Fécamp's writings, monastic context, and students prove that an interior connection with God was desired by and intended for traditional monks in the eleventh century.

When the picture of traditional monasticism transforms into a more emotionally alive one, where monks sought emotional connection with God by many different and innovative means, the narrative of the development of medieval Christianity is transformed. Such emotional inwardness has been habitually characterised by medievalists of all kinds (historians, art historians, and literary scholars alike) as a 'self-awareness' or 'individuality' only cultivated in the world outside of the monastery or after the eleventh century. It has been traditionally seen as a feature of the later Middle Ages, the world of chivalric vernacular literature, of dialectical arguments in the cathedral schools and universities, of romance and autobiography.[36] Part of this is because of an anachronistic conception of individuality: to certain scholars, individual religious quests seemed to be possible only outside of a community's control; on the monastic spectrum, therefore, individualism could only be found in eremitic monasticism, which critiqued the coenobitic 'ritualism, the rigidity for the sake of unity, and the interminable *laus perennis* (perennial praise)'.[37] Blinded by modern conceptions of the self,[38] scholars have been resistant to the notion that inner penance could have been located in the mechanisms and structures of coenobitic life, apparently antithetical to introspection.[39] According to this line of thinking, in order to be truly 'passionate and introspective', monastic prayers needed to be 'outside the framework of the established liturgy', because only then could they 'become more personal'.[40]

Some studies on *lectio divina* (divine reading) in the monastery have worked against this anachronism, following the idea that, since Augustine, medieval Christianity and monasticism cultivated 'self-conscious reader[s]'.[41] To Augustine and others, the medieval 'self' was contingent upon knowledge of God – as Augustine says in his soliloquies, '*Noverim me, noverim te*' ('[To] let me know myself [is to] let me know you [God]').[42] But despite this newfound openness to the potential 'individualism' inherent in monastic practices of reading, many scholars maintain that traditional monasticism was 'constricting' to the individual[43] and insist the notion of 'inner life' is a phenomenon still best associated with later medieval private devotion.[44] Even John of Fécamp's interiority is seen by some scholars as a precocious exception rather than a part of a larger emotional culture in traditional monasticism.[45] This book will work to correct the record, showing how, a generation before Anselm, John, his brethren at Fécamp, and Christians under John's influence around Europe were striving to cultivate introspective prayer and an affective connection with God, fostering inner lives in their lived religious experience while simultaneously remaining members of an eleventh-century monastic community.[46]

Affective piety in the eleventh-century male monastery

In addition to changing the way we understand monastic interiority, John of Fécamp's example will complete our understanding of the development of medieval affective devotion. 'Affective piety' is a term that scholars often use without fully defining, usually in cases where devotion to the suffering Christ is involved, especially in cases of highly emotive piety from the post-twelfth-century period.[47] Generally considered one of the first medievalists to draw attention to this trend, R.W. Southern, in his classic work *The Making of the Middle Ages*, characterised this type of devotion in the following way: 'The theme of tenderness and compassion for the sufferings and helplessness of the Saviour ... opened up a new world of ardent emotion and piety.'[48] For Southern, this 'new world' began with Anselm of Canterbury. Others have followed Southern's model, locating the 'newness' of emotionality with various movements and people, usually all in the twelfth century, and usually all revolving around 'the pathos of Christ's suffering', 'the body of [the] tortured son ... [with] graphic depictions of the suffering body, depictions which are designed to stimulate an emotional response ... [which are] majestic [and yet] disfigured'.[49]

John's trailblazing affectivity does not conform to this definition, however. John's tearful, compassionate use of the suffering Christ was merely *a part* of his larger programme for proper contemplation of God. John confronts his reader with affective images of the crucified Christ only at a certain stage of his devotional process; they are not the only things that make John's contemplative method affective or unique. John is instead primarily concerned with affecting emotional devotion in his reader, using various tools, the suffering Christ merely one among them, to do so.

Introduction

Moreover, John does not embrace the image of the crucified Christ because he is showing his *humanity*, but instead because Christ's *suffering* allows him to be the best avatar for the suffering sinner. In this book, therefore, I will refer to John's type of devotion as 'affective', allowing my narrative to fit into the wider scholarly discourse; but, when I do, I will be referring to a kind of piety that does not neatly fit into 'affective piety' as it is commonly defined. Instead, I will define it as John did – as a programme of emotional openness in prayer not necessarily centred on the crucified Christ, but in fact on the Christian's awareness of his sinful self.

John spent his whole life defining his brand of piety through three recensions of the *Confessio theologica*. In this book, and Chapter 1 especially, I will focus on the affective terminology that John created, and on the mechanisms of affective experience that John laid out. In so doing, I have largely chosen to leave modern affect theory by the wayside. This is a conscious decision. Several scholars of medieval religion have embraced William Reddy's formulation of 'emotives'[50] as an appropriate label for the process of medieval contemplation, showing how medieval devotional emotion, when articulated, is both descriptive and performative, both encapsulating the emotion of religious experience and instigating it. Some medievalists, like Robert Glenn Davis, have rightly noted that this formulation is reductive, being 'in danger of collapsing into a simple notion of performance, wherein emotions become the means of exercising rational agency towards a determinate goal … for managing individual, collective, and political life'.[51] These medievalist-critics have found it helpful to instead engage instead with affect theory, which, following Gilles Deleuze and Brian Massumi, among others, distinguishes *affect* (feeling that is subliminal, visceral, intense, prepersonal, and beyond the limits of the cognitive) from *emotion* (affect that has been named, rationalised, signified, and made subjective).[52] There is an extent to which these theorists' privileging of affect is more appropriate to later medieval mystical contemplation, which aims to 'disrupt and transform' the 'cognizing and volitional self'.[53] In the case of John of Fécamp, however, feeling is very much cultivated both cognitively *and* emotionally, used as a tool to approach the divine in prayer. In fact, John does not believe that he is able to feel on his own – instead, he believes that *God* affects the deepest love and feelings he desires, and that the only way he can come close to earning God's most instinctual and 'pre-personal' affect (*affectus*) is if he forces himself to initiate emotional introspection. The distinction which affect theorists draw between cognition and intense visceral feeling, therefore, does not accurately represent John's understanding, nor does it represent the affective practices of his monastic context, which encouraged the use of intellectual engagement, ritual praxis, and emotional modelling to cultivate feeling.[54] Plus, John does not consistently use vocabulary that distinguishes 'affect' (*affectus*) from the 'passions' (*passiones*), or emotion from feeling.[55] In these ways, John certainly shows, as Barbara Rosenwein has noted repeatedly elsewhere, that the Middle Ages was not an unenlightened age of unbridled emotion, but was instead an age where emotion was very intentionally employed and cultivated, and where, at least in the monastery, it was seen as the highest virtue, a gift of God's grace.[56] But the best way to explain how John understood affectivity is to rely on *his* words, and not the words of modern affect theorists or historians of emotion, to describe the methodology for devotional feeling that he hoped to nurture in his *Confessio theologica*.

This book does not intend to provide a unicausal explanation for the emergence of affective piety in the medieval Christian landscape. I am not claiming that John or the traditional medieval monastery were originators of affective piety, nor am I claiming that John's monastery was unique in its affective practices. By showing how John's affective devotion was defined, what inspired it, how it was employed and disseminated, and what particularly monastic uses it had, I explore how affective piety worked in one of its earliest historical moments and contexts. This, in turn, may help us to better understand the motivations for its later medieval transformations, in addition, of course, to being of intrinsic interest in and of itself.

Chapter outline

To achieve the loftiest aims of this study, we must venture through the nitty-gritty details of John of Fécamp's text, of his monastic context, and of his devotional legacy.

The first chapter of this book provides the foundation for the subsequent ones. In it, I analyse John's *Confessio theologica*. I sketch out the stages of John's devotional prescriptions, defining his goals for his monastic reader, his requirements for achieving inwardness, his use of affectivity and emotion, and his reliance on the models of the suffering Christ, the crying Mary Magdalene, and the prayerful Hannah. Along with providing this exposition, valuable in and of itself in how it clarifies John of Fécamp's ideas and reveals the full scope of a text – his *Confessio theologica* – that has been principally understood through its excerpts elsewhere, Chapter 1 also provides the battery of themes, metaphors, and vocabulary that John uses, defining the ideas that then undergird the rest of my study.

Introduction

In the second chapter, I address what about John's *Confessio theologica* is new and innovative, and what about it was drawn from traditional (or earlier but not so traditional) sources. To better establish John's inheritance, I survey the eleventh-century library at Fécamp, and I focus on John's childhood influences from Ravenna, from Cluny (via Ravenna and Saint-Bénigne de Dijon), and from John's mentor, William of Volpiano. I work to show that classic texts, such as those by Gregory the Great, use affective devotion, demonstrating that affective prayer was never quite as foreign to the early monastic mind as some medievalists might believe. Establishing John's sources will show the extent to which the *Confessio theologica* emanates from the larger monastic context as well as from his own personal history, and also how much was new about John and his work – his interest in the affective parallels between the crucified Christ and the suffering Christian, the committed intensity of his longing for the divine, and his codifying and reforming of the emotional process of a Christian's prayerful approach to God.

Chapter 3 explores how John's devotional philosophy in the *Confessio theologica* – particularly its emotional reform priorities – was present in the religious culture at his monastery. I will show that John's affective ideas were present in the liturgical ceremonies, homilies, books, and letters that comprised his monastery's devotional culture. I will then explore the complex relationship between emotional reform and monastic discipline, as such affective rhetoric seems to have played this dual role at Fécamp.

In the fourth chapter, I demonstrate that John's teachings on emotional reform were not confined to his monastic community at Fécamp; they also motivated his involvement with church-wide reform initiatives led by the papacy, and, perhaps surprisingly, coloured his interactions with the secular world. As the abbot of the most prominent abbey in Normandy, John wrote against heresy at the behest of the pope, criticised bishops' infringement on abbatial rights, wrote letters of spiritual advice to fellow monks and holy women, and regularly interacted with the lay lords and dukes of Normandy. This chapter shows how John's prayerful efforts were not restricted to contemplation inside the monastery, but were also connected by John to his wider institutional responsibilities, thereby influencing his use and experience of his political, social, and economic actions as abbot.

The final chapter examines John's legacy after his death, both at Fécamp and in the wider medieval landscape. I first show how John's students and direct inheritors elaborated on the devotional seeds that John's *Confessio theologica* planted: a cult to the Precious Blood of Christ was established at Fécamp; John's students Maurilius of Rouen and Gerbert of Saint-Wandrille wrote affective prayers to a crucified Christ; Guibert of Nogent, a Norman monk, wrote his own memoir in the style of Augustine's *Confessions* after John; and, most famously, Anselm of Bec wrote his prayers and meditations, following in the steps of the greatest Norman abbot of the generation before him, John of Fécamp. The chapter moves on to examine how certain concepts embraced by John changed in the hands of Cistercians. It concludes by discussing how John's *Confessio theologica* circulated in the later Middle Ages, often attributed in manuscripts to Anselm or Bernard or Augustine, and considered by later medievals to be a part of their type of affective devotion.

Through the lens of a single abbot whose life spanned the course of the eleventh century, and a single monastic foundation whose devotional culture evidenced some of the earliest instances of affective piety, we will see how traditional monks embraced emotional devotion a generation before Anselm of Canterbury. We will observe the inner workings of eleventh-century monastic prayer practices and note their implications. We will witness how monastic reform slowly transformed monks' livelihood through both external regulations and internal devotional practices. We will understand the extent to which monks actively shaped their religious emotions through their worldly actions so that they could have fuller, more intimate relationships with their God. And, hopefully, we will alter the scholarly narrative, reclaiming the monk as a feeling, prayerful creature, affective piety as an early medieval monastic practice, and John of Fécamp as one of the most important touchstones for eleventh-century monasticism and Christian devotion.

Notes

1 '*per illa salutifera vulnera tua, quae passus es in cruce pro salute nostra, ex quibus emanavit ille pretiosus et vivificus sanguis … vulnera hanc animam peccatricem, pro qua etiam mori dignatus es; vulnera eam igneo et potentissimo telo tuae nimiae charitatis. Vivus es, sermo Dei, et efficax et penetrabilior omni acutissimo gladio. Tu gladius bis acute cordis duritiam scinde, et vulnera hanc animam peccatricem, atque altius penetra ad intima potenti virtute, et sic da capiti meo aquam immensam, oculisque meis verum lacrimarum fontem nocte ac die currentem infunde ex nimio affectu et desiderio visionis pulchritudinis tuae, ut lugeam iugiter cunctis diebus vitae meae, nullam in praesenti vita recipiens consolationem, donec te in caelesti thalamo merear videre dilectum et pulcherrimum sponsum Deum et Dominum meum*' (*CT*, pp. 180–1).
2 *Meditations of Saint Augustine*, trans. Matthew J. O'Connell (Villanova, PA: Augustinian Press, 1995), pp. 9–20; André Wilmart, *Auteurs spirituels et textes dévots du moyen âge latin* (Paris: Librarie Bloud et Gay, 1932), pp. 173, 175, 178;

Introduction

André Wilmart, 'Formes successives ou parallèles des "Meditations de Saint Augustin"', *Revue d'ascétique et de mystique* 68 (1936), 337–57; Jean Leclercq and Jean-Paul Bonnes, *Un maître de la vie spirituelle au XIe siècle* (Paris: Vrin, 1946), pp. 13–50; Thomas H. Bestul (ed.), *A Durham Book of Devotions* (Toronto: Pontifical Institute of Mediaeval Studies, 1987), pp. 1–18.

3 For more on John's circulation in the Late Middle Ages, see Stephen A. Hurlbut, *The Picture of the Heavenly Jerusalem in the Writings of Johannes of Fécamp, De Contemplativa Vita, and in the Elizabethan Hymns* (Washington, DC: St. Alban's Press, 1943); see also Chapter 5, below.

4 Thomas H. Bestul, *Texts of the Passion: Latin Devotional Literature and Medieval Society* (Philadelphia: University of Pennsylvania Press, 1996), pp. 26–38; Rachel Fulton, *From Judgment to Passion: Devotion to Christ and the Virgin Mary, 800–1200* (New York: Columbia University Press, 2002), pp. 1–192; Ewert Cousins, 'The Humanity and Passion of Christ', in Jill Raitt, Bernard McGuinn, and John Meyendorff (eds), *Christian Spirituality: High Middle Ages and Reformation* (New York: Crossroad, 1987), pp. 375–91.

5 Marlene Villalobos Hennessy, 'Passion Devotion, Penitential Reading, and the Manuscript Page: "The Hours of the Cross" in London, British Library Additional 37049', *Mediaeval Studies* 66 (2004), 216; Bestul, *Texts of the Passion*, p. 37.

6 Bestul, *Texts of the Passion*, pp. 36–8; Sarah McNamer, *Affective Meditation and the Invention of Medieval Compassion* (Philadelphia: University of Pennsylvania Press, 2010), pp. 58–85; Anne Derbes, *Picturing the Passion in Late Medieval Italy* (New York: Cambridge University Press, 1996), pp. 1–11; A.S. Lazikani, *Cultivating the Heart: Feeling and Emotion in Twelfth- and Thirteenth-Century Religious Texts* (Cardiff: University of Wales Press, 2015), pp. 1–24; Nicole Rice, *Lay Piety and Religious Discipline in Middle English Literature* (New York: Cambridge University Press, 2008), pp. 1–16.

7 André Wilmart, 'Deux préfaces spirituelles de Jean de Fécamp', *Revue d'ascétique et de mystique* 69 (1937), 3–44; Wilmart, *Auteurs spirituels*, pp. 125–35.

8 The four prayers of John of Fécamp that I refer to here often are cited by their numbering in the *Meditations of St Augustine* as collected in the PL: *Liber meditationum*, c. XXXV, PL 40, cols 928–30; *Liber meditationum*, c. XXXVI, PL 40, cols 930–2; *Liber meditationum*, c. XXXVII, PL 40, cols 933–4, and *Liber meditationum*, c. XXXVII, PL 40, cols 934–6. The *Confessio theologica* was likely written during John's priorship; for more on this, see Chapter 1. Stéphane Lecouteux has recently revised the date of the start of John's priorship, changing it from 1016 to 1023: Stéphane Lecouteux, 'Réseaux de confraternité et histoire des bibliothèques: L'exemple de l'abbaye bénédictine de la Trinité de Fécamp' (PhD dissertation, Université de Caen Normandie/École Pratique des Hautes Études, 2015), vol. I, p. 71.

9 McNamer, *Affective Meditation*; Gerard Sitwell, *Spiritual Writers of the Middle Ages* (New York: Hawthorne Books, 1961), pp. 25–42; Brian Patrick McGuire, 'John of Fécamp and Anselm of Bec: A New Language of Prayer', in Santha Bhattacharji,

Rowan Williams, and Dominic Mattos (eds), *Prayer and Thought in Monastic Tradition: Essays in Honour of Benedicta Ward SLG* (New York: Bloomsbury, 2014), pp. 153–66.

10 In this book, I will use the phrases 'affective piety' and 'affective devotion' in order to better dialogue with previously written scholarship.

11 Alison Beach, as co-editor of the forthcoming *Cambridge Companion to Medieval Monasticism in the Latin World*, has called for an end to the use of the anachronistic term 'Benedictine' to describe monasticism before the twelfth century. I will embrace this idea here, but will occasionally use the term in order to speak to the scholarly narrative that has characterised traditional monasticism as 'Benedictine'.

12 Véronique Gazeau and Monique Goullet, *Guillaume de Volpiano: Un réformateur en son temps (962–1031)* (Caen: CRAHM, 2008), pp. 1–16.

13 Over the last thousand years, several myths about John have been perpetuated. He has been called nephew of William of Volpiano, a doctor, a scribe, a musician, a writer of prayers unconfirmed to be his own. While I do not directly address these myths in this book, I have identified sources in the Fécamp manuscript evidence that could be parlayed for the purpose; for example, Rouen, BM, ms. 978 (I57) might link John to his medical identity, and Rouen, BM, ms. 477 (A191) might provide clues as to whether John was a scribe.

14 Tom License, *Hermits and Recluses in English Society, 950–1200* (New York: Oxford University Press, 2011), pp. 32–4.

15 Véronique Gazeau, *Normannia monastica: Prosopographie des abbés bénédictines* (Caen: CRAHM, 2007), pp. 105–10; Elisabeth van Houts, 'The Ship List of William the Conqueror', in *History and Family Traditions in England and the Continent, 1000–1200* (Brookfield, VT: Varorium, 1999), pp. 159–83.

16 Lucien Musset, 'La vie économique de l'abbaye de Fécamp sous l'abbatiat de Jean de Ravenne (1028–1078)', in *L'abbaye bénédictine de Fécamp: Ouvrage scientifique du XIIIe centenaire (658–1958)* (Fécamp: EMTN, 1959), vol. I, pp. 67–79, 345–9.

17 Marie Fauroux, *Recueil des actes des ducs de Normandie (911–1066)* (Caen: Société d'Impressions CARON 1961); Michaël Bloche, 'Le chartrier de l'abbaye de la Trinité de Fécamp: étude et édition critique, 928/929–1190' (PhD dissertation, École nationale des chartes, 2012).

18 Jean-François LeMarignier, 'L'exemption de Fécamp au début du XIe siècle', in *Étude sur les privilèges d'exemption et de juridiction ecclésiastique des abbayes Normandes depuis les origines jusqu'en 1140* (Paris: Archives de la France Monastique, 1937), pp. 288–340; Benjamin Pohl and Steven Vanderputten, 'Fécamp, Cluny, and the Invention of Traditions in the Later Eleventh Century', *Journal of Medieval Monastic Studies* 5 (2016), 1–41.

19 François Avril, 'Notes sur quelques manuscrits bénédictins normands du XIe et du XIIe siècle', *Mélanges d'archéologie et d'histoire* 77 (1965), 209–48; François Avril, 'Notes sur quelques manuscrits bénédictins normands du XIe et du XIIe siècle', *Mélanges d'archéologie et d'histoire* 76 (1964), 491–525; Geneviève Nortier, *Les*

bibliothèques médiévales des abbayes bénédictines de Normandie: Fécamp, Le Bec, Le Mont Saint-Michel, Saint-Évroul, Jumièges, Saint-Wandrille, Saint-Ouen (Paris: Paul Lethielleux, 1971); J.J.G. Alexander, *Norman Illumination at Mont St. Michel* (Oxford: Clarendon Press, 1970); Stéphane Lecouteux, 'Sur la dispersion de la bibliothèque bénédictine de Fécamp. Partie 1: Identification des principales vagues de démembrement des fonds', *Tabularia* 7 (2007), 1–50.

20 Betty Branch, 'The Development of Script in Eleventh- and Twelfth-Century Manuscripts of the Norman Abbey of Fécamp' (PhD dissertation, Duke University, 1974); Betty Branch, 'Inventories of the Library of Fécamp from the Eleventh- and Twelfth-Centuries', *Manuscripta* 23 (1979), 159–72; Betty Branch, 'William Peccator et les manuscrits de Fécamp 1100–1150', *Cahiers de civilisation médiévale* 26 (1983), 195–207.

21 David Chadd (ed.), *The Ordinal of the Abbey of the Holy Trinity Fécamp (Fécamp, Musée de la Bénédictine, Ms 186)*, 2 vols (London: Henry Bradshaw Society, 1999).

22 Karin Brockhaus, *L'abbatiale de la Trinité de Fécamp et l'architecture normande au moyen âge* (Caen: Société des Antiquaires de Normandie, 2009); Lindy Grant, 'Fécamp et l'architecture en Normandie', *Tabularia* 2 (2002), 83–94; Lucile Tran-Duc, 'Les princes normands et les reliques (Xe–XIe siècles): Contribution du culte des saints à la formation territoriale et identitaire d'une principauté', in Jean-Luc Deuffic (ed.), *Reliques et sainteté dans l'espace médiéval* (Paris: PECIA, 2005), pp. 525–64; Lucile Tran-Duc, 'De l'usage politique du Précieux Sang dans l'Europe médiévale', *Tabularia* 8 (2008), 89–106; Jacques Le Maho, 'Aux sources d'un grand pèlerinage normand: L'origine des reliques fécampoises du Précieux Sang', in Catherine Vincent (ed.), *Identités pèlerines* (Rouen: Publications de l'Université de Caen, 2004), pp. 45–66; Annie Renoux, *Fécamp: Du palais ducal au palais de dieu* (Paris: CNRS, 1991).

23 See works by Wilmart and: Gérard Mathon, 'Jean de Fécamp, théologien monastique?', in Louis Gaillard (ed.), *La Normandie bénédictine au temps de Guillaume le Conquérant (XIe siècle)* (Lille: Facultés Catholiques, 1967), pp. 485–500; Gillian Evans, 'Mens devota: The Literary Community of the Devotional Works of John of Fécamp and St. Anselm', *Medium Aevum* 43.2 (1974), 105–15; Fay Anne Martineau, 'Envisioning Heaven with Faith, Imagination, and Historical Relevance: Selected Writings from Early and Medieval Christianity' (PhD dissertation, Harvard University, 2007); Martine Pastor, 'Jean de Fécamp, "Un auteur sans amour-propre"', *Annales du patrimoine de Fécamp* 2 (1995), 36–41; Hugh Feiss, 'John of Fécamp's Longing for Heaven', in Jan Swango Emerson and Hugh Feiss (eds), *Imagining Heaven in the Middle Ages* (New York: Garland Publishing, 2000), pp. 65–81.

24 The only attempts at synthesising the various aspects of Fécamp's devotional practices with its political and economic cultures have been undertaken by French historians writing sweeping histories of the abbey for a popular audience, some from as long ago as 1663 and others as recently as 1987: Robert Soulignac, *Fécamp et sa campagne à l'époque des ducs de Normandie: 911–1204*

(Fécamp: EMTN, 1987); Gourdon de Genouillac, *Histoire de l'abbaye de Fécamp et ses abbés* (Fécamp: A. Marinier, 1875); A.-J.-V. Leroux de Lincy, *Essai historique et littéraire sur l'abbaye de Fécamp* (Rouen: Librarie de la Bibliothèque de la Ville, 1840); Arthur Långfors, 'Histoire de l'abbaye de Fécamp: En vers français du XIIIe siècle', *Annales academiae scientiarum Fennicae* B 22 (1928), 7–208; Guillaume Le Hule, *Le thresor ou abbrégé de l'histoire de la noble et royalle abbaye de Fescamp* (Fécamp: Banse Fils, 1684); Arthur Du Monstier, *Neustria pia, seu de omnibus et singuilis abbatiis et prioratibus totius normaniae* (Rouen: Joannem Berthelin, 1663).

25 For a useful survey of this historiography, see Tjamke Snijders, *Manuscript Communication: Visual and Textual Communication in Hagiographical Texts from the Southern Low Countries, 900–1200* (Turnhout: Brepols, 2015), pp. 18–32. Classic studies on monastic reform include Giles Constable, *The Reformation of the Twelfth Century* (New York: Cambridge University Press, 1996); Gerhart B. Ladner, *The Idea of Reform: Its Impact on Christian Thought and Action in the Age of the Fathers* (New York: Harper Torchbooks, 1967); Giles Constable, 'Renewal and Reform in Religious Life: Concepts and Realities', in Robert L. Benson and Giles Constable (eds), *Renaissance and Renewal in the Twelfth Century* (Toronto: Medieval Academy Reprints for Teaching, 1991), pp. 37–67.

26 Maureen Miller, 'Reconsidering Reform: A Roman Example', in David C. Mengel and Lisa Wolverton (eds), *Christianity and Culture in the Middle Ages: Essays to Honor John Van Engen* (Notre Dame, IN: University of Notre Dame Press, 2015), pp. 123–40; Julia Barrow, 'Ideas and Applications of Reform', in Thomas F.X. Noble and Julia M.H. Smith (eds), *The Cambridge History of Christianity* (New York: Cambridge University Press, 2008), vol. III, pp. 345–62; Steven Vanderputten, *Monastic Reform as Process: Realities and Representations in Medieval Flanders, 900–1100* (Ithaca, NY: Cornell University Press, 2013).

27 Snijders, *Manuscript Communication*, p. 27. They do not remain unexplored for the slightly later context, however. See, for example, Barbara Rosenwein, *Generations of Feeling: A History of Emotions, 600–1700* (New York: Cambridge University Press, 2016), pp. 88–113; Damien Boquet and Pirsoka Nagy, *Medieval Sensibilities: A History of Emotions in the Middle Ages*, trans. Robert Shaw (Cambridge: Polity, 2018), pp. 69–103.

28 Damien Boquet, 'Affectivity in the Spiritual Writings of Aelred of Rievaulx', in Marsha L. Dutton (ed.), *A Companion to Aelred of Rievaulx (1110–1167)* (Boston: Brill, 2017), p. 168.

29 Bede K. Lackner, *The Eleventh-Century Background of Cîteaux* (Washington, DC: Cistercian Publications, 1972), pp. 92–112; Jean Leclercq, 'The Monastic Crisis of the Eleventh and Twelfth Centuries', in Noreen Hunt (ed.), *Cluniac Monasticism in the Central Middle Ages* (New York: Macmillan, 1971), pp. 217–37; Norman F. Cantor, 'The Crisis of Western Monasticism, 1050–1130', *American Historical Review* 66 (1960), 47–67; John Van Engen, 'The "Crisis of Coenobitism" Reconsidered: Benedictine Monasticism in the Years 1050–1150', *Speculum* 61.2 (1986), 269–304.

30 For an example of the persistence of this narrative, see Gert Melville, *The World of Medieval Monasticism: Its History and Forms of Life* (Collegeville, MN: Liturgical Press, 2016), p. 90.

Introduction

31 M.B. Pranger, 'Bernard the Writer', in Brian Patrick McGuire (ed.), *A Companion to Bernard of Clairvaux* (Leiden: E.J. Brill, 2011), pp. 220–48.
32 Exceptions include Renie S. Choy, *Intercessory Prayer and the Monastic Ideal in the Time of the Carolingian Reforms* (New York: Oxford University Press, 2017), pp. 8–10; Susan Boynton, 'Prayer as Liturgical Performance in Eleventh- and Twelfth-Century Monastic Psalters', *Speculum* 82 (2007), 896–931; Adam Cohen, 'Art, Exegesis, and Affective Piety in Twelfth-Century German Manuscripts', in Alison I. Beach (ed.), *Manuscripts and Monastic Culture: Reform and Renewal in Twelfth-Century Germany* (Turnhout: Brepols, 2002), pp. 45–68; Isabelle Cochelin, 'Obedience or Agency?', in Sébastien Baret and Gert Melville (eds), *Oboedientia: zu Formen und Grenzen von Macht und Unterordnung im mittelalterlichen Religiosentum* (Münster: Lit Verlag, 2005), pp. 229–54.
33 Cassandra Potts, *Monastic Revival and Regional Identity in Early Normandy* (Woodbridge: Boydell Press, 1997), pp. 36–80; Barbara Rosenwein, *To Be the Neighbor of Saint Peter: The Social Meaning of Cluny's Property, 909–1049* (Ithaca, NY: Cornell University Press, 1989), pp. 109–43.
34 Jörg Sonntag, 'Obedience in High Medieval Monastic Sources: Some Brief Remarks in Light of Ritual', in Mirko Breitenstein, Julia Burkhardt, Stefan Burkhardt, and Jens Röhrkasten (eds), *Rules and Observance: Devising Forms of Communal Life* (Berlin: Lit Verlag, 2014), pp. 253–63.
35 Monique Scheer, 'Are Emotions a Kind of Practice (And is That What Makes Them Have a History)? A Bordieuian Approach to Understanding Emotion', *History and Theory* 51 (2012), 193–220.
36 Classic studies include Charles Homer Haskins, *The Renaissance of the Twelfth Century* (Cambridge, MA: Harvard University Press, 1955); Colin Morris, *The Discovery of the Individual, 1050–1200* (Toronto: University of Toronto Press, 1987); Richard Southern, *The Making of the Middle Ages* (New Haven, CT: Yale University Press, 1992), pp. 219–57.
37 Lackner, *The Eleventh-Century Background of Citeaux*, p. 145. This opposition between community and individual is the kind of statement critiqued by Susan Boynton in her discussion of public vs. private prayer (see n. 32 above), and in Caroline Walker Bynum, 'Did the Twelfth Century Discover the Individual?', in *Jesus as Mother: Studies in the Spirituality of the High Middle Ages* (Berkeley: University of California Press, 1982), pp. 82–109; Suzanne Verbender, *The Medieval Fold: Power, Repression, and the Emergence of the Individual* (New York: Palgrave Macmillan, 2013), pp. 25–60.
38 For a critique of claims that medieval people did not have a sense of self akin to the modern or twentieth-century sense, see Ronald J. Ganze, 'The Medieval Sense of Self', in Stephen J. Harris and Bryon L. Grigsby (eds), *Misconceptions About the Middle Ages* (New York: Routledge, 2008), pp. 103–16 and John Jeffries Martin, *Myths of Renaissance Individualism* (New York: Palgrave Macmillan, 2004).
39 The 'radical individualism' and the 'mystical anarchism' that comes with later medieval mysticism is troubled in Sara S. Poor and Nigel Smith (eds), *Mysticism and Reform, 1400–1750* (Notre Dame, IN: University of Notre Dame Press, 2015),

pp. 1–9; and Jeffrey F. Hamburger and Hildegard Elisabeth Keller's 'A Battle for Hearts and Minds: The Heart in Reformation Polemic', in Sarah S. Poor and Nigel Smith (eds), *Mysticism and Reform* (Notre Dame, IN: University of Notre Dame Press, 2015), p. 338.

40 Constable, *The Reformation of the Twelfth Century*, p. 274.

41 Brian Stock, *After Augustine: The Meditative Reader and the Text* (Philadelphia: University of Pennsylvania Press, 2001), p. 13; Duncan Robertson, *Lectio Divina: The Medieval Experience of Reading* (Collegeville, MN: Liturgical Press, 2011).

42 Stock, *After Augustine*, pp. 20, 58–9; Caroline Walker Bynum, 'Jesus as Mother and Abbot as Mother', in *Jesus as Mother*, p. 130; Bynum, 'Did the Twelfth Century Discover the Individual?', p. 88.

43 Phyllis G. Jestice, *Wayward Monks and the Religious Revolution of the Eleventh Century* (Leiden: E.J. Brill, 1997), p. 14.

44 Jennifer Bryan, *Looking Inward: Devotional Reading and the Private Self in Late Medieval England* (Philadelphia: University of Pennsylvania Press, 2008); Ben Morgan, *On Becoming God: Late Medieval Mysticism and the Modern Western Self* (New York: Fordham University Press, 2013). Certain studies, however, do not ignore the cultivation of the 'interior' during the early Middle Ages, such as Piroska Zombory-Nagy, 'Les larmes du Christ dans l'exégèse médiévale', *Médiévales* 27 (1994), 37–49; Piroska Nagy, *Le don des larmes au moyen âge. Un instrument en quête d'institution (Ve–XIIIe siècle)* (Paris: Albin Michel, 2000); Sandra J. McEntire, *The Doctrine of Compunction in Medieval England: Holy Tears* (Lewiston, NY: Edwin Mellen Press, 1991).

45 Ineke van 't Spijker, *Fictions of the Inner Life: Religious Literature and Formation of the Self in the Eleventh and Twelfth Centuries* (Turnhout: Brepols, 2004), pp. 21, 39, 55; Bestul, *Texts of the Passion*, pp. 36–8; Stock, *After Augustine*, p. 63.

46 For more on the idea of lived religious experience vs. religious discourse, see Caroline Walker Bynum, *Wonderful Blood: Theology and Practice in Late Medieval Northern Germany and Beyond* (Philadelphia: University of Pennsylvania Press, 2007), pp. 19–21; Andrew J. Romig, *Be a Perfect Man: Christian Masculinity and the Carolingian Aristocracy* (Philadelphia: University of Pennsylvania Press, 2017), pp. 1–12.

47 Scholars have repeatedly ignored work on early, particularly Anglo-Saxon, affectivity; examples of that work include: Frances McCormack, 'Those Bloody Trees: The Affectivity of Christ', in Alice Jorgensen, Frances McCormack, and Jonathan Wilcox (eds), *Anglo-Saxon Emotions: Reading the Heart in Old English Language, Literature, and Culture* (New York: Ashgate, 2015), pp. 143–61; Scott DeGregorio, 'Affective Spirituality: Theory and Practice in Bede and Alfred the Great', *Essays in Medieval Studies* 22 (2005), 129–39, at 131; Barbara C. Raw, *Anglo-Saxon Crucifixion Iconography and the Art of Monastic Revival* (New York: Cambridge University Press, 1990); Celia Chazelle, *The Crucified God in the Carolingian Era: Theology and Art of Christ's Passion* (Cambridge: Cambridge University Press, 2001); Juliet Mullins, Jenifer Ní Ghrádaigh, and Richard

Introduction

Hawtree (eds), *Envisioning Christ on the Cross: Ireland and the Early Medieval West* (Portland, OR: Four Courts Press, 2013).
48 Southern, *The Making of the Middle Ages*, p. 232.
49 Bestul, *Texts of the Passion*, p. 37.
50 William Reddy, *The Navigation of Feeling: A Framework for the History of Emotions* (Cambridge: Cambridge University Press, 2001), pp. 125–6; Both Sarah McNamer and Niklaus Largier agree with Reddy's assessment; McNamer, *Affective Meditation*, p. 12–13; Niklaus Largier, 'Inner Senses–Outer Senses: The Practice of Emotions in Medieval Mysticism', in C. Stephen Jaeger and Ingrid Kasten (eds), *Codierung von Emotionen im Mittelalter/Emotions and Sensibilities in the Middle Ages* (New York: De Gruyter, 2003), pp. 3–15.
51 Robert Glenn Davis, *The Weight of Love: Affect, Ecstacy, and Union in the Theology of Bonaventure* (New York: Fordham University Press, 2017), pp. 21, 23.
52 Brian Massumi, *Parables for the Virtual: Movement, Affect, Sensation* (Durham, NC: Duke University Press, 2002).
53 Davis, *The Weight of Love*, p. 26.
54 Ruth Leys, 'The Turn to Affect: A Critique', *Critical Inquiry* 37.3 (2011), 434–72 and *The Ascent of Affect: Geneology and Critique* (Chicago: Chicago University Press, 2017).
55 The word 'emotion' is really an invention of the nineteenth century – see Thomas Dixon, *From Passions to Emotion: The Creation of a Secular Psychological Category* (Cambridge: Cambridge University Press, 2003), pp. 1–25. In this study, therefore, I will use the word(s) 'emotion(al)' only to allow my narrative to fit into the wider scholarly discourse of the history of emotions; but, when I do, I am not referring to the nineteenth-century secularised meaning of the word 'emotion'; see Jan Plamper, *The History of Emotions* (New York: Oxford University Press, 2015), p. 38.
56 Barbara Rosenwein, 'Worrying about Emotions in History', *American Historical Review* 107.3 (2002), 821–45.

1

Reforming the reader's interior: defining emotional reform and affectivity in John of Fécamp's *Confessio theologica*

To the best of our knowledge, John of Fécamp wrote only one major treatise in the course of his fifty-five years at the monastery of Fécamp. Unlike the expansive corpus of Anselm of Canterbury (1033–1109) or Lanfranc of Bec (1005–89), John revised a single work at different moments in his priorship and abbacy, choosing not to write new works.[1] This is a significant fact. Ultimately, as this book will show, John seemed to have felt that his *Confessio theologica* was the core of what he had to teach his monks, his noble female acquaintances, and the wider Anglo-Norman audience of his work.

The *Confessio theologica*'s central argument is the following: Christians desiring a connection to the divine needed to work to reform their devotional *emotions*, not just their devotional actions. John demands readers 'enter into the interior of [their] mind[s]'.[2] For John, even the most devout Christian was in need of a *conversio* – a turning back to God – because even the most devout Christian relapsed into habitual behaviours, dulling his or her awareness of the divine. At the pinnacle of that divine awareness was the paradoxical experience of *caritas* – suffering that heals, pain that soothes, love that wounds. Each time it was read, John's *CT* was meant to create such an awareness – and, thereby, an inward *conversio* – in its Christian reader.

John outlines a comprehensive theory of contemplative practice in his *Confessio theologica*; in its printed edition, the treatise includes over seventy pages of prose alongside four oft-excerpted prayers. To provide the foundation for the chapters that follow, this chapter will examine the *CT* in its entirety. I will analyse John's theory of contemplative practice through a close reading of his text, defining terms, ideas, and devotional objectives which will lay the foundation for the rest of my book.

The *Confessio theologica* as a book for monks

When André Wilmart, Jean Leclercq, and Jean-Paul Bonnes wrote their pioneering studies of John of Fécamp, they postulated that John initially composed the *Confessio theologica* (Theological Confession) for his own spiritual edification when he was prior of Fécamp.[3] They believed that John also revised the *CT* two more times before his death in 1078: two copies of a second recension, which a scribe called the *Libellus de scripturis et verbis patrum collectus ad eorum presertim utilitatem qui contemplativae vitae sunt amatores* (Little Book of Extracts from the Scriptures and Words of the Fathers, Especially Useful for Those Who are Lovers of Contemplation, hereafter *Libellus*), were sent first to an anonymous nun, c. 1030, and then thirty years later to the Empress Agnes of Poitou (1025–77), c. 1060. A third recension, called the *Confessio fidei* (Confession of Faith) by a scribe in its lone surviving manuscript, was written in response to the Berengar of Tours (c. 999–1088) Eucharistic controversy, around 1050.[4]

Before I jump into the content of John's treatise, a brief discussion of the questions of recension and reception is important to our understanding of John's text's construction and, more importantly, of John's audience. Few scholars since Wilmart, Leclercq, and Bonnes have examined the complete first recension of the *CT* in their work on John; most rely instead on his work's more famous extracts, four prayers excerpted from the *Libellus* and published in the late medieval Pseudo-Augustinian collection of prayers called the *Meditations of St Augustine*.[5] This selective reading of John obscures the meaning of John's words and prevents an accurate identification of John's contemporary audience.

Since the only published critical edition of the *Confessio theologica* dates to 1946, and since that edition only examines the so-called first recension, relying on only one manuscript and one manuscript fragment, it goes without saying that the recensions of John's work demand further study (work that, admittedly, I will not do here).[6] Leclercq and Bonnes relied on these two manuscripts for their edition because they were (and continue to be) the only identified surviving manuscripts of the earliest recension of the *Confessio theologica*: Paris, BnF, ms. lat. 3088 (fols 1–6v), an eleventh-century fragment of unknown origin and of only six folia,[7] and Paris, BnF, ms. lat. 1919, a twelfth-century manuscript from a Cistercian or Premonstratensian abbey in Champagne, perhaps around Troyes.[8] In contrast, second recension manuscripts of the *Libellus* version surviving from the later eleventh and twelfth centuries far outnumber those of the first and third – there are eleven in total – indicating that this was the version of John's work most widely read by his contemporaries. Only one known manuscript of the third *Confessio fidei* recension survives, making that recension even harder to trace than the first, and also causing some scholars to doubt it to be authentically John's at all.[9]

No matter the recension, though, John's *Confessio theologica* was read extensively by, and was likely initially composed for, a male monastic audience. Wilmart argued that John of Fécamp's writings were *effusions de sa prière intime*,[10] sincere records of John's own private prayer that were then disseminated to his monastic brethren once they got wind of the existence of such personal texts. To support this notion (and to support his dating of the *CT* to John's priorship at Fécamp), Wilmart cited the passage below, where John refers to the need to be obedient to his own abbot in his daily life:

> Grant, O Lord, that I always love my abbot, your servant, and all my seniors and brothers with sincere and humble charity [*RB*, ch. 71]; that from my heart I feel deep sorrow in their evils and sins and adversities; that from my heart I feel deep joy in their goods and virtues and advances; that I never set anything before your love, but love you in all things and above all things [*RB*, ch. 72]. Give me true humility and obedience, true submission and mortification, so that unrestrained judgment lives not in me, nor my own will to lead [cf. *RB*, ch. 5]. Give to me simplicity, innocence, and wholeness of mind, continuous custody of my heart and mouth, so that I condemn and despise no one, doubt the merits of no one, render evil for evil to no one, but walk in the simplicity of my heart before you always.[11]

Wilmart takes John's first-person supplications literally, and interprets them as biographical facts: John refers to his abbot, therefore he is composing this text when he was prior; John speaks in the first person, therefore the *CT* is a private confessional text written from John's point of view. In 1946, Leclercq and Bonnes followed Wilmart's lead, likewise claiming that John's *CT* was '*liée à sa vie personelle*' and was initially a product of his own monastic life.[12]

It is certainly likely that John wrote the *Confessio theologica* as Fécamp's prior. It was not uncommon for a prior to write a manual of spiritual advice to his monks: Anselm of Canterbury wrote his *Prayers and Meditations* while he was prior at Bec, which served to model proper devotional behaviours to the monks in his care.[13] But Wilmart, Leclercq, and Bonnes's confidence that John wrote the *CT* for his *own* spiritual edification is problematic: the passage above merely shows that the *Confessio theologica* was initially written with a *monastic* audience in mind, long before John sent the manuscript to a nun or Agnes. The passage above constantly draws from the precepts of the Rule of St Benedict, as I indicate in brackets, both directly excerpting the *RB*'s prescriptions and indirectly reflecting them in original prayerful language. John also emphasises loving 'all [his] seniors and all [his] brothers', an explicit reference to the monastic community. These comments suggest that John certainly composed his first recension with fellow followers of the *RB* in mind.[14] These and other *RB*-inspired passages from the *CT* are the principle passages that are omitted in the second *Libellus* recension, likely as part of an effort to make John's text more accessible to a wider, non-monastic audience, chiefly of noble women.[15]

In addition, it is clear from manuscript evidence that all three of the recensions of John's text, even the *Libellus* recension, were read by a substantial male monastic audience in John's lifetime. The evidence for this conclusion is as follows: all three manuscripts of John's complete text that survive from the eleventh century (two *Libellus*, one *Confessio fidei*[16]) are from male monastic houses; all nine (seven *Libellus*, one *Confessio fidei*, one *Confessio theologica*[17]) that survive from the twelfth century are too; and these numbers do not include the likely countless unidentified monastic manuscripts that feature unattributed excerpts of John's prayers and other works (like Paris, BnF, ms. lat. 3088's edition of the *CT*, mentioned above).[18] Moreover, many of these early manuscripts survive from monasteries that were strongly connected to Fécamp's monastic network, foundations that were either reformed by John's mentor and Fécamp's first abbot, William of Volpiano (962–1031), or whose abbots maintained strong connections with John himself during the eleventh century.[19] Thus, while the *Libellus* sometimes circulated with a dedicatory letter to an empress or a nun,[20] John's contemplative prescriptions were not targeted exclusively (or even primarily) at a female audience. John's text was originally composed for monks, and, while later adapted to an expanded audience that included women, it was still read by and circulated among John's male brethren.

The *Confessio theologica* as a book for personal use

At the end of his *Confessio theologica*, John summarises the purpose of the text he has written:

> Therefore not out of the temerity of presumption, but out of the great avidity of my desire for you [God] I have applied myself to this little compilation of readings for your praise, in order that I might always have a short and handy word about God with me, and from the fire of reading it, as many times as I grow cool, I may be reignited in your love. For since we are placed in the midst of snares, we easily grow cold in our heavenly longing. And so we lack

a constant defence, so that, having been roused, we run back to you, our true and highest good, whenever we slide away. But pardon me, I ask, O Lord, pardon me, a most unworthy and unhappy slave speaking too long with you about you. Pardon me, a wretch, O Holy One. For I have opened my lips to you out of an excessive love of your name.[21]

This passage provides us with some clues about John's envisioned use for his *Confessio theologica*: John wants his text to be for personal edification and prayer. Indeed, medieval copies of the *CT* and *Libellus* seem to conform to John's stated purpose, usually circulating in small manuscripts that could easily have been carried on a person.[22] Following the biblical injunction to always have a prayer on one's lips, John's *CT* thus aims to provide reflections and prayers to readers in handy, pocket-sized form.

The personal nature of the *Confessio theologica* is also seen in the tone John adopts for the book. The treatise is written entirely in the first person. However, the purpose of John's text is not to tell the story of his own life – there are no biographical details in the text; nor is it to write for his own spiritual edification alone – shortly after its initial composition, he sends it out to a nun, in 1030. John's retention of the first person 'I' in his *Libellus* recension – a treatise he specifically revised to send to a nun in 1030 and an empress in 1060 – is a clue for us. Neither a nun nor Agnes is the 'I' of Abbot John, and yet he retains the first-person speaker. Like so many prayerful medieval texts written in the first person, John's text's 'I' aims to provide a contemplative model for any reader to use in his or her own devotional practice.[23] This creates a 'text ... [that] does not so much express the inner thoughts of the *author*, but functions rhetorically by constructing a speaking *exemplum* that an audience can respond to or even model its conduct upon'.[24] John's 'I' is a performative 'I', a means by which the reader could speak and appropriate John's confessional words for him or herself.[25] The tone of the *Confessio theologica* is a private one: by reading John's text in the first person, the individual reader could better rouse himself to an embrace of the contemplative method that John is prescribing. Like monks in a *calefactorium*, John's readers would use the *CT* to warm up their prayer, thus better stirring, reawakening, and emotionally reforming their love for God.[26] While the *RB* regulates communal action, the *CT* is John's attempt to regulate internal devotion – one reader at a time.

John believes that the chief way to 'be reignited in [God's] love' is to make oneself aware of how, even in the regular prayerful actions of his life, one has not yet aligned right *action* with right *feeling*. John defines this problem explicitly in the *CT*, inviting his reader to speak along with the text:

> Give me contrition of heart, even a font of tears, especially when I bring you my requests and my prayers, while I chant the psalmody of your praise, while I contemplate or make known the mystery of our redemption, the manifest judgment of your mercy [i.e. engage with doctrinal instruction] … while I, albeit unworthily, stand in attendance of your altars, desiring to offer that marvellous and heavenly sacrifice, worthy of all reverence and devotion [i.e. celebrate the Eucharist].[27]

This is the *CT*'s chief purpose: the reader must work to reform his emotional palate, to *feel* as connected as possible to God in his own heart and with his own tears while performing pious actions. Fulfilling his monastic duties (singing the psalms, studying doctrine, celebrating the Eucharist) is not enough. In an article on medieval monastic prayer, Amy Hollywood has raised the very issues that John himself is grappling with in his treatise. She writes:

> To many modern ears, the repetition of the Psalms [required by the *RB*] … will likely sound rote and deadening. Some modern Western conceptions of the mystical, spiritual, or religious life insist that it be an immediate and spontaneous engagement with the divine. From this perspective, one might well ask of the *Rule*: What of the immediacy of the monk's relationship to God? What of his personal feelings in the face of the divine? What spontaneity can exist in the monk's engagement with God within the context of such a regimented and uniform prayer life? If the monk is reciting another's words rather than his own, how can the feelings engendered by these words be his own and so be sincere?[28]

It is not just modern minds that wonder – eleventh-century minds did too. In spiritual practice, beyond right action, what is the right *feeling* an individual monk should have in relationship to the divine? And how can he instigate such feeling – such emotional reform – in such a regular existence of persistent, regimented prayer?

The *Confessio theologica* provides its answers to these questions – and prescribes proper devotional feeling – over the course of three untitled parts.[29] Like the beginning of Augustine's *Confessions*, Part I of the *CT* is an extended opening invocation of God and a definition and glorification of each member of the Trinity, a warm-up of sorts. In this part especially, John often excerpts quotations from the liturgy, from the Bible and the Psalms, and from the Church Fathers in order to provide an orthodox definition and praise of the divine in the words of the authorities. (He claims at one point early on that 'my words are the words of the Fathers'.[30]) Having paid due homage to the divine in Part I, Part II proceeds to instruct the reader, reviewing the need for faith, prayer, and a neglect of earthly things in order to achieve God's grace and eventual redemption. The longest and most original part of John's *CT* is Part III, where the ideal affective state of the prayerful reader is defined. In this section, John in effect proposes a method for personal emotional reform that engenders a tearful, pleading, prayerful, emotional turmoil with the aid of the emotional examples of the crucified Christ, Mary Magdalene, and Hannah, and by modelling the performance of an intense, internal self-examination in the eyes of God. By the end of the work, John's *CT* has not *described* a method for prayer to its readers, but has rather *inflicted* it upon them. One can imagine a reader, upon reaching the end of the *CT*, not feeling passively instructed but frenzied and weepy.

John reminds his readers throughout the *Confessio theologica* that 'in this present life, saturated with miseries and errors, the perfection of the contemplative life is not achievable'.[31] John's *CT* promises, therefore, no divine union or ultimate peace as a result of the prayer it prescribes – that is not its use, after all.[32] Rather, John's *CT* attempts to awaken the reader to his own imperfect self, shaking him from rote devotion and prompting within him impassioned excitations of prayer. By speaking directly as and for the individual, the *CT* works to perform its method on each single reader, awakening in him the proper affective state of prayer. John (after Augustine) calls this a *conversio* in his text: a turning (or returning) towards God. Just how the *CT* does this, what the contours of its method for emotional reform is, and what this 'conversion' attempts to achieve, will be the focus of the remainder of this chapter.[33]

Reforming the interior at the site of the heart

In his work *In Isaiam*, Richard of Saint-Victor (1110–73), writing about a hundred years after John of Fécamp's death, praised Jerome (347–420) for his diligence at digging for the truth in things. Richard says that Jerome 'knew how obscure truth is, how deep it lies buried … by how much work it is reached, how practically no one ever succeeds, how it is dug out with difficulty and then only bit by bit'.[34] John, like Jerome before him and Richard after him, believed that the true method for efficacious prayer was buried deep inside the emotional core of his readers, and he wrote his whole *Confessio theologica* as an attempt to create a contemplative process by which it could be teased out of them.

For John, the first step in this process is for the reader to move from exterior praise of God to interior feeling,[35] to heighten the 'interior senses of [one's own] soul'.[36] To love God and truly connect to him in prayer, John says, one must not just perform the right words publicly, but rather use those words to open up an 'inmost' vision.[37] It is that inner vision, that interior, that is judged by God after all – the *intentions* behind the words, and not the words, are what matters in prayer.[38] Public professions of faith performed by rote are the empty things of earth, but inner vision and feeling is the substance of God.[39] This idea of interior/exterior in fact mirrors a monastic plan, where the area outside the monastery's walls (*extra terminos*) is an area where non-monastics can visit, and the area inside the walls (*infra terminos* or *interior domus*) is the space where the individual monk's real soulful work occurs, the cloister of the soul (*claustrum animae*).[40] When defining these exterior and interior spaces in the *CT*, John himself even alludes to walled space, imagining metaphorical walls within the contemplative self that serve to stop up earthly influence and protect the soul when it is in silent retreat.[41]

John's instruction to his reader to go inside himself follows his idea that, though God is found inside every single being,[42] human beings are too often outside of themselves.[43] The goal of contemplation according to the *Confessio theologica*'s method is to recognise the presence of God that is already inside the human soul. This recognition, to John, is actually an act of recall, of unforgetting the seal of God that was always set on the reader's heart.[44] This effort of memory works to call God into the reader's soul and to have him 'penetrate more deeply to the inmost parts by [his] powerful virtue'.[45] By calling God into the self, the reader will create a revulsion for the self that neglected God for so long,[46] replacing it with an inner hunger for God,[47] a hunger that will never fully be sated while the reader is alive.[48]

Once the necessity of this interior journey is established, John quotes Augustine's *Confessions*, asking: 'in what place do you dwell in me, God?'.[49] God's place, it turns out, is the human heart;[50] and it is the heart that is the site of the contemplative reform in the reader. Following Augustine's description of Ambrose in the *Confessions*, John's reader will also '[seek] out the meaning':[51]

> Give me a contrite heart, a pure heart, a sincere heart, a devout heart, a chaste heart, a sober heart, a mild heart, a gentle heart, a calm heart, a most serene heart, a heart full of desire for you ... Cleave the hardness of my heart in order that that font may flow out for which my soul exceedingly seethes with desire ... in order that my tears may become to me bread day and night ... Free me from the quarrels and contentions that my wretched mind suffers there where the squabbling multitude of men is found ... in order that loosed from all cares, I may freely sit at the feet of the Lord Jesus Christ and may listen intently to what heavenly wisdom teaches.[52]

The main obstacle to allowing God to dwell within, for John, is a hardened heart.[53] John notes that in heaven where there is an eternal vision of God, there is no place for any 'sharpness of gall'.[54] A hard heart prevents divine vision, and prevents God's mercy from penetrating 'deep within (*intus*) the sinner'.[55] In order to attain a true connection with God through prayer, the heart first needs to be broken with repentance (*contritum*), 'torn' (*scinde*) and un-'hardened' (*duritiam cordis mei*). Only then can God 'pour [himself] from heaven into [one's] heart'.[56]

With this heartfelt embrace of God, John's reader would finally be able to match his external recitations with an authentically fervent, internal feeling; he would finally be able to say 'This I confess with my mouth, this I believe in my heart, and for this I give you thanks.'[57] John not only instructs his reader to *open* his heart to God in the *CT*, but, more tellingly, he invites the reader to *inscribe* the love and commandments of God onto his heart 'so that [he] will never forget and can never erase it'.[58] Once opened, the reader will finally be 'delivered from the noise that [otherwise] seizes the heart of man'.[59] Surprisingly, this longed-for openness is not a blissful, calm state. John explains that a truly open-hearted man is actually in a constant state of suffering, broken by constant repentance,[60] crushed by constant 'sacrifice'.[61] Real 'misery', to John, is that of a 'sinful soul' whose heart is 'unfeeling' (*insensibilis*)[62] and distant from God; but, perhaps ironically, once the heart is broken and God is let in, there is still only 'plaintive notes and excessive wailings and deep sighs of the heart'.[63] This miserable state of suffering, however, brings the sinner closest to God. Suffering, tears, and despair are signs of a contemplative practice that is effective. John cries repeatedly in the *CT* for *interior* tears – tears stemming from the heart, tears that extend from feeling.[64] Such suffering opens the heart to senses that can point the sinner towards God: smells, sounds, sights, and tastes are discovered, and the heart develops eyes, ears, and a mouth through which the reader can receive the divine.[65] Such openness comes with an intense feeling of suffering. But this, John believes, is much less painful than the ultimate consequences of a life of hard-hearted exterior living. John writes that his *CT* is ultimately written 'so that with the very palate of my heart I may feel'.[66]

The use of feeling, emotion, and *affectus* in John's devotional programme

Contrary to the image of the unfeeling monk, endlessly repeating rote verses of prayer, John's programme called for intense emotion on the part of the devotee. For while heaven is a place of serenity, both for God – 'You

[God] love, without passion; are jealous, without anxiety; repent, yet grieve not; are angry, yet serene'[67] – and for Christians – 'They see and desire to see: without anxiety they desire, without disgust they are sated'[68] – the temporal realm was a place so apt to harden the heart of the sinner that only intense feeling could break it open to God's love: 'With the penalty of sin, moreover, the hardened mind tolerates this, that it is able to see its own sins, [but] it is not able to weep.'[69] This inability to feel and suffer while on this earth, John reasons, makes the devotee blind to the true consequence of his sin. As in the model of Christ's suffering on the cross, only suffering and feeling can truly propel the devotee towards the divine in John's view. So, once the devotee has moved into his own heart, he must now break that heart so that it can feel.

And what, exactly, must the heart feel? A complex of emotions that can be neatly summed up by one of the most frequently used terms in the John's treatise: *caritas*.[70] John defines *caritas* as when 'the soul of the devout mind, burning with an excessive love for Christ, gaping for Christ, sighing for Christ, desiring to see Christ his lone love, possesses nothing sweet except for moaning and crying'.[71] John's *Confessio theologica* often speaks of the paradox of *caritas*, calling it a wounding love, a healing pain, a tender agony. *Caritas* pierces the heart like an arrow of love; its affection causes torment:[72]

> Come, tears, I beseech you, in the name of Jesus Christ my Lord, come; fill my heart, wet my eyes, moisten my cheeks, sprinkle me with crying, flow over my face, give me bitter wailing, generate sweet pardon ... He who brought forth water from the rock[73] and mercifully infused the sinful woman inwardly,[74] at the same time as kindly took her up outwardly, may he himself by his own most holy command speak to you, delayed tears, in order that you may so make drunk my heart with your inundation, desiring you and seeking you, so [the heart] cannot keep itself from crying. As long as it is salutary to weep, as long as it is salutary to repent, hasten, O tears that I wish for, that with my whole mind I seek, in order that I may cry bitterly day and night unceasingly from the wounds of my soul: lest the times granted to repentance pass away, lest the days granted to living well flow by without cause, let the Spirit of God, good teacher and illuminator of Mother Church, who from a hard heart produces tears and gives to penitents fruits worthy of repentance, descend into my heart in order that he may strike streams from above and below [the heart], made as it is of stone and iron.[75]

Given today's popular conception of crying and love as less 'rational' and more 'spontaneous' emotion, John's evocation of them may seem contrived. With our modern sensibilities, we might be sceptical of any crying monk who had been reading the *CT*, suspecting that, by crying, the monk was merely following orders for right action, and not necessarily feeling John's prescribed suffering. But, for John's eleventh-century monastic readers, such deliberate crafting of affective experience was common, and no less genuine than an unprompted bout of tears. The *RB* describes the process of monastic learning as a process of internalisation, where repetition means deeper understanding and not (as a modern audience might suspect) rote memorisation. Through reiteration of John's contemplative prescriptions, a monk would come 'to observe without effort, as though naturally, from habit, no longer out of fear of hell, but out of love for Christ, good habit, and delight in virtue'.[76] The process of *lectio divina* in the monastery was also derived from the belief that genuine knowledge followed repetitive behaviour:[77] repetitive behaviour could indeed yield more sincere feeling in its participants.[78] The *Confessio theologica*'s prescriptions may seem contrived to a modern reader – but they may well have been effective in fostering genuinely emotional prayer in John's monastic audience.

John did not believe, however, that a human could cultivate right emotion without divine help, no matter how hard he might try. Ever since John Cassian, monks had believed that right emotion in prayer was performed (or rather *affected*) on them by God (*afficio*); the resulting affective experience was therefore passively received by a Christian who allowed God to bestow the emotion, or affect, upon him (*affectus*).[79] John's *Confessio theologica* embraces this point, its first-person speaker pleading with or even ordering God in the imperative to affect such feeling in the devotee's self. 'Do [this for me] (*Fac*)', 'Give [this to] me (*Da mihi*)', and 'I beg you (*Rogo*)' are the commands used by the *CT*'s speaker to plead with God that he *afficit* the grace of emotional *affectus*.[80] John shares this age-old notion that emotion is granted to the devotee through the largesse of God.[81] Prayerful emotion is experienced, not wholly created, by John's readers – it is affected on them by God.[82] As he writes in the passage above: 'Let the Spirit of God ... who from a hard heart produces tears, and gives to penitents fruits worthy of repentance, descend into my heart.'[83] Still, while only God can provide the right feeling, Christians are expected to try to cultivate *caritas*, all the while begging for God's help.

The word *affectus* is important in the history of Christian devotion, and plays an outsize role now in its scholarship thanks to the term 'affective piety', so its appearance in the *CT* merits a brief note. John's *CT* only explicitly uses the word *affectus* twice. The first time, John quotes Augustine on the state of heavenly bliss, where devotees finally come face to face with God: in heaven, inhabitants are always the recipients of the right affection (*affectu*) from God, which streams like rays from God's sunlike presence.[84] In the second mention, which will be discussed more extensively below, John shows his reader how the right longing for God (*affectu*) can be cultivated on this earth with the help of the image of the crucified Christ. In each of these cases, the *CT* reminds its readers how praying for the proper *affectus* in turn could make devotees more receptive to these emotions and stronger combatants in the fight for refuge 'away from the turmoil of the thoughts of this age'.[85] Moreover, these efforts, John says, will cause the memory of a specific *affectus* to live on in the devotee, by being more easily revivable in the future.[86]

John's use of the model of the crucified Christ

To bolster his specific prescriptions for suffering, tears, and emotional devotion to God, John provides the readers of the *CT* with three biblical exemplars for right devotion and right feeling: Christ on the cross (Matthew 27:27–44; Mark 15:16–32; Luke 23:26–43; John 19:16–27), Mary Magdalene crying over Jesus's empty tomb (John 20:11), and Hannah tearfully praying for a child (1 Samuel 1–2). John envisions each of these biblical figures in order to better induce a proper emotional reformation in his readers. He invites his readers to empathise with all three characters and to adopt these characters' emotional states for themselves.

John's use of the vision of the crucified Christ is the model for devotion most frequently invoked in the *CT*, and the model that is most embraced by later medieval 'affective piety'. John's *CT* defines *caritas* as the right emotion for the devotee to feel when praying – an experience of divine love through suffering. No other model embodies *caritas* more powerfully than the obedient Son's torture and death for the sake of love. Fittingly, most of John's explicit mentions of the word '*caritas*' are made in connection with Jesus's crucifixion.[87] By peppering his *CT* with images of the suffering Christ, John shows that 'it is by [Christ's] blood that we have access to [God]'.[88] Here, John acknowledges both that Jesus's atonement literally allows Christians 'access' to heaven after death, and that Jesus's *blood* – the material proof of his suffering – allows Christians to *feel* emotionally in contemplation, granting them interior access to God while they are on this earth.

The *Confessio theologica*'s most distinctive use of the crucifixion, however, does not merely present an image of Jesus's suffering *caritas*. It also attempts to crucify the *reader*, shaping the reader into Christ himself so that he can better feel the painful lengths Christ went for the sake of godly love. John uses the following image to spark in his reader the same affective experience of the crucified Christ:

> Through those saving wounds which you suffered on the cross for our salvation and from which flowed the precious and vivifying blood by which we have been redeemed with propitious graciousness ... wound this sinful soul of mine for which you were willing even to die; wound it with the fiery and powerful dart of your excessive *caritas*. You are the living Word of God, efficacious and more piercing than every sharpest sword. You, double-edged sword, cleave my hardness of heart and wound this sinful soul, and pierce more deeply to the inmost parts with your powerful virtue. Give me an abundant source of water and pour into my eyes a true font of tears running day and night out of excessive feeling [*affectu*] and desire for the vision of your beauty, so that I may grieve constantly all the days of my life, taking no consolation in the present life, until I merit to see you, my God and my Lord, as a beloved and beautiful spouse in your heavenly chamber.[89]

This passage distils the essence of John's distinctive use of the crucifixion in his *CT*.[90] Here, the prayerful speaker of the *CT* asks that the image of the wounded Christ in turn work to wound the sinner and penetrate the tough shield of the human heart so that the sinner can weep day and night. This notion of wounding and penetrating the heart is an image common in the Bible, particularly in the Song of Songs, and thus common also to both contemporary monastic literature and later medieval mystical writings.[91] But beyond making biblical references and speaking in rhetorical tropes, John is doing something very specific here: as John's devotee looks at Christ's bleeding wounds in his mind's eye, the vision of those wounds (and the *caritas* that they signify) affect a wound in the devotee's own soul.[92] The soul becomes wounded as Christ's body is wounded; and instead of bleeding from the wound, the soul cries abundant tears from the wound – its wounds weep. The devotee's very act of engaging with this crucified image is a painful one – the image 'pierces', 'cleaves', 'wounds', and it is not consoling. The image of the crucified affects an emotional crucifixion of the devotee. But it is a crucified suffering that is a sign of *caritas* – it is a 'dart of love' – and, as a result, it is the most effective (*efficax*) technique that John offers to his reader to receive the feeling (*affectu*) of weeping for closeness to God. The passage invites its reader to engage in an empathy so extreme he longs to become the crucified Christ and to make the ultimate sacrifice – at least, emotionally.[93] This is as close to God as a human can get.

John even emphasises the connection between the tears that pour from the wounded heart of the sinner and the blood that gushes from the wounds of Christ by using parallel language throughout his work;[94] John's devotee-speaker longs to be a 'holocaust' and a 'sacrifice of a broken spirit'.[95] John thus bombards his reader with the model of Christ.

Another passage from the *CT* expands the scope of John's use of the crucified Christ as a model for his reader to follow:[96]

> Dearest one, I beseech you through your passion and cross, fill my heart with your inextinguishable love, with your constant remembrance, so that like a burning flame I may entirely blaze in the sweetness of your love ... write with your finger in my heart the sweet memory of your mellifluous name, a memory never erased by any forgetfulness. Write on the tablets of my heart your commandments and will, your laws and right doing, so that I may always and everywhere have you, Lord of immense sweetness, and your precepts before my eyes. How sweet are your words to my throat. Grant me a tenacious memory, so that I forget them not.[97]

Where is the reader's crucifixion in this passage? Rachel Fulton has argued that medieval people would have seen this 'writing' on the heart as a kind of 'inscriptive wounding'; much as a stylus would wound the skin of parchment during the act of writing.[98] 'Writing' here, then, becomes parallel to the earlier wounding of the heart, whose tough shield the devotee asks Christ to penetrate with his two-edged sword; John calls for Christ to help pierce the sinner in a new way.[99] The devotee wants his heart – now unhardened – to be wounded continuously ('always and everywhere') by the 'memory' of Christ's own passion. There is a kind of self-perpetuating circularity here: the devotee asks for the vision and memory of the wounded Christ to create a wounding of his own heart, and these wounds in turn will serve as a constant reminder for him of the model of Christ's passion and *caritas*, which will continue to wound him.

John's use of the models of Mary Magdalene and Hannah

Perhaps because Jesus's human life is less important to John than the emotional model of the crucifixion, John is not interested in devotion to the Virgin Mary in his *Confessio theologica*, unlike many of the affective writers who come after him. The Virgin, in fact, is mentioned only once, obliquely, in the whole treatise.[100] Alongside the crucified Christ, however, John refers the *Confessio theologica*'s readers to two other biblical models: Mary Magdalene and Hannah. This is unusual before the twelfth century, particularly the use of Hannah.[101] Nonetheless, both the Magdalene and Hannah are showcased by John in the same way that the crucified Christ is: in all three recensions of John's work, they serve as archetypes for right emotional devotion and behaviour for John's readers, whether male or female.

Mary Magdalene appears several times in the *Confessio theologica*, primarily as a model for tearfulness.[102] In fact, in the *Confessio theologica*, John highlights how the Magdalene went through all of the stages that John's treatise prescribes. He mentions Mary Magdalene as a model for his first stage of prayer – interiority – saying that God 'mercifully infused the sinful woman inwardly, at the same time that he kindly took her up outwardly'.[103] Mary Magdalene thus serves as a model of someone who reformed her exterior actions *and* her interior connection to God. John mentions Mary Magdalene again after he has established the desirability of tears in Part III of the *CT*, showing her to be a relevant emotional model as well, exemplifying a persistent, tearful, loving, *caritas*-filled devotion to God. In John's formulation, Mary Magdalene returns again and again to the action of seeking God; through her, John relates another virtue to his reader's practice of prayer – the virtue of persistence. Since John acknowledges that the reader's prayer will never be satisfied with a heavenly vision on this earth, patience and persistence are important.[104]

John's most involved depiction of Mary Magdalene's spiritual persistence is the following:

> Let my eyes, O Lord, bring down allotments of waters, with you, for whom all things are possible and nothing difficult, merciful and forgiving. But just like that woman who was seeking you, O Lord, while you were lying in the tomb, had been inundated with so many tears, and had desired to see you whom she loved with such great fervour of mind, that although others were receding that woman did not recede, who, full of your excessive love, approached to visit the place of burial again and again. She stood, she persevered, she found finally what she desired. For to that one loving you above the rest, and seeking you more zealously than all, you deigned to appear first of all, since the power of such great perseverance was love. Therefore with what zeal, with what tears, or with what constancy of holy longing must we seek, fear, and love you, night and day through all the days of our life, the Lord of all things now reigning in heaven and holding all things under your command?[105]

Christ shows right *caritas* and inspires proper suffering in the viewer. Mary Magdalene's example helps to cultivate *continual* suffering once it is achieved; she shows the stamina required. With the aid of such persistence, the devotee can then say: 'so that my tears become to me bread day and night ... give me the best part, which Mary chose and which I myself have chosen formerly and preferred through the inspiration of your grace, in order that I, absolved from all my cares, may freely sit at the feet of the Lord Jesus Christ and may listen intently to what heavenly wisdom teaches'.[106] In this image, John alludes to Mary sitting at Jesus's feet, tearful and devoted, while Martha busies herself about the house.[107] It is no coincidence, then, that the monks of Fécamp had a relic of Mary Magdalene, who was such a potent exemplar from their abbot's *CT*.[108]

The third biblical model invoked by John in the *CT* is one from the Hebrew Bible: Hannah.[109] While scholars have previously examined Mary Magdalene as a sometime feature of affective piety, Hannah has not been discussed, and her presence seems to be one of John's unique contributions.[110] In 1 Samuel 1, Hannah is a barren woman. Like Mary Magdalene, Hannah is persistent and tearful (in Hannah's case, it is because she longs for a baby); and yet, though God is silent in her repeated request for a child, she never stops praying, and she persists in her tearful prayers (1 Samuel 1:10). For John's monks, Hannah likely served as a poignant model. It was Hannah whom the priest Eli accused of being drunk when, tearfully praying, she 'spoke *in her heart*,[111] and only her lips moved' ('*loquebatur in corde suo, tantumque labia illius movebantur*'; 1 Samuel 1:13–14); Hannah's interior plea, then, would have resonated with John of Fécamp's own prescription that prayer come from an open heart.

When John mentions Hannah, he emphasises all of these points: her tears, her persistence, and her special, internal, self-altering prayer:

> I recall, O Lord, I recall, holy one, that holy woman who came to the tabernacle intending to ask, who sought with many tears a son to be given to her, concerning whom the Scripture reports that her countenances after her tears and prayers were no more changed into different things. I recall, I say, such great faith and such great constancy, and I am twisted with pain and confounded with shame, because I most wretchedly do no such thing.[112]

John continues:

> For if the woman who was seeking a son wept in this way, and in weeping persevered, how ought the soul who seeks God to wail and in wailing to persist? Let my soul, I beseech, wail, O my God, let it wail and let it not cease from wailing, having been pierced by a heavenly visitation.[113]

The image of Hannah praying allows John to remind his reader of the intent behind his entire *CT* project: to teach his reader how to pray. For it is not just John's wish to turn his reader towards the experience of *caritas*, or to get his reader to cry continual tears; it is John's intent to teach his reader how to pray correctly, with the right internal connection, with an open heart, and with catalysed, reformed feeling. Hannah, then, serves as a means for tying all of John's observations together and bringing his monk-reader back to the main goal of his *CT*: to create 'this little compilation of readings for

[God's] praise' to incite proper, fervent, emotional prayerful activity in his monastic readers so that they 'may be reignited in [God's] love'.[114]

Conclusion

John of Fécamp's *Confessio theologica* has often been called the beginning of medieval affective piety; but this chapter attempts to move beyond John's current status as the beginning of a devotional trend and instead to locate the role of emotion in John's larger devotional purpose. The mere fact that John calls to mind a crucified body is not a sufficient evidence of his 'affectivity'; and, in view of his larger treatise, his chief interest is not in Jesus's humanity. To understand what John's affective piety is, we must look to the larger programme of his *CT*. In doing so, we learn that he is reaching for the example of Christ alongside other examples of Mary Magdalene and Hannah; we learn that his chief interest in all of these exemplars is the perfected emotional devotion that they model for his reader. Moreover, we learn that these characters and their lives are not the focus for John, but rather that they serve as vehicles carrying the devotee towards a greater goal, as the means to an end. John asks, how can a monk stay emotionally awake in his prayerful actions? How can a devotee know that he is doing the right thing while he is praying, when prayer, as a task, is never satisfied with a heavenly vision or reassurance from God? How can a monk improve and reform his devotion? Look at these biblical models, John says. Are you really suffering in your love for God, as Christ did on the cross? Are you really persistent in your tearful emotion, as Mary Magdalene was at the tomb? Are you really heartfelt and constant in your prayer, as Hannah was in the sanctuary, even though you have no assurance that God is listening? If you are really doing all of these things, John says, then, monk-reader, you are fully engaged in the act of true prayer.

John's *Confessio theologica*'s attention to the reform of the inner emotion of its readers' prayer seems remarkable for his eleventh-century context. Monastic leaders in the beginning of the eleventh century have traditionally been viewed as less concerned with *how* one prayed and more concerned *that* one prayed, more concerned with right external action than right internal emotion. But John's attention to exactly the reverse persists throughout his *CT* and throughout all of his actions as abbot of Fécamp. So where did his idea for an internal, emotional reform of prayer come from? And just how innovative was it in the wider context of European monasticism? Those are the questions of the next chapter.

Notes

1 John's writings are notoriously difficult to identify today because they circulated anonymously. I acknowledge therefore that he could have written more than has been identified.
2 'Ingrediar in interiore mentis meae' (*CT*, p. 167).
3 Note that John did not title his own work '*Confessio theologica*'. The name is a variation from a twelfth-century manuscript of John's work (Paris, BnF, ms. lat. 1919), where the book is called '*liber confessionum*' in the titular rubric (see fol. 1 of that manuscript). The word '*theologica*' was added in the sixteenth-century printed edition entitled *Confessio theologica tribus partibus absoluta* (Paris: M. Vascovanum, 1539). Stéphane Lecouteux has recently revised the date of the start of John's priorship, changing it from 1016 to 1023 (until 1028) in 'Réseaux', I, p. 71.
4 Leclercq and Bonnes, *Un maître*, pp. 37–44. For more on these recensions, their manuscripts, and their readership, see Lauren Mancia, 'Affective Devotion and Emotional Reform at the Eleventh-Century Monastery of John of Fécamp' (PhD dissertation, Yale University, 2013), pp. 88–162.
5 The differences between the *Confessio theologica* and the *Libellus* recensions are less significant to the larger meaning of John's text than earlier scholars have believed. Both versions cover roughly the same content, and are divided into three parts, though the *Libellus* is reordered and a little shorter; and, while the *Libellus* recension presents John's four prayers extracted as separate meditations, the texts of those prayers exist in full as integrated parts of the prose of the first recension, *Confessio theologica*. For example, John's most famous prayer, so-called *Meditations of St Augustine* prayer 37b, occurs at the end of the *CT*, on pp. 180–1. Moreover, the themes and phrases of these prayers are found in the larger text of the *Confessio theologica*. *Meditations of St Augustine* prayer 37a's metaphors of the 'fountain of life' and the 'thirsty soul' and its desire for the gift of tears, reoccur throughout the *CT*. The differences between the *Confessio theologica* and *Confessio fidei*, on the other hand, are more significant, and will be discussed in Chapter 4.
6 The only translation of John's work exists in French: *La Confession théologique*, trans. Philippe de Vial (Paris: Cerf, 1992).
7 Where they overlap, both *Paris* 1919 and *Paris* 3088 have texts of the *Confessio theologica* that align almost perfectly, and both contain the same explicits and the same subsequent *Lamentation* text following the *CT* (a text edited in Leclercq and Bonnes, *Un maître*, pp. 166–83). That *Paris* 3088's leaves are from the end of the *CT* is helpful because it confirms that the manuscript is indeed a copy of the first recension of John's work: it does not contain the separately enumerated prayers (which would make it part of the *Libellus* recension) or a fourth part on the Eucharist (which would make it part of the *Confessio fidei* recension).
8 Stéphane Lecouteux has traced the connections between Fécamp and the Cistercian houses in Champagne (of which community *Paris* 1919 is a part). He has shown that Paris, BnF, ms. lat. 5318 (a collection of saints' lives from Fécamp)

was a model for a Cistercian compilation of saints' lives at Clairvaux and diffused to other Cistercian abbeys under the name *Liber de natalitis*. Lecouteux also suspects that books from Saint-Bénigne (for instance, Vatican City, Biblioteca Apostolica Vaticana, Ottob. lat. 120) were likewise associated with this lineage of hagiographical manuscripts stemming from Fécamp. 'Réseaux', I, pp. 139–43.

9 On the dispute over the *Confessio fidei*'s authenticity, see Vincent Serralda, 'Étude comparée de la "Confessio Fidei" attribuée à Alcuin et de la "Confessio Theologica" de Jean de Fécamp', in Walter Beschin (ed.), *Mittellateinisches Jahrbuch* (Stuttgart: Anton Hiersemann, 1988), pp. 7–27; Warren Pezé, 'Aux origines de la Confession de Saint Martin', *Revue Mabillon* 86 (25 n.s.) (2014), 5–44.

10 Wilmart, 'Deux préfaces spirituelles', p. 25, n. 11.

11 '*Praesta, Domine, ut famulum tuum abbatam meum et omnes seniores fratresque meos sincere et humili caritate semper diligam malis et peccatis atque adversitatibus eorum ex corde condoleam, bonis et virtutibus atque profectibus eorum ex corde congaudeam, amori tuo nunquam aliquid praeponam, sed te in omnibus et super omnia diligam. Da mihi veram humilitatem et oboedientiam, veram subiectionem atque mortificationem, ut liberum arbitrium non vivat in me neque propria voluntas ducat me. Da mihi simplicitatem, innocentiam et integritatem mentis, iugem custodiam cordis atque oris, ut nullum damnem aut respuam, de nullius meritis diffidam, nulli malum reddam pro malo, sed ambulem in simplicitate cordis mei coram te semper*' (*CT*, pp. 133–4).

12 Leclercq and Bonnes, *Un maître*, p. 28.

13 Teresa Webber, 'Cantor, Sacrist, or Prior? The Provision of Books in Anglo-Norman England', in Katie Bugyis, Margot Fassler, and Andrew Kraebel (eds), *Medieval Cantors and their Craft: Music, Liturgy, and the Shaping of History, 800–1500* (Woodbridge: York Medieval Press/Boydell & Brewer, 2017), pp. 172–89.

14 Mancia, 'Affective Devotion and Emotional Reform', pp. 88–162; Fulton, *From Judgment to Passion*, p. 166.

15 This, in combination with the fact that the majority of the eleventh- and twelfth-century manuscripts that circulated in John's lifetime were *Libellus* manuscripts prefaced by dedicatory letters to women, has caused some to argue that an audience of women chiefly consumed John's work, namely McNamer, *Affective Meditation*, 60. McNamer here refers specifically to the *Libellus* recension. However, because most of the *Libellus* manuscripts enjoyed a circulation at male monastic houses, it is unlikely that John wrote his texts solely for women; see also Davis, *The Weight of Love*, p. 131.

16 Of the *Libellus*: Metz, Médiathèque de Metz, ms. 245 and Paris, BnF, ms. lat. 13593. Of the *Confessio fidei*: Montpellier, Bibliothèque interuniversitaire de Montpellier, ms. H309.

17 Of the *Libellus*: Zwettl, Zisterzienserstift Zwettl, Cod. 164 and Cod. 225; Vienna, Österreichische Nationalbibliothek, Cod. 1580 and Cod. 1582; Barcelona, Archivo de la Corona de Aragón, Ripoll 214; Munich, Bayerische Staatsbibliothek, Clm. 11352 and Clm. 12607. Of the *Confessio theologica*: Paris, BnF, ms. lat. 1919. Of the *Confessio fidei*: Troyes, Bibl. mun., ms. 2142 (fols 180v–189r).

18 For more on this, see Chapter 5.
19 Among the eleventh-century manuscripts: Metz, Médiathèque, ms. 245 was from Saint-Arnoul de Metz, a monastery that was reformed by John's mentor William of Volpiano in 996/7, and that maintained a correspondence with John of Fécamp in the 1050s (see Chapter 3); Montpellier, Bibliothèque interuniversitaire de Montpellier, ms. H309 is from Saint-Bénigne de Dijon, William of Volpiano's monastery, John's alma mater, and a monastery of which John was abbot from 1052 to 1054; *Paris* 13593 has a possible Bec origin (and Fécamp connection thereby – see Lauren Mancia, 'Praying with an Eleventh-Century Manuscript: A Case Study of the Enigmatic Paris, BnF, ms. lat. 13593', in Thomas Barton, Susan McDonough, Sara McDougall, and Matthew Wranovix (eds), *Boundaries in the Medieval and Wider World* (Turnhout: Brepols, 2017), pp. 153–77). Among the twelfth-century manuscripts: Ripoll 214 is from the monastery of Santa Maria de Ripoll in Catalonia, a monastery that has William of Volpiano listed in its necrology, likely because of its connection with Cuxa (see Stéphane Lecouteux's 'Deux fragments d'un nécrologe de la Trinité de Fécamp (XIe–XIIe siècles). Étude et édition critique d'un document mémoriel exceptionnel', *Tabularia* 16 (2016), 1–89. Note that there is no surviving *Confessio theologica* manuscript from Fécamp itself, although the unattributed *Paris* 3088 might be.
20 The existence of a dedicatory letter does not necessarily have anything to do with the readership of the particular manuscript, since dedicatory letters often circulated with their texts as a kind of foreword to attract attention, regularly having no bearing on the audience of the manuscripts themselves: Giles Constable, *Letters and Letter Collections*, Typologie des sources du moyen âge occidental 17 (Turnhout: Brepols, 1976); Christian Høgel and Elisabetta Bartoli (eds), *Medieval Letters: Between Fiction and Document* (Turnhout: Brepols, 2015).
21 'Idcirco non praesumptionis temeritate, sed magna tui desiderii auiditate huic defloratiunculae ad laudem tuam operam dedi, ut breve et manuale verbum de Deo mecum semper haberem, ex cuius lectionis igne, quoties tepefio, in tuum reaccendar amorem. Quoniam enim in medio laqueorum positi sumus, facile a caelesti desiderio frigescimus. Assiduo itaque indigemus munimento, ut expergefacti ad te nostrum verum et summum bonum, cum defluximus, recurramus. Sed ignosce, rogo, Domine, ignosce mihi indignissimo et infelici tecum de te divtius colloquenti servo. Ignosce, pie, mihi misero. Amore enim tui nominis nimio labia mea tibi aperui' (*CT*, p. 182).
22 There are several such cases in the eleventh- and twelfth-century examples. Pages from *Paris* 3088, the earliest fragment of the *CT*, measure long and narrow at 26 cm × 17.5 cm. The same is true for its *Libellus* editions: Metz, Médiathèque, ms. 245, for instance, is even longer and narrower, measuring 31.8 cm × 17.3 cm; Paris, BnF, ms lat. 13593, an edition of John's *Libellus* prayers, is as small as a book of hours, measuring 20.3 cm × 15.2 cm.
23 This kind of performative 'I' is common in medieval writing according to A.C. Spearing, *Medieval Autographies: The 'I' of the Text* (Notre Dame, IN: University of Notre Dame Press, 2012).

24 Italics my emphasis. See Chapter 5; Thomas H. Bestul, 'Self and Subjectivity in the Prayers and Meditations of Anselm of Canterbury', in Roman Majeran and Edward Iwo Zielinski (eds), *Saint Anselm: Bishop and Thinker: Papers Read at a Conference Held in the Catholic University of Lublin on 24–26 September 1996* (Lublin: University Press of the Catholic University of Lublin, 1999), p. 151.

25 The *CT* has thus been called a monumental moment for the development of silent reading, see Paul Saenger, *Space between Words: The Origins of Silent Reading* (Stanford, CA: Stanford University Press, 1997), p. 202. Sarah McNamer agrees, calling this an 'impassioned "I"': McNamer, *Affective Meditation*, pp. 67–73.

26 This performative instigation of emotions is akin to the 'emotives' described in Reddy, *The Navigation of Feeling* (see Introduction, above). The idea that emotion is performative and performable is also discussed in Davis, *The Weight of Love*, pp. 6, 19.

27 '*Da mihi cordis contritionem, et lacrimarum fontem, praecipue dum preces et orationes meas tibi affero, dum tuae laudis psalmodiam decanto, dum mysterium nostrae redemptionis manifestum misericordiae tuae iudicium recolo vel profero, dum sacris altaribus, licet indignus, assisto, cupiens offerre illud mirabile et caeleste sacrificium omni reverentia et devotione dignum*' (*CT*, p. 173).

28 Amy Hollywood, 'Song, Experience, and the Book in Benedictine Monasticism', in Amy Hollywood and Patricia Z. Beckman (eds), *The Cambridge Companion to Christian Mysticism* (New York: Cambridge University Press, 2012), p. 65.

29 The idea that prescribed feelings of the past can be recovered by historians is discussed by Barbara Rosenwein, *Emotional Communities in the Early Middle Ages* (Ithaca, NY: Cornell University Press, 2006), p. 196.

30 '*Dicta mea dicta sunt patrum*' (*CT*, p. 121). There is more on this in Chapter 2.

31 '*In hac quidem vita miseriis erroribusque plenissima haberi non potest contemplativae perfectio vitae*' (*CT*, p. 174).

32 For more on how this contrasts with the writings of Anselm of Canterbury and others, see Chapter 5.

33 For more about 'conversion' or 'confession' being an act of understanding and recognition of God by Christians, see Elizabeth C. Parker and Charles T. Little, *The Cloisters Cross: Its Art and Meaning* (New York: Abrams, 1994), pp. 72–5, 175–95; see also Chapter 2, below.

34 As quoted in M.D. Chenu, *Nature, Man, and Society in the Twelfth Century: Essays on New Theological Perspectives in the Latin West* (Toronto: University of Toronto Press, 1997), p. 313.

35 The process of moving from the exterior to the interior also mirrors the process of *lectio divina*. See, for instance, Jean-François Cottier, *Anima mea: Prières privées et textes de dévotion du moyen âge latin* (Turnhout: Brepols, 2001), p. 110.

36 '*interioribus sensibus animae meae*' (*CT*, p. 179). This idea is also found elsewhere in medieval texts; for instance, Piroska Nagy, 'Religious Weeping as Ritual in the Medieval West', *Social Analysis* 48.2 (2004), 123.

37 '*intimae visionis*' (*CT*, p. 172).

38 *CT*, p. 124.
39 *CT*, p. 156.
40 Phillip C. Adamo, *New Monks in Old Habits: The Formation of the Caulite Monastic Order, 1193–1267* (Toronto: Pontifical Institute of Mediaeval Studies, 2014), p. 183. On the *interior domus*, see Melville, *The World of Medieval Monasticism*, pp. 189–90. Melville also discusses like images of the 'inner household' and 'soul's cloister' (*claustrum animae*) on pp. 318–20.
41 Cf. *CT*, pp. 137, 158.
42 *CT*, p. 114.
43 This is an intentional paraphrase from Augustine's *Confessions* 10.27.38.
44 *CT*, p. 172.
45 '*Atque altius penetra ad intima potenti virtute*' (*CT*, p. 181).
46 For more on how both Augustine and Anselm do this, see Karl F. Morrison, 'Framing the Subject: Humanity and the Wounds of Love', in Karl F. Morrison and Rudolph M. Bell (eds), *Studies on Medieval Empathies* (Turnhout: Brepols, 2013), p. 10.
47 *CT*, p. 144.
48 *CT*, pp. 159, 173.
49 '*Et quis locus in me est, quo veniat in me, Deus meus?*' (*CT*, p. 110).
50 This focus on the heart and on inscription on the heart is biblical: cf. Jeremiah 31:33, 'But this is the covenant that I will make with the house of Israel after those days, says the Lord: I will put my law within them, and I will write it on their hearts; and I will be their God, and they shall be my people.' Thanks to Travis Stevens for pointing this out.
51 Augustine, *Confessions* 6.3: 'When [Ambrose] read, his eyes scanned the page and his heart sought out the meaning, but his voice was silent and his tongue was still.'
52 '*Da mihi cor contritum, cor purum, cor sincerum, cor deuotum, cor castum, cor sobrium, cor mite, cor mansuetum, cor tranquillum, cor serenissimum, cor tui desiderio plenum ... scinde duritiam cordis mei ut emanet fons iste cuius desiderio nimis aestuat anima mea ... ut lacrimae meae fiant mihi panis die ac nocte. Libera me iurgiis et contentionibus quas ibi patitur misera mens, ubi est litigans hominum multitudo ... ut a cunctis absolutus curis liber ad pedes Domini Iesu Christi sedeam et intente audiam quid caelestis sapientia doceat*' (*CT*, pp. 133, 136).
53 The obsession with the heart (the 'palate of the heart', a 'hardened heart') is akin to Augustine's obsession with the heart in his *Confessions*. For instance, *CT*, pp. 144, 172 is parallel to *Confessions* 5.13.23 and *Confessions* 7.16.22; see Lauren Mancia, 'Reading Augustine's *Confessions* in Normandy in the Eleventh and Twelfth Centuries', *Tabularia* 14 (2014), 195–233.
54 '*Amaritudo et omnis fellis asperitas in regione tua locum non habet*' (*CT*, p. 156).
55 '*et peccatricem mulierem intus misericorditer infundit*' (*CT*, p. 152).
56 '*tu infunde caelitus cordibus nostris*' (*CT*, p. 127).
57 '*Hoc ore confiteor, hoc corde credo, et pro hoc tibi gratias ago*' (*CT*, p. 141).

Emotional monasticism

58 '*in pectore meo dulcem memoriam tui melliflui nominis nulla unquam oblivione delendam*' (*CT*, p. 172). Mary Carruthers has spoken about this idea of the memory as a writing tablet upon which to inscribe thoughts in *The Craft of Thought: Meditation, Rhetoric, and the Making of Images, 400–1200* (New York: Cambridge University Press, 1998), p. 102.

59 '*Confugiat mens mea sub umbram alarum tuarum ab aestibus cogitationum huius saeculi*' (*CT*, p. 143).

60 '*Da mihi cor contritum, cor purum, cor sincerum, cor devotum, cor castum, cor sobrium, cor mite, cor mansuetum, cor tranquillum*' (*CT*, p. 133).

61 '*ut sacrificium spiritus contribulati et cordis contriti*' (*CT*, p. 172).

62 '*Desiderat desiderio magno divisiones aquarum, peccatrix anima mea: sed obriguit misera, insensibilis facta est*' (*CT*, p. 151).

63 '*Et inter has quarerelas nimiosque ploratus ac profunda cordis suspiria, assumis maestam et anxiam mentem super alta iuga montium*' (*CT*, p. 160).

64 *CT*, p. 136.

65 *CT*, pp. 157, 176–7. For more on the divine awakening of the senses in monastic writing, see R. Hale, '"Taste and See, for God is Sweet": Sensory Perception and Memory in Medieval Christian Mystical Experience', in Ann Clarke Bartlett (ed.), *Vox Mystica: Essays on Medieval Mysticism in Honor of Professor Valerie M. Lagorio* (Rochester, NY: D.S. Brewer, 1995), pp. 3–14; Rachel Fulton, '"Taste and See That the Lord is Sweet" (Ps. 33:9): The Flavor of God in the Monastic West', *Journal of Religion* 86.2 (2006), 169–204.

66 '*Ut ipso cordis palato sentiam*' (*CT*, pp. 176–7).

67 '*Amas, nec aestuas. Zelas et securus es. Paenitet te et non doles. Irasceris et tranquillus es*' (*CT*, p. 112); cf. Augustine's *Confessions* 1.4.4.

68 '*Vident et videre desiderant: sine anxietate desiderant, sine fastidio satiantur*' (*CT*, p. 159).

69 '*De paena autem peccati hoc obdurata mens sustinet, ut peccata sua videre possit, flere non possit*' (*CT*, pp. 151–2). This relationship between emotion and sin is also noted in Rosenwein, *Emotional Communities in the Early Middle Ages*, p. 49.

70 *Caritas* is mentioned with incredible frequency throughout the *Confessio theologica*: it can be found in *CT*, pp. 119, 127, 129, 130, 133, 140, 155, 156, 158, 159, 161, 171, 172, 173, 175, 179, 181, 182. At the beginning of the *CT*, God himself is identified as *caritas*: '*Tu vere Patris et Filii caritas, unitas, et sanctitas*' (*CT*, pp. 119). John also quotes Augustine's *Confessions* supporting this point, saying '*O aeterna veritas, et vera caritas, et cara aeternitas! Tu es Deus meus*' (*CT*, p. 161; from *Confessions* 7.10.16). This is somewhat different from how other scholars have depicted the medieval definition of *caritas* (as fellow-feeling) in other contexts; see, for instance, Romig, *Be a Perfect Man* or Morrison, 'Framing the Subject'. The connection between *caritas* and Augustine will be discussed further in Chapter 3.

71 '*Incipit pars tertia in qua mens devota a nimio Christi amore flagrans, Christo inhians, Christo suspirans, Christum quem solum amat videre desiderans, nihil dulce habet nisi gemere et flere*' (*CT*, p. 142).

Reforming the reader's interior

72 'Tuae enim caritatis iaculo vulneratus sum ... Anxius et sitibundus ad te volando curro' (*CT*, p. 155). The idea of *caritas* as a wounding arrow is a rhetorical trope found often in monastic writing (and derived in part from the Song of Songs); see Chapters 3 and 5, below.
73 The passage comes from Psalm 127:16, and according to Leclercq and Bonnes, is reminiscent of a prayer from the *Precum libelli*, which will be discussed further in Chapter 2.
74 The 'sinful woman' mentioned here is Mary Magdalene.
75 '*Venite lacrimae obsecro, in nomine Domini mei Jesu Christi venite; implete cor meum, irrigate oculos meos, humectate genas meas, aspergite me fletibus, fluite super faciem meam, date mihi planctum amarum, generate dulcem veniam ... Qui eduxit aquam de petra et peccatricem mulierem intus misericorditer infundit, pariterque benigne foris suscepit, ipse suo piisimo iussu vobis tardantibus dicat, ut cor meum vos desiderans, et vos quaerens, vestra ita inebrietis inundatione, ut se a fletibus temperare nec velit, nec possit ... Donec salubre est flere, donec salubre est paenitere, festinate lacrimae quas opto, quas tota mente mea peto: ut pro vulneribus animae meae indesinenter diebus ac noctibus defleam: ne tempora indulta poenitentiae pereant; ne dies ad bene vivendum concessi, sine causa fluant, Spiritus Dei, bonus doctor et illuminator matris ecclesiae, qui ex duro corde producit lacrimas, et dat paenitentibus dignos paenitentiae fructus, descendat in cor meum, ut cudat ex eo saxeo et ferreo irriguum superius, et irriguum inferius*' (*CT*, pp. 151–2).
76 *RB* 7:67–9, as quoted in Hollywood, 'Song, Experience, and the Book', p. 64.
77 For more on this process, see Conrad Leyser, '*Lectio divina, oratio pura*: Rhetoric and the Techniques of Asceticism in the *Conferences* of John Cassian', in Giulia Barone, Marina Caffiero, and Francesco Scorza Barcellona (eds), *Modelli di santità e modelli di comportamento: contrasti, intersezioni, complementarità* (Turin: Rosenberg & Sellier, 1994), pp. 133–44; Robertson, *Lectio Divina*; Mary Agnes Edsall, 'Reading Like a Monk: Lectio Divina, Religious Literature, and Lay Devotion' (PhD dissertation, Columbia University, 2000); Jean Leclercq, *The Love of Learning and the Desire for God: A Study of Monastic Culture* (New York: Fordham University Press, 1982).
78 Hollywood, 'Song, Experience, and the Book', pp. 77–8; Scheer, 'Are Emotions a Kind of Practice'; Frederick Paxton, 'Performing Death and Dying at Cluny in the High Middle Ages', in Bruce T. Morrill, Susan Rodgers, and Joanna E. Ziegler (eds), *Practicing Catholic: Ritual, Body, and Contestation in Catholic Faith* (New York: Palgrave Macmillan, 2006), pp. 43–57; Morrison, 'Framing the Subject', p. 31; Christopher Swift, 'The Penitent Prepares: Affect, Contrition, and Tears', in Elina Gertsman (ed.), *Crying in the Middle Ages: Tears of History* (New York: Routledge, 2011), pp. 79–101.
79 Hollywood, 'Song, Experience, and the Book', pp. 64–9.
80 '*Fac*' appears in *CT*, pp. 145, 173, 177, 179; '*Da mihi*' appears in *CT*, pp. 180, 181; '*Rogo*' appears in *CT*, pp. 181, 182.
81 Cf. *CT*, p. 180.

82 Cf. *CT*, p. 178.
83 Cf. n. 75 above.
84 'Its delight is exclusively in you. In an unfailing purity it satiates its thirst in you. It never at any point betrays its mutability. You are always present to it, and it concentrates all of its *affection* on you. It has no future to expect. It suffers no variation and experiences no distending in the successiveness of time' ('*Tu solus es, te perseverantissima castitate hauriens mutabilitatem suam nusquam et nunquam exerit et in te sibi semper praesente, ad te toto affectu se tenet, non habens futurum quod expectet nec in praeteritum traiiciens quod meminerit, nulla vice variatur nec in tempore ullo distenditur*') (*CT*, p. 166); cf. Augustine's *Confessions* 12.11.12.
85 '*Confugiat mens mea sub umbrum alarum tuarum ab aestibus cogitationum huius saeculi*' (*CT*, p. 143).
86 For more on the relationship between memory and affect, see Mary Carruthers, *The Book of Memory: A Study of Memory in Medieval Culture* (New York: Cambridge University Press, 1990), p. 54.
87 Of the mentions of *caritas* listed above, the following *italicised* pages indicate instances when *caritas* is connected implicitly or explicitly to the model of the crucified Christ: *CT*, pp. 119, 127, 129, *130*, 133, *140*, 155, 156, 158, 159, 161, *171*, *172*, *173*, *175*, *179*, *181*, *182*.
88 '*Per eius sanguinem habemus accessum ad te*' (*CT*, p. 140).
89 '*per illa salutifera vulnera tua, quae passus es in cruce pro salute nostra, ex quibus emanavit ille pretiosus et vivificus sanguis quo sumus redempti propitiabili dignatione ... vulnera hanc animam peccatricem, pro qua etiam mori dignatus es; vulnera eam igneo et potentissimo telo tuae nimiae charitatis. Vivus es, sermo Dei, et efficax et penetrabilior omni acutissimo gladio. Tu gladius bis acute cordis duritiam scinde, et vulnera hanc animam peccatricem, atque altius penetra ad intima potenti virtute, et sic da capiti meo aquam immensam, oculisque meis verum lacrimarum fontem nocte ac die currentem infunde ex nimio affectu et desiderio visionis pulchritudinis tuae, ut lugeam iugiter cunctis diebus vitae meae, nullam in praesenti vita recipiens consolationem, donec te in caelesti thalamo merear videre dilectum et pulcherrimum sponsum Deum et Dominum meum*' (*CT*, pp. 180–1).
90 This also happens to be part of one of the four prayers excerpted in the *Libellus*; see Introduction, above.
91 Note that the conflation of love with the sight of God's wounds here is similar to an image found in the Rothschild Canticles (Figure 8); see Chapter 5, below, and Jeffrey Hamburger, 'The Visual and the Visionary: The Image in Late Medieval Monastic Devotions', in *The Visual and the Visionary: Art and Female Spirituality in Late Medieval Germany* (New York: Zone Books, 1998), p. 127. There is a gender inversion here: the male monk wants to be pierced with a dart or a lance, assuming the 'female' position. While I will not dwell on this here, an important book on such gender issues is L.C. Engh, *Gendered Identities in Bernard of Clairvaux's Sermons on the* Song of Songs: *Performing the Bride* (Turnhout: Brepols, 2014).
92 Note that the word *vulnera* also means sins – it is used as such in the *RB*, ch. 46 – so there is a *double entendre* here too. The Christian's sinfulness causes his

suffering, and the sinner's *vulnera* require him to be crucified and to obtain visual *vulnera* to brand him a sinner. The tears of contrition even flow from the wound (i.e. sin) in the sinner's soul.

93 Morrison defines empathy as metaphorical identity that strives to be literal – I am you – so such extremity is an empathic act; Karl Morrison, '*I Am You*': *The Hermeneutics of Empathy in Western Literature, Theology, and Art* (Princeton, NJ: Princeton University Press, 1988).

94 See the parallel use of forms of *emanare* for both tears and blood in John's text. In *CT*, p. 181, concerning blood: 'Wherefore I pray for the clemency of your goodness through those salvific wounds which you suffered on the cross for our salvation, from which flowed the precious and life-giving blood by which we have been redeemed with propitious graciousness' ('*Quapropter precor clementiam bonitatis tuae per illa salutifera vulnera quae passus es in cruce pro salute nostra, ex quibus emanavit ille praetiosus et vivificus sanguis quo sumus redempti propitiabili dignatione*'). And in *CT*, p. 180, concerning tears: 'In a contrite spirit, producing a true font of tears constantly flowing out of much love and desire for you' ('*in animo contrito, producens verum fontem lacrimarum iugiter emanantem ex multo amore et desiderio tuo*').

95 *CT*, pp. 172, 180, 183.

96 This excerpt is also a part of a *Libellus* prayer.

97 '*Carissime, obsecro per passionem et crucem tuam, reple cor meum tua inextinguibili dilectione, tua continua recordatione, tua continua recordatione, adeo ut totus sicut flamma urens ardeam in tui amoris dulcedine ... scribe digito tuo in pectore meo dulcem memoriam tui melliflui nominis nulla unquam oblivione delendam. Scribe in tabulis cordis mei mandata et voluntatem tuam, legem et iustificationes tuas: ut te immensae dulcendinis Dominum, et praecepta tua semper et ubique habeam prae oculis meis. Quam dulcia faucibus meis eloquia tua. Da mihi tenacem memoriam, ut non obliviscar ea*' (*CT*, p. 172).

98 See Fulton, *From Judgment to Passion*, pp. 164–5. The idea of writing on the 'tablets of the heart' is also seen in later medieval manuscript illumination, when books sometimes were made in a heart-shaped format (and scribes literally wrote on them), or the so-called 'charters of Christ'. See Carruthers, *The Craft of Thought*, p. 102; Jessica Brantley, *Reading in the Wilderness* (Chicago: University of Chicago Press, 2007), pp. 189–91; and Miri Rubin, *Corpus Christi: The Eucharist in Late Medieval Culture* (New York: Cambridge University Press, 1991), pp. 306–8.

99 This kind of *imitatio* on the part of the sinner is discussed in Caroline Walker Bynum, *Fragmentation and Redemption: Essays on Gender and the Human Body in Medieval Religion* (New York: Zone Books, 1991), pp. 126–45.

100 *CT*, p. 121.

101 On John's originality here, see Chapter 2; on how John's use of Hannah and Mary Magdalene differs from how these two female biblical figures are used later, see Chapter 5.

102 John is one of the earliest monks to portray Mary Magdalene as a pillar of steadfast love of Christ: most other writers only use her after the end of the eleventh

century. See Chapters 2 and 5; and see also Fiona Griffiths, *Nuns' Priests' Tales: Men and Salvation in Medieval Women's Monastic Life* (Philadelphia: University of Pennsylvania Press, 2018), pp. 67–76.

103 '*Qui eduxit aquam de petra et peccatricem mulierem intus misericorditer infundit, pariterque benigne foris suscepit*' (*CT*, pp. 151–2).

104 Some scholars have noted that this persistent longing is one of John's unique contributions to affective devotion. For more on this, see Chapter 2.

105 '*Deducant oculi mei, Domine, divisiones aquarum, te miserante et donante, cui omnia possibilia sunt et nihil difficile. Similiter vero illa quae te Domine in sepulcro iacentem quaerebat, tantis lacrimis inundaverat tantoque mentis fervore te, quem amabat, videre desideraverat ut recedentibus aliis ipsa non recederet, et tuo nimio amore plena, locum sepulturae iterum iterumque visura adiret. Stetit, perseveravit, invenit tandem quod desideravit. Illi enim te prae caeteris amanti, et studiosius omnibus quaerenti, primitus apparere dignatus es, quia virtus tanti amoris perseverantia fuit. Quo itaque studio, quibus lacrimis, quaue sancti desiderii instantia nocte ac die per omnes dies vitae nostrae te omnium Dominum iam in caelis regnantem et omnia sub tuo imperio tententem, quaerere, venereari et amare debemus?*' (*CT*, p. 178).

106 '*ut lacrimae meae fiant mihi panis die ac nocte ... da mihi partem illam optimam quam Maria elegit et quam ego ipse elegi olim et praeelegi per inspirationem gratiae tuae ut a cunctis absolutus curis liber ad pedes Domini Jesu Christi sedeam et intente audiam quid caelestia sapientia doceat*' (*CT*, p. 136).

107 See Giles Constable, *Three Studies in Medieval Religious and Social Thought* (New York: Cambridge University Press, 1995), pp. 3–141. See also Katherine Ludwig Jansen, *The Making of the Magdalen: Preaching and Popular Devotion in the Later Middle Ages* (Princeton, NJ: Princeton University Press, 2000), p. 38. For more on John's sources, see Chapter 2, below.

108 Bishop Hugh of Lincoln is recorded to have actually eaten some of Fécamp's relics of Mary Magdalene in the twelfth century: 'Bishop Hugh of Lincoln's Devotion to Relics', in John Shinners (ed.), *Medieval Popular Religion, 1000–1200: A Reader* (Toronto: Toronto University Press, 2007), pp. 181–3.

109 Both the Mary Magdalene and the Hannah texts quoted above appear in the *Libellus* prayer excerpts.

110 Hannah is seen as a symbol of *Ecclesia* (versus Penninah's *Synagoga*), or as a personification of Christian sacrifice (and an exemplar for the practice of monastic oblation) in literature before the eleventh century. John is the first medieval writer to use Hannah as a devotional exemplar (he is followed by Peter Damien and Abelard, though neither uses Hannah as robustly as John does). John's invocation of Hannah as a prayerful exemplar paralleled what monks were already familiar with from the liturgy, since at Lauds on ferial Wednesdays monks would sing her canticle from 1 Samuel 2:1–10 (*Chadd* I, p. 161). Fran Altvater, 'Barren Mother, Dutiful Wife, Church Triumphant: Representations of Hannah in 1 Kings Illuminations', *Different Visions: A Journal of New Perspectives on Medieval Art* 3 (2011), 1–29. For more on this, see Chapters 2 and 5.

111 Italics are here my emphasis.
112 'Recordor, Domine, recordor, pie, illius sanctae mulieris quae ad tabernaculum rogatura venit, quae multis lacrimis dari sibi filium petiit, de qua Scriptura refert, quod vultus eius post lacrimas et preces non sunt amplius in diversa mutati. Recordor, inquam, tante fidei tantaeque constantiae: et dolore torqueor, et verecundia confundor, quia ego miserrimus nil tale facio' (CT, pp. 177–8).
113 'Si enim ita flevit, et in fletu perseveravit mulier quae quaerebat filium, quomodo plangere, et in planctu persistere debet anima quae quaerit Deum? Plangat obsecro anima mea, Deus meus, plangat, et a planctu non desinat caelesti visitatione compuncta' (CT, p. 178).
114 It is interesting that John uses the examples of two women – the Magdalene and Hannah – for his audience of male monks. Medieval men's reaching for female examples is not new – many scholars have written on the subject, most notably Caroline Walker Bynum (in *Jesus as Mother*) and Fiona Griffiths (in *Nuns' Priests' Tales*). It is worth noting that the fact of these female exemplars does not confirm a female audience for John's *CT* – male monks were speaking in Hannah's voice all the time when they sang her canticle in the liturgy, for instance.

2

Dicta mea sunt dicta patrum?: tradition and innovation in John's *Confessio theologica*

Of all the texts John could have written, why a treatise on right feeling in prayer? Why not instead a treatise on proper liturgical behaviour, or a commentary on the *RB*, or some other work regulating monastic action as was typical for monastic reformers at the time? John's choice to write about emotional reform instead of behavioural reform in his *Confessio theologica* was in many ways a natural extension of his experience of monastic policies and training in Ravenna (from his early life until c. 1010), at Saint-Bénigne de Dijon (from c. 1010 to 1023), and at Fécamp (from 1023 to 1028 as prior under William of Volpiano, and then from 1028 to 1078 as abbot). But, in other ways, John's *Confessio theologica* went beyond his models, both selectively excerpting extant ideas and elaborating his own focus on an emotional experience of prayer and meditation, which would come to be embraced by monks and other Christians until the end of the Middle Ages.

This chapter will trace John's sources for the *Confessio theologica*, and, in so doing, will show how John's monastic training and particular pedigree combined to inspire a distinctive text that was all his own. I will begin by showing how John's treatise was very much a product of his monastic context. Relying on foundational texts present in the majority of monastic libraries (psalms, the Song of Songs, *libelli precum*, and Gregory on Job, among others), John's *CT* was, as he claimed, 'the words of the Fathers'.[1] Even the extensive excerption and quotation in his writings followed monastic practice promoted by Benedict of Aniane (747–821) and Smaragdus of Saint-Mihiel (760–840).[2] I then turn more specifically to the particular combination of sources John encountered as a novice in Ravenna and as a young monk in Dijon. I will show how John's unique formation created a perfect storm of ideas on introspection, emotion, and contemplation without which the *CT* could not have been written. I will also show how John's use of sources from his own monastic education and formation was an intentional extension of reform ideals popular in the eleventh century: taking cues from Ravennate hermits, Cluniac abbots, and his own mentor William of Volpiano (960–1031), John likely felt compelled to embrace, perpetuate, and deepen their ideas of reform at Fécamp. Yet, even with its extensive quotation and excerption of patristic and biblical authorities, and even with its implicit citation of the reform ideals popular at the time, John's *Confessio theologica* would have read as innovative to his monastic readership. First, many of the ideas John quoted from his Ravennate or his Saint-Bénigne training were new to Normandy. Second, John revived ideas long dormant in the wider medieval world, adapting the tone of Augustine's *Confessions*, for example, or training a spotlight on Hannah. Finally, even the traditional ideas cited were rewoven to create an innovative text filled with longing and a focus on interior reform.

By understanding the sources of John's *Confessio theologica*, we can understand how he positioned his treatise within the frameworks of age-old monastic discourse and eleventh-century reform rhetoric; how his particular biography shaped his ideas and allowed for an introduction of Italian and Byzantine ideas into Normandy; how he recombined the words of the Fathers to reveal his particular devotional interests; and how the ideas he revived were very much connected to monastic reform ideals. Moreover, in exploring John's sources, we can assess the extent of John's invention, and we can acknowledge the deep-rooted early medieval and monastic foundations of later medieval affective piety that have been largely overlooked by scholars.

The influence of monastic culture and curriculum

First and foremost, John was inspired by the monastic curriculum of the eleventh century. To some extent, this was required: the extensive citation of patristic authorities was so essential in the central Middle Ages that Lanfranc, for instance, refused to approve Anselm's *Monologion* in their absence.[3] That John embraced the words of these monastic authorities, though, does not indicate that his own texts were not original – indeed, as we will see, the sources he selects emphasise the problems in which he is most interested. Some of the sources for John's *CT* were staples of the daily life of medieval European monastics, like the *libelli precum* of the early and central Middle Ages or the psalms. Others might have been taught in the schoolroom of the monastery, like Gregory the Great's (fl. 590–604) *Moralia in Job*. In this section, I will outline the ways in which John's *CT* drew on these monastic sources.

The influence of psalms and the libelli precum

Penitential prayer was a mainstay of monastic life. From Columbanus (543–615) to the Carolingians, the medicine of penance was essential for a sinful soul and was best achieved through prayer.[4] The original book of prayer for medieval Christians, the psalter, deeply influenced John's sense of metaphor, depiction of heaven, and penitential tone.[5] Modelling the proper approach to God and devotional feeling, the psalms served medieval Christians as *formulae* for prayer.[6] Quotations from the psalms would be appropriate to a treatise like John's, which prescribed the most effective devotional practice, and they were interspersed throughout the *Confessio theologica*'s text, seamlessly undergirding John's observations and invocations. As an example, one of the psalms that appears most frequently in the *CT* is Psalm 41. Reading its full text here, one can see whole phrases that serve as essential refrains in John's work:

> As a deer longs for flowing streams, / so my soul longs for you, O God. My soul thirsts for God, for the living God.[7] / When shall I come and behold the face of God? / My tears have been my food day and night,[8] / while people say to me continually, 'Where is your God?' /... Why are you cast down, O my soul, and why are you disquieted within me? / Hope in God; for I shall again praise him, my help and my God. / ... Deep calls to deep at the thunder of your cataracts / all your waves[9] and your billows have gone over me. /... I say to God, my rock, 'Why have you forgotten me? Why must I walk about mournfully because the enemy oppresses me?'[10] / As with a deadly wound[11] in my body, my adversaries taunt me, while they say to me continually, 'Where is your God?' Why are you cast down, O my soul, and why are you disquieted within me?[12]

John's *CT* has first and foremost taken its tone from the psalm above: it, too, questions God and the sinner's soul and is filled with deep longing for God.[13] Actual metaphors employed by the psalmist are also employed by John: the deer, the tears, the waves and thunder.[14] Most important, though, are the two lines that John lifts from this psalm. First, '[m]y tears have been my food day and night' is a line that John repeats again and again; and second, the idea that sins are glaring 'wound[s]' in the sinner's body is also adopted by John – likely made more attractive by the antecedent echo of Christ's wounds.

Beyond the psalms, the prayer texts that were most directly influential for the *CT* were those physically appended to the psalter in medieval books: the *libelli precum* produced in monasteries from the Carolingian period through the eleventh century.[15] While no *libellus precum* survives from the monastery of Fécamp, it is unlikely that John did not encounter such books in his lifetime. The confessional formulas and themes that are seen in John's work are found in the private prayers to the Trinity, Christ, the Virgin, and others of the *libelli*;[16] and the prayers to the Cross and rituals for confession found therein were also likely influences on John's *CT*.[17]

The *libelli precum* often address the crucified Christ directly in the prayers for the Adoration of the Cross and Good Friday with the goal of eliciting proper penitence and confession on the part of their monk-readers.[18] See, for instance, this passage from a *libellus* (Perugia, Biblioteca Comunale Augusta, MS I 17, fols 123r–124v):

> Almighty and merciful God ... although I am wounded and weighed down with all evils, I cry out to you and await mercy from you, so that, by these psalms which I have sung in the sight of your divine majesty, you may deign to give indulgence for all my sins, most holy Lord, and deign to bestow pardon and eternal rest on all my living relatives and the deceased faithful.[19]

One can hear in this passage the desperate call for a vision of God and the tone of the sinner's attentive wail, both reminiscent of John's own work. Elsewhere, prayers in *libelli precum* contain what Renie Choy calls a '"litany of possessives," containing the grammatical construction, 'You are my [noun] ... I confess to you my Lord God ... my king. My author. My life. My salvation ..."'[20] Such litanies are more than just definitions of Christ; rather, they are absolutes for a proper Christian life,[21] and John uses them to this end.[22] Moreover, the prayers for the Adoration of the Cross invite the sinner to kiss Christ on various parts of his body, engaging the reader in a performative relationship with the body of Christ in addition to emphasising the salvific mechanism of prayer.[23] The *libelli precum*'s prayers attempt to instruct readers with their words and immerse them in a scene that engenders correct feelings.

However, prayers to the crucified God in the *libelli* more often focus on the cross's power to save and the crucified Jesus's promise of salvation rather than the humanlike suffering of God. Prayers for the Adoration of the Cross from *libelli* exemplify this embrace of the cross's salvific power (rather than the suffering of Christ):

> Made in the likeness of men, and found dressed as a man, indeed taking on a true man in the true God, humbled and obedient unto death, even death on the cross. You have redeemed us with your precious blood, unstained lamb rising from the dead, ascending to heaven, you sit on the right hand of God the all-powerful Father, whom the angels worship, and I, unhappy

sinner, I adore you prayerfully, confessing my sins and I pray that just as you have made me, through the cross, partake of the mysteries of your death and redemption, so through the power of this sacrosanct cross you may extinguish and destroy all my vices and sins and against all spiritual evils and artifices of the ancient enemy.[24]

Lord Jesus Christ, maker of the world, who – although shining in glory and coeternal and coequal with the Father and the Holy Spirit – deigned to assume flesh from the immaculate virgin and suffered your glorious palms to be nailed on the gibbet of the cross, that you might break asunder the gates of hell and free the human race from death, have pity on me oppressed with evil deeds and the weight of my iniquities. Do not abandon me, most pious father, but indulge me in those things which I impiously bear. Hear me, prostrate before your most glorious and worshipful cross, so that in these days I should merit to stand by you, pure and pleasing in your sight, freed from all evil things, and consoled by your help, always my lord. Through you Jesus Christ, savior of the world.[25]

These prayers emphasise the redemptive power of Christ crucified. In the first prayer, the cross inspires confession on the part of the sinner so that he might 'through the power of this ... cross' 'extinguish' all sin and achieve redemption. In the second prayer, the body of Christ is emphasised, but it is resplendent because it promises salvation: Christ's palms are 'glorious', his body 'shining', his cross 'worshipful'. While the crucified Christ hangs 'nailed on the gibbet of the cross' in this prayer, he is not pathetic (as is the 'impious' sinner); rather, he is 'coeternal and coequal with the Father and the Holy Spirit' and the 'savior of the world'.

John's prayers also admit that redemption is made possible through the act of the crucifixion. But, in contrast to those in the *libelli precum*, John's prayers, with their enumeration of Christ's torments, their conflation of Christ's wounds with the sinner's tears, and their comparisons of the pathetic body of Christ with the pathetic state of the sinner, are actually quite distinct in their focus. By comparing the body of the sinner with the body of Christ and creating a voice for the sinner that actively longs for a simultaneous suffering and co-crucifixion between sinner and God, John proves himself more interested in the pathos and emotional use of the image than its salvific power. With his references to the *vulnera* of his sins, John finds the wounds of Christ important loci of empathy. Like the *libelli precum*, John bombards the reader with images of the crucified God in order to cause the sinner to feel pathetic by comparison; but, unlike the *libelli*, John also hopes that the image of the crucified God will incite feelings in the sinner that will be the first step to righting his spiritual attentions.

Dicta mea sunt dicta patrum?

Sources from the monastic library

The monastic practice of *lectio divina* – the tradition of mastering a text so that 'the page is literally embodied, incorporated'[26] – made it only natural for John's writing to reflect his education and, even more, his internalisation of texts found at the monasteries in Fécamp, Dijon, and Ravenna. In the following section I will show how major themes in John's *Confessio theologica* were accessible in the texts populating the monastic libraries of the eleventh century. Where I can, I will note when a copy of such texts was found in the library of Fécamp. I will also indicate the ways in which John's *CT* elaborates on extant ideas found in the writings of many of his contemporaries. But I will likewise show how John sometimes deviates from the authorities and from his contemporaries writing on the same issues, honing traditional themes for new purposes.

The literature of contrition in the monastery was extensive before the eleventh century, and it is from this corpus that John primarily draws. Chief among these texts was Gregory the Great's *Moralia in Job*, of which Fécamp had not one, but two copies.[27] The *Moralia* speaks of the 'two-edged sword of compunction, piercing with terror and tenderness, fear and delight'.[28] The *Moralia* is a prescription for 'self-examination and self-restraint ... a roadmap for the soul'.[29] Like Augustine's *Confessions* (John's chief model, to be discussed below), John's *CT*, and the Book of Job itself, the *Moralia* speaks from a place of personal crisis: in all four sources, its speakers attempt to clarify the relationship between a sinful man and his omnipotent God.[30] Further like the *CT*, the *Moralia* insists that 'one must always scrutinise the soul for hidden sins and repent of them, even if one does not know what they are'.[31] Gregory insists 'Job's sin was assuming he was not guilty. When afflicted with such terrible losses, he ignored the opportunity – indeed, the obligation – to repent.'[32] The contrast between Job and Christ is a lesson that Gregory extracts for his monks. By refusing to submit to God's will because he believed himself perfect, Job sinned; Christ, perfect, submitted to God's will anyway, out of obligation. Gregory's statement is exhortatory: he used the biblical story of Job as a warning to his monks. Even the most humble and ascetic monk could not think himself free from the need to do penance; the embrace of suffering (in the mode of Christ on the cross) and tears was required both for contrition and as evidence that the monk was wholly subservient to the will of God.[33] Gregory states that the more advanced a monk, the more diligent he needs to be with his self-scrutiny: 'the more I subtly understand [God's] speaking, the more humbly I examine myself'.[34]

In view of Gregory's instructions, John's obsessive desire for self-examination through proper emotion appears justified. While the relentlessness of John's longing is unprecedented in Gregory, his longing itself mimes Gregory's prescriptions. He adopts Gregory's phrases. He implements his concepts. He paraphrases excerpts from Job itself.[35] His writings are given titles attributed to Gregory when they circulate in manuscript elsewhere in Europe.[36] And yet, there are some differences. While Gregory insists that Job's problem is his ignorance of God's plan,[37] John remains keenly aware of the grace needed. Yet the tone and sense of John's *CT* borders on hysteria and self-abnegation, pre-empting consolation (let alone the level of consolation attained by Gregory in the *Moralia*). Moreover, though he prescribes contrition and observes Job's sin, Gregory does not model the process of interior examination to the extent that John does in his *CT*. It is almost as if John created the introspective text a monk would turn to after being convinced by Gregory that he needed to engage in self-examination.

The chief distinction between the *Moralia* and the *Confessio theologica* is the absence in the former of any passage or link to interiority prescribed by the latter. While the distinction between 'interior' thought and 'exterior' action comes from a monastic rhetoric that existed before the eleventh century,[38] the investigation of the *interior homo* became more widespread in the eleventh century, reflecting a new anxiety about sinfulness and proper self-excavation.[39] But John's *CT*, a book that allowed a monk to 'always have a short and handy word of God with [him]',[40] was a unique vehicle focused on the means to facilitate a monk's interior cultivation. Paul Saenger, in fact, notes that John is the first Christian writer to use the word *meditatio* in a text intended for spiritual use.[41] Perhaps taking a cue from Augustine, but certainly unlike Gregory, John emphasises that to gain knowledge of God through contemplation, it is required that one first gain knowledge of oneself.

Alongside the *Moralia*, many monastic texts prescribing contrition longed for the so-called 'gift of tears' as a sign of having achieved true repentance – just as the *CT*'s speaker cries out repeatedly for his tears to flow. Following Augustine's model in the *Confessions*, Athanasius, Cassiodorus, Bede, Alcuin, Ambrose Autpert, Isidore, Benedict of Aniane, Gregory the Great, and Smaragdus of Saint-Mihiel (among others) advocated for weeping as evidence of a true spiritual practice.[42] Each of these authors believed that inner experience was not wholly cultivated by outward discipline and that tears, therefore, were emitted as a sign of true inner humility, compunction, inspiration, and grace.[43] Weeping as a ritual for compunction, therefore, could not be prescribed or adopted in the way that genuflecting, singing, or any other exterior action could be: only the grace of God could give a sinner the 'gift' of tears.[44] Crying was evidence of God's affect working on the sinner, bestowing grace and penitence; it was evidence that God was present.[45] As we will see below, several of John's other models also drew upon this early tradition.

Tears in monastic practice, then, were a sign of God's grace. Ademar of Chabannes (988–1034), John's contemporary at Saint-Martial in Limoges, for instance, writes of a monk who envisioned 'the Lord, hanging on the cross, weeping a great river of tears. [The monk] who saw this, astonished, could do nothing other than pour forth tears from his eyes.'[46] The difference, however, was that John depicted tears as a reflection of an interior emotional attitude purposefully cultivated, not merely as a God-given inner grace. Further, according to the *CT*, tears were a sign of the sinner's recognition of his own imperfection. Tears were a sign of the sinner's *preparedness* for seeing God on this earth, a sign of the sinner's open emotional state and inward awareness as he plans to meet and recognise God: they are not in this context evidence of contact with God himself. The self-scrutiny described in the *CT* results in tears if done correctly; the tears are an outward sign of the contemplative work the sinner has done (not just that God's grace has bestowed). In John's conception, God's grace is needed in the election of the sinner to heaven and for the sinner's ultimate salvation, but not in the sinner's readying of himself for contemplation. That transformation, rather, is controlled and channelled in the method outlined by John in his *CT*, and tears are the desired result of that work (if they are to be effective). Tears are *achieved*; they are not spontaneous outpourings solely resulting from grace, as they are for Ademar's visionary monk.

The combination of self-scrutiny and explicitly cultivated emotion found in John of Fécamp's writings also affects his use of the image of the crucified Christ. There is a long-standing misconception that Christ's crucified suffering was invented by John or Anselm of Canterbury. This is not true. The suffering Christ is incontestably present in earlier Anglo-Saxon writings, and even, to some extent, in Carolingian writings.[47] Contemporaries of John were manifestly interested in the crucified Christ. Richard of Saint-Vanne (970–1046) was apparently particularly devoted to the crucified Christ,[48] making a pilgrimage to Jerusalem in 1027 that was sponsored by John's literal next-door neighbour, Duke Richard II of Normandy (978–1026) (see Map 2).[49] An influx of relics connected to the Crucifixion were sent to the West in the tenth and eleventh centuries and were collected and celebrated by John's contemporaries Ademar of Chabannes, Odilo of Cluny (d. 1049), and Richard of Saint-Vanne.[50]

Despite the presence of the crucified Christ in earlier writings, John's use of the crucified figure is distinct, specifically in the manner in which Christ figures in John's approach to emotional reform. Each of John's contemporaries, however, limited devotion to the crucified Christ to an elite group, either as proof of a person's religious exceptionalism or in reference to an abbot's role as the Christlike head of a monastery. Richard of Saint-Vanne, for instance, 'relied on his devotion as a means of demonstrating his exceptional situation as someone gifted with exclusive charisma, a status continuously nurtured by means of explicit identification with Christ and his suffering ... It also underscored the notion that his virtuosity was beyond reach for most others.'[51] John, instead, was interested in *every* sinner's potential likeness to the pathetic state of the crucified God. Indeed, what makes John unique is the 'possibility of identity between Christ and the desiring soul' in his prayers:

> I call to you, I cry out to you in a loud voice, and with all my heart I call you into my soul; enter into it, mold it to your likeness so that you may possess it as a soul without a spot or wrinkle. Sanctify me as the vessel which you made for yourself; rid it of sin, fill it with grace, and keep it full. Thus I will become a worthy temple for you to dwell in, here, and for all eternity.[52]

The conflation between sinner and God in this excerpt ('mold it to your likeness' ... 'as the vessel which you made for yourself' ... 'I will become ... worthy for you to dwell in') draws parallels between sinner and God, no matter the sinner's status or identity. Whereas contemporary writers call the suffering Christ to mind only in association with certain chosen Christians, John's prayers democratically present meditation on the crucified Christ as a method useful to any sinner. By isolating his own sinful inadequacy, and by connecting it with the pain suffered by the crucified God, the sinner can recognise the distance between himself and God and use that pain, along with tears and meditation, to assess his relationship with the divine. The crucified then becomes a tool in the emotional work required for the sinner's interior self-excavation that is unique to John's *CT*.

Sources from John's novitiate in Ravenna

The monastic sources discussed above for John's *Confessio theologica* were common to most European monks. Other texts influencing the *CT*, however, were shared only with those who had John's particular formation, those from Ravenna at Sant'Apollinare in Classe[53] and those at Saint-Bénigne de Dijon in Burgundy. Sant'Apollinare exposed John both to ideals local to

Dicta mea sunt dicta patrum?

Ravenna – such as those of Romuald of Ravenna (951–1027) – and, thanks to its proximity to Byzantium, also to those Eastern Christian motifs more alive in Ravenna than elsewhere in Europe. And John's time at both Sant'Apollinare and Dijon allowed him to gain a familiarity with Cluniac ideals as well, since Maiolus of Cluny (d. 994) had reformed Sant'Apollinare about twenty years before John became a novice there, and William of Volpiano, his mentor at Dijon, had trained at Cluny.[54]

In this section, we will assess the influences on John from Ravenna. Though John likely left Sant'Apollinare in the early days of the eleventh century, his connection to the Ravennate monastery was one he maintained throughout his life. John brought the *vita* of Sant'Apollinare to the monastery of Fécamp during his abbacy.[55] He corresponded with Romuald's hagiographer Peter Damian (1007–72) while abbot at Fécamp.[56] Most relevant to this study, he used Romuald's example as direct inspiration for his *CT*. The ideas planted when he was an oblate in Ravenna bore fruit when he was writing as a prior at Fécamp.

Though Romuald was an abbot at Sant'Apollinare in the 970s, he left the monastery to live as a hermit many years before his death in 1027.[57] Peter Damian's *vita* of Romuald depicts a solitary devotee who uses both the language of monastic life and liturgy to talk directly to God[58] and the example of the desert fathers who lived as hermits to better foster that divine connection.[59] Hermits were more and more prevalent in the eleventh century, appearing in the forests around John and William of Volpiano's monasteries in Normandy and Lorraine; but the inspiration for such an eremitical movement emanated from Byzantium through Italy (namely Ravenna).[60] Importantly, unlike other hermits, Romuald seems to have been able to model the lifestyle of a hermit *without* contradicting the obedience to the abbot required in coenobitic monasticism. Colin Phipps argues that while Romuald himself retired to a hermit's cell, he advocated that his coenobitic followers use the cloister of the heart – the retreat into individual, interior prayer – as their cells. Phipps says that while Romuald was thus 'properly eremitic', his model nevertheless provided an 'institutional answer' to those monks bound by the *RB*.[61] This promotion of interior retreat, combined with Romuald's core principles of solitude and humility, had a particular influence on John's *CT*.[62] We can imagine that as an abbot, John might have been particularly relieved to find in Romuald an exemplar that could promote trendy eremitical ideals while still encouraging obedience among his coenobitic readership.[63]

The greatest impression on John, however, came through Romuald's use of tears in devotion. Romuald's *vita* shows its subject addressing

God in the overwrought way found both in John's *CT* and in Augustine's *Confessions*: 'Dear Jesus, well-loved Jesus, why do you abandon me? Have you lifted me entirely from the hands of my enemies?'[64] But, as with Hannah and Mary Magdalene, weeping was key to Romuald's route to perfection. Tears marked Romuald's conversion from his life as a duke's son to his life as a penitent hermit;[65] Peter Damian claims that they were an outward sign of his internal reform and true internal piety.[66] In the *vita*, it is tears that evidence a great 'compunction' in Romuald's 'whole heart', melting him so that he is no longer kept from feeling.[67] Such an invocation of the *palatium cordis* parallels John's desire for continual weeping in his *CT*.

Ideas of Byzantine origin that he encountered in Italy appear in John's work as well. Evidence for the transmission of Greek ideas to Normandy through Italians can be found in works of Italo-Norman intellectuals[68] like Anselm of Canterbury and Lanfranc of Bec, whose writings evidence a tremendous familiarity with eastern Byzantine sources and motifs.[69] Rouen, just a short distance from Fécamp, was one of the foremost western repositories of Byzantine icons from Sinai,[70] and the Norman Duke Richard II had a particularly strong connection to St Catherine's monastery there.[71] Despite of the lack of direct evidence of the connection between Byzantium and Sant'Apollinare,[72] evidence of connection between Byzantium and John's *CT* hints at what John might have learned during his time in Ravenna. The Byzantine liturgical rite practised at Sant'Apollinare in Ravenna and elsewhere in eastern Italy was likely a particular source of inspiration for John, with its feasts for the Invention and Exaltation of the True Cross, which did not come to the rest of western Europe until the mid-eleventh century.[73] The Byzantine focus on the suffering (as opposed to the divine triumph) of Christ on the cross in art and prayer could have inspired the enumeration of Christ's torments and the focus on Christ's bloody crucifixion in John's *Confessio theologica*.[74] And the Byzantine writers present in Latin translation in Fécamp's library might also provide a clue to John's intellectual formation at Ravenna. For instance, one Greek author, John Chrysostom (d. 407), wrote a series of sermons on Hannah,[75] works that are found only at Fécamp among the monastic libraries in Normandy, though none of them showcases Hannah as a prayerful model, but instead as a symbol of the Church.[76] John's insistence on an internal, embodied piety towards Christ and on an emotional approach to Jesus instead of a rational one was a technique favoured by middle Byzantine authors like Symeon the New Theologian (949–1022).[77] The tearful brand of asceticism embraced by Gregory of Nazianzus (329–90) and Ephraem the Syrian (306–73) also reappears in John's *CT*.[78] John's Ravennate pedigree from Sant'Apollinare in

Dicta mea sunt dicta patrum?

Classe could, therefore, have brought him into contact with eastern sources, albeit now untraceable, which likely inspired certain of the most innovative pieces of the *CT*.

The influence of William of Volpiano

As his mentor at Dijon and his abbot at Fécamp, William of Volpiano was perhaps the most influential and persistent monastic presence in John's life. A disciple of Maiolus of Cluny,[79] William of Volpiano concurrently served as abbot at the monastery of Saint-Bénigne de Dijon from 990, the monastery of Saint-Arnoul de Metz from 996, and the monastery of Fécamp from 1001,[80] along with thirty other houses. John likely first encountered William's reform policies upon his arrival at Saint-Bénigne de Dijon around 1010. Beginning in 1023,[81] John worked directly under Abbot William as prior of Fécamp, striving to implement William's ideas on the reforming community at Fécamp while the abbot travelled between his various monasteries. By the time John succeeded William as abbot of Fécamp in 1028, he had lived for at least eighteen years under his influence.[82] He maintained William's liturgical reforms at Fécamp after William's death[83] and worked to honour William's legacy both by burying him in the crypt of Fécamp in 1031 and by acquiring (and maybe even editing) one of the first copies of his *vita* for the monastery of Fécamp.[84] Bearing in mind John's efforts to preserve his predecessor and mentor's legacy, what of William's ideas persist in John's *Confessio theologica*?

Over the course of the early eleventh century, William developed an international reputation for reforming monastic houses with 'severity'.[85] William's reforming zeal was influenced by his experiences at Cluny.[86] While the extent of Fécamp's corruption before 1001 might have been a fiction constructed to legitimise both the piety of the Norman dukes and the role of William as a founding father,[87] William's efforts seem to focus on material and behavioural changes rather than emotional or internal ones. According to contemporary chronicles, *vitae*, and charters, William is depicted as a reformer regulating external action at his monastic foundations. In the *Libellus de revelatione, aedificatione et auctoritate Fiscannensis monasterii* (a chronicle from Fécamp written in the late eleventh century), William was called on by monastic houses to better impose the *RB* on monks,[88] to introduce proper liturgical customs and the proper singing of psalmody,[89] to reform the scriptoria at each monastery,[90] and to rebuild the monastic schools so as to improve the practice of reading at each monastery.[91] The charter given by Duke Richard II to William of Volpiano in 1006 to formalise his position at Fécamp asserts that Richard enjoined William to eliminate the depravity and 'increase the religious rigour' at Fécamp by aligning its monks' activities with those prescribed by the *RB*.[92] Rodulfus Glaber (985–1047) chronicles William's transformations: improved liturgical rites, increased interest from pilgrims, new pedagogical resources, and reconsidered relationships with lay donors.[93]

At first sight, therefore, it might seem that William of Volpiano's reforming zeal was grounded in external regulation; as such, it may seem not to bear on John's emphasis on emotional reform. But there are some clues in the very few extant texts that William's reforms went deeper than external behaviour and penetrated realms relevant to the *CT*. We can even go beyond explicit descriptions of William's reforms to the vehicles of their dissemination, first, to the books that were in the Fécamp library during William's abbacy from 1001 to 1028, and, second, to a perpetuator of William's reform, that is, to one of his most effective disciples, John of Fécamp.

Eleven manuscripts survive from the time of William's abbacy at Fécamp.[94] The majority of these books were made at Fécamp itself between 1001 and 1028, though two, Paris, BnF, ms. lat. 1714 and pieces of Paris, BnF, ms. lat. 1805, were likely brought from Saint-Bénigne de Dijon by William in 1001 or even by John in 1023.[95] These books reveal the cross-pollination between the multiple houses of which William was abbot (St Bénigne's *vita*, for instance, numbers among those included at Fécamp),[96] and each of these manuscripts certainly speaks to one or more aspects of William of Volpiano's external, behavioural reforms. Four of the books contain collections of *vitae*, intended to help in revising Fécamp's liturgical programme and in teaching grammar at Fécamp's school.[97] Several of the books likely worked to facilitate reading at the monastery, allowing for more rigorous exegetical instruction.[98] Two of the books, Smaragdus of Saint-Mihiel's *Diadema monastica* and *Expositio in regular sancti Benedicti*, were explicit regulators of monastic life according to the *RB*.[99] Jean Leclercq states that Smaragdus's impetus for writing his works on monastic life was the monastic capitulary of 817, formulated at Monte Cassino: 'Let the abbots scrutinize the *Rule*, word for word, in order to understand it well, and, with their monks, let them endeavor to practice it.'[100] One can thus imagine William following this well-established principle, guided by Smaragdus in his reform of the lifestyle of Fécamp's monks. John's *CT* also reflects the principles of these texts, reasserting the importance of obedience to the *RB* and alluding to it both implicitly and explicitly.

John's *Confessio theologica* absorbed more from these texts than simple behavioural instructions, however: the quality of John's emotional reforms also stems from these books. Two codices among these early texts, Paris, BnF, ms. lat. 3330 and *Paris* 1714, seem to have been principal influences on John. Each codex is a thematic collection that focuses on fostering internal as well as external reforms. *Paris* 3330 contains Smaragdus's *Diadema monastica*, which could have influenced John's understanding of the use of tears in his *CT*, as it contains sections on compunction, prayer, penitence, and, most distinctively, a whole chapter on the gift of tears.[101] *Paris* 3330 also contains a collection of *vitae* of the desert fathers, whose eremitic spirituality and emphasis on individual compunction greatly influenced John's own.[102] When bound together, the volume with Smaragdus on tears plus the exempla of the hermits' spirituality might have been an especially practical codex of inspiration to John when writing his *CT*.

Paris 1714 was arguably an even stronger influence on John's *Confessio theologica*. Stéphane Lecouteux has concluded that the book was taken from Saint-Bénigne after 1001, likely by John of Fécamp himself as he made the trek to take up his priorship.[103] Whether John took the codex after a request from William or on his own volition, we cannot be certain. This manuscript, however, confirms a source at the monastery of Fécamp for John's brand of tearful, interior piety, one that stems from Saint-Bénigne de Dijon. After all, John could have read Smaragdus anywhere[104] – his was a very popular monastic text, by no means exclusive to the monastery of Fécamp.[105] But the particular combination of texts in *Paris* 1714 did not circulate in Normandy until it was brought from Saint-Bénigne. That either John or William then chose to bring the manuscript from Burgundy to Normandy in this early moment tells us something about the reforming spirit at Fécamp by 1023.

Paris 1714 contains several texts: the sermons of St Ephraem;[106] the Rule of St Basil (329–78);[107] the *vita* of Mary of Egypt (344–421);[108] the sermons of Caesarius of Arles (470–542);[109] an unedited sermon;[110] a sermon of John Chrysostom to Theodore of Mopsuestia (350–428);[111] and, at the end of the original manuscript, an unedited sermon purportedly of Isidore of Seville (560–636).[112] At first glance, *Paris* 1714 seems to be a collection of sermons warning against sinful practices,[113] read aloud during mealtimes and other moments during the monastic day by the abbot himself.[114] In accordance with William's efforts to reform the Fécamp monks' external behaviours, Caesarius's texts, for instance, instruct the reader on how he must control himself in order to guarantee his soul's salvation. Caesarius records a litany of sins easily committed by sinners in this life, and then prescribes the medicine of penance (*medicamentum paenitentiae*)[115] in order to guarantee the health of the soul. Caesarius's prescription for penance is described only in general terms, and only once does he order a penitent to engage in tears as John would.[116] But, like John's *CT*, written to 'make [the reader] penitent night and day for the sins of [his] soul',[117] the mandate of contrition is the theme of the collection of writings in *Paris* 1714. The Rule of St Basil and the two concluding sermons likewise laid out rules for external practices of penitence learned from ascetic models, including prayer, vigils, and fasting.

Thematically, then, this collection imported from Saint-Bénigne is typical for a monastery of its time, aligned with the general prescriptions of Gregory's *Moralia*. However, the specific texts included to explore this penitential theme are not. The *De compunctione cordis* of St Ephraem[118] was more often encountered indirectly in medieval Europe through the writings of other authors like Smaragdus.[119] Even so, there are copies of Ephraem's text at three of the monasteries associated with William of Volpiano's reform (Gorze, Saint-Arnoul de Metz, and Cluny), suggesting that Saint-Bénigne's copy may have derived from (or inspired) these manuscripts as part of William's own reform programme.[120] Yet, regardless of where William had originally encountered the text of St Ephraem, it is clear that Ephraem's text influenced John's *CT*.

Ephraem's *De compunctione cordis*, as the name suggests, is, like the other sermons contained in *Paris* 1714, a text about penance. But unlike the rules and sermons with which it is collected, Ephraem's penance is actually about interior contrition, about self-knowledge as demonstrated by tears, and about the usefulness of crying for the redemption of the *vulnera* of sin. Ephraem makes two key arguments in his *De compunctione cordis* that later show up in John of Fécamp's *CT*: one regards the need for crying, and the other is the conflation of sins with wounds (*vulnera*) that bleed and putrefy like Christ's, and that are healed by the salve of tears. Ephraem asks for a 'fountain of tears', as does John.[121] Nowhere in his *De compunctione cordis* does Ephraem invoke images of the suffering Christ. Yet, interestingly, Ephraem has a very particular 'physiognomy of asceticism', one that characterises a monastic life as an 'institution of penitence' achieved by 'introspection as a spiritual form of mortification'.[122] The compiler of *Paris* 1714 highlighted the tearful motifs in Ephraem's text by including the sermon from John Chrysostom at the end of the collection, which also is about tears.[123] And the two eremitical texts at the end of the manuscript – the Rule of St Basil[124] and the *vita* of Mary of Egypt[125] – bring an ascetic flavour to *Paris* 1714's collection, perhaps alluding to Romuald's tearful eremitism.[126] One can then imagine that the extremity of the behaviours described by Ephraem, Chrysostom, Basil, and the author of Mary of Egypt's *vita* modelled the longings for tears and suffering for John, making a strong argument for *Paris* 1714 being at the *CT*'s root.

Dicta mea sunt dicta patrum?

We know that *Paris* 1714 was present at Fécamp during the time of William's abbacy. But can we be sure that its ideas were a part of the reform principles preached by William himself, or was the adoption of this manuscript's ideas in the *CT* a product of John's will alone?[127] Steven Vanderputten has observed that monastic reform movements happen at monasteries in generational waves, and that the first waves are often more logistical (implementing rules, customs, etc.), while the second wave can be more nuanced.[128] According to that model, William's reforms could have been solely regulations of external behaviour, while John's reforms (as part of the second generation at Fécamp) could have delved deeper, addressing the emotional.

But three records of William's voice indicate that the prescriptions of *Paris* 1714 might also have been encouraged by Fécamp's first abbot. At William's monastery of Fruttuaria, in the Easter Sepulchre drama central to the Easter liturgy, the tearful Mary Magdalene was a particular focus, and the monk who was playing her was instructed in the customary to prostrate himself repeatedly before both the tomb and the resurrected Christ.[129] A particular emphasis on proper contrition and tearful penance was also preached and modelled by William himself at Saint-Bénigne de Dijon in a sermon on the feast of St Bénigne. On that day William, 'burst forth tearfully with these words: "You have come together, brothers and sisters, the flock redeemed by the price of Christ's blood ... In [the Church] you are washed and renewed from the guilt of ancient sin by the waters of saving baptism" ... [when he was finished], it [was] impossible to record what weeping, how many tears, what lamentation was made throughout the whole church.'[130] William's rhetoric on renewal from the guilt of sin therefore instigated a 'fountain of tears' from his audience, perhaps indicating that Ephraem's tearful model was embraced by William as well. Finally, a prayer attributed to William and recorded in the eleventh-century copy of John's *CT* collected at Saint-Arnoul de Metz (Metz, Médiathèque, ms. lat. 245) also hints that William valued characteristics similar to those reflected in *Paris* 1714.[131] The prayer contains a penitential refrain from the abbot on behalf of his monastic brothers, '*Absolvas me et omnes fratres nostros*' ('Absolve me and all of our brothers'); it also argues that monks must remember the model of Augustine, the ways he confessed to God with heartfelt emotion (*cordis affectu*) and asked for tears to cleanse his sinful soul,[132] much as John himself does in his *CT*.

These hints indicate that by focusing on Mary Magdalene's penance, devotional tears, and the Augustinian rhetoric of the heart in his *CT*, John of Fécamp could have been extending the model of William of Volpiano's reforming influence. In light of this evidence, we may imagine that William requested John bring *Paris* 1714 with him from Saint-Bénigne de Dijon in order to deepen the penitential education of the monks at Fécamp now that their correct behaviours had been established by William himself. We can further imagine that the writing of the *CT* might, in some way, have been an extension of the spirit of William's reforms on the part of his prior, John of Fécamp. And yet, these scraps of evidence of William's tearfulness and devotional advice pale in comparison to John's *CT* and the affective devotional focus at his monastery in his time.[133] Therefore, while it is possible that John's work focused on kernels planted by William, its extensive elaboration on these themes likely registered as distinct from William's own promotion of them to the monks at Fécamp.

The influence of Cluny

Tracing William's influence on John makes the strongest case for John's *Confessio theologica* to have emerged out of the reforming spirit sweeping medieval monasteries. When dealing with the eleventh century, such spirit cannot be divorced from the influence of Cluny. Still, because William of Volpiano was himself a monk at Cluny, it is difficult to fully distinguish which influences on John's *CT* were Volpianian and which were Cluniac.[134] Moreover, though the monastery of Saint-Evroult was the only Norman monastery to administratively connect itself to the great abbey,[135] many monks came from Cluny to Fécamp and other monasteries in Normandy.[136] John's particular pedigree was strongly connected to the abbey of Cluny, for he was a novice at a monastery that had itself been reformed by the abbot Maiolus of Cluny in the years 971–72.[137] It is unsurprising, then, that Cluniac priorities generally infuse John's *CT*. On the simplest level, John's emphases on the *RB*, the virtues of obedience, and the idea of a spiritual army are all principles shared with contemporary Cluniac writings.[138]

John's *Confessio theologica*, however, was also inspired more directly by certain idiosyncratic aspects of Cluniac exemplars. In the late eleventh century, there were two manuscripts from Fécamp that contained lives of the abbots of Cluny: Paris, BnF, ms. lat. 5290 contained the lives of saints Odo (d. 942), Maiolus (d. 994), and Odilo of Cluny (d. 1049);[139] and Rouen, BM, ms. 1400 (U3) contained a different version of the life of Odilo of Cluny involving a Eucharistic miracle as proof of Odilo's sanctity.[140] Moreover, Fécamp manuscripts Paris, BnF, ms. lat. 5329 and Rouen, BM, ms. 1404 (U20) both also contained sermons of Abbot Odo's.[141] Since Maiolus and Odilo were both still alive during portions of John's lifetime, the example of Odo was potentially more legendary for him, though the examples of each of these Cluniac abbots likely contributed to the emotional practices prescribed in the *CT*.[142]

Like William of Volpiano at Fécamp, much of Odo of Cluny's reforming zeal was directed towards questions of monastic rules and exterior reforms.[143] But both Odo's *Occupatio* and his *vita* emphasise his concern for the interiors of his monks as well. His *Occupatio* emphasised the importance of the mental discipline of monastic practice, hoping that monks would not only follow the rules but also align their physical behaviours with the desires of their hearts, much like the interior reform prescriptions of John.[144] According to the *vita* of Odo written by John of Salerno (d. 990),[145] Odo advocated combating the depravity of the world with private prayer, focusing both on constructing spaces for private prayer (such as oratories in buildings) and on advocating for an intimacy with Christ (best fostered by prayer's inward gaze).[146] Odo was also particularly interested in proper contrition,[147] and his ideas about contrition were associated especially with Mary Magdalene's tears.[148] Though the feast of Mary Magdalene was established by Gregory the Great before Odo's time,[149] it was not regularly celebrated at Cluny until Odilo's abbacy. Yet in Odo's time, her example had become particularly poignant[150] as an example of proper contrition, advocating access to repentance through suffering.[151] A sermon of Odo's[152] contained in the Fécamp library uses Mary Magdalene's *exemplum* to foster proper penance: Odo claims that the Magdalene's tears allowed her to experience a spiritual resurrection, one that paralleled the physical resurrection of her brother Lazarus, and one also accompanied by tears.[153] In this way, both Mary Magdalene and Lazarus fell into the category of proper penitents, as Mary of Egypt (in *Paris* 1714) was a penitent woman who was ultimately promised salvation.[154] In his sermon, Odo says:

> She enters continuously the palace of her heart, and in the cavern of her breast she erects for herself a worthy consistory, makes her conscience a piece of papyrus, her groaning the pen, and her tears the ink ... she has considered herself, examined herself, has herself become her own judge and advocate, has placed herself before her own face, has examined her pieces of papyrus, which are written with the ink of iniquity, has opened her own filthiness, has acknowledged her own badly fallen life.[155]

The example of the Magdalene, therefore, served as a model for the recognition of the sinful self that Odo felt was required in the process of contrition and prayer.[156] Odo thus anticipated the embrace of the Magdalene which occurred in the later eleventh and twelfth centuries.[157] And such internal reform through the Magdalene's repentance was not only prescribed for the *individual* at Cluny: Hallinger and Leclercq both claim the repentance demonstrated by the Magdalene was also a metaphor for the reforms of the *Church* embarked upon by Cluny in Odo's time.[158]

There is much of Odo's influence in John's *Confessio theologica*. Like Odo, John shows that proper penitence is achieved when one delves into one's interior soul and confronts one's sins properly through prayer and intimate connection with Christ. Like Odo, John's need for proper contrition is expressed through the example of Mary Magdalene. The presence of the Magdalene in other texts in Fécamp's eleventh-century library testify to the efforts made to collect evidence of her example in John's spiritual environment.[159] Yet, John goes beyond Odo in his use of the Magdalene and her tears as a model for contemplation.[160] To John, it is not just her penitence that one should admire, and it is not just her behaviour that models internal reform. Rather, Mary Magdalene's tears and 'spiritual ardour to see' God are what John finds most exemplary. It is *how* she suffers and waits to see God, how she longs to make a connection with him in contemplation, that is the model of reform for John's reader. By using the Magdalene to exemplify contemplative emotional and penitential behaviours in his texts, John distinguishes himself from Odo's model of contrition and of reform, and from earlier medieval writers who draw on Mary Magdalene as well.[161]

Unlike Odo, who died before John's lifetime, Maiolus and Odilo of Cluny were John's contemporaries and might have served as living exemplars. Maiolus's stress on humility and obedience may have proved foundational for John's writings, though this is hard prove, since Maiolus left no writings of his own behind.[162] Odilo's embrace of the cross and its devotion in penitential practice potentially served as active inspirations for John.[163] Odilo's devotion to the cross may have been particularly influential, since, like John, he used the image of the crucified Christ to foster proper compunction in the sinner.[164] According to Peter of Blois (1135–1203), Odilo's devotion to the cross was inspired by the example of the desert fathers, who Odilo claimed meditated each day on the Passion upon receiving the Eucharist.[165] Odilo, like Odo, believed that reform began with monastic penitence: the cross, Christ's instrument, inspired the act of penitence required for such redemption,[166] and the behaviour of the Virgin Mary and Mary Magdalene around the cross inspired the penitential behaviour required of Christian devotees.[167] Despite this parallel emphasis on the cross, however, Odilo's image of Jesus crucified remains a triumphant image, not a suffering and pathetic one, as in John's work.[168] Therefore, by using the images of the Magdalene and the cross to foster contrition, John was likely speaking in accordance with the Cluniac abbatial rhetoric of his time; but by focusing on the Magdalene's longing for God and for communion with a suffering God, John had created his own distinctive approach that highlighted the emotional involvement required in proper penitential behaviours.

John's revival of Augustine's *Confessions*

The sources for John's work discussed in the previous sections of this chapter are all texts that were being read in one way or another in John's time: the Ravennate sources might only have been read in Ravenna, and the focus on the Magdalene might have been particularly popular at Cluny, but these ideas, adopted by John, were alive in Europe in the eleventh century. The final section of this chapter details John's interest in a source that was by and large *not* being read by his contemporaries: Augustine's *Confessions* (c. 397–400).

Before the eleventh century, *Confessions* was one of the least-often-read texts from the Augustinian corpus. When it was read in the early Middle Ages, it was typically mined for doctrinal excerpts and was largely limited to a manuscript presence in florilegia of quotations of Augustine's writings.[169] Pierre Courcelle argues that John of Fécamp's *Confessio theologica* changed the way that medieval people read the text of *Confessions*: with John, it was no longer a resource to buttress orthodoxy, but instead became interesting for its affect, its tone, its prayerful nature. Courcelle observes that John adopted Augustine's manner of addressing God and his vocabulary of prayer, and that it was only after John's model that a multiplicity of authors (including Anselm and Bernard of Clairvaux) did the same.[170] In addition to adopting Augustine's tone, John embraced Augustine's notion of 'inwardness'[171] and his desire for God following Augustine's characterisation of his own text in his *Retractiones*.[172] Most importantly, John re-excerpted Augustine's text in order to interpret it as an advice manual for the proper contemplation of God so that it might serve as the backbone of John's own method of contemplation.[173] John quoted so extensively from the passages of *Confessions* that pertain to the problems encountered during contemplation that if one knew Augustine's text only through John's excerpts, one would not learn the story of Augustine's life, nor would one have a strong sense of Augustine's doctrinal or exegetical expositions.

John excerpts Augustine's spiritual journey in order to make it universally applicable, eliminating autobiographical details. Like Augustine, John advises a sinner to force himself inside his own heart, where he can best confront and acknowledge his sinfulness to better repent and prepare himself to see God.[174] Once inside the heart and in touch with God, the sinner then can hope to be so possessed with love for God that he will abandon all of his worldly cares and focus on prayer to God without cease.[175] However, just as one of the most distinctive characteristics of John's *Confessio theologica* was the unachievable nature of divine solace and satisfaction, Augustine's own path away from sinfulness is never fully achieved or complete.[176] John's sinner remains uncertain of his abilities to feel and love God with the appropriate fervour and inadequate to the task of fully eradicating his own sinfulness, just as Augustine, despite his revelatory conversion in Book 9 of *Confessions*, is constantly aware of regressive tendencies:

> And sometimes you cause me to enter into an extraordinary depth of feeling marked by a strange sweetness. If it were brought to perfection in me, it would be an experience quite beyond anything in this life. But I fall back into my usual ways under my miserable burdens. I am reabsorbed by my habitual practices. I am held in their grip. I weep profusely, but still I am held. Such is the strength of the burden of habit. Here I have the power to be, but do not wish to be. There I wish to be, but do not have the power.[177]

Imperfect in this life like John's sinner, Augustine is also left inadequate in God's sight with only the solace of his own tears. For both John's and Augustine's sinners, these tears, then, allow for continual conversion, the repeated turning away from and confessing to sin.[178] To both Augustine and John, a Christian is never stable in his purity; rather, he is always striving to be more perfect, moving towards or away from perfection. The goal of a Christian, then, is to always approach Christ with the fervour of a convert who has only just recognised him as God. Each regression, each moment of tepidity, is cherished because it allows for the potential for a Christian to reawaken his desire for God as if he was falling in love with him (reconverting to him, turning back towards him, performing a *conversio*) for the first time.

John's interest in Augustine's *Confessions* seems to have informed his own text as well as to have inspired a revival of the text around the Norman monastic world.[179] At Fécamp itself there was a fervent campaign to acquire Augustinian texts between the eleventh and twelfth centuries, perhaps due to John's central interest in *Confessions*.[180] By the twelfth century, Fécamp's copy of *Confessions* had been passed around the Norman network, allowing copies to be made at Jumièges,[181] Bec, and Saint-Evroult; and, by the Late Middle Ages, it appeared in the monasteries of Saint-Ouen[182] and Lyre.[183] Moreover, subsequent medieval authors famous for drawing extensively from Augustine's *Confessions* were themselves likely inspired by these Norman copies: Goscelin of Saint-Bertin (d. c. 1107), whose *Liber confortatorius* was written from the Flemish abbey of Saint-Bertin (linked to Norman houses through its manuscript exemplars)[184] and Guibert of Nogent (d. 1124), once a monk at the Norman abbey of Saint-Germer-de-Fly, whose autobiography was famously modelled on the *Confessions*.[185] Therefore, while John's depiction of contemplative experience was in no way new to the corpus of Christian writings, his reliance on Augustine's *Confessions* was new and effective for his historical moment such that one can trace the impact of his revival of this text on the medieval world after him.

John's mix of influence and innovation

By looking at John's sources, one can better understand the ways that his monastic readers might have seen his work both as part of their tradition and as innovative. Drawing on sources written and compiled by monastic authors as early as Gregory and as contemporary as William of Volpiano, John wrote a treatise that reflected his identity as a Benedictine monk and drew on sources specific to his education in Ravenna and Saint-Bénigne de Dijon. Moreover, because of his adoption of certain ideas that were part and parcel of the reforms of William of Volpiano, Romuald of Ravenna, and the abbots of Cluny, one imagines that John considered his *Confessio theologica* as an extension of those reforms, as a furtherance of the ideas put forward by the great abbots who went before him. If John as a young oblate was taught by Romuald that a proper monk fostered certain eremitical values, it would make sense that he would integrate those values into his *CT*. If John as a young prior was in charge of implementing the reforms begun at Fécamp by William of Volpiano, it would likewise make sense that he would write a treatise to apply those teachings to his brethren's devotional practices. In these ways, by writing his *CT*, John was following the reforms of his abbatial *exempla* and the mentors of his life.

But John did not take others' ideas verbatim without elaborating on them and making them his own. John pieced together prescriptions for contrition from others, creating a full-fledged interior reform process: the idea of forging an internal connection with God came from Odo of Cluny; the idea of opening one's heart came from Augustine;[186] the idea of suffering and crying came from Ephraem and Romuald. But the packaging of these ideas and the resulting emotional, interior reform proposed by John, was entirely John's own. While William chiefly was interested in the rules, liturgy, and behaviour of the newly reformed monks of Fécamp, John chiefly was attentive to the proper interior behaviour of Fécamp's monks. The cultivation of an intense longing for God through prayer, the particular employment of the models of Mary Magdalene, Hannah, and the suffering, crucified Christ, and the unrelenting cycle of striving towards perfection were pieced together by John from various sources, allowing John to stand on the shoulders of monastic authorities while saying something new about the desperate spiritual ardour required in contemplation. It allowed him to paint a picture of the correct emotional attitude one should have in prayer. And his new prayerful attitude, his fresh use of the suffering Christ as a model for the suffering sinner, and his lengthy elaboration on how a Christian should examine his inner self to rouse proper feelings for the divine, allowed John to be considered a reformer in his own right by the generations of Fécamp monks who came after him.[187] Beyond Ravennate, Cluniac, Volpianian, and general monastic precedents, John's *CT* specified the detailed emotional excavation required in a monk's prayer process, elevating the stakes for monastic introspection as never before.

Notes

1. 'My words are the words of the Fathers. Read that which we say in such a way that you consider yourself to be rereading the words of the Fathers, and with the whole striving of your mind, render eagerly and sincerely to your redeemer what thanksgiving you are able' (*'Dicta mea dicta sunt patrum. Sic ista quae dicimus, lege ut putes te patrum verba relegere, et toto mentis adnisu quas vales actiones gratiarum tuo redemptory alacriter sinceriterque persolve*') (*CT*, p. 121).
2. Choy, *Intercessory Prayer*, pp. 10–12, citing Smaragdus's *Diadema monastica*.
3. Eileen Sweeney, *Anselm of Canterbury and the Desire for the Word* (Washington, DC: Catholic University of America Press, 2012), p. 6.
4. Albrecht Diem, 'The Stolen Glove: On the Hierachy and Power of Objects in Columbanian Monasteries', in K. Pansters and A. Plunkett-Latimer (eds), *Shaping Stability: The Normation and Formation of Religious Life in the Middle Ages* (Turnhout: Brepols, 2016), pp. 64–5.
5. Cottier, *Anima mea*, pp. xl–xli, lii–liii; André Wilmart, 'Formes successives'.
6. Rachel Fulton, 'What's in a Psalm? British Library MS Arundel 60 and the Stuff of Prayer', in Valerie Garver and Owne Phelan (eds), *Rome and Religion in the Medieval World: Studies in Honor of Thomas F.X. Noble* (New York: Routledge, 2014), pp. 235–52.
7. Cf. *CT*, p. 159.
8. Cf. *CT*, p. 136.
9. John refers to waves and tempests several times in the *CT*, pp. 143, 151, 152, 153, 154, 157, 168.
10. This series of questions, and the series of questions that end this quotation from the psalm, are all reminiscent of both the *CT* and Augustine's *Confessions*.

Dicta mea sunt dicta patrum?

11 This compares with John's reference to his sins as wounds (*vulnera*).
12 'Quemadmodum desiderat cervus ad fontes aquarum ita desiderat anima mea ad te Deus sitivit anima mea ad Deum fortem; vivum quando veniam et parebo ante faciem Dei fuerunt mihi lacrimae meae panis die ac nocte dum dicitur mihi cotidie ubi est Deus tuus ... quare tristis es anima mea et quare conturbas me spera in Deo quoniam confitebor illi salutare vultus mei Deus meus ad me ipsum anima mea ... abyssus ad abyssum invocat in voce cataractarum tuarum omnia excelsa tua et fluctus tui super me transierunt ... dicam Deo susceptor meus es quare oblitus es mei quare contristatus incedo dum adfligit me inimicus dum confringuntur ossa mea exprobraverunt mihi qui tribulant me dum dicunt mihi per singulos dies ubi est Deus tuus. quare tristis es anima mea et quare conturbas me spera in Deum quoniam adhuc; confitebor illi salutare vultus mei et; Deus meus.'
13 This is common in monastic prayer; see Aden Kumler, 'Handling the Letter', in Kristen Collins and Matthew Fischer (eds), *St. Albans and the Markyate Psalter: Seeing and Reading in the Twelfth Century* (Kalamazoo, MI: Medieval Institute Publications, 2017), p. 81.
14 Robertson, *Lectio divina*, p. 139.
15 Pierre Salmon, *Analecta liturgica: Extraits des manuscrits liturgiques de la Bibliothèque vaticane* (Vatican City: Biblioteca Apostolica Vaticana, 1974); André Wilmart, *Precum libelli quattuor aevi karolini* (Rome: Ephemerides Liturgicae, 1940); Susan Boynton, '*Libelli Precum* in the Central Middle Ages', in Roy Hammerling (ed.), *A History of Prayer* (Leiden: Brill, 2008), pp. 255–318; Boynton, 'Prayer as Liturgical Performance'.
16 The tradition of John's *Confessio theologica* in manuscript also reflects his connection to the *libelli precum* tradition. The *libelli precum* manuscripts often were connected to psalters or *flores psalmorum*; prayers were not contained in independent collections until Anselm. John's own works were also collected on occasion with the Psalms (for instance, in Metz, Mediathèque, ms. 245). For more on this, see Thomas H. Bestul, 'The Collection of Private Prayers in the "Portiforium" of Wulfstan of Worcester and the "Orationes Sive Meditationes" of Anselm of Canterbury', in Raymonde Foreville (ed.), *Les mutations socio-culturelles au tournant des XIe–XIIe siècles* (Paris: CNRS, 1984), pp. 357–60.
17 Susan Boynton, *Shaping a Monastic Identity: Liturgy and History at the Imperial Abbey of Farfa, 1000–1125* (Ithaca, NY: Cornell University Press, 2006), p. 89.
18 Boynton, *Shaping a Monastic Identity*, p. 102.
19 As translated by Boynton in '*Libelli Precum* in the Central Middle Ages', p. 920.
20 Renie Choy, '"The Brother Who May Wish to Pray by Himself": Sense of Self in Carolingian Prayers of Private Devotion', in Santha Bhattacharji, Rowan Williams, and Dominic Mattos (eds), *Prayer and Thought in Monastic Tradition: Essays in Honour of Benedicta Ward, SLG* (New York: Bloomsbury, 2014), p. 102.
21 Choy, '"The Brother Who May Wish to Pray by Himself"'.
22 Cf. *CT*, p. 140.

23 Boynton, 'Libelli Precum in the Central Middle Ages', p. 915.
24 Translation is as cited in Boynton, 'Libelli Precum in the Central Middle Ages', p. 922.
25 As cited in Fulton, From Judgment to Passion, p. 150–1.
26 Ivan Illich, In the Vineyard of the Text: A Commentary to Hugh's Didascalicon (Chicago: University of Chicago Press, 1993), p. 54.
27 The Moralia is listed on the eleventh-century library list for Fécamp, even though its manuscript has not been identified as extant: Branch, 'Inventories', p. 170.
28 Gregory's Moralia in Job, Book 23, PL 76 col. 292; as quoted by Benedicta Ward in her Introduction to Anselm, p. 55. Cf. John's 'You are the living Word of God, and efficacious and more piercing than every sharpest sword. You, double-edged sword, cleave my hardness of heart and wound this sinful soul, and pierce more deeply to the inmost parts with your powerful virtue' (CT, pp. 180–1).
29 Carole Straw, 'Job's Sin in the Moralia of Gregory the Great', in Franklin T. Harkins and Aaron Canty (eds), A Companion to Job in the Middle Ages (Turnhout: Brill, 2016), pp. 72–3.
30 Straw, 'Job's Sin', p. 74.
31 Straw, 'Job's Sin', p. 100.
32 Straw, 'Job's Sin', p. 100.
33 Gregory is cited as the first medieval writer to define the gift of tears; Damien Boquet and Piroska Nagy, Sensible moyen âge: Une histoire des émotions dans l'Occident médiéval (Paris: Seuil, 2015), p. 72.
34 Mor 32.3.4: 'nunc quanto te loquentem subtilius intellego, tanto memetipsum humilius investigo'.
35 Cf. CT, p. 153–4.
36 Paris, BnF, ms. lat. 13593, for instance, is called the Reclinationem anime, a title usually given to Gregory's works; see Elizabeth Kuhl, 'Education and Schooling at Le Bec: A Case Study of Le Bec's Florilegia', in Benjamin Pohl and Laura Gathagan (eds), A Companion to the Abbey of Le Bec in the Central Middle Ages (11th–13th Centuries) (Leiden: Brill, 2017), pp. 248–78.
37 Straw, 'Job's Sin', p. 92.
38 Piroska Nagy, 'Individualité et larmes monastiques: Une experience de soi ou de Dieu?', in Gert Melville and Markus Schürer (eds), Das Eigene und Das Ganze. Zum individuellen im mittelalterlichen Religiosentum (Münster: Lit Verlag, 2002), 107–30; van 't Spijker, Fictions of the Inner Life, p. 16.
39 Susan R. Kramer and Caroline W. Bynum, 'Revisiting the Twelfth-Century Individual: The Inner Self and the Christian Community', in Gert Melville and Markus Schürer (eds), Das Eigene und das Ganze. Zum individuellen im mittelalterlichen Religiosentum (Münster: Lit Verlag, 2002), p. 65.
40 Cf. Chapter 1.
41 Saenger, Space between Words, p. 144.
42 All of these authors are counted among the listed and extant manuscripts from Fécamp's library in the eleventh century.

43 McEntire, *The Doctrine of Compunction*, p. 38.
44 Nagy, 'Religious Weeping'; Nagy, *Le don des larmes au moyen âge*.
45 Patrick Henriet, *La parole et la prière au moyen âge: Le verbe efficace dans l'hagiographie monastique des XIe et XIIe siècles* (Brussels: DeBoeck Université, 2000), p. 146.
46 As quoted in Daniel Callahan, *Jerusalem and the Cross in the Life and Writings of Ademar of Chabannes* (Turnhout: Brill, 2016), pp. 22–3, from Ademar's *Chronicon* 3.46.
47 See Introduction, above.
48 Steven Vanderputten, *Imagining Religious Leadership in the Middle Ages: Richard of Saint-Vanne and the Politics of Reform* (Ithaca, NY: Cornell University Press, 2015), pp. 67–8; Giles Constable, 'The Cross in Medieval Monastic Life', in David C. Mengel and Lisa Wolverton (eds), *Christianity and Culture in the Middle Ages: Essays to Honor John Van Engen* (Notre Dame, IN: University of Notre Dame Press, 2014), pp. 242–3.
49 Callahan, *Jerusalem and the Cross*, p. 10.
50 Callahan, *Jerusalem and the Cross*, p. 11.
51 Vanderputten, *Imagining Religious Leadership*, pp. 69, 71. See also the discussion of exceptional abbots in Liège in Helena Vanommeslaeghe, 'Wandering Abbots: Abbatial Mobility and *stabilitas loci* in Eleventh-Century Lotharingia and Flanders', in Steven Vanderputten, Tjamke Snijders, and Jay Diehl (eds), *Medieval Liège at the Crossroads of Europe: Monastic Society and Culture, 1000–1300* (Turnhout: Brepols, 2017), p. 6, 7, 22–3.
52 Fulton, *From Judgment to Passion*, p. 163.
53 Leclercq and Bonnes, *Un maître*, p. 130; E. Bougaud and M. Joseph Garnier (eds), *Chronique de l'abbaye de Saint-Bénigne de Dijon* (Dijon: Darantiere, 1875), p. 152; Neithard Bulst, *Untersuchungen zu den Klosterreformen Wilhelms von Dijon (962–1031)* (Bonn: Ludwig Röhrscheid, 1973), p. 40.
54 With a link to the hermits in and around Ravenna, William may have been another of John's sources for Romuald's teachings: Bulst, *Untersuchungen zu den Klosterreformen*, p. 40; Mathieu Arnoux, 'Un Vénitien au Mont-Saint-Michel: Anastase, moine, ermite, et confesseur (d. vers 1085)', *Médiévales* 28 (1995), 73; and Jean-Marie Sansterre, 'Ermites de France et d'Italie, XIe–XVe siècle', in André Vauchez (ed.), *Le monachisme bénédictin d'Italie et les bénédictins italiens en France face au renouveau de l'érémitisme à la fin du Xe et au XIe siècle* (Rome: École française de Rome, 2003), p. 41.
55 Apollinare's *vita* is added to the back of Paris, BnF, ms. lat. 1632 in a mid- to late-eleventh-century hand.
56 Peter writes a defence of the hermitic life in a letter to John of Fécamp in *Peter Damian Letters. The Fathers of the Church: Mediaeval Continuation* (Washington, DC: Catholic University of America Press, 1990), letter 152.
57 Derek Baker, '"The Whole World a Hermitage": Ascetic Renewal and the Crisis of Western Monasticism', in Mark Anthony Meyer (ed.), *The Culture of Christendom*

(London: Hambledon Press, 1993), p. 213. Special thanks to Edward Schoolman and Kathryn Jasper for their bibliographic advice on Romuald and Ravenna.
58 Margaret Gibson, *Lanfranc of Bec* (Oxford: Oxford University Press, 1978), pp. 1–2.
59 Nagy, *Le don des larmes au moyen âge*, p. 223; Henrietta Leyser, *Hermits and the New Monasticism: A Study of Religious Communities in Western Europe, 1000–1150* (New York: St. Martin's Press, 1984), pp. 24–5; Lackner, *The Eleventh-Century Background of Cîteaux*, p. 131–50, 167–216; Jestice, *Wayward Monks*, pp. 157–8.
60 Baker, '"The Whole World a Hermitage"', p. 207. There were several hermits in Normandy in the eleventh century: Anastasius the Venetian was near Mont Saint-Michel; there were hermits around Saint-Wandrille and Saint-Evroult; and Herluin of Bec was near Bec; see Marjorie Chibnall, *The World of Orderic Vitalis: Norman Monks and Norman Knights* (Woodbridge: Boydell and Brewer, 1984), p. 81; Leyser, *Hermits and the New Monasticism*, p. 16.
61 Colin Phipps, 'Romuald – Model Hermit: Eremitical Theory in Saint Peter Damian's *Vita Beati Romualdi*, Chapters 16–27', in W.J. Shiels (ed.), *Monks, Hermits and the Ascetic Tradition: Papers Read at the 1984 Summer Meeting and the 1985 Winter Meeting of the Ecclesiastical History Society* (Oxford: Basil Blackwell, 1985), pp. 74–5.
62 Anne Wagner, 'De l'humilité de l'abbé Richard', in Noëlle Cazin and Philippe Martin (eds), *Autour de la congrégation de Saint-Vanne et de Saint-Hydulphe: L'idée de réforme religieuse en Lorraine* (Bar-le-duc: Société des lettres, sciences et arts, 2006), pp. 231–63.
63 See also Chapter 3.
64 Peter Damian's *Vita Romualdi*, ch. 2; as quoted in Nagy, *Le don des larmes au moyen âge*, p. 171.
65 Henriet, *La parole et la prière*, pp. 146–59, 363–8.
66 Nagy, *Le don des larmes*, pp. 150–1, 163, 229; Bouquet and Nagy, *Sensible moyen âge*, pp. 105–8.
67 Peter Damian's *Vita Romualdi*, ch. 16; as cited in Nagy, *Le don des larmes au moyen âge*, p. 174. Patrick Henriet and Anne Wagner say that 'l'insistance sur "le don des larmes" est une nouveauté liée à la réforme monastique du XIe siècle', in 'Les moines du XIe siècle entre érémitisme et cénobisme', in Anne Wagner (ed.), *Les saints et l'histoire* (Rosny-sous-Bois: Bréal, 2008), p. 235.
68 Elisabeth van Houts, 'Qui étaient les Normands? Quelques observations sur des liens entre la Normandie, l'Angleterre, et l'Italie au début du XIe siècle', in David Bates and Pierre Bauduin (eds), *911–2011: Penser les mondes normands médiévaux. Actes du colloque international de Caen et Cerisy (29 septembre–2 octobre 2011)* (Caen: CRAHAM, 2016), pp. 129–46.
69 Maylis Baylé has attributed the presence of Italian and Byzantine motifs in Normandy to the same Italo-Normans: Maylis Baylé, 'L'influence des Italiens sur l'art roman de Normandie: Légende ou réalité?', *Cahier des Annales de Normandie* 29 (2000), 45–64. See also Giles E.M. Gasper, *Anselm of Canterbury and His*

Dicta mea sunt dicta patrum?

Theological Inheritance (New York: Routledge, 2004), pp. 30, 34, 53; Mathon, 'Jean de Fécamp, théologien monastique?', p. 487; Stephen J. Shoemaker, 'Mary at the Cross, East and West: Maternal Compassion and Affective Piety in the Earliest Life of the Virgin and the High Middle Ages', *Journal of Theological Studies* 62.2 (2011), 593–4, 598.

70 Barbara Baert, 'Heraclius, l'exaltion de la croix et le Mont-Saint-Michel au XIe s.: une lecture attentive du ms. 641 de la Pierpont Morgan Library à New York', *Cahiers de civilisation médiévale* 51 (2008), 3–20; Christine Walsh, 'The Role of the Normans in the Development of the Cult of St. Katherine', in Jacqueline Jenkins and Katherine J. Lewis (eds), *St. Katherine of Alexandria: Texts and Contexts in Western Medieval Europe* (Turnhout: Brepols, 2003), pp. 19–35; Nagy, *Le don des larmes au moyen âge*, pp. 235–41, 248–53; *Anselm*, p. 27; Shoemaker, 'Mary at the Cross, East and West', 591.

71 Shoemaker, 'Mary at the Cross, East and West', 601; Callahan, *Jerusalem and the Cross*, p. 10.

72 A library list does not survive from Sant'Apollinare from John's time, so we cannot be sure of the Greek titles collected there.

73 Joseph Szövérffy, '"Crux Fidelis": Prolegomena to a History of the Holy Cross Hymns', *Traditio* 22 (1966), 1–41.

74 Shoemaker, 'Mary at the Cross, East and West', 580; Miri Rubin, *Mother of God: A History of the Virgin Mary* (New Haven, CT: Yale University Press, 2009); Derbes, *Picturing the Passion*; see Introduction, above.

75 Robert C. Hill, 'St. John Chrysostom's Homilies on Hannah', *St. Vladimir's Theological Quarterly* 45.4 (2001), 333–4.

76 Giles Gasper has noted that Fécamp is the lone house in the Anglo-Norman world to collect the works of John Chrysostom; Giles Gasper, *Anselm of Canterbury and His Theological Inheritance* (Burlington, VT: Ashgate, 2004), p. 51. John Chrysostom's works also appeared at Fécamp in: Rouen, BM, ms. 440 (A298) and BM, ms. 82 (A208); Paris, BnF, mss. lat. 1872, 1919, 2101, 2079, 2401, and 3776; and Vatican City, Biblioteca Apostolica Vaticana, Vat. Reg. lat. 633 pt. 1 and Vatican City, Biblioteca Apostolica Vaticana, Vat. Ottob. 120. For more on early medieval models of Hannah being about her symbolic nature rather than her prayerful nature, see Griffiths, *Nuns' Priests' Tales*, pp. 164–6 and Altvater, 'Barren Mother, Dutiful Wife, Church Triumphant', pp. 1–29.

77 Hannah Hunt, 'The Reforming Abbot and his Tears: Penthos in Late Byzantium', in Eugenia Russell (ed.), *Spirituality in Late Byzantium: Essays Presenting New Research by International Scholars* (Newcastle upon Tyne: Cambridge Scholars Publishing, 2009), p. 15.

78 Compare the *CT* with Gregory's words here: 'O fountains of tears, sowing in affliction that they might reap in joy! O cry in the night, piercing the clouds and reaching unto Him that dwelleth in the heavens! O fervor of spirit, waxing bold in prayerful longings against the dogs of night and frost and rain and thunders and hail and darkness!' As quoted in Rosemary Radford Ruether, *Gregory of*

Nazianzus: Rhetor and Philosopher (Oxford: Clarendon Press, 1969), p. 149. Sally Vaughn has written on Gregory's influence on another Italo-Norman, Anselm of Canterbury; Sally Vaughn, 'Anselm of Le Bec and Canterbury: Teacher by Word and Example, Following in the Footprints of His Ancestors', in Benjamin Pohl and Laura Gathagan (eds), *A Companion to the Abbey of Le Bec in the Central Middle Ages (11th–13th Centuries)* (Leiden: Brill, 2017), pp. 57–94.

79 Maiolus's role as William's mentor is discussed extensively in ch. 5 of *Glaber*, p. 265. The comparisons between Cluny and William's first foundation at Saint-Bénigne are extensive; for more on the architectural and liturgical comparisons between the houses, see Carolyn M. Malone, *Saint-Bénigne de Dijon en l'an mil, "Totius Gallie basilicis mirabilior": interprétation politique, liturgique, et théologique* (Turnhout: Brepols, 2009); Carolyn M. Malone, 'Interprétation des pratiques liturgiques à Saint-Bénigne de Dijon d'après ses coutumiers d'inspiration clunisienne', in Isabelle Cochelin and Susan Boynton (eds), *From Dead of Night to Dark of Day* (Turnhout: Brepols, 2005), pp. 221–50; Kenneth John Conant, 'Cluny II and Saint-Bénigne at Dijon', *Archaeologia* 99 (1965), 179–94; Watkin Williams, 'William of Dijon: A Monastic Reformer of the Early XIth Century', *Downside Review* 52 (1934), 525.

80 The chronicle of Saint-Bénigne says that William arrived at Fécamp with fifty monks from Saint-Bénigne (Bougard and Garnier, *Chronique de l'abbaye de Saint-Bénigne de Dijon*, p. 156).

81 Stéphane Lecouteux has recently revised this date, changing it from 1016 to 1023: Lecouteux, 'Réseaux', I, p. 71.

82 Bulst, *Untersuchungen zu den Klosterreformen*, p. 40. John's ultimate election as abbot is also detailed in Bougard and Garnier, *Chronique de l'abbaye de Saint-Bénigne de Dijon*, p. 197.

83 *Chadd* I, pp. 2, 25.

84 Paris, BnF, ms. lat. 5390, fols. 222–230r. On John being a potential editor of the text, see Gazeau and Goullet, *Guillaume de Volpiano*, pp. 19, 26. On the primacy of Fécamp's copy, see Bulst, *Untersuchungen zu den Klosterreformen*, p. 322.

85 Sigebert of Gembloux's *Chronicon* says '[c. 1027], monastic observance flourished through notable abbots: in France and Burgundy Odilo of Cluny, notable for his piety, and William of Dijon, honorable for his severity' ('*Florebat hoc tempore aecclesiastica religio per abbates nominabiles; in Francia quidem et Burgundia per Odilonem Cluniacensem pietate insignem, per Guilelmum Divionensem severitate reverendum*'), in Ludwig Conrad Bethmann (ed.), *Chronicon*, MGH Scriptores 6 (Hanover, 1844), p. 356.

86 *Libellus de revelatione, aedificatione, et auctoritate Fiscannensis monasterii*, PL 151, cols 701–24, at col. 726. For the complete list of monasteries reformed by William, see Bulst, *Untersuchungen zu den Klosterreformen*, p. 160.

87 Eleanor Searle, *Predatory Kinship and the Creation of Norman Power, 840–1066* (Berkeley: University of California Press, 1988); Christopher Brooke, 'Princes and Kings as Patrons of Monasteries: Normandy and England', in *Il monachesimo*

Dicta mea sunt dicta patrum?

    e la riforma ecclesiastica (1049–1122) (Milan: Vita e Pensiero, 1971), pp. 125–52; Potts, *Monastic Revival and Regional Identity*.

88 *Libellus de revelatione*, PL 151, cols 720–1. The *Libellus* emphasises that William's customs derived from those of the church of '*B. Majolum*', in other words, Maiolus of Cluny. Glaber also mentions William's imposition of the *RB*: 'Then this man of the Lord gathered to that place a group of monks under the *RB*, so numerous in their persons and abounding in the study of virtue that they exceeded three times the number of the past clerics' (*Glaber*, p. 273).

89 *Glaber*, p. 273. For more on William's reforms at Fécamp, see David Hiley, *Western Plainchant: A Handbook* (Oxford: Clarendon Press, 1993), pp. 578–80; Gazeau and Goullet, *Guillaume de Volpiano*; Neithard Bulst, 'La réforme monastique en Normandie: Étude prosopographique sur la diffusion et l'implantation de la réforme de Guillaume de Dijon', in Raymonde Foreville (ed.), *Les mutations socio-culturelles au tournant des XIe–XIIe siècles* (Paris: CNRS, 1984), pp. 317–30; Gregorio Penco, 'Il movimento di Fruttuaria e la riforma Gregoriana', in *Il monachesimo e la riforma ecclesiastica (1049–1122)* (Milan: Vita e Pensiero, 1971), pp. 229–39; Williams, 'William of Dijon'.

90 John Munns, *Cross and Culture in Anglo-Norman England: Theology, Imagery, Devotion* (Woodbridge: Boydell Press, 2016), p. 53.

91 For more on the establishment of schools as part of monastic reform programmes, see David Knowles, *The Monastic Order in England: A History of Its Development from the Times of St Dunstan to the Fourth Lateran Council, 943–1216* (New York: Cambridge University Press, 1963), p. 85; Lackner, *The Eleventh-Century Background of Cîteaux*, p. 132.

92 '*crescende religionis preesse institui*' (Faur, p. 80).

93 Gazeau and Goullet, *Guillaume de Volpiano*, pp. 50–5, 64–9, 111–15, 21–2; *Libellus de revelatione*, PL 151, col. 726.

94 Lecouteux, 'Réseaux', I, pp. 390–2. These include Paris, BnF, ms. lat. 989, fols 8–75 (hagiographies); Paris, BnF, ms. lat. 1714 (containing writings of Ephraem the Syrian); BnF, ms. lat. 1805 (saints' lives, including the *passio* of St Bénigne); BnF, ms. lat. 1872, fols 104–9 (life of Saint Maur); BnF, ms. lat. 3330 (Smaragdus of Saint-Mihiel's *Diadema monachorum* and *De vita sanctorum patrum heremitarum*); BnF, ms. lat. 4210 (Smaragdus of Saint-Mihiel's *Expositio in regula sancti Benedicti*); BnF, ms. lat. 5359 (saints' lives); Rouen, BM, ms. lat. 465 (A217) (Augustine's *De consensu evangelistarum libri IV*); Rouen, BM, ms. lat. 524 (I49) (Isidore's *Liber officiorum* and Bede's *De temporum ratione*); Rouen, BM, ms. lat. 528 (A362) (Bede's *Expositio in Marcum*); and Rouen, BM, ms. 532 (A395) (Augustine's *Enchridion, De diversis haeresibus*, and *Contra haereticos*).

95 Saint-Bénigne's chronicle describes William as wanting to bring things with him to Fécamp: Bougard and Garnier, *Chronique de l'abbaye de Saint-Bénigne de Dijon*, p. 89; Lecouteux, 'Réseaux', I, pp. 390–2, 472, 499.

96 Paris, BnF, ms. lat. 989, BnF, ms. lat. 1805 (which includes the *passio* of Saint Bénigne), BnF, ms. lat. 1872, and BnF, ms. lat. 5359.

97 Lecouteux, 'Réseaux', I, p. 512. Lecouteux argues that William of Volpiano likely also introduced a sacramentary, antiphoner, tonary, and customary at Fécamp, all now lost.
98 These include Rouen, BM, ms. lat. 465 (A217) (Augustine's *De consensu Evangelistarum libri IV*); Rouen, BM, ms. lat. 524 (I49) (Isidore's *Liber officiorum* and Bede's *De temporum ratione*); Rouen, BM, ms. lat. 528 (A362) (Bede's *Expositio in Marcum*).
99 Paris, BnF, ms. lat. 3330 (Smaragdus de Saint-Mihiel's *Diadema monachorum* and *De vita sanctorum patrum heremitarum*); BnF, ms. lat. 4210 (Smaragdus of Saint-Mihiel's *Expositio in regula sancti Benedicti*).
100 From the *Capitula Aquisgranensia* I, *Consuetudines Monasticae* III (Monte Cassino, 1907), p. 116, as quoted in Leclercq, *The Love of Learning and the Desire for God*, p. 46.
101 *PL* 102, cols 674–5; Nagy, *Le don des larmes au moyen âge*, pp. 147–8.
102 Paris, BnF, ms. lat. 3330 contains *vitae* of the hermit desert fathers. Note that Romuald was also inspired by these *vitae*; see Emily A. Bannister, '"From Nitria to Sitria": The Construction of Peter Damian's *Vita Beati Romualdi*', *European Review of History* 18.4 (2011), 501.
103 Lecouteux, 'Réseaux', I, p. 551.
104 Teresa Webber, *Scribes and Scholars at Salisbury Cathedral, c. 1075–c.1125* (Oxford: Clarendon Press, 1992), p. 114.
105 In one edition of John's *Confessio theologica*, Vienna, Cod. 1580, John's text is collected with both Smaragdus's *Diadema* and the *De compuctio cordis* of St Ephraem.
106 From fols 1–52v. The text is edited in Joseph Mercati (ed.), *S. Ephraem Syri opera: textum Syriacum Graecum Latinum ad fidem codicum recensuit* (Rome: Sumptibus Pontificii Instituti Biblici, 1915). Any Latin quotations from Ephraem, however, are transcribed directly from Paris 1714.
107 From fols 53r–63v. This text is edited in *PL* 103, cols 683–700. The text is titled *Regula S. Basilii* in the manuscript, but it is elsewhere called the *De admonitio ad filium spiritualem*; James Francis Le Pree, "Pseudo-Basil's *De admonitio ad filium spiritualem*: A New English Translation', *The Heroic Age: A Journal of Early Medieval Northwestern Europe* 13 (2010), www.heroicage.org/issues/13/lepree2.php.
108 From fols 64r–78v; *BHL* 5417.
109 From fols 79r–143r; Caesarius of Arles, *Sermones, nunc primum in unum collecti et ad leges artis criticae ex innumeris mss. recogniti*, ed. Dom G. Morin (Turnhout: Brepols, 1953).
110 Incipit reads '*Jeronimus dixit: Scire debemus quia diabolus*' at fol. 143.
111 At fol. 146v. Text is edited in *PG* XLVII, col. 309.
112 Incipit reads '*Occultam malitiam blandi*' at fol. 149. Note that a similar collection is considered a reformed monastery's 'syllabus' in Steven Vanderputten and Tjamke Snijders. 'Echoes of Benedictine Reform in an Eleventh-Century Booklist from Marchiennes', *Scriptorium* 63.1 (2009), 77–88.

Dicta mea sunt dicta patrum?

113 While only Caesarius explicitly speaks to an audience of monks in these particular sermons, all four sermon authors warn against the kinds of sinful behaviour that the world outside of the monastery encourages. John also warns against the sins of the body, and praises the solitary retreat of monastic life as an antidote to such sin in *CT*, pp. 134, 137.

114 Leclercq notes that sermon collections like these often were read from twice a day, once in the morning, before manual work or in the refectory, and then in the evening, when work was over: Leclercq, *The Love of Learning and the Desire for God*, pp. 167–72. There is a record of the *lectiones ad prandium* of Fécamp from the thirteenth-century ordinal of Fécamp: Denis-Bernard Grémont (ed.), 'Lectiones ad prandium à l'abbaye de Fécamp au XIIIe siècle', *Cahiers Léopold Deslisle* 20 (1971), 3–41. According to that edition, it appears that this book was read from during mealtimes in April on the feast day of Mary of Egypt ('*IIII. Non. Aprilis, Marie Egyptiacae, in Libro Effrem*').

115 Fols 100v, 110v, 121r, and 123v, among others. Cf. *CT*, p. 132.

116 Fol. 83v: 'in abstinence or in tears' ('*in abstentia vel in lacrimis*').

117 '*Et pro vulneribus animae meae nocte et die paenitentiam faciam*' (*CT*, pp. 135–6).

118 I have quoted the Latin as it appears in *Paris 1714*. For more on Ephraem's transmission to the medieval west, see: Albert Siegmund, *Die Überlieferung der griechischen christlichen Literatur in der lateinischen Kirche bis zum zwölften Jahrhundert* (Munich: Filser-Verlag, 1949); Scott G. Bruce, 'The Lost Patriarchs Project: Recovering the Greek Fathers in the Medieval Latin Tradition', *Religion Compass* 12 (forthcoming); and David Ganz, 'Knowledge of Ephraim's Writings in the Merovingian and Carolingian Age', *Hugoye: Journal of Syriac Studies* 2.1 (1999), p. 40.

119 See *Diadema monachorum* of Smaragdus of Saint-Mihiel at *PL* 102, cols 680–1; Margot Schmidt, 'Influence de saint Ephrem sur la littérature latine et allemande du début du moyen-age', *Parole de l'Orient: Revue semestrielle des études syriaques et arabes chrétiennes* 4.1 (1973), 325–41; G. Bardy, 'Le souvenir de S. Ephrem dans le haut moyen-âge latin', *Revue du moyen âge latin* 2 (1946), 297–300.

120 For a transcription of the eleventh-century library list at Gorze, see Anne Wagner, *Gorze au XIe siècle: Contribution à l'histoire du monachisme bénédictin dans l'Empire* (Turnhout: Brepols, 1996), p. 166. There, at item no. 273–4, is *Libri Effrem duo in singulis volumnibus*. Morin confirms this in his edition of the Gorze catalogue: Dom G. Morin, 'Le catalogue des manuscrits de l'abbaye de Gorze au XIe siècle', *Revue bénédictine* 22 (1905), 1–14. Wagner notes that the sermons of Ephraem were contained in volumes at Saint-Arnoul de Metz lost in 1944 (Metz, Médiathèque, ms. 223 and Metz, Médiathèque, ms. 134). The library list from the monastery of Cluny from the twelfth century, published in Léopold Delisle, *Inventaire des Manuscrits de la Bibliothèque Nationale: Fonds de Cluni* (Paris: Librarie H. Champion, 1924), contains the Rule of St Basil (at nos. 65 and 71), and a copy of St Ephraem (no. 77), both no longer extant. A borrowing list from the library of the eleventh-century monastery of Cluny

Emotional monasticism

indicates that the *Vitae Mariae Egyptiacae*, the *Dicta Sancti Basilii*, and the *Effrem de compunctione* were all at Cluny in the mid-eleventh century, if not earlier; see André Wilmart, 'Le convent et la bibliothèque de Cluny vers le milieu du XIe siècle', *Revue Mabillon* 11 (1921), p. 110. The Cluniac Ephraem, however, appears to have been in the tradition of Paris, BnF, ms. lat. 18095 rather than *Paris 1714*, though whether it pre- or post-dates William's time at Cluny is unknown.

121 Ephraem says: 'Blessed is he who remembers to be dedicated to that tremendous one, he who swims in a fountain of tears to wash and cure the wounds of his soul. Blessed is he who will create such clouds as to put forth a shower of tears, through which the flames of sin can be extinguished' ('*Beatus quis per recordatus fuerit dedice illa tremmenda et festi naverit lacrimarum fontibus ablvi et animae suae vulnera per curare. Beatus qui fuerit effectus tamquam nubes ad proferendam pluviam lacrimarum per quas possit extinguere flammas peccatorum*') (fol. 34r). John similarly says: 'And so that I can be delivered [into heaven] with the most purity and devotion, give me the compunction and the peace to flee, keep silent, and remain quiet, and make me penitent night and day for the wounds of my soul ... Tear my hardened heart so that desire might flow very ardently from this fountain. Make it so that [this fountain] waters me from the base to the head' ('*Et ut hoc purius et devotius agere possim, da mihi luctum et quietem ut fugiam, taceam et quiescam et pro vulneribus animae meae nocte et die paenitentiam faciam ... Scinde duritiam cordis mei ut emanet fons iste cuius desiderio nimis astuat anima mea. Da mihi irriguum inferius et irriguum superius*') (*CT*, pp. 135–6).

122 Arthur Vööbus, *Literary Critical and Historical Studies in Ephrem the Syrian* (Stockholm: Etse, 1958), pp. 94, 96, 106.

123 Chrysostom's sermon addresses two biblical passages having to do with tears: Jeremiah 9:1 ('O that my head were water and my eyes a fountain of tears!') and Isaiah 22:4 ('Let me alone, I will weep bitterly; labour not to comfort me'). Chrysostom writes in his sermon that the only way to save one's lost soul is to submit to the depths of tearful mourning.

124 On the Rule of St Basil's connection with hermitic movement, see Baker, '"The Whole World a Hermitage"', p. 216. Ephraem and Basil had a long tradition of mutual association: see Vööbus, *Literary Critical and Historical Studies*, pp. 34, 42, and Dom. O. Rousseau, 'La rencontre de saint Ephrem et de saint Basile', in *L'orient syrien: Revue trimestrielle d'études et de recherches sur les églises de langue syriaque* 2.1 (1960), pp. 261, 269, 271.

125 The specific version of Mary's life included in *Paris 1714* is told by an Abbot Zosimus, who narrates her story as an example of an intensely penitent former sinner. Ruth Mazo Karras interprets this particular story as one that, for the Middle Ages, would have emphasised the eremitic over the coenobitic life; Ruth Mazo Karras, 'Holy Harlots: Prostitute Saints in Medieval Legend', *Journal of the History of Sexuality* 1.1 (1990), 6–7; Jane Stevenson, 'The Holy Sinner: The Life of Mary of Egypt', in Erich Poppe and Bianca Ross (eds), *The Legend of Mary of Egypt in Medieval Insular Hagiography* (Portland, OR: Four Courts Press, 1996), pp. 19–50.

Dicta mea sunt dicta patrum?

126 Leyser, *Hermits and the New Monasticism*.
127 Stéphane Lecouteux believes that it was John who transported the manuscript from Saint-Bénigne de Dijon. Perhaps he brought it not at William's request, but rather of his own volition; Lecouteux, 'Réseaux', I, p. 551.
128 Vanderputten, *Monastic Reform as Process*, pp. 143ff.
129 Alain Rauwel, 'Circulations liturgiques, circulations dévotes dans l'espace abbatial: Autour de Guillaume de Dijon', in Michael Lauwers (ed.), *Monastères et espace social. Genèse et transformation d'un système de lieux dans l'Occident médiéval* (Turnout: Brepols, 2014), p. 383. The *Quem quaeritis* play was widely circulated in medieval Europe; see David A. Bjork, 'On the Dissemination of the *Quem quaeritis* and the *Visitatio sepulchri* and the Chronology of Their Early Sources', *Comparative Drama* 14 (1980), 46–69.
130 *Glaber*, p. 293.
131 This prayer is edited in Jean Leclercq, 'Prières attribuables à Guillaume et à Jean de Fruttuaria', in *Monasteri in alta Italia dopo le invasioni saracene e magiare (sec. X–XII)* (Turin: Deputazione Subalpina di Storia Patria, 1966), pp. 159–66. William reformed Saint-Arnoul de Metz in 996/97; Bulst, *Untersuchungen zu den Klosterreformen*, p. 160.
132 Leclercq, 'Prières attribuables à Guillaume et à Jean de Fruttuaria', p. 161.
133 There is more on this in Chapter 3.
134 Lecouteux, 'Réseaux', I, p. 520.
135 David Bates, *Normandy before 1066* (New York: Longman, 1982), p. 223.
136 Véronique Gazeau, 'Les abbés bénédictins dans la Normandie ducale', in *L'étranger au moyen âge* (Paris: Publications de la Sorbonne, 2000), pp. 248–9.
137 Bulst, *Untersuchungen zu den Klosterreformen*, p. 317.
138 Steven Vanderputten, 'Oboedientia: Réformes et discipline monastique au début du XI siècle', *Cahiers de civilisation médiévale* 53 (2010), 255–66; Steven Vanderputten, 'Crises of Cenobitism: Abbatial Leadership and Monastic Competition in Late Eleventh-Century Flanders', *English Historical Review* 127.525 (2012), 259–84.
139 *BHL* numbers 6292, 6294 (Odo); *BHL* 5182 (Maiolus); *BHL* 6282 (Odilo).
140 *BHL* 6281.
141 Incipit *Exigitis domini mei divites in opem eloquente* in BnF, ms. lat. 5329; and his sermon for the feast of St Benedict in Rouen, BM, ms. 1404 (U20).
142 Henriet, *La parole et la prière*, pp. 55–70, 207–18.
143 Lackner, *The Eleventh-Century Background of Cîteaux*, pp. 47–8.
144 Note that the *Occupatio* enjoyed limited popularity in its own moment in the Middle Ages: *Odonis abbatis Cluniacensis Occupatio*, ed. Antonius Swoboda (Leipzig: B.G. Teubner, 1900); Christopher A. Jones, 'Monastic Identity and Sodomitic Danger in the *Occupatio* by Odo of Cluny', *Speculum* (2007), 1–53.
145 This is the same edition contained in the Fécamp manuscript Paris, BnF, ms. lat. 5290, *BHL* 6292, 6294.
146 Gerard Sitwell (ed.), *St. Odo of Cluny: Being the Life of St. Odo of Cluny by John of Salerno* (New York: Sheed and Ward, 1958), p. 135; Carolyn M. Malone,

Saint-Bénigne de Dijon en l'an mil, 'totius Gallie basilicis mirabilior': Interprétation politique, liturgique et théologique (Turnhout: Brepols, 2009), p. 227; Isabelle Rosé, Construire une société seigneuriale: Itinéraire et ecclésiologie de l'abbé Odon de Cluny (fin du IXe–milieu du Xe siècle) (Turnhout: Brepols, 2008), pp. 519–22.

147 Rosé, Construire une société seigneuriale, pp. 609–10.

148 Dominique Iogna-Prat, 'La Madeleine du Sermo in veneratione sanctae Mariae Magdalenae attribué à Odon de Cluny', Mélanges de l'École française de Rome 104.1 (1992), 37–70; Dominique Iogna-Prat, Agni immaculati: Recherches sur les sources hagiographiques relatives à saint Maieul de Cluny (Paris: Cerf, 1988).

149 Stevenson, 'The Holy Sinner', p. 25.

150 Iogna-Prat, 'La Madeleine', p. 58.

151 Nagy, Le don des larmes au moyen âge, p. 260; Madeleine Fournié, 'L'unum necessarium à Jumièges: Le culte de sainte Marie-Madeleine', in Jumièges: Congrès scientifique du XIIIe centenaire (Rouen: Lecerf, 1954), p. 991.

152 Odo's sermon, Iogna-Prat believes, was not actually written by Odo, but was instead likely written at Vezelay, circulating under Odo's name. The sermon happens to circulate with one of John's prayers – the Lamentation – in an eleventh-century manuscript from southern England, Cambridge, Fitzwilliam Museum, McClean ms. no. 7, fols 113–16 (discussed further in Chapter 4). The sermon was read on Easter Sunday in the Fécamp refectory (see 'Lectiones ad prandium', ed. Grémont), a nice accompaniment to the Easter drama featuring the Magdalene and performed at Fécamp (discussed further in Chapter 3).

153 Zombory-Nagy, 'Les larmes du Christ'; Iogna-Prat, Agni immaculati, pp. 45–50.

154 Iogna-Prat, Agni immaculati, p. 53.

155 'Intrat continuo palatium cordis sui et in spelunca pectoris, collocat sibi dignum consistorium, facit cartham conscientiam suam, stilum gemitum, et lacrymas atramentum ... consideravit se, quaesivit se a se, facta est ipsa sibi iudex et advocata, posuit se ante faciem suam, aspexit carthas suas, atramento iniquitatis scriptas, aperuit foeditatem suam agnovit male lubricatam vitam suam'; from Homelie II, n. 11, as quoted by Iogna-Prat, 'La Madeleine', p. 56.

156 Rachel Fulton notes that Mary Magdalene was considered by medieval Christians to be particularly 'other' to Christ, unlike the male saints, who were thought to be more akin to him. Such a feeling of separation might therefore have been useful to a monk who felt himself to be distant from Christ on account of his own sin. See Rachel Fulton, 'Anselm and Praying with the Saints', in Karl F. Morrison and Rudolph M. Bell (eds), Studies on Medieval Empathies (Turnhout: Brepols, 2013), p. 130.

157 Griffiths, Nuns' Priests' Tales, pp. 60–7.

158 Kassius Hallinger, 'The Spiritual Life of Cluny in the Early Days', in Noreen Hunt (ed.), Cluniac Monasticism in the Central Middle Ages (New York: Macmillan 1971), p. 42; Jean Leclercq, Regards monastiques sur le Christ au moyen âge (Paris: Mame-Desclée, 2010), p. 117; Jean Leclercq, Monks on Marriage: A Twelfth-Century View (New York: Seabury, 1982), pp. 123–46; Malone, Saint-Bénigne de Dijon en l'an mil, p. 135.

Dicta mea sunt dicta patrum?

159 Several Fécamp manuscripts from the eleventh century contain sermons on the Magdalene, including a Pseudo-Augustinian sermon contained in Paris, BnF, ms. lat. 2019 (on fol. 56v), and one from Hrabanus Maurus in Paris, BnF, ms. lat. 3776/2253, in addition to that from Rouen, BM, ms. 1404 (U20) discussed above.
160 Nagy, *Le don des larmes au moyen âge*, p. 264.
161 Note that the Magdalene had a prominent role in the Easter drama at William of Volpiano's monastery of Fruttuaria, as well as at the monastery at Fécamp (see Chapter 3). Alain Rauwel, 'Circulations liturgiques', p. 383.
162 Maiolus's *vita* by Syrus of Cluny conveys these ideas, *BHL* 5179: see Iogna-Prat, *Agni immaculati*, pp. 119, 329.
163 Constable, *Three Studies in Medieval Religious and Social Thought*, p. 179; Jacques Hourlier, *Saint Odilon: Abbé de Cluny* (Louvain: Bibliothèque de l'université, 1964), pp. 145–6.
164 Odilo apparently meditates on the cross on his deathbed for this reason, invoking proper penitence: 'Un opuscule inédit de saint Odilon de Cluny', *Revue bénédictine* 16 (1899).
165 Peter of Blois says this in Ep. 123, *PL* 207, col. 363, as quoted by Hourlier, *Saint Odilon*, pp. 146–7. See also Dominique Iogna-Prat, 'La croix, le moine, et l'empereur: Dévotion à la croix et théologie politique à Cluny autour de l'an mil', in Michel Sot (ed.), *Haut moyen âge: Culture, éducation, société. Études offertes à Pierre Riché* (Paris: Publidix/Éditions européennes Erasme, 1990), pp. 449–75.
166 See Sermon 15 in *PL* 149, col. 685, as cited by Leclercq in *Regards monastiques sur le Christ*, pp. 119–20.
167 Iogna-Prat, 'Le croix, le moine, et l'empereur', pp. 449–75. Odilo even adopted the feast of Mary Magdalene and the feasts for the Exaltation and Invention of the Cross for the first time at Cluny.
168 *CT*, p. 124.
169 Pierre Courcelle, *Les Confessions de saint Augustin dans la tradition littéraire: Antécédents et postérité* (Paris: Études augustiniennes, 1963), p. 254.
170 Courcelle, *Les Confessions de saint Augustine*, pp. 263–4.
171 Denys Turner, *The Darkness of God: Negativity in Christian Mysticism* (New York: Cambridge University Press, 1995), p. 66.
172 In his *Retractiones* (the relevant passages of which were excerpted at the beginning of most medieval copies of *Confessions*, including Fécamp's), Augustine states that his *Confessions* should 'praise the just and good God, and into him excite the human intellect and affection. At least, as far as I'm concerned, they accomplished this in me when they were written and they do when they are read'; as quoted by Linda Olson, 'Did Medieval English Women Read Augustine's *Confessiones*? Feminine Interiority and Literacy in the Eleventh and Twelfth Centuries', in Sarah Rees Jones (ed.), *Learning and Literacy in Medieval England and Abroad* (Turnhout: Brepols, 2003), p. 71.
173 Mancia, 'Reading Augustine's *Confessions*'.
174 Cf. *CT*, p. 144; *Confessions* 1.5.5.
175 Cf. *CT*, p. 149; paraphrasing *Confessions* 1.6.7.

176 Cf. *CT*, p. 161.
177 *Confessions* 10.40.65.
178 Confession as a tool for continual conversion has been discussed by Karl Morrison, *Conversion and Text: The Cases of Augustine of Hippo, Herman-Judah, and Constantine Tsatsos* (Richmond, VA: University of Virginia Press, 1992), p. 47; it is also mentioned by Gregory the Great, St Benedict, and other earlier medieval monastic authors.
179 See Part II of Mancia, 'Reading Augustine's *Confessions*'.
180 Twenty Augustinian texts were collected at Fécamp in the eleventh century.
181 Though Jumièges has no extant medieval library list, an extant eleventh-century manuscript of *Confessions* from that library contains an ownership note from the twelfth century on fol. 214v, placing a copy of the book in the Jumièges library from at least the twelfth century onwards; see Nortier, *Les bibliothèques médiévales*, p. 149.
182 By the late fourteenth century, Saint-Ouen had a copy of *Confessions*: the earliest library list from Saint-Ouen is from between 1372 and 1378, contained in Rouen, Archives départementales de Seine-Maritime, 14H17, fol. 7v, a register of loans made between 1372 and 1378 from the library. On that list, *Confessions* is listed as article number 36; see Henri Dubois (ed.), *Un censier normand du XIIIe siècle: Le Livre des jurés de l'abbaye Saint-Ouen de Rouen* (Paris: CNRS, 2001), pp. 12–14.
183 The manuscript is recorded to be at Lyre in a seventeenth-century catalogue of manuscripts from that monastery, in Paris, BnF, Dupuy 651, fols 252r–252v, listed as *D. August. Lib. Confess.* on fol. 252v.
184 Alexander, *Norman Illumination*, pp. 1–64.
185 See Chapter 5.
186 Augustine likely got it from late antique Christian monks, see Paul C. Dilley, *Monasteries and the Care of Souls in Late Antique Christianity* (New York: Cambridge University Press, 2017), pp. 110–47.
187 See Chapter 5; Leroux De Lincy, *L'abbaye de Fécamp*, p. 263; Bates, *Normandy before 1066*, pp. 195, 213.

3

Reforming the monastic community: the uses of John's devotional method within the walls of Fécamp

The devotional method prescribed in John of Fécamp's *Confessio theologica* was not confined to the pages of that abbot's treatise; rather, an eleventh-century monk would have been presented with John's emotional devotion in a variety of media at the monastery of Fécamp. In examining the manuscripts, sermons, liturgical rituals, letters, and images that were circulating around John's eleventh-century monastery, one can see that the ideas of emotional reform contained in the *Confessio theologica* were being reinforced at many other junctures of the monastery's spiritual and intellectual life. The importance of right interior feeling, the emphasis on wounding love and *caritas*, and the emotional avatars of the crucified Christ, Mary Magdalene, and Hannah were all stressed in a variety of ways throughout a monk's day and year over a lifetime at the Norman monastery. Some of these motifs contained in texts or ceremonies would have been present at any monastery in the eleventh century; but some of them were unique to John's monastery. In view of the pervasiveness of these themes at Fécamp, the emotional reforms prescribed by John's *CT* begin to seem less like the hopeful musings of an abbot and more like the thoughtful expression or even codification of a wider programme of emotional reform at the monastery.

I: The *Confessio theologica*'s motifs in the Fécamp monk's wider devotional curriculum

At every stage of his life at Fécamp, a monk would have encountered aspects of the *Confessio theologica*'s prescriptions for emotional devotion. He would have received instruction about proper feeling, prayer, and *caritas* – and the efficacy of the examples of Christ, Mary Magdalene, and Hannah in

Sermons given to novices entering the monastery

These are the words that every eleventh-century monk at Fécamp would have heard his abbot speak on his first day at the monastery:[1]

> Our cross is the fear of the Lord. Therefore just as someone crucified no longer has the power of moving or turning his own limbs any way in accord with the motion of his own mind, so also ought we to fasten our wills and desires, not according to that which is pleasant to us and delights us at present, but according to the law of the Lord, to the place where that [law] has bound us.[2]
>
> And indeed, my brothers, as long as we are in the body, we sojourn apart from the Lord. Sojourners do not long for the native land without a tear. If you long for what you do not have, shed tears. For whence will you say to God: 'Thou hast set my tears in thy sight'? Whence will you say to God: 'My tears have been my meat day and night'? They have been my meat: they have consoled the one who groans, they have fed the one who hungers. My tears have been my meat day and night.[3]

From his very first moments at Fécamp, therefore, a monk would have heard the teachings that were fundamental both to John's *CT* and to Fécamp's devotional message.[4] The first passage quoted above asks novices to become Christ through their commitment to the monastic livelihood, 'apply[ing] to [them]selves' a metaphorical crucifixion of discipline and rule, just as John's *CT* asks for the image of the crucified to wound its reader, making him into Christ. In the second passage above, tears are upheld as a chief and right desire for every monk, and the paradoxical idea that weeping and pain serve as comfort is here introduced to the Fécamp novice in his first moments as a member of the community. These passages laid the foundation from which the new monk would extract his purpose and motivation for the rest of his life. When such a monk encountered passages alluding to the crucified or the consolation of tears as ideals in the *CT* and other devotional documents at Fécamp, then he would already have been primed by the background of this introductory sermon to recognise them as foundational, to perceive their meaning, and to integrate them into his monastic life. And, fittingly, when the monk performed the death ritual for one of his brethren, which also involved performing the crucifixion,[5] he would likely think back to his orientation at the monastery, aware that the crucifixion bracketed a monk's life at Fécamp, ushering him in as a novice and out as a corpse.

Manuscripts from Fécamp's library

When a Fécamp monk was assigned a book to read at Lent,[6] or when he took a book out of the monastery's new library to read after Matins or Prime,[7] treatises in the spirit of the *Confessio theologica* that were exclusively dedicated to contemplation were few and far between. Nevertheless, of the books collected in Abbot John's time, many of which are listed on Fécamp's eleventh-century library list,[8] several titles supplemented the *CT* as models of proper contemplative behaviour and interior feeling for the monastic reader. Some of these texts were typical for an eleventh-century monastery: Smaragdus's *Diadema monastica*[9] or Ambrose's (c. 340–97) *De fuga saeculi*[10] are just two of the books from the monastic canon that show up in the Fécamp library that advocate rejecting the world and embracing suffering and the contemplative life. In *De fuga saeculi*, for instance, Ambrose encourages readers to use Christ's passion to model the rejection of the world.[11] If a monk were seeking to supplement his understanding of devotional models of the *CT*, such as Hannah, for example, whose canticle the monks would sing in the liturgy and on ferial Wednesdays, he need not look further than the lavish eleventh-century copy of Augustine's *De civitate dei*, which could provide a reader with more background on Hannah.[12] There, in Book 17, Augustine spends a chapter glossing Hannah's canticle; the monk-reader could thereby enhance his understanding of this pious woman by learning Augustine's exegesis of her prayerful words.

Other texts in the Fécamp library, however, were less common elsewhere and more closely aligned with the *CT*'s prescriptions. Ephraem the Syrian's *De compunctione cordis*, for instance, calls for a contemplative to cultivate tears in order to open his heart.[13] A Fécamp monk even had the unique opportunity to read *the* earliest copy of Augustine's *Confessions* in Normandy, a book whose tear-filled pages and mournful tone directly inspired the *Confessio theologica* and was subsequently introduced by Fécamp to the other monasteries in its network.[14] Most striking of all, several books in Fécamp's eleventh-century library prescribing proper penance contain readers' markings highlighting the passages that recommend tearful contrition.[15] Therefore, while there were many titles whose messages would have dovetailed nicely with John's own available at the monastery, several may have been specially collected, or at least could have been particularly read, with John's devotional prescriptions in mind.

The abbot's performance in Good Friday's depositio drama

The Fécamp monk not only heard the words of sermons and read the words of books that accorded with the ideas of the *Confessio theologica*; he also witnessed the actions of his abbot, who would often model certain devotional behaviours to his brethren. The monastic ideal of teaching by example was widespread: in Normandy, in the generation after John, Lanfranc at Saint-Etienne in Caen and Anselm at Bec embraced this precept,[16] and the Bec priors and abbots who came before Anselm emphasised similar modelling.[17] This teaching by example yielded a kind of *affectus*: the abbot's model would not only work to instruct his monks intellectually, but would also affect them emotionally, bringing them into another *habitus*, a new state of mind and heart.[18]

Above all other motifs from the *Confessio theologica*, it was the utility of the image of the suffering Christ that was chiefly modelled by the Fécamp abbot for his community. The Fécamp monk would have most memorably encountered this in the ritual of the deposition (*depositio*) drama that took place during the Good Friday liturgy, two days before Easter Sunday. The *depositio* drama played at Fécamp much as it did at many of the monasteries reformed by William of Volpiano.[19] At all of these monasteries, during the *depositio*, the celebrant imitated the events after the crucifixion, taking the cross down from the altar, cradling and kissing the body of Christ on the cross, and then burying the cross in a kind of sepulchre.[20] At Fécamp, however, the *depositio* drama had its own customs that on occasion were distinct from those practised elsewhere. For instance, at Fécamp, the drama was chiefly performed by the abbot (which, in the eleventh century, would mean John of Fécamp). Moreover, while elsewhere the celebrant was assisted by deacons and priests,[21] at Fécamp, the abbot alone would cradle and kiss the cross before performing the entombment of the body of Christ along with his assistants,[22] and then the abbot alone on Easter Eve would remove the cross from the sepulchre, unaccompanied when miming Christ's resurrection.[23] Additionally, at Fécamp, after the abbot took down the cross, the congregation watched him take a private moment to make a 'very long genuflection' (*tam longa fiat genuflexio*) and handle the cross with 'great reverence' (*cum magna reverentia*).[24] At Fécamp, I would argue that such a pronounced genuflection would have been a moment of prayerful devotion to a crucified body that was seen in the *CT* and elsewhere as an enactment of right *caritas*; it would have been a moment to try out the contemplative methods that centred on the suffering images that filled the devotional culture of Fécamp. Phrases from the *Confessio theologica* such as 'I ask you through that most holy effusion of your precious blood … give me contrition of heart, even a font of tears, especially while I … stand in attendance at your altars'[25] may have been constructed so as to be recalled during this exact moment both by John as abbot and by his monks looking on. What John's prayers yearn for – a reflection on the imagined vision of the scene of the crucifixion – the abbot here literally and materially demonstrates for the benefit of his community. Annually, the Fécamp monk witnessed a dramatisation of the kind of appreciation of the crucified Christ that was preached in his novitiate, emphasised in the *Confessio*, and apparent in other readings from the library.

Audience participation in the drama of the Easter liturgy

Monks at Fécamp were not only witnesses to such liturgical productions; they were also participants in its performances, learning by enacting concepts prescribed by John's treatise and emphasised elsewhere. A chief example of the kinaesthetic opportunity given to Fécamp monks to dramatise their devotional lessons came two days after the *depositio* drama in the Easter Sunday *Quem quaeritis* play.[26] The Easter drama as it was performed at Fécamp particularly encouraged a dramatic embodiment of the example of Mary Magdalene, paralleling the function of the avatar that was encouraged in the *Confessio theologica* and in the relic of Mary Magdalene that was at the monastery.[27] Like many Easter dramas from the same period, the *Quem quaeritis* play occurred in the Fécamp liturgy between Matins and Lauds at Easter after the abbot had enacted the resurrection of a cross that he had buried in the sepulchre during the *depositio* drama two days before.[28] During this short play, four of the Fécamp monks were chosen to play the roles of the three Marys who visited Jesus's tomb and the angel who appeared to them there. In front of the congregation, these four monks engaged in a dialogue where they re-enacted the biblical scene, annually witnessing the revelation of the resurrection in real time.

Like the *depositio* drama, the Easter drama occurs in liturgies elsewhere, but Fécamp's has some particularly local distinctions. For our purposes, there are two significant ways in which the Fécamp Easter play is distinct, both of which resonate with John's *Confessio theologica*'s themes. First, the Fécamp customs explicitly outline its actors' particular costumes, props and stage directions.[29] Because of this, we know that Fécamp's play is the earliest

Emotional monasticism

extant to distinguish Mary Magdalene from the other two Marys: while other plays dress all three Marys in white, Fécamp's play puts the Magdalene in red.[30] A thirteenth-century antiphoner-hymnal from Fécamp accords with this distinction, featuring an initial in which three women – the central one in a red cloak – stand behind a sepulchre and next to an angel (Figure 1).[31] This dramatic highlighting of the Magdalene would have followed on the heels of a special sermon that every monk at Fécamp would have heard the night before, in which Mary Magdalene is called the most devout of all

Figure 1 An initial with the three Marys at the tomb (thirteenth century)

the women at the tomb because she desired to see the testament of Jesus's blood at his sepulchre.[32] It also would have followed the ritual washing of the feet that the monks performed three days before, on Maundy Thursday, through which Fécamp monks 'entered more deeply into the role model of the sinful woman [than at other contemporary monasteries]' by specifically 'using the hair of their tonsure to dry the poor people's feet' just as the Magdalene supposedly did.[33] Easter week, then, was a time for Mary Magdalene to be presented as the prime exemplar of *caritas* for the monks at Fécamp, just as John uses her in the *CT*.[34]

Fécamp's drama also differs from other *Quem quaeritis* plays in the directions it gives to the three Marys at the tomb. While elsewhere the Marys are advised to wander as if seeking something before meeting the angel at the sepulchre,[35] at John's monastery, the Mary's need to wander *quasi querela*, as if mourning. This emotional dimension is not delivered with the exact language that John himself uses in the *CT*; nevertheless, it is parallel to John's way of seeking and connecting with God through tears and conveys the prescriptions for weeping seen elsewhere in the library. Because of this liturgical drama, the Fécamp monk would not just have read about the importance of Mary Magdalene as a model mourner in John's *CT*, he would not just have heard about the virtues of her devotion in sermons; he also would have witnessed or even performed the concept at Easter, absorbing yet more deeply another consistent theme of Fécamp's devotional culture.

II: *Caritas*, harming to help, and monastic discipline

The foregoing discussion presented the moments when the Fécamp monk might have encountered in his devotional practice the emotional reform instructions inhering in John of Fécamp's *Confessio theologica*. Comparisons between the *CT* and Fécamp's other devotional literature extends our exploration of affectivity at Fécamp beyond re-enactments either by abbot or monk in religious practice. In this section, I present evidence of its further use. The evocation of *caritas* actually served a practical use as well as a religious one: it promoted a certain style of monastic discipline alongside its more interior, spiritual objectives.

To examine this pragmatic application, I turn now to another work of John's, one that is, in fact, the only specimen of his writing found in Fécamp's eleventh-century library.[36] The work is a letter 'to unruly monks' (*ad monachos dyscolos*), a missive that John sent to renegade monks who had left Fécamp to live as hermits in the Norman countryside. John's letter is a warning to the rebellious monks that their spiritual deliverance could occur only by living under the will of an abbot – not by the guidance of their own will or religious fervency. He says:

> Read among the rest where it is said [in the *RB*, ch. 49]:
> 'Whatever each wants to offer to God, let him bring it before his abbot, and let it be done with the abbot's prayer and consent, because what is done without the blessing of the spiritual father will be attributed to presumption, and for vainglory, not for heavenly reward' ... Hear, brother, and understand plainly: if long-lasting testing, and the rooting out of vices, and the rule and will or permission of the abbot has led you to so exceptional a life, or rather if your own will has seduced you.[37]

At first glance, this letter appears to be about obedience, about John's desire as a leader of coenobitic monks to contain the pestilence of eremitism that threatened his abbatial control. After all, it is John's job as abbot to enforce the *RB* and to keep his monks in line. What makes this letter most intriguing for our purposes, however, is that John goes on to employ what we have heretofore identified exclusively as *devotional* rhetoric in his condemnation of such disobedient behaviour. Drawing on the meaning of *caritas* used in his *Confessio*, John emphasises the salutary nature of 'cruel' punishment and the healing properties of suffering:

> Finally, if some deceit or transgression has intervened, we commit what must be expunged to your philosophical argumentation; *caritas* does not hide. Surely your inner eye did not rightly discern that I [John] am shedding innocent blood or that I am cruel in the death of our sons.[38] Notice who of us is crueller: for we know that God is the one who kills and makes alive,[39] and that it is proper to himself to forgive sins ... and [God] teaches his disciples to absolve the one whom he resuscitates; nevertheless, even this we discover, as long as the fault remains, no one is by any means able to be absolved.[40]

Taken in part from Hannah's own biblical language, John emphasises here that abbatial obedience is a devotional instruction as well as a practical one: it is required for salvation, even if it appears to be 'scatter[ing] blood'. It follows, then, that abbatial punishment for acts of disobedience, while seemingly cruel, is in fact *caritas*, because it effects correct absolution through suffering. Were he not to punish the disobedient, but rather rely on the wayward monk to correct his behaviour by means of his own 'inner eye', he would be denying proper *caritas*, and thus, would actually 'kill' the disobedient monk's spiritual self by leading him, instead, to damnation.[41]

John then ends his letter using the example of Christ to explicitly connect the practical concerns of obedience to the higher aims of devotional practice:

> If you boast of speaking with the tongues of angels through the goal of contemplation, you have lost *caritas*, which is the bond of perfection. God is *caritas*; he who feels in opposition to *caritas* loses God; he who loses God has nothing; he who hates himself, or feigns to love another than himself, that very one kills himself, who of his own accord flees from the yoke of obedience; he who flees from the yoke of obedience, who withdraws from obedience, withdraws from Christ, who became obedient to the father unto death. For in this you have lost the benefit of obedience, when you have at the base shaken the neck from under the yoke of the rule: he who brandishes arms against obedience acts against Christ; he who acts against Christ is the antichrist. In this indeed it more clearly stands evident than the light of day that *I* have not poured out the blood of our sons, but those very sons have killed themselves. What more [can I say]?[42]

Here, John comes full circle, making clear the adaptive use of the devotional model of the crucified Christ. Christ's suffering through his obedience evidenced a closeness to God that a monk must strive to imitate in his own obedience to his abbot, to the *RB*, and to the yoke of the monastic life. A monk who decides that he can live alone as a hermit without the *RB* of an abbot has lost the 'yoke of obedience' *and* the ability to feel right *caritas*, and has therefore distanced himself from Christ *both* in action and in feeling and thus, in essence 'killed' himself.[43] Without the right brand of exterior discipline, John argues, a monk has no hope of finding God in his interior practice of contemplation; such exterior discipline, no matter how 'cruel' it may seem, is certainly less fatal than a life without it. In order to enforce monastic discipline at Fécamp, therefore, John enforces contemplative discipline as well, using the concepts of salutary suffering, *caritas*, and Christological avatarism that are encouraged by the *CT* and in other devotional practices around his monastery to link monastic obedience and divine punishment.[44] In John's formulation, the pairing of pain and suffering with devotion in the *CT* and elsewhere in Fécamp's devotional culture incited an interior reform that paralleled, enforced, and upheld the exterior reform that John undertook.

If we apply the precepts of John's letter to the image of the Fécamp monk witnessing the abbot cradle the body of Christ in the *depositio* drama on Good Friday, we can see how abbatial modelling at the monastery could have served to promote the abbot's own authority. In the drama, the *abbot* alone is with Christ and therefore assumes the role as his vicar and as the supreme judge of his monks while they are on earth.[45] The *CT* often stresses that the crucifixion itself is an implicit reminder of Christ's obedience to God;[46] and this is a fact that was also stressed by the abbot in his sermon for novices when he asked them to cultivate obedience by 'crucify[ing]' their wills and desires.

Our modern sensibilities might cause us to approach these recommendations cynically, assuming the abbots used this devotional rhetoric simply to enforce their power and manipulate their brethren. Indeed, the concept of 'affective lordship' has been applied by Thomas Bisson to 'lord-abbots' like Robert of Torigny (1106–86), who used such domineering behaviour to keep others in line.[47] Abbots like Geoffrey of Vendôme (1093–1132) used similarly violent rhetoric in his letters to Hildebert of Lavardin (1055–1133), attempting to control the archbishop or his own disobedient monks.[48] As early as the fourth century, abbots like Shenoute (348–466) literally beat their misbehaving monks to death at the White Monastery in Egypt, using the threat of death as an intimidation tactic while simultaneously claiming to have acted in concert with God.[49] Affective instruction has been used by many cultures and many time periods as a means of effective physical discipline and emotional control,[50] and, by the twelfth century, emotional practices of *caritas* specifically often led to legal *conventio* with juridical (and, sometimes, physical) force.[51] It is therefore not a stretch to imagine that the emotional devotional prescriptions at Fécamp could have had a purposeful disciplinary use in their monastic context, and that John and other abbots could have chosen the devotional reform most useful in promoting their own power and stability.

Yet, despite the authoritarian tone that John and others used to exact obedience, and despite the ways in which Fécamp's devotional motifs helped to position the abbot, to the eleventh-century monk, the emphasis on monastic obedience and abbatial authority would also have been a rhetorical means to a devotional end. While the monastic emphasis on obedience worked to elevate abbatial power, it was not blind surrender to authoritarian rule, but rather willing submission that ultimately generated authentic virtue in the obedient monk.[52] Obedience was not seen as oppression by a power-hungry abbot, but rather a way towards perfection for all; it was desperately sought after by monks so that they could attain God with the support of a community of equals.[53] Disobedience and free will yielded evil and sin (cf. Adam and Eve), so obedience in community (cf. Christ) was the only answer. As Amy Hollywood says, 'although the monk begins following the *RB* and obeying the abbot out of fear, through the repeated practice of injunctions, he will come "to observe without effort, as though naturally, from habit, no longer out of fear of hell, but out of love for Christ, good habit, and delight in virtue" (*RB* 7:67–9)'.[54]

This observation thus reveals a practical-cum-devotional use for Fécamp's particular set of devotional motifs, a use that I here call 'harming to help': the idea that discipline, though seemingly causing suffering and 'spilled blood', ultimately leads to deliverance and salvation (it is, in John's words, 'innocent blood'). In revisiting what we have already learned about John's *CT*, we come to see how many of its themes come together in this larger theme of compassionate cruelty: suffering, crying, and feeling pain were the means to achieving efficaciousness in prayer. In revisiting Fécamp's wider devotional culture, we can also trace this idea of 'harming to help' in library books, letters, and even in manuscript frontispieces. John's devotional prescriptions for seeming cruelty in the *CT* (suffering, wounding, and tears), and his elevation of the image of the crucified were understood and applied in his eleventh-century monastic context in specific ways. While requiring exterior discipline and obedience, 'harming to help' rhetoric was likely embraced by the monks of Fécamp as a device to kindle obedience and simultaneously cultivate their own interior divine virtue and ability to move closer to God. It was, in Karl Morrison's words, 'cruelty as a method of redemptive love'.[55]

'Harming to help' in John's Confessio theologica

Throughout the *Confessio theologica*, John of Fécamp speaks of spiritual death in the same terms that he used in his letter to the disobedient hermit-monks: man is 'killed' by his faults and saved by Christ's grace. In the case of the *monachos dyscolos*, these faults are incorrect *exterior* practices (the monks have left the *RB* and their abbot to live as hermits); however, in the *CT*, disobedience is *internal* and is determined by a process of self-reflection outlined by John in his text. To 'break the bonds of sin' through contemplation, the reader of the *CT* must cultivate a state of constant lamentation, always straining to be conscious of his unworthiness and sinfulness. The devotee, newly aware, must ultimately ask God to 'tear out with loving hands' his sinfulness (notice how the violence of 'tear out' is softened with the adjective 'loving').[56] In his treatise, John of Fécamp depicts God as a force of violent correction, a sword that would 'write on the tablets of [the reader's] heart [God's] commandments and will, your laws and right doing, so that I may always and everywhere have you, Lord of immense sweetness, and your precepts before my eyes'.[57] Inner discipline, to achieve salvation, needed to be cruelly inflicted and inscribed, much as outer discipline was achieved in John's *monachos dyscolos*.

Nowhere is this 'cruel' corrective clearer than in John's final prayer of the *CT*:

> Through those saving wounds which you suffered on the cross for our salvation and from which flowed the precious and vivifying blood by which we have been redeemed with propitious graciousness ... wound this sinful soul of mine for which you were willing even to die; wound it with the fiery and powerful dart of your excessive *caritas*. You are the living Word of God, efficacious and more piercing than every sharpest sword. You, double-edged sword, cleave my hardness of heart and wound this sinful soul, and pierce more deeply to the inmost parts with your powerful virtue. Give me an abundant source of water and pour into my eyes a true font of tears running day and night out of excessive feeling and desire for the vision of your beauty, so that I may grieve constantly all the days of my life, taking no consolation in the present life, until I merit to see you, my God and my Lord, as a beloved and beautiful spouse in your heavenly chamber.[58]

In John's prayer, the monk-reader is a sinful soul, disobedient and deserving of punishment by the powerful, piercing dart of God's love. John uses the vision of the crucified Christ as a mechanism to transform the monk's emotional approach to God: the monk, wounded by that image, can finally be led to spiritual health; his internal disobedience can be violently corrected and reshaped into the right emotional affect so that it may ultimately lead to salvation. When read next to John's letter to the *monachos dyscolos*, this passage from the *CT* resonates with the disciplinary language employed in the monastery. John prescribes right *caritas* and obedience to his disobedient hermit-monks; he argues that his abbatial 'cruelty' works to 'make [his brethren] alive' and is 'proper' to their correction. Like Christ, who is 'both victor and victim, and therefore victor, because the victim',[59] the corrected monk (only seemingly victimised) will triumph through his suffering.[60] In this light, John's authoritative letter is of a piece with his *Confessio theologica*, both documents working to lead his brethren towards spiritual health through harsh physical and emotional discipline. Christ, then, is invoked as an example of such right discipline in the eleventh century, not as an example of relatable humanity as he will be in later centuries.

'Harming to help' in Fécamp's library

Such salutary 'cruelty' is not John's own invention – it is a convention that he is drawing on from earlier precedents, particularly from the *RB* and patristic texts against heresy. The *RB* is very clear on how 'harsher corrections' for the most delinquent brethren are signs of right 'compassion' and *caritas* that will restore spiritual health to sick brothers. The *RB* explicitly states that punishment is executed so that 'false' monks may be 'heal[ed]',[61] dovetailing nicely with John's 'harming to help' rhetoric. It is likely, then, that it was not eremitism per se that catalysed John's writing to the *monachos dyscolos*,[62] but rather the monks' throwing off of their obedience and deference to John as abbot – an abuse that could only, according to the *RB*, be corrected by the compassionate cruelty of the abbot himself.[63] For this reason, John's letter likely had important didactic potential for non-hermit monastic audiences at Fécamp that merited its prominence in that monastery's eleventh-century library.

The 'harming to help' philosophy espoused by John and by the *RB* had an even earlier precedent: Augustinian texts against early Christian heretics. According to Augustine, Christian heretics needed to be treated differently from non-Christian unbelievers. Unlike pagans, Augustine claims, one needed to repress 'false' Christians like the Donatists or the Arians in order to save them.[64] The Donatists were an especially good example for Augustine, because they saw themselves as rigorists – holding that their behaviour was saintlier than that of mainstream Christians. In his letter *On the Correction of the Donatists*, Augustine demanded that despite their self-proclaimed sanctity, despite their appearance of godliness (cf. John's description of the proud hermits), imperial officials must recognise the danger of the Donatists and 'use force to snatch [their] souls from hell'.[65] Here again is 'cruelty as a method of redemptive love': the Donatists are being punished in order to save them.[66] Augustine says:

> What does it profit [the Donatists], therefore, if they have both the voice of angels in the sacred mysteries, and the gift of prophecy [1 Corinthians 13:1–2, cf. John's *monachos dyscolos* letter[67]] … yet because they do all these things apart from the Church, not 'forbearing one another in love', nor 'endeavoring to keep the unity of the spirit in the bond of peace'; insomuch as they have not *caritas*, they cannot attain eternal salvation, even with all those good things which profit them not.[68]

Augustine justifies this forcefulness, because he believes the Donatists were not '"endeavoring to keep the unity of the spirit in the bond of peace"'.

Moreover, he uses the same Corinthians quotation and reference to *caritas* that John does in his letter to the hermits.[69] For both Augustine and John, a heretic's heart had to be opened to the truth by means of forceful discipline (like the dart of love in John's *Confessio theologica*).[70]

Augustine's letter was known to the eleventh-century monks at Fécamp: it is bound in at least three different Fécamp manuscripts from John's time.[71] Furthermore, it seems that under John, the monastery of Fécamp was particularly fond of collecting texts against heresy: over the course of John's abbacy, 18 per cent of the titles collected fall into this category.[72] Part of this might reflect the Fécamp monks' involvement in combating many of their own eleventh-century iterations of the Donatists found both in Normandy and around Fécamp's network: in the early eleventh century, 'Manicheans' and other heretics were condemned near John's hometown of Ravenna and William of Volpiano's hometown of Turin, among other places.[73] In one manuscript from the library, the letter from Augustine mentioned above is bound with the Fécamp monk Durandus of Troarn's refutation of the eleventh-century heretic Berengar of Tours, thus tying Durandus's contemporary efforts directly to the patristic model.[74]

Still, more often than not, monks using such anti-heretical rhetoric around eleventh-century Fécamp were writing not against heretics in the traditional sense but rather against 'false' monks who were practising an 'incorrect' faith, and therefore, like the Donatists, may have claimed to be rigorists but were actually 'false' Christians.[75] John applied this Augustinian rhetoric in much of his writings concerning spiritual guidance,[76] especially throughout his *CT*, when Christ is often explicitly thanked for guiding the reader against any kind of 'heretical perversion'.[77] John's fellow abbot, Warin of Metz, also uses such rhetoric in a letter to John, working to correct what he felt was John's un-monastic arrogance, which he likens to 'the heresy of the Donatists'.

> Although we [at Metz] are indeed sinners, nevertheless we confess Christ. We hold the catholic faith: we take the baptism and Eucharist of Christ, we read and keep to the extent of our ability the *RB*, we stand in the battle line of Christ against the common foe; we strike, and we are sometimes struck; with God sustaining, we stand, and sometimes, with infirmity impeding, we waver; if we fall due to frailty, we rise again with God lifting us up, and yet we do not sink to the point of despair in our faltering moments. And I believe that each faithful monk is just as able to keep and to save his own soul with the help of God in our poor and meagre place [i.e. Metz],

won with respect to both riches and (that which is more dangerous) religion, as in any wealthier and more religious [place, implying Fécamp]; unless perhaps someone, knowing more than it is fitting to know, should transfer the heresy of the Donatists, who said that the 'true religion' was *only* in Africa, and should transfer that same pestilence from Africa to Normandy, asserting that no monk is able to be saved *except* in the monastery of Fécamp.[78]

Warin is not here condemning John of Fécamp as a Donatist – instead, he uses the heretical label to assert his abbatial independence. Warin's reference to Donatism thus shows how earlier heretics served as examples when John and his contemporary abbots argued about proper monastic behaviours. No matter how fervent in their devotion, no matter their appearance of orthodoxy, even fellow abbots could run the risk of becoming Donatists in need of compassionate correction when they misinterpreted monastic rules.

'Harming to help' in Fécamp's manuscript images

Only two frontispiece illustrations remain among the extant eleventh-century books from Fécamp, likely saved from post-medieval excision because they were left unfinished by their medieval artists. It turns out, however, that these two remaining images from Fécamp also promote the 'harming to help' motif popularised in various guises at the monastery. The manuscript images, both those from anti-heretical texts and depictions of Church Fathers triumphing over heretics, feature parallel programmes with a unique iconography.[79] Paris, BnF, ms. lat. 2079 (Figure 2) is a copy of Augustine's *Contra Faustum* featuring a frontispiece on fol. 1v of Augustine triumphing over Faustus the Manichaean (fl. c. 383).[80] Paris, BnF, ms. lat. 1684 (Figure 3), also made at Fécamp during the second half of the eleventh century, is a copy of Athanasius's (296–373) *Contra Arianos*, and it features a frontispiece on fol. 1r of Athanasius triumphing over the heretic Arius (c. 256–336). Also included in the codex in the same scribal hand is Vigilius Tapensis's (d. c. 490) *De trinitate*, another diatribe written against a heretic who did not believe in the Trinity.[81]

Though likely made by two different artists, the visual parallels between these two frontispieces are striking. In both images, we see the Church Father haloed and wearing the clerical vestments of a monk-bishop: in Athanasius's case, as per the Eastern tradition, his monastic status is denoted by a simple belted robe; in Augustine's case, as per the Western tradition, his monastic

Figure 2 Augustine triumphing over Faustus the Manichean (eleventh century)

status is denoted by a tonsure.[82] The heretics are both wearing shorter garments, indicating their lower (and perhaps even their courtly or military) ranks, showing themselves to be more of this world than of the Church. The Fathers' robes are noticeably plainer and more kempt than those of the

Reforming the monastic community

Figure 3 Athanasius triumphing over Arius (eleventh century)

heretics. Both bishops have cuffs that are not ornamented[85] in contrast to Faustus's and Arius's more opulent, decorated cuffs. In *Paris 2079* (Figure 2), Faustus looks dishevelled, with the stubble of a beard growing, and perhaps even with an unkempt tonsure. Both pairs are contained within similar architectural frames: rounded arches with simple, undecorated capitals and bases. Important for the purposes of this chapter, both heretics are tonsured,

99

shown to be monks, seeming as legitimately Christian as the Fathers who discipline them; and Augustine uses an abbatial crosier to silence Faustus – a crosier whose shape would have been recognisable to Norman monks in the late eleventh century as an arm of abbatial authority.[84] The crosier and dress of the monk-bishop figure in each image would have been conflated with the dress of a Norman abbot. In *Paris 2079*, Augustine, for instance, looks very similar to a Norman-made image of St Vulfran (c. 640–703), the founding abbot of Saint-Wandrille, a monastery closely linked with Fécamp.[85] While the positioning of the figures in each of the images is not precisely the same, the desired effect is identical. In *Paris 2079* (Figure 2), Faustus topples down mid-argument, pointing at his book defiantly all the while, his gaze locked with Augustine's; Augustine, silent and commanding in his stance, raises his own book, which he gingerly clutches in the folds of his robe, and uses the point of his crosier to spear Faustus directly in the mouth. In *Paris 1684* (Figure 3), Arius also continues to gesture towards his book while being wrestled to the ground; Athanasius points his long finger accusingly at Arius, while using his left foot to step on the heretic's throat and his cross-lance to pierce through the heretic's heart. Such intense targeting of the throat and mouths of Arius and Faustus is likely connected with metaphors addressing the dangers of heresy from Augustine's own writings and with more contemporary writings from the eleventh century: Augustine describes Faustus as being able to 'lure [with his] smooth language';[86] Paul of Saint-Père de Chartres (fl. c. 1000), in 1022, characterised heretics in Orléans as 'reply[ing] with the tongues of snakes',[87] as, indeed, it was the mouth of a snake through which 'humankind had been seduced to disobey God'.[88] The spear through the mouth of the vanquished also calls to mind iconographic precedents. Particularly rich for the monastic houses of Normandy was the image of the scribe Gelduin (fl. tenth century) and St Michael triumphing over the devil, who is shown speared through the mouth in several manuscripts from Mont Saint-Michel.[89] Given the close relationship between the Mont Saint-Michel and Fécamp scriptoria, it would not be surprising if a shared illustrator made these images, or if the Fécamp artist was inspired by the Mont Saint-Michel manuscript.[90]

Despite the hints of inspiration from images of Michael and the dragon, the two Fécamp images share an otherwise unique iconography for their time. I have not found another illustrated medieval image of Athanasius and Arius in any format; and, while there are many depictions of Augustine and his heretical interlocutors, they are more often than not depicted in mid-disputation. Two manuscripts from Mont Saint-Michel, one of the *Contra Felicianum* and one of the *Contra Faustum*, share certain characteristics with the Fécamp manuscripts: here, again, we see the heretic wearing shorter garments and tonsured; both heretic and Augustine are arguing from the authority of a codex; and, even without his crosier, Augustine in each case is given a halo, less-ornamented dress, and a more distinguished seat to the right of the image to emphasise his triumph and favour.[91] The parallels between the bodies of Augustine and Christ in this image also make a clear point about who is in the right.

I have found only one other example of a full figure triumphing over a heretic in the manner of Michael and the dragon: in an image from Canterbury from 1020, Arius lies beneath John the Evangelist's feet, summarising his central heresy, which claims that the Son of God was created.[92] He says in the picture: *erat tempus quando non erat* ('there was a time when [Jesus] was not'), and he is bested by John's opening words *in principio erat verbum et verbum erat apud deum et deus erat verbum; hoc erat in principio* ('In the beginning was the Word, and the Word was with God, and the Word was God; by this we know that [Jesus] was in the beginning'). By this we see the authority that John uses to subvert Arius's heresy is scriptural authority: his pen is raised, but he does not pierce Arius's throat, and he does not even make contact with Arius's body, which lies cramped between the frame of the image and the platform on which John stands. Significantly, it is not the authority of a monk-bishop that triumphs here, as it is in the Fécamp images; and it is also not a *violent* triumph, as it is in the Fécamp images.

The iconography of these two Fécamp frontispieces, with their tonsured figures and their violent victories, parallels the 'harming to help' rhetoric used elsewhere in the Fécamp monastery. In a like manner to Warin, John, and Augustine, the Fécamp artists' depictions of Faustus and Arius emphasise 'false' religion's deceptive power and threat in the monastic sphere. In the Fécamp images, Arius and Faustus have tonsures: they look like monks. Like the renegade monks from Fécamp, or like John of Fécamp to Abbot Warin, they are not pagans or dragons or devils, but *appear* to be true religious;[93] and only abbots Augustine and Athanasius can see them (and punish them) for the dissemblers they are. Once Augustine's, Benedict's, and John's approaches to the correction and reform of 'heretical' behaviour and 'false' monks are considered, the meaning behind the violence of the Fécamp iconography comes into even sharper focus: in the Fécamp images, Augustine and Athanasius are not disputing the heretics (as they are elsewhere) but instead are dominating them, stepping on their necks and piercing their mouths and hearts. They are acting as disciplining abbots and good pastors,[94] harming 'false' monks, stifling their words, in order to help them and to save them from being misled. We can then imagine Faustus as one of John's disobedient hermits, and we can imagine Augustine's spear as a 'dart of love'.[95] When a monk at Fécamp opened his monastery's copy of *Contra Faustum* or *Contra Arianos*, he would have understood the opening images not just as depictions of the Fathers triumphing over heretical devils; he also would have seen these postures of dominance as gestures of *compassionate* correction, acts for the good of the heretic's spiritual self.

All of this helps to further uncover the eleventh-century meaning of the *Confessio theologica*'s passages on wounding and Fécamp's emphasis on the crucified Christ and the crying Magdalene: they rest on the foundation of this 'harming to help' trope. John finds in the crucifixion a pairing of cruelty with love, epitomising his definition of *caritas* and resonating with the method that he and other abbots were employing against disobedient monks of all types. The pairing of pain and suffering with devotion in John's *CT* incited an interior reform that paralleled the rhetoric of exterior reform that John and others employed for disobedient Christians elsewhere. By noting this rhetorical resonance, we see that John's insistence in the *CT* on the suffering of Christ is not an attempt to emphasise Jesus's humanity, nor is it purely an attempt to bolster his own abbatial power. He uses Christ's wounded example as a model for proper affective correction that would lead to the promise of heaven, and which the Fécamp monks, with the reinforcement of their wider devotional culture, would have understood as such.

Conclusion

This chapter has shown that John's devotional prescriptions in the *Confessio theologica* were not idiosyncratic; rather, they were part of a much larger effort at the monastery of Fécamp to reform exterior behaviour and interior spiritual practice, to align it with the examples of Christ, Hannah, and Mary Magdalene, and to cultivate *caritas* for the sake of redemption. Moreover, when seen within the wider devotional context at Fécamp, John's early prayers to a wounded, suffering Christ in the *CT* are revealed as clear extensions of rhetoric alive elsewhere in the monastic context. To a monk at Fécamp, Christ's obedient acts and his painful emotions would have worked hand in hand as *exempla* for the monastic experience enforced by the *CT*, the *RB*, the Fécamp liturgy, sermon literature, frontispiece images, and patristic curriculum. John put forward Christ on the cross not in order to stress how human he was in his flesh, but rather to demonstrate his monklike obedience, his willing submission to punishment and pain. As a result, John's *CT* would have been particularly calibrated to the concerns of a monastic audience in their cloistered confines with their disciplined, contemplative, emotional goals.

The parallels between Fécamp's devotional culture and John's text, and between eleventh-century monastic rhetoric of obedience and Fécamp's wider devotional rhetoric, stand alone as sufficient testament to the pervasive and complicated devotional experience of which John's *CT* would have been a part. But who created such a complicated programme at Fécamp? Did it all stem from John's guidance, from the template of the *CT*? Or was it all in place already, and did John's *CT* simply strengthen an already richly complicated heuristic environment?

The question of intentionality cannot easily be answered. There is some evidence that John was indeed in charge of the transformations at the monastery of Fécamp and that it was he who implemented the inflections of the monastery's devotional culture. We have already discussed the innovations of John's *CT* next to his influences,[96] so the appearance of the particular novelties of the *CT* elsewhere at Fécamp could be a sign of John's influence on the monastery's culture. Moreover, it was John under whose watch the Fécamp library grew from thirteen codices in 1028 to eighty-seven in 1078.[97] As abbot, John likely dictated the speed of the copying in the scriptorium and prioritised which text was to be copied first.[98] Therefore, it is under John's gaze that the anti-heresy titles in the library grew, that the frontispiece programme was made, and that Augustine's *Confessions* were copied.[99] Further, as abbot, according to the *RB*, John was responsible for assigning each monk a book to read during Lent;[100] and he even had a hand in guiding the reading habits of the patrons of the monastery, William the Conqueror and his wife.[101] All of this evidence seems to suggest that John had a preeminent role in shaping both the devotional culture and instruction at and around the monastery in the eleventh century.

But, even if these emphases at Fécamp were John's own, it is unclear that he would have described them as such. Drawing from age-old patristic precedent and the guidance of the *RB*, John likely saw himself as forming a series of prescriptions and rituals that solidly adhered to monastic tradition and purpose while simultaneously, subtly refreshing an inner connection with God. There are no extreme elaborations of John's devotional philosophy at Fécamp – no gory crucifixes survive dating from the eleventh century, no radical deviation from tradition in John's motifs. But that is what is so brilliant about John's *CT*'s suggestions for reform: he is making the space for invigorating affective engagement with God within the limits of the orthodoxy and obedience required. He is conservative while still being innovative enough to reinvigorate devotional culture at the monastery. His reform is incremental while still being particularly directed towards emotional, interior transformation. After all, to him, his words are merely the words of the Fathers (*dicta me sunt dicta patrum*).

These investigations are significant for scholars of affective piety who have often in the late medieval context attributed the devotee's focus on Christ's suffering to his God's relatable humanity. With this chapter's investigations, we can add another oft-neglected dimension to our understanding of the medieval embrace of the suffering Christ in affective devotion: his obedient *caritas*, or his embrace of suffering and correction for its salvific importance. Monks reading John of Fécamp wanted to embrace the image of the suffering Christ because it modelled the perfect devotee: one who would suffer his *vulnera* because of their healing power. His words resonated with and were informed by reform prescriptions, exterior and interior, that pervaded the culture of his monastery in the eleventh century. The crucified Christ and his particular suffering were indeed useful to monks, inspiring affective prayer even in the eleventh century in ways foundational for, if different from, later medieval interpretations.

Notes

1 This sermon is found in Fécamp homiliary Paris, BnF, ms. lat. 3776. Betty Branch dates the book to the second half of the eleventh century, claiming that it was once bound with Paris, BnF, mss. lat. 2253 and 5390. Branch, 'The Development of Script', pp. 94–6.
2 This sermon is attributed to Cassian, and is contained in *PL* 49, col. 196A: '*Crux nostra timor Domini est. Sicut ergo crucifixus quis iam non pro animi sui motu membra sua quoquam movendi vel convertendi habet potestatem: ita et nos voluntates nostras ac desideria, non secundum id quod nobis suave est ac delectat ad praesens, sed secundum legem Domini, quo nos illa constrinxerit, applicare debemus.*'
3 This sermon is attributed in the Fécamp manuscript to Isidore of Seville, but elsewhere to Augustine, *PL* 38, col. 195: '*Etenim, fratres mei, quamdiu sumus in corpore, peregrinamur a Domino. Non desiderat patriam peregrinatio sine lacryma. Si desideras quod non habes, funde lacrymas. Nam unde dicturus es Deo: Posuisti lacrymas meas in conspectu tuo? Unde dicturus es Deo: Factae sunt mihi lacrymae meae panis die ac nocte? Panis mihi factae sunt: consolatae sunt gementem, paverunt esurientem. Factae sunt mihi lacrymae meae panis die ac nocte.*'
4 We can see similar language being used in other eleventh- and twelfth-century sermons for novice formation: Jean Leclercq, 'Textes sur la vocation et la formation des moines au moyen âge', in *Corona Gratiarum: Miscellanea Patristica, Historica, et Liturgica Eligio Dekkers O.S.B. XII Lustra Complenti Oblata* (Bruges: Sint

Pietersabde, 1975), vol. II, p. 178; Isabelle Cochelin, 'Peut-on parler de noviciat à Cluny pour les Xe–XIe siècles?', *Revue Mabillon* 70 (1998), 17–52; Caroline Walker Bynum, *Docere verbo et exemplo: An Aspect of Twelfth-Century Spirituality* (Cambridge, MA: Harvard University Press, 1979), pp. 122ff.; Constable, 'The Cross in Medieval Monastic Life', pp. 236–7.

5   Jörg Sonntag, 'On the Way to Heaven. Rituals of *Caritas* in High Medieval Monasteries', in Gert Melville (ed.), *Aspects of Charity: Concern for One's Neighbor in Medieval Vita Religiosa* (Berlin: Lit Verlag, 2011), p. 45: 'The cilice was strewn with ashes in the form of a cross; the dying monk was positioned on the cilice in the form of a cross; a wooden cross was laid on his head; he wore his *cuculla* – the symbolization of the cross; if the brother was still conscious, the monks read him the episode of Christ's crucifixion.'

6   RB, 67–9. This practice is supported by loan lists that survive from monasteries from the Carolingian period onwards: Anne Lawrence, 'Anglo-Norman Book Production', in David Bates and Anne Curry (eds), *England and Normandy in the Middle Ages* (London: Hambledon Press, 1994), p. 79; Bates, *Normandy before 1066*, p. 81; James Westfall Thompson, *The Medieval Library* (Chicago: University of Chicago Press, 1939), p. 231; Karl Christ, 'In Caput Quadragesimae', *Zentralblatt für Bibliothekswesen* 60 (1943), 33–59.

7   This prescription is from William of Volpiano's customs at Fruttuaria; see Luchesius G. Spätling and Petrus Dinter (eds), *Consuetudines Fructuarienses-Sanblasianae* (Siegburg: Franciscum Schmitt Success, 1985), vol. I, pp. 19, 30. It is likely that Fécamp's customs were modelled on those of Fruttuaria, which was William's earlier, major foundation.

8   Rouen, BM, ms. 1417 (U45), fol. 55v. For more on the date of these lists, see Branch, 'Inventories'. Manuscripts not on the eleventh-century inventory may have been housed in the chapter house, or in some other location that caused them to be left off the list from John's time; see Teresa Webber, 'Monastic Space and the Use of Books in the Anglo-Norman Period', *Anglo-Norman Studies* 36 (2013), p. 238.

9   Paris, BnF, ms. lat. 3330 (fols 7–60v), a late-tenth-century manuscript.

10 Paris, BnF, ms. lat. 2639, an eleventh-century manuscript.

11 On fols 89r–v, Ambrose invites his readers to scourge themselves for their sinfulness in a way reminiscent of Christ's own scourges. This passage is marked with an 'r' in the margins, so, at one point in Fécamp's history, it resonated enough with a monastic reader to merit a reader's mark; for more on readers' marks, see M.B. Parkes, *Pause and Effect: An Introduction to the History of Punctuation in the West* (Berkeley: University of California, 1993), p. 67.

12 Paris, BnF, ms. lat. 2055 is discussed in Branch, 'The Development of Script', p. 73. In Book 17, ch. 4, of *De civitate dei*, Augustine glosses Hannah's canticle. For more on this, see Chapter 4, below.

13 Paris, BnF, ms. lat. 1714, as discussed in Chapter 2. There is a record of a reading from this manuscript in the *lectiones ad prandium* of Fécamp from

the thirteenth-century ordinal, published in 'Lectiones ad prandium', ed. Grémont, p. 20.

14 Vatican City, Biblioteca Apostolica Vaticana, Vat. Reg. lat. 755, which dates to 1051. For more on the dating of this manuscript, its resonance with the *CT*, its primacy in the Norman context, and its possible solicitation by John himself, see Chapter 2, and Mancia, 'Reading Augustine's *Confessions*'.

15 See n. 11 above; the same manuscript contains Ambrose's *De paradyso* and has several passages on the use of tears notated by the same monastic reader; see, for instance, the highlighted passage on fol. 152r. Paris, BnF, ms. lat. 1684, another eleventh-century manuscript, contains the later addition of an anonymous prayer on fol. 128v, which includes a passage on the use of tears. Vatican City, Biblioteca Apostolica Vaticana, Vat. reg. lat. 500, also from the eleventh century, contains a collection of the sayings of the Fathers; on fol. 146r a reader has marked the sayings of Abba Arsenius, who always kept a handkerchief on his person, because tears of compunction so often fell from his eyes.

16 Priscilla D Watkins, 'Lanfranc at Caen: Teaching by Example', in Sally N. Vaughn and Jay Rubenstein (eds), *Teaching and Learning in Northern Europe, 1000–1200* (Turnhout: Brepols, 2006), pp. 70–97; Sally N. Vaughn, 'Anselm of Bec: The Pattern of His Teaching', in *Teaching and Learning in Northern Europe*, pp. 98–127.

17 Vaughn, 'The Pattern of his Teaching', pp. 104, 106, 114.

18 This definition of *affectus* follows Cassian's; see Chapter 1 and Hollywood, 'Song, Experience, and the Book', p. 67.

19 Comparable liturgies were at Saint-Bénigne de Dijon, Fruttuaria, and Cluny. For more on the *depositio* drama, see Pamela Sheingorn, *The Easter Sepulchre in England* (Kalamazoo, MI: Medieval Institute Publications, 1987); Colin Morris, *The Sepulchre of Christ and the Medieval West* (New York: Oxford University Press, 2005); Elizabeth Parker, 'The Descent from the Cross: Its Relation to the Extra-Liturgical Depositio Drama' (PhD dissertation, Institute of Fine Arts, New York University, 1975); Sandro Sticca, 'The Montecassino Passion and the Origin of the Late Passion Play', *Italica* 44.2 (1967), 211; Wm. L. Smoldon, 'The Easter Sepulchre Music-Drama', *Music and Letters* 27.1 (1946), 2; Karl Young, *The Drama of the Medieval Church* (Oxford: Clarendon Press, 1933), p. 13; Solange Corbin, *La deposition liturgique du Christ au Vendredi Saint: Sa place dans l'histoire des rites et du théâtre religieux (analyse de documents portugais)* (Paris: Les Belles Lettres, 1960). The *depositio* drama is said by Parker to have originated at Metz (Amalarius of Metz discusses it in his work, see Parker, 'The Descent from the Cross', p. iii); if this is true, William of Volpiano may have encountered the drama at Metz or the monasteries under the Gorze reform that he visited before his journey to reform Fruttuaria and Fécamp.

20 Munns, *Cross and Culture*, pp. 146–54.

21 I have compared Fécamp's liturgy to that of houses influenced by William of Volpiano's customs, namely, Cluny, Fruttuaria, and Saint-Bénigne de Dijon, and to that of Norwich, which was directly influenced by Fécamp's customs. Cf.

Kassius Hallinger (ed.), *Consuetudines Cluniacensium antiquiores cum redactionibus derivatis* (Siegburg: Franciscum Schmitt, 1983); Petrus Dinter (ed.), *Liber tramitis aevi odilonis abbatis* (Siegburg: Franciscum Schmitt 1980); Spätling and Dinter (eds), *Consuetudines Fructuarienses-Sanblasianae*; J.B.L. Tolhurst (ed.), *The Customary of the Cathedral Priory Church of Norwich* (London: Henry Bradshaw Society, 1948). The Saint-Bénigne customary is contained in Paris, BnF, ms. lat. 4339; there, the feast for Good Friday (*De passio domini*) begins on fol. 82v. See more comparative liturgies in Yvonne Rokseth, 'La liturgie de la passion vers la fin du Xe siècle', *Revue de Musicologie* 31.89/92 (1949), 1–58; Louis van Tongeren, *Exaltation of the Cross: Toward the Origins of the Feast of the Cross and the Meaning of the Cross in the Early Medieval Liturgy* (Leuven: Peeters, 2000).

22 *Chadd* I, p. 231.
23 *Chadd* I, p. 237.
24 *Chadd* I, pp. 230–1. For more on the sorrowful significance of such a long genuflection, see Richard C. Trexler, 'Legitimating Prayer Gestures in the Twelfth Century: The *De penitentia* of Peter the Chanter', *History and Anthropology* 1 (1984), 97–126. Susan Boynton has commented on the potent drama of a similar moment in the liturgy at the abbey of Farfa: Boynton, *Shaping a Monastic Identity*, p. 98.
25 '*Rogo te per illam sacratissimam effusionem praetiosi sanguinis tui, quo sumus redempti, da mihi cordis contritionem, et lacrimarum fontem, praecipue dum sacris altaribus ... assisto*' (*CT*, p. 173).
26 The earliest incarnation of the Fécamp drama survives in a liturgical manuscript from the early twelfth century, Rouen, BM, ms. 244 (A261); a thirteenth-century version is in *Chadd*; and an additional copy from the fourteenth century is Rouen, BM, ms. 253 (A538). David Chadd argues that the late-twelfth-/early-thirteenth-century ordinal contained customs copied from an earlier Fécamp ordinal, perhaps made under William of Volpiano or, more likely, John of Fécamp (*Chadd* I, p. 15); Lecouteux agrees that the liturgy at Fécamp was very conservative, in 'Réseaux', I, pp. 461, 484; these observations help argue that the Easter drama was practised under John. I have compared this with similar Easter plays at Gorze from the tenth century (Dominique Berger, *Le drame liturgique de Paques du Xe au XIIIe siècle: Liturgie et théâtre* (Paris: Éditions Beauchesne, 1976), p. 80); from the tenth-century *Regularis Concordia*; and from monasteries reformed by William of Volpiano, namely Fruttuaria, Saint-Ouen, Mont Saint-Michel. For more on comparable liturgies, see Diane Dolan, *Le drame liturgique de Pâques en Normandie et en Angleterre au moyen-age* (Paris: Presses universitaires de France, 1975), pp. 72–3; David A. Bjork, 'On the Dissemination of the *Quem quaeritis* and the *Visitatio sepulchri* and the Chronology of their Early Sources', in Clifford Davidson, C.J. Gianakaris, and John H. Stroupe (eds), *The Drama of the Middle Ages: Comparative and Critical Essays* (New York: AMC Press, 1982), pp. 1–24.
27 Cf. Chapter 1.
28 *Chadd* I, p. 237.
29 See, for instance, *Chadd* I, p. 238.

30 A comparison between Fécamp's dramas and others can be found in Dolan, *Le drame liturgique de Pâques*, p. 58.
31 The initial is on fol. 120v, Rouen, BM, ms. 245 (A190); here, the Marys are in red, white, and blue; as the manuscript is from the thirteenth century, the blue may have been a development in the later customs of the monastery. This scene is also emphasised in a Gospel book made for Fécamp in the late eleventh century, Rouen, BM, ms. 29 (A165): on fol. 66r, the name of Mary Magdalene is specially flourished, causing it to stand out from the names of *Maria Jacobi* and *Salomae*.
32 The sermon read on Holy Saturday is contained in the Fécamp eleventh-century homiliary Paris, BnF, ms. lat. 3776, fols 47v–49v; it is from Hrabanus Maurus's *Commentary on Matthew* and examines Matthew 23.
33 Sonntag notes that the monks at Hirsau and Fruttuaria, unlike other places in Europe, added the hair to this drying ritual (Sonntag, 'On the Way to Heaven', pp. 38, 47).
34 Such an emphasis on the Magdalene could also have been connected to Fécamp's relics from her; see Chapter 1.
35 C. Clifford Flanigan, 'Medieval Liturgy and the Arts: Visitatio Sepulchri as Paradigm', in Eva Louise Lillie and Nils Holger Peteren (eds), *Liturgy and the Arts in the Middle Ages* (Copenhagen: Museum Tusculanum Press, 1996), p. 16.
36 *Epistola ad monachos dyscolos* was bound as part of a larger codex with the letters of Augustine in Paris, BnF, ms. lat. 1928; see Branch, 'Inventories', p. 171. In the same hand following this letter, on fol. 173v, there is an excerpt from a synod at Caen dated to 1042. This suggests that John's letter was written before 1042. Jean Leclercq notes that often such letters were read aloud as sermons to monks by their abbots in Jean Leclercq, 'Recherches sur d'anciens sermons monastiques', *Revue Mabillon* 36 (1946), 1–14.
37 '*Lege inter caetera ubi dicitur: "Quidquid unusquisque offerre vult Deo, abbati suo suggerat, et cum eius fiat oratione et voluntate, quia quod sine benedictione patris spiritalis fit, praesumptioni deputabitur et vanae gloriae, non mercedi" ... Audi, frater, et subtiliter intellige: si diuturna probatio vos, et vitiorum excoctio, et abbatis imperium et voluntas vel permissio ad tam egregiam vitam provexit, aut potius propria voluntas illexit*' (CT, p. 218).
38 The rhetoric here refers to spiritual death, following Hannah's canticle, John's CT, and Paul's Letter to the Ephesians 2:4.
39 This is a direct quotation from Hannah's canticle: 'The Lord puts to death and gives life' ('*Dominus mortificat et vivificat*') (1 Samuel 2:6).
40 '*Denique, si aliquis simulatio vel transgressio intercursit, vestrae philosophicae argumentationi committimus expurgandum: charitas non quaerit angulos. Sane non rite discrevit interior oculus vestrorum me sanguinem innocentem fundere, aut crudelem in filiorum nostrorum morte fore. Quis nostrum crudelior existat advertite: scimus namque quia Deus est qui mortificat et vivificat ... et quem resuscitat, discipulis praecipit absolvere: verumtamen et hoc rescimus quia, quamdiu culpa manet absolui quisquam nequaquam valet*' (CT, p. 219).

41 This dovetails with prescriptions found in the *Moralia in Job* (cf. Chapter 2), where Gregory discusses the 'divine whips' that are ultimately salutary for the sinner. See, for instance, *Mor* 32.4.5. Note that here, 'inner eye' is a kind of bad interiority, in contrast with the good introspection prescribed by John's *CT*.
42 Italics my emphasis. '*Si linguis hominum loquar et angelorum, charitatem autem non habeam, nihil mihi prodest. Si gloriamini angelorum lingua loqui per scopon contemplationis, charitatem perdidistis, quod est vinculum perfectionis. Deus charitas est: qui contra charitatem sentit, Deum perdit; qui Deum perdit, nihil habet: qui seipsum odit, alium se fingit amare; ipse seipsum perimit, qui sponte sua obedientiae iugum refugit; qui obedientiae iugum refugit; qui obedientiae derogat, Christo derogat, qui factus est patri obediens usque ad mortem. In hoc enim fructum obedientiae perdidistis, cum de sub iugo regulae collum fundis excussitis: ergo qui contra obedientiam arma vibrat, contra Christum facit; qui contra Christum facit, antichristus est. In hoc siquidem luce clarius patet quia non ego effudi sanguinem filiorum nostrorum, sed ipsi filii se peremerunt. Quid plura?*' (*CT*, pp. 219–20).
43 The *vincula caritatis* is an assurance against vainglory even among monks in the Carolingian period, see Choy, *Intercessory Prayer*, p. 93.
44 Monasteries, in fact, were often called *caritatis schola*; Sonntag, 'On the Way to Heaven', p. 52.
45 Fécamp abbot's demonstration of this special relationship with the crucified Christ through the *depositio* drama is not wholly surprising; according to the *RB*, the abbot was considered the special vicar of Christ, acting in the place of Christ in the monastery (*RB*, 2.1–3).
46 *CT*, p. 138.
47 Thomas N. Bisson, *The Crisis of the Twelfth Century* (Princeton, NJ: Princeton University Press, 2009).
48 G. Giordanengo (ed. and trans.), *Geoffroy de Vendôme, Oeuvres*, Sources d'histoire médiévale 26 (Paris: Éditions du CNRS, 1996), letter 32 (from 1102), and letters 92 and 93 (1107–10), concerning disobedient monks.
49 Rebecca Krawiec, *Shenoute and the Women of the White Monastery: Egyptian Monasticism in Late Antiquity* (New York: Oxford University Press, 2002), pp. 40–50; Dilley, *Monasteries and the Care of Souls*, pp. 130–1.
50 Catherine Lutz, 'Emotion, Thought, and Estrangement: Emotion as a Cultural Category', *Cultural Anthropology* 1.3 (1986), 287–309.
51 Bruce C. Brasington, 'From Charitable Sentiments to Amicable Settlements: A Note on the Terminology of Twelfth Century Canon Law', in Gert Melville (ed.), *Aspects of Charity: Concern for One's Neighbor in Medieval Vita Religiosa* (Berlin: Lit Verlag, 2011), pp. 1–10; Lars Arne-Dannenberg, 'Charity and Law. The Juristic Implementation of a Core Monastic Principle', in *Aspects of Charity: Concern for One's Neighbor in Medieval Vita Religiosa*, pp. 11–28.
52 Cochelin, 'Obedience or Agency?'; Talal Asad, 'On Discipline and Humility in Medieval Christian Monasticism', in *Genealogies of Religion: Discipline and Reasons of Power in Christianity and Islam* (Baltimore, MD: Johns Hopkins University

Press, 1993), pp. 125–67; Katherine O'Brien O'Keeffe, *Stealing Obedience: Narratives of Agency and Identity in Later Anglo-Saxon England* (Toronto: University of Toronto Press, 2012); Giles Constable, 'The Authority of Superiors in the Religious Communities', in George Makdisi, Dominique Sourdel, and Janine Sourdel-Thomine (eds), *La notion d'autorité au moyen âge. Islam, Byzance, Occident* (Paris: Presses universitaires de France, 1982), pp. 189–210; Gert Melville, 'Der Mönch als Rebell gegen gesatzte Ordnung und religiöse Tugend. Beobachtungen zu Quellen des 12. und 13. Jahrhunderts', in Gert Melville (ed.), *De ordine vitae. Zu Normvorstellungen, Organisationsformen und Schriftlichkeit im mittelalterlichen Ordenswesen* (Munster: Lit Verlag, 1996), pp. 153–86.

53 Leon Strieder, *The Promise of Obedience: A Ritual History* (Collegeville, MN: Liturgical Press, 2001).

54 Hollywood, 'Song, Experience, and the Book', p. 64.

55 Morrison, 'Framing the Subject', p. 36.

56 '*Da mihi, quaeso, lacrymas ex tuo affectu internas quae peccatorum meorum possint solvere vincula, et coelesti jucunditate semper repleant animam meam*' (contained in John's *Libellus* only, also in *Meditations of St Augustine* no. 36, PL 40, cols 931–2).

57 '*Scribe in tabulis cordis mei mandata et voluntatem tuam, legem et iustificationes tuas: ut te immensae dulcedinis Dominum, et praecepta tua semper et ubique habeam prae oculis meis*' (*CT*, p. 172).

58 '*per illa salutifera vulnera tua, quae passus es in cruce pro salute nostra, ex quibus emanavit ille pretiosus et vivificus sanguis quo sumus redempti propitiabili dignatione ... vulnera hanc animam peccatricem, pro qua etiam mori dignatus es; vulnera eam igneo et potentissimo telo tuae nimiae charitatis. Vivus es, sermo Dei, et efficax et penetrabilior omni acutissimo gladio. Tu gladius bis acute cordis duritiam scinde, et vulnera hanc animam peccatricem, atque altius penetra ad intima potenti virtute, et sic da capiti meo aquam immensam, oculisque meis verum lacrimarum fontem nocte ac die currentem infunde ex nimio affectu et desiderio visionis pulchritudinis tuae, ut lugeam iugiter cunctis diebus vitae meae, nullam in praesenti vita recipiens consolationem, donec te in caelesti thalamo merear videre dilectum et pulcherrimum sponsum Deum et Dominum meum*' (*CT*, pp. 180–1).

59 *CT*, 122: '*Pro nobis tibi victor et victima, et ideo victor quia victima.*'

60 Sonntag, 'On the Way to Heaven', pp. 29–54.

61 See *RB*: ch. 27 (how the abbot should care for 'brothers who have behaved wrongly with the utmost concern', and how such *caritas* is a sign of 'compassion' and love); ch. 28 (on how 'harsher correction' should be applied to brothers who do not amend after repeated corrections in order to 'heal' this sick brother 'like a wise physician'); ch. 30 (on how boys who cannot understand the seriousness of the penalty of excommunication should 'be subject to strict fasting or punished with severe beatings to heal them'); ch. 64 (on how only once the abbot is satisfied can the excommunicated be totally satisfied); ch. 70 (on how punishments should be doled out only by the abbot, and not at random). For more on the connection between 'harming to help' and the *RB*, see Morrison, 'Framing the Subject', p. 35.

62 In fact, once in a while, John granted his consent to certain monks who desired to become hermits during his abbacy, showing that he did not have a problem with hermits per se. Leyser, *Hermits and the New Monasticism*, pp. 18–19, 78–86; Licence, *Hermits and Recluses in English Society*, p. 33; M. Arnoux, 'Ermites et ermitages en Normandie (XI–XII siècles)', in André Vauchez (ed.), *Ermites de France et d'Italie (XIe–XVe)* (Rome: École française de Rome, 2003), pp. 119, 124.

63 John might also have been following the example of his mentor William of Volpiano, who the *Chronicle of Saint-Bénigne de Dijon* claims was harsh in the disciplining of his own monks; see Jestice, *Wayward Monks*, p. 184 and Bulst, *Untersuchungen zu den Klosterreformen*, p. 195.

64 Romig, *Be a Perfect Man*, pp. 22–7, 144; James J. O'Donnell, 'Augustine: His Time and Lives', in Eleaonore Stump and Norman Kretzmann (eds), *The Cambridge Companion to Augustine* (New York: Cambridge University Press, 2001), p. 14.

65 Augustine, letter 185, ch. 2, Almut Mutzenbecher (ed.), *Retractionum libri II*, Corpus Christianorum Series Latina 57 (Turnhout: Brepols, 1984), pp. 47–51; as cited by Morrison, 'Framing the Subject', pp. 36–7.

66 Morrison, 'Framing the Subject', p. 36. Morrison also discusses the paradox of love and hate (a 'malevolent sympathy') and the role of 'correcting punishment' in the other works of Augustine in *'I Am You'*, pp. 89, 152, 188.

67 The full quotation from 1 Corinthians 13:1–2 is: 'If I speak with the tongues of men, and of angels, and have not *caritas*, I am become as sounding brass, or a tinkling cymbal. And if I should have prophecy and should know all mysteries, and all knowledge, and if I should have all faith, so that I could remove mountains, and have not *caritas*, I am nothing.' ('*Si linguis hominum loquar, et angelorum, caritatem autem non habeam, factus sum velut æs sonans, aut cymbalum tinniens. Et si habuero prophetiam, et noverim mysteria omnia, et omnem scientiam: et si habuero omnem fidem ita ut montes transferam, caritatem autem non habuero, nihil sum.*')

68 '*Quid ergo eis prodest si et linguam in sacris mysteriis habeant angelicam, et prophetiam ... tamen quia separati haec agunt, non sufferentes invicem in dilectione, neque studentes servare unitatem spiritus in vinculo pacis, charitatem utique non habendo, etiam cum illis omnibus quae nihil eis prosunt, ad aeternam salutem pervenire non possunt*', from Philip Schaff (ed. and trans.), *St. Augustine: The Writings against the Manichaeans and against the Donatists*. Select Library of the Nicene and Post-Nicene Fathers of the Christian Church 4 (Buffalo, NY: Christian Literature Company, 1974), p. 417.

69 Morrison, 'Framing the Subject', p. 37; Augustine, *Retractionum libri II*, pp. 12, 18, 31–2, 39–40.

70 Peter Brown likens this kind of Augustinian discipline to the Christian struggle 'inside' reflected by Augustine's *Confessions*. Syllogistically, it could be likened to the practice of interior, emotional reform in John's *CT*. For more on Augustine's policy of disciplining the Donatists, see Peter Brown, *Augustine of Hippo: A Biography* (Berkeley: University of California Press, 1969), pp. 227, 236, 245.

71 Paris, BnF, ms. lat. 1970, where the letter is found on fol. 1r; Bern, Burgerbibliothek, Bongars ms. 162, where the letter is found on fol. 33v; and Paris, BnF, ms. lat. 2720, where the letter is found on fol. 1r.

72 Most of these titles were acquired as part of collections of texts against heresy, and not merely as happenstance or as parts of the *opera* of a single author. Other patristic works – theology, letters, sermons – make up 20 per cent of the library. About 25 per cent of the remaining collection was made up of Gospel books or Bible texts or texts of biblical exegesis, 10 per cent was hagiographical texts, and 27 per cent was other miscellaneous texts: law, rules, histories, etc. (see Branch, 'Inventories'). The library at Fécamp acquired the following *contra* heretics texts under John: Paris, BnF, ms. lat. 2055 (Augustine's *De civitate dei contra paganos*); BnF, ms. lat. 2079 (Augustine *Contra Faustum*); BnF, ms. lat. 1872 (Augustine, *Contra Rufinum*); BnF, ms. lat. 2019 (Augustine's homilies against the Arians); BnF, ms. lat. 1805 (Jerome against heretics); BnF, ms. lat. 989 (anonymous sermons against heretics); Bern, Burgerbibliothek, Bongars ms. 162 (Augustine, *Contra Donastistas*); Vatican City, Biblioteca Apostolica Vaticana, Vat. Reg. lat. 107 (Augustine, *Contra Manicheos*); Rouen, BM, ms. 477 (A191) (Augustine, *De catechizendis rudibus, Contra Arianos, De vera religione*); Rouen, BM, ms. 471 (A271) (Augustine, *Contra Felicium*); Rouen, BM, ms. 489 (A254) (Boethius, *Liber contra Eutychen et Nestorium*); Rouen, BM, ms. 427 (A143) (Ambrose, *Contra Arrium*); Rouen, BM, ms. 532 (A395) (Augustine and Bede, *Contra hereticos*); Rouen, BM, ms. 2101 (Augustine, *Contra Julianem*, a Pelagian heretic); Rouen, BM, ms. 478 (A71) (Augustine, *Contra academicos*); Rouen, BM, ms. 425 (A178) (Athanasius, *De singulis nominibus adversus novellam heresem*). Soon after John, Fécamp also acquired: BnF, ms. 1970 (containing a letter of Augustine against the Donatists); BnF, ms. lat. 2628 (Macarius of Rome against Arianism); BnF, ms. lat. 2720 (Augustine's sermons against the Donatists, bound with Durandus of Troarn against Berengar); BnF, ms. lat. 5080 (Petrus Alphonsus against the Jews).

73 Lauren Mancia, 'John of Fécamp and Affective Reform in Eleventh-Century Normandy', *Anglo-Norman Studies* 37 (2015), 167. See also Chapter 4.

74 Paris, BnF, ms. lat. 2720. Durandus was a Fécamp monk and John's cross-bearer before he became abbot at Saint-Troarn (*Gazeau*, p. 372). See also Chapter 4.

75 Edward Peters, *Heresy and Authority in Medieval Europe* (Philadelphia: University of Pennsylvania, 1980), p. 71.

76 John of Fécamp, in a prefatory letter to his *CT* sent to an anonymous nun, explicitly gives the name of heresy to incorrect practices of devotion: 'From which place it is known that the perusal of this book must be especially for those who do not allow their minds to be made dark by carnal desires and earthly longing. Therefore, when this is read with tears and enough devotion, then the meek reader tastes of what sweetness lies within the palate of her heart. Light cannot penetrate blind eyes; if it is thus, no indeed, because it is thus, prideful and disdainful minds cannot presume to touch the secret and sublime words of divine language, lest by chance they slip into error. From [this state of blindness] it also happens that the majority fall into a pit of eternal damnation through heresy, dragging others with them into death, because the mysteries of the divine scriptures, the roots of which are in heaven, become clear to no one among the

perfect.' ('*Unde sciendum est quod huius libelli lectio illis praesertim debetur qui mentes suas carnalibus desideriis et terrenis concupiscentiis obetenebrari non sinunt. Quando autem ista leguntur cum lacrimis et devotione nimia, tunc mitis lector ipso cordis palato sapit quid dulcendis intus lateat. Si ita est, immo quia ita est, eloquiorum divinorum archana et sublimia verba tangere non praesumat superba et fastidiosa mens, ne forte labatur in errorem, quia caecis oculis lumen intueri non potest. Hinc etenim actum est ut plerique per haeresim in aeternae damnationis baratrum ruerent, alios secum in mortem trahentes, quia Sacrae Scripturae mysteria, quorum radices in caelo sunt, nemini perfectorum hic tota patent.*') (CT, p. 207). See also Chapter 4.

77 'haeretica pravitate' (CT, 141).

78 Italics here are my emphasis. Warin of Metz, Letter to John of Fécamp, PL 147, cols 470A–B: '*Etenim etsi peccatores sumus, Christum tamen confitemur; catholicam fidem tenemus, baptismum et eucharistiam Christi suscepimus, regulam Sancti Benedicti legimus, et pro posse servamus, in acie Christi contra communem hostem stamus; ferimus, et ferimur aliquando; Deo sustinente stamus, aliquando infirmitate impediente vacillamus; si fragilitate cadimus, Deo relevante resurgimus, nec tamen usque ad desperationem deficimus. Et credo ita in nostro, et divitiis, et (quod periculosius est) religione exiguo et paupere loco, quemque monachum fidelem posse animam suam cum Dei adjutorio servare et salvare, sicut in quocunque ditiori et religiosiori, nisi forte aliquis plus sapiens quam oportet sapere, haeresim Donatistarum, qui dixerunt in sola Africa veram esse religionem, eamdem pestem ab Africa in Normanniam transferat, et asserat nullum monachum, nisi in solo Fiscamni monasterio posse salvari.*' For more on the battle imagery here, see Katherine Allan Smith, *War and the Making of Medieval Monastic Culture* (Woodbridge: Boydell Press, 2011); Constable, 'Renewal and Reform', p. 42.

79 These frontispieces have been noted in various iconographical studies as having similar programmes, but no conclusions have been drawn about the significance of this iconography: Alexander, *Norman Illumination*, p. 102, n. 1; p. 234, n. 1; Avril, 'Notes sur quelques manuscrits bénédictins normands du XIe et du XIIe siècle', pp. 504–14; François Avril, *Manuscrits normands XI–XIIeme siècles* (Rouen: Musée des Beaux Arts, 1975), pp. 25–7. Further discussion of these frontispieces can be found in Mancia, 'John of Fécamp and Affective Reform'.

80 The *Contra Faustum* is contained on fols 1–172 of the manuscript, written by a single scribe. There are then some later additions of miracle texts and homilies on saints in the back pages of the manuscript. The Fécamp scribe Antonius produced the book at Fécamp during the later years of John's abbacy (Branch, 'Development of Script', pp. 128–9).

81 Branch, 'Development of Script', pp. 113–16. The Athanasius text is incomplete (fols 1–67); it is followed by various other writings (mostly letters) of Athanasius, and also includes another anti-Arian text by Vigilius Tapensis, *Solutiones objectionum Arianorum* (fols 117–26).

82 Thanks to Jennifer Ball for her help in identifying the vestments in these illuminations.

83 Athanasius's cuffs are green here; the green could have served as an undercoat for a simple gold (in contrast with the heretic's jewelled, ornamented cuffs).
84 The iconography of Athanasius's cross-lance type specifically comes from Ottonian ivories of Last Judgment scenes, invented in Germany or in England in the late tenth century. See Alexander, *Norman Illumination*, p. 91. For more on the comparative shape of eleventh- and twelfth-century Norman crosiers, see Pierre Bolotte and Paul Feuilloley, *Trésors des abbayes normandes* (Rouen: Musée des Antiquités, 1979), object nos. 270, 272, and 275, pp. 243–4.
85 An image is in *Trésors des abbayes Normandes*, object no. 167, p. 140. This image of St Vulfran is in a late-eleventh-century manuscript of the *Gesta abbatum Fontanellensium* from Saint-Wandrille, Le Havre, BM, ms. 332, fol. 62.
86 Augustine, *Confessions* 5.3.3: '*per inlecebram suaviloquentiae*'.
87 Peters, *Heresy and Authority in Medieval Europe*, p. 71: '*viperino ore responderunt*'. This rhetoric is likely following Psalm 108, whose language of vengeance includes a reference to the 'lying tongues' (*lingua dolosa*) of heretics.
88 Herbert L. Kessler, 'A Sanctifying Serpent: Crucifix as Cure', in Karl F. Morrison and Rudolph M. Bell (eds), *Studies on Medieval Empathies* (Turnhout: Brepols, 2013), p. 166.
89 Mont Saint-Michel, Avranches, BM, ms. 50, fol. 1v. A picture is in Monique Dosdat, *L'enluminure romane au Mont Saint-Michel* (Rennes: Ouest-France, 2006), p. 35. Alexander discusses the iconography of St Michael in Avranches, BM, ms. 50 as from Byzantine sources in Alexander, *Norman Illumination*, p. 86. Another Mont Saint-Michel-made copy of Michael and the dragon is in a copy of Augustine, *Enarrationes in Psalmos* from before 1060, Avranches, BM, ms. 76, fol. Av. A picture is in Dosdat, *L'enluminure romane*, p. 13.
90 On the connection between Fécamp and Mont Saint-Michel, see Alexander, *Norman Illumination*, pp. 235–6.
91 I here refer to an image in an eleventh-century manuscript of *Contra Felicianum* from Mont Saint-Michel: Avranches, BM, ms. 72, fol. 97; and to the frontispiece of an eleventh-century Mont Saint-Michel manuscript of the *Contra Faustum*: Avranches, BM, ms. 90, fol. 1r. For more on the *Contra Felicianum* image (and for a picture), see Alexander, *Norman Illumination*, pp. 86, 101, plate 22. For more on the connection between the *Contra Faustum* image and the proliferation of dialogue and disputation in the eleventh century (and for a picture), see Alex J. Novikoff, 'Toward a Cultural History of Scholastic Disputation', *American Historical Review* 117.2 (2012), 330–64. Pierre Courcelle notes that the earliest image of Augustine with a heretic comes from the tenth-century *Contra Jovinianum* from Einsiedeln in Pierre Courcelle, 'Quelques illustrations du *Contra Faustum* de saint Augustin', in Jeanne Courcelle-Ladmirant (ed.), *Oikoumene* (Catania: VDM Publishing, 1964), pp. 1–99. For heretics and manuscripts elsewhere, see Diane J. Reilly, *The Cistercian Reform and the Art of the Book in Twelfth-Century France* (Amsterdam: Amsterdam University Press, 2018), pp. 181–8.

Reforming the monastic community

92 The image is from Christ Church, Canterbury, c. 1020, now Hanover, Kestner-Museum WM XXIa 36, fol. 147v.
93 Italics here are my emphasis.
94 In *De civitate dei*, Augustine notes in Book 15, ch. 7 that his notion of a 'good pastor', like Abel or Melchisedech, is also relevant to his treatise against Faustus the Manichean. For more, see Chapter 4.
95 Compare this image and Figure 8; for more on the 'dart of love' as actualised in the Rothschild Canticles, see Chapter 5.
96 See Chapter 2.
97 Branch, 'The Development of Script'. Note that the thirteen codices under William are merely those identified by palaeographers; in the absence of a library list, it is hard to have a definitive number.
98 Herman A. Peterson, 'The Genesis of Monastic Libraries', *Libraries and the Cultural Record* 45.3 (2010), 320–32; Karl Christ, *The Handbook of Medieval Library History*, trans. Theophil M. Otto (Metuchen, NJ: Scarecrow Press, 1984); Karl Christ, 'In Caput Quadragesimae', *Zentralblatt für Bibliothekswesen* 60 (1943), 33–59.
99 John as prior of Fécamp also likely had a hand in the organisation of the Fécamp library's collection. A letter survives in which the prior of Fécamp requests that of Saint-Bénigne to return certain books to Fécamp's library, indicating that such was the prior's responsibility at John's monastery: Georges Chevrier and Maurice Chaume (eds), *Chartes et documents de Saint-Bénigne de Dijon: Prieurés et dépendances des origines à 1300* (Dijon: Imprimerie Bernigaud et Privat, 1933), pp. 14–15.
100 *RB*, chs 67–9. This practice is supported by loan lists that survive from monasteries from the Carolingian period onwards: D. Nebbiai-Dalla Guarda, 'Les listes médiévales de lectures monastiques. Contribution à la connaissance des anciennes bibliothèques bénédictines', *Revue bénédictine* (1930), 271–327; Lawrence, 'Anglo-Norman Book Production', p. 79; Bates, *Normandy before 1066*, p. 81.
101 In Paris, BnF, ms. lat. 1872, on fol. 102v, there is a letter from John to William, bestowing ten books as gifts.

4

Reforming monks in the temporal world: John's devotional principles cultivated in the secular landscape

John of Fécamp found many ways to teach his monks how to distinguish between devotion that was truly felt and devotion that was merely performed: his *Confessio theologica*, his letters, and the devotional culture at this monastery all embraced his contemplative instructions. But John also acknowledged that there were limited benefits to being wholly absorbed in the 'cloister of the soul'; in fact, to John, the world outside of the monastery was surprisingly useful to a monk's religious cultivation. In his *CT*, John explicitly admits that 'it is necessary for us to believe rightly *and* to live well, for the one without the other has no perfection'.[1] John, as abbatial pastor of his flock, trusted that engaging in the temporal world also nurtured attention to prayer for both his monastic brethren and himself.

In this chapter, I will argue that part of John's interest in the world outside the monastery stemmed from his responsibility to care for the souls of his monks. His chief source for understanding these pastoral responsibilities was Gregory the Great. In the *Moralia in Job*, a foundational text for John's *CT*, and in his *Pastoral Care*,[2] Gregory the Great addresses the pastoral role of the abbot to his brethren.[3] Gregory explains that a good pastor does not care for his flock by selfishly withdrawing from the world around him, but by engaging with it – by directing and correcting his sheep and by providing for them.

> There are some who undertake the care of the flock, but desire to be so at leisure for their own spiritual concerns as to be in no way occupied with external things. Such persons, in neglecting all care for what pertains to the body, by no means meet the needs of those who are put under them. And certainly their admonition is for the most part despised; because, while they find fault with the deeds of sinners, but nevertheless afford them not the necessaries of the present life, they are not at all willingly listened to. For the

word of doctrine does not penetrate the mind of one that is in need ... Let pastors, then, so glow with ardor in regard to the inward affections of those they have the charge of as not to relinquish provision also for their outward life. For, as we have said, the heart of the flock is set against preaching, if the care of external succor be neglected by the pastor.[4]

Pastors, Gregory argues, must care for both the spiritual *and* the worldly needs of those entrusted to them, for those in their care cannot tackle larger spiritual issues when their most essential material needs are unmet. The proper pastoral care of souls, therefore, requires an abbot to pay attention to both the internal spiritual world and the external, physical world. The abbot pastor plays the role of Christ, attending to the souls and the bodies of the monks in his care.[5] Gregory goes on to say that a good pastor builds his own spiritual knowledge in four stages: first he learns about Christ through the Scriptures; next he experiences Christ through his own suffering and contemplation; then he uses 'experience in life' to help him comprehend God; and finally he uses 'experience in discerning the needs of the Church and its subjects' to fortify his understanding of the divine.[6]

In this section, I will show how John's political and economic actions in the world beyond the cloister were at their core pastoral, attempting to affect proper devotional emotions directly or indirectly in the wider Norman world, and ultimately serving to bolster contemplative and devotional feeling in others and in himself.[7] As abbot of the monastery of Fécamp, John had significant administrative, political, and economic duties that would seem to distract from the focused introspection required by his *CT*. In fact, in John's time, the monastery of Fécamp gained such plentiful economic revenue that it allowed the abbey to remain prosperous well into the thirteenth and fourteenth centuries, indicating that its abbot was most likely spending significant time away from his devotional duties in securing these resources.[8] Historians analysing important abbots have often interpreted abbatial engagement with the world in a black-and-white way, either as a task despised by brilliant spiritual abbots longing for the solitude of the monastery or a task revealing of the cunning minds of abbots who were actually political lords in their hearts.[9] Some historians have even claimed that abbots only engaged in the world when they were so spiritually exceptional that they could claim to be able to withstand the temptations of the world. Here, I will paint a more nuanced picture, showing how John's worldly, pastoral actions, though seemingly far from prayerful, were also directed towards his contemplative prescriptions and his desire for being awake to proper devotional emotion.

Scholars have long recognised that medieval monasteries regularly broke with the ideals of heavenly isolation from the secular world, engaging synergistically in the aristocratic and economic world and requiring monks and abbots to develop shrewd economic skills and political acumen.[10] Property administration was considered a necessary evil by abbots of monasteries from the time of Benedict of Nursia, who begrudgingly understood that monasteries needed material support for their devotional activities.[11] Moreover, many historians have cited this monastic engagement with the world as the chief cause for the 'Gregorian' reform of the eleventh century and the 'new monasticism' of the twelfth – that monks had become so worldly that the Church sought to finally separate the secular and ecclesiastical spheres, and that new orders of monks sought to correct the opulent worldliness of older monasteries.[12] Few historians, however, have shown how sometimes monastic engagement with the world ultimately served to reinforce and intensify devotional practices in the monastery.[13] This chapter will do just that, and, in so doing, will work to change the way in which historians of monastic reform have understood the role of the secular world in eleventh- and twelfth-century monastic transformations.

I will begin this chapter by detailing how John understood his role as a pastor. I will then show how he performed that role, sometimes providing direct spiritual ministrations to the world outside his monastery's walls, at other times tending to the physical needs of his monks as a means of indirectly facilitating their salvation. In his fight against the Eucharistic heresy of Berengar of Tours, in his correspondence with male and female lay outsiders, and in his interactions with lay members of the confraternity of Fécamp, John directly provided for Christian souls in matters of spiritual import. In his care for the monastery of Fécamp's material property and rights, John attended to secular matters while more indirectly nurturing monastic spiritual potential and affluence. In the end, John's worldly engagements were in service of his *Confessio theologica*'s spiritual purpose: they worked to elicit more genuine cravings for the contemplative life and for proper contrition, serving as distractions or tests that would ultimately effect the profession of (*confessio*) and return to (*conversio*) God. In the *Moralia*, Gregory remarks that 'some monks flee from the action of the world, but they exercise in themselves no virtues. These [monks], indeed, sleep from stupefaction, not from serious design, and therefore they never behold the things of the interior, because they have laid their head, not upon a stone, but upon the earth.'[14] John's material trials served as active means to interior, contemplative heavenly ends.

The Fécamp abbot as pastor in the temporal world

In the period between 1055 and 1065, Fécamp's library acquired one of its most opulent eleventh-century books: a copy of *De civitate dei* (Paris, BnF, ms. lat 2055).[15] The manuscript was modelled after an exemplar at Mont Saint-Michel and was lavishly decorated with gold and illuminations (unfortunately excised in the centuries since the Middle Ages). Though we know that John had a robust curatorial influence on less lavish documents in the Fécamp library, such as Ephraem's *De compunctione cordis* or Augustine's *Confessions*,[16] the expense of this new book, and the decision to outsource it to the finer scriptorium at Mont Saint-Michel, suggests that in this case especially Abbot John ordered the work himself. John likely did this in part to fill in a gap in the Fécamp library, which did not have a copy of the classic Augustinian text. But I would argue that with this particular illuminated volume as a showpiece in his monastery's library, John's understanding of the value of his pastoral abbacy is affirmed: *De civitate dei* represented more to John than just a reminder of the ultimate monastic goal (the heavenly City); it was also a text that clarified the 'religious imperative to the quotidian interactions of a high medieval world'.[17] Fécamp's copy of Augustine's *De civitate dei* particularly highlighted the value of monastic interactions with the world through the fact of its sumptuous illuminations and the content of its marginal annotations.

Augustine's *De civitate dei* was one of the chief texts read by medieval monks, particularly those seeking information on how terrestrial peace could guarantee the city of God.[18] Jocelyn Hilgarth has noted that medieval monks were therefore more interested in the second half of Augustine's opus, where the Church Father details how the city of man might reflect the city of God.[19] Corroborating Hilgarth's observation, the Fécamp copy of *De civitate dei* chiefly evidences monastic reading through marginal annotations following Book 9, bespeaking an interest in the spiritual use of worldly action.[20] But the notations in Fécamp's *De civitate dei* particularly worked to point its readers to models of good pastors, those whose worldly behaviour had a spiritual valence. On fol. 150v of the Fécamp copy, for instance, the marginal notes highlight Augustine's interpretation of Abel as a prefiguration of Christ the Shepherd (or, to put it in Gregory's terms, *Christus pastor*). Augustine distinguishes between Cain (founder of the Earthly City) as a bad pastor, and Abel (a type of Christ) as a good one.[21] Likewise, on fol. 171r, the annotator highlights Augustine's interpretation of Melchisedech as another good pastor.[22] To Augustine, Melchisedech reveals the potential for a good pastor to be both king and priest, both an acceptor of tithes and a purveyor of the Eucharist.[23] Like Abel with his sheep or Melchisedech with his offerings, John, even in his worldly activity, was invested in the spiritual care of his monks.[24]

The pastors highlighted as models in Fécamp's copy of *De civitate dei* may have resonated personally with John of Fécamp because of his childhood: Melchisedech, Abel, and Abraham were chief models for the monks at Sant'Apollinare in Classe in Ravenna, where John was a novice. The church in Ravenna contains seventh-century apse mosaics of the Transfigured Christ as Shepherd (a kind of transfigured *Christus pastor*, in the dome of the apse, Figure 4) and of Melchisedech, Abel, and Abraham (to the left of the altar, Figure 5).[25] The iconography of the latter mosaic presents the three Old Testament figures as types for Christ: just as Abel sacrificed his sheep to God, Abraham offered his son Isaac, and Melchisedech offered bread and wine to Abraham's army, so too did God sacrifice Christ, who was at once a lamb (Abel), a son (Abraham), and the Eucharist (Melchisedech). These three figures, therefore, would have been linked together in John's mind not only because of his reading of Augustine, but also because they presented some of the earliest Christian images from John's childhood in

Figure 4 Apsidal vault mosaic from Sant'Apollinare in Classe, Ravenna (sixth century)

Figure 5 Sacrifices of Abel, Melchisedech, and Abraham mosaic from
Sant'Apollinare in Classe, Ravenna (sixth century)

Ravenna. Additionally, John's former mentors were also outspoken about the 'pastoral responsibilities' of abbots. Romuald of Ravenna considered abbots *pastors* in the world (despite being at times a reclusive hermit), as did Odo of Cluny, William of Volpiano, and Leo IX, the pope for whom John served as legate.[26] William, in fact, according to Rodulfus Glaber, went out of his way to rebuild Fécamp as a pilgrimage church and to open a school at the monastery because he was 'father and pastor': he was invested in both his interior spiritual life and his worldly actions.[27]

The combined impact of John's library, the mosaics of his early childhood, and his mentors primed him to value the role of abbot as pastor. So, it is no surprise that later in life, John became a champion of the pastor-abbot. Sometime between 1055 and 1067, John joined forces with Archbishop Maurilius of Rouen (d. 1067, a former Fécamp monk) to write to the bishop of Evreux. In the letter, John and Maurilius condemn bishops who do not grant abbots autonomy in their practice of the *cura animarum*.[28] In his own *Confessio theologica*, following Augustine's *Confessions*, John repeatedly addresses Christ as *pastor*[29] and distinguishes Christ's duties as a good pastor:

> You have set me loose from original bonds and have joined me to the flock among your adopted sons ... I give thanks to you who separated me from the empty commerce of this world and grants me the enjoyment of the love and company of your slaves: you give me salvation and rest of body and soul, and freedom suitable to your holy service, you free me from the emptiest encumbrances of this age for the profit of my soul for the sake of your mercy alone.[30]

Since the *RB* refers to the abbot as the Christlike figure who pastors the monks in the monastery,[31] one can imagine that these duties were easily transferable to the abbot. It is then not hard to read the passage in this way:

> You [the abbot] have set me loose from original bonds and have joined me to the flock among your adopted sons ... I give thanks to [the abbot] who separated me from the empty commerce of this world and grant[s] me the enjoyment of the love and company of [the abbot's] servants: [the abbot] give[s] me salvation and rest of body and soul, and freedom suitable to [Christ's] holy service, [the abbot] free[s] me from the emptiest encumbrances of this age for the profit of my soul for the sake of [Christ's] mercy alone.

John likely understood his pastoral responsibilities to his flock as both physical and spiritual, as did Christ.[32] Like Melchisedech, John could both deal in the world and be a holy man. In order to keep his monks from the corruption of the world, to provide them with food and health, and to give them the leisure to go to church and to ultimately 'profit' their souls, the abbot must himself be in the wider world. So, while some of John's interactions with the world outside of the monastery were obviously for the spiritual good of those with whom he was interacting, other interactions were only indirectly undertaken for spiritual purposes. In the case of those especially, John, like Christ, had to sacrifice his own leisure and safety for the good of his flock.

Directing devotional behaviour in the wider world

Berengar of Tours

Around 1050, a new heresy became the grave concern of elite churchmen in medieval Europe: Berengar of Tours had written in several places that the bread of the Eucharist was merely symbolic and experienced no material change in the mass.[33] Pope Leo IX (1002–54) had denounced Berengar in 1050 and called both John and Abbot Lanfranc of Bec to Rome in summer 1050, hoping that they might assist him in Berengar's final condemnation.[34] Several Italo-Norman monks also wrote treatises denouncing Berengar and upholding the real presence in the mid-1050s, most of them engaged with the secular world: Lanfranc (*De corpore et sanguine domini*);[35] Guitmund of Aversa (d. 1094, from Bec); Durandus of Troarn (d. 1088), abbot of Saint-Martin of Troarn but formerly a Fécamp monk and John's own 'cross-bearer' (*De corpore et sanguine domini*);[36] and our own John, who in the 1050s completely reworked his *Confessio theologica* into what scholars have called his *Confessio fidei*, transforming large passages so that they would serve to combat Berengar and reassert the real presence.[37] John's alterations in the 1050s have been called less 'personally fervent' and 'more discursive' than the original *CT*, 'confront[ing] heresy by affirming an array of orthodox tenets including Trinitarian doctrines'.[38] Indeed, John transforms the first three parts of his *Confessio theologica* for his *Confessio fidei*, omitting his *Libellus*'s prayers and infusing his *Confessio fidei* with many more quotations from the Fathers. But, most significantly, John adds a fourth part to his original three, a part entirely dedicated to the theology of the Eucharist. He uses this fourth part to emphasise the real presence of Christ[39] and the process of transubstantiation,[40] but he also uses this discourse on the Eucharist to build on themes already present in his original *CT* and to connect the sacrament to his own devotional interests.[41]

It is not surprising that one of John's chief fights outside his monastery's walls was against Berengar. Monks celebrated mass daily, making this threat to the central focus of their lives no small matter.[42] The Fécamp monks had in particular been responsible for converting much of Normandy to orthodox Christian practice.[43] But, by exercising his duty to combat the Eucharistic heresy, John was also taking the opportunity to reassert his specific devotional priorities regarding prayer. The connection between the sacrament and prayer was by no means John's own – Gregory the Great considered the Eucharist to be 'the most important and most potent form of prayer' because it allowed Christians to experience momentary harmony and union with Christ.[44] But the way that John depicts the Eucharist in his *Confessio fidei* ties the sacrament specifically to his idea of interior prayer: John sees a Christian's taking of the Eucharist as a literal embodiment of that emotional work. For instance, he says:

> O holy bread, O living bread, O beautiful bread, O clean bread, you who have descended from heaven and give life to the world, come into my heart and cleanse me from every defilement of the flesh and spirit, enter into my soul and sanctify me both without and within.[45]

Here, John asks that the 'bread' come into a sinner's heart. On the one hand, the 'bread' is a metonym for Christ, and John simply asks for Christ to descend into the sinner's heart in symbolic form. But throughout the *Confessio fidei*, John seems to embrace the action of the Eucharist as a literal ingestion of the divine that might inspire the Christian, now a vessel literally containing Christ, to do the inner emotional excavation required to retain proper interior contemplation. For instance, in another passage, John says:

> For it is correct that the sacrament is great and ineffable, in which your actual flesh is eaten and your actual blood is drunk. O mystery to be feared and revered, the human gaze is beaten back for gazing at [your majesty]. Through the very sacrosanct and vivifying mystery of your body and blood ... shine brightly on me, ignite me, illuminate and sanctify me, your vessel, empty me of malice, fill me with grace, and wholly preserve me, in order that I may eat the food of your flesh for the salvation of my soul: for by eating you I may live according to you, may advance thanks to you, may arrive at you, [and] may rest in you. For the very one who eats you lives on because of you.[46]

John here holds the internalisation of Christ in the Eucharist as a real physical practice that might direct a Christian to an authentic emotional practice. He sees the Eucharist (Christ) as the match that will relight the spark of Christological devotion in the sinner through intuition (*intuitus*) and introspection (*inspicium*).[47] By penetrating the interior of the sinner, the Eucharist will be inside the sinner while the sinner is still outside himself,[48]

Reforming monks in the temporal world

and will suddenly become 'the sweet food of [his] heart'[49] that will activate the sinner's true devotion. Berengar's theory – that the Eucharist does not provoke a physical, material change in bread, but is merely a change of being and spirit – reduces the power of this parallel for John, who wants this material internalisation of God to elicit the physical results of tears (which are related to Christ's bleeding wounds,[50] and which in turn are related to the Eucharistic wine[51]). Moreover, Berengar proposed that a Christian use his senses to ascertain truth, concluding that, since the Eucharist tastes like bread and not like flesh, there is no real presence; but this runs contrary John's *Confessio fidei*'s method of 'knowing' God through a process of introspection. John therefore needed to attack Berengar's privileging of essence and representation over introspection.[52] And this is why, unlike Lanfranc and Durandus, John was not interested in refuting Berengar's heretical positions about the involvement of the will of God in his *Confessio fidei*,[53] but was instead focused on combating the parts of Berengar's heresy that allowed him to highlight and further empower his own spiritual programme.

The fight against Berengar raged much beyond John's spiritual prerogatives, however, and likely required John to get involved in the world in ways that tested his own contemplative focus. William the Conqueror (fl. 1066–87) summoned Berengar to a court at Brionne so that scholars from around Normandy (including John) could publicly condemn his position.[54] At the council of Rouen around 1055 (which John likely attended), Archbishop Maurilius (the former monk of Fécamp) required Norman clerics to regularly read and enforce a profession of Eucharistic orthodoxy against Berengar.[55] John's words were even excerpted as a prayer for ordained priests – both monks and non-monks – to say during the mass that incorporates this profession against Berengar.[56] Still, John made sure that his *Confessio fidei* made its way to the monks of whose souls he was primarily in charge. The only complete surviving eleventh-century copy of John's revised text (Montpellier, Bibliothèque Interuniversitaire de Montpellier, H309) is from Saint-Bénigne de Dijon, the very monastery where John trained and where he was abbot from 1052 to 1054,[57] right at the time of the Berengar controversy.[58] A second eleventh-century copy, now lost, was at Glastonbury, an English monastery connected with Fécamp in the late eleventh century.[59] As he did with his *CT*,[60] John spread his *Confessio fidei* around his own monastic network, taking the opportunity to channel his energies towards the further emotional reform of monks. In a way, John follows a pattern from prayer (*Confessio theologica*) to polemic (*Confessio fidei*) that is seen elsewhere in medieval Christian writings; Anselm, for instance, writes prayers in the 1070s and then moves on to more polemical treatises.[61] Paul Arne-Dannenberg argues that the late eleventh and twelfth centuries become moments of systematisation, when more emotional Christian values are turned into juridical forces in order to better build the institution of the Church.[62] That is what we see here from John, who uses a diatribe against a heretic to set in stone (or, at least, in parchment) his ideas about prayer.

Letters to monks and women

As with his penning of the *Confessio fidei*, John's tending to monks and abbots outside of Fécamp's walls was more often than not an attempt to provide spiritual advice. Most of his letters, therefore, preach a contemplative focus rather than an active one – ironically, John engages with the world to encourage others to leave it in order to focus on devotion and prayer.

We have already seen ways in which John took care of the souls of other monks in Europe: he passed around the works of Ephraem and Augustine's *Confessions* to Norman houses that William had reformed.[63] John's *Confessio theologica* itself also made its way to monastic houses associated with Fécamp: Metz, Saint-Bénigne de Dijon, and Bec all had copies.[64] John's lasting impact on these monasteries is confirmed by his presence in their necrologies after his death in 1078.[65]

But in addition to disseminating books he found to be important around his monastic network, John also wrote to his fellow abbots around Normandy. Some of John's letters are simple bureaucratic necessities, recognising the authority of new abbots for abbeys among Fécamp's dependent houses.[66] Others, however, are more pastoral, making sure that abbots near and far from Fécamp are themselves good shepherds to their monastic flocks. We have already seen three such letters, two between John and the Abbot Warin of Metz and one from John to the rebellious monks, all attempts by John to discipline monks and abbots into performing what he feels are the correct practices.[67] Another of these letters, known as the *Tuae quidem* letter, actually circulates as a preface to John's full *CT*.[68] *Tuae quidem* shows us that John was as interested in monastic friendship as his contemporaries were,[69] and that he was specifically interested in the *caritas* that was exchanged in correspondence.[70] Such *caritas* was often corrective advice coming from John, who took it upon himself to shepherd his fellow monks towards truths that would benefit their spiritual selves.[71] This letter is no exception: John is concerned with the decadence of clerics and abbots surrounding him, and is reminding his abbot-correspondent of the tears and penance needed for every contrite sinner to eventually be united with the divine. Abbots, John claims, have become richer than bishops, so that there is no more difference between the clerics of the secular world and the abbots cultivating their friendship. John here particularly criticises abbots who use the example of the work of greater abbots in the world (like Maiolus of Cluny, who is mentioned in certain copies by name) to justify their conduct as political operatives removed from the tasks of the cloistered life.[72] Instead, John states, abbots should follow the example of Christ himself, who in the Sermon on the Mount models how clerics should eschew money and the temptations of this world. Monks, he claims, have only one task: ascending the contemplative ladder to God.[73] John's *Tuae quidem* letter therefore serves as the perfect preamble for the *Confessio theologica*: it is a guide for divesting oneself of the secular world and renewing one's own contemplative aspirations.

Even when writing to female recipients, John is sure to instruct the male clerics and monks who will also read those letters on an abbot's proper pastoral duties.[74] In his letter to the Empress Agnes of Poitou (1025–77), written around 1063/64, John lashes out at the 'dogs of Scylla' who might question whether it is proper for a monk to speak to women.[75] With the same acerbic ferocity that characterised his letter to disobedient hermit monks, John launches into an extensive discourse (irrelevant to his female addressee) for the 'wretched', 'prevaricat[ing]' 'blind leaders of the blind' who might criticise his address to the empress as an unmonastic distraction.[76] John asserts that his address to this 'venerable handmaid of Christ' (*venerabilis Christi ancilla*) is also for the self-proclaimed virtuous male religious who should learn a lesson from Agnes's desire for contemplative instruction:

> There are some less proficient [Christians] who pretend [to have seen] God in their imagination, since they do not know how to intelligently contemplate that wondrous and uncircumscribed light, scattered formless in temporal things. What is the eye of contemplation to them, then, other than a snare of perdition? Such people are to be admonished that, content with the exercise of the active life alone, they not presume to ascend the mountain of contemplation. For it is written that the animal man does not perceive the things which are of the spirit of God, and that it is death to know things according to the flesh. For the human spirit, unless it repulses the desire of external things, does not penetrate internal things, since the more subtly it looks on invisible things, the more perfectly it scorns visible things.[77]

The 'less proficient' here addressed is not Agnes, who has, by writing to John, already established herself as part of a group interested in proper contemplation. Instead, John momentarily ignores Agnes to instruct the religious around him of the need for contemplation in their distractingly active lives. Many medieval church leaders and abbots upheld women as paradigmatic spiritual exempla for their male monastic brethren (Aelred of Rievaulx, Goscelin of Saint-Bertin, even Augustine in the *Confessions*[78]), and here, John proves himself to be no exception.

Of course, John is not just writing this letter for the male readers who might intercept it; he is also writing it to his female lay addressee, Agnes.[79] Like many male monks before and after him, John saw his care of lay and religious women as part of his pastoral duties, particularly by improving their devotional practices.[80] John performed these duties in Normandy by establishing female monasteries like Montivilliers and bestowing the veil upon several noble women; but his most famous exercise of these duties came through his letters to women. In 1030–50, John wrote a letter to an anonymous nun, likely of Notre-Dame-aux-Nonnais in Troyes;[81] a few years later, in 1063/64, he wrote to the Empress Agnes, who by then had ceased serving as regent and had committed herself to a convent in Rome. Like the *Tuae quidem* letter, John's letters to Agnes and to the anonymous nun survive because they circulate with his copies of the *CT* as prefaces, indicating that they were initially sent along with copies of John's treatise and then kept in the subsequent copies made thereafter.[82] These letters have prompted some scholars to claim that John of Fécamp would not have written his *Confessio theologica*'s affective prescriptions at all were it not for the requests by these women.[83] While the work of this book should dispel the notion that John's affective tendencies were exclusively geared to or prompted by a female audience, it is indeed important to note women's role in perpetuating and disseminating John's 'script for the performance of prayer' more widely:[84] Agnes, having heard of his *CT* elsewhere, seems to have written to John wanting a copy for herself;[85] and John, in sending it, encouraged her to disseminate it to other interested parties.[86]

John's letters to women indicate his own desire to share his method for contemplation with women as well as men, encouraging all Christians to remain focused on devotion to Christ in the face of worldly pleasures.[87] In the letters, John explicitly praises both Agnes and the anonymous nun for avoiding the temptations of this world.[88] He suggests that, to best combat these temptations, Agnes and the nun replace them with a truly felt interest in holding 'sacred vigils and [singing] psalmody, not sleepily but intently'.[89] In both of his letters, John cites concepts and uses language which come directly from his *CT*: the nun must 'take pleasure in the solitude of prayer, as much as is allowed';[90] 'sweetly and frequently cr[y]';[91] her soul must 'repel exterior desires from itself, so they do not penetrate the interior';[92] in praying, she 'tastes of what sweetness lies within with the palate of his heart'[93] and 'chooses the best part always, as much as is allowed for herself, with the blessed Mary'.[94] John's letters, therefore, become for these women précis of his longer treatise advising them in contemplative matters.

The crux of my argument, however, is that letters were instructive to more than their addressees: they were also instructive to John himself.[95] After summarising his contemplative method in his letter to Agnes, John says, 'And it is just by [teaching readers like you] that the one practising the active life [i.e. John] converts, assuming the wings of the contemplative life.'[96] Here, John claims that it is precisely through his pastoral actions, for example, teaching lay women about contemplation, that his own devotional life is enabled. Through his ministry to these women, through their longing for better connection with God, he too can awaken his own contemplative engagement. John explicitly characterises Agnes's letter as a potential moment for his own spiritual 'warming'.[97] Initially, impressed with her fervour, John muses 'if only there were a fire in me to make my heated mind develop'.[98] By the end of his letter, he finds himself kindling his own devotional emotion: 'Brilliant exemplar of holy widowhood, accept, I ask, this little anthology from my *waking* mind.'[99] The occasion to deliver Agnes advice, and the 'brilliant exemplar' of her spiritual desire, has *awakened* John's contemplative soul. By ministering to these women in the world, John is able to spread the word about his spiritual practices. But it is through this outside engagement that he is given the opportunity to augment *his own* spiritual practices, refreshing his own desire for God in the process of awakening others'.

John's administration of Fécamp's property and its devotional effects

While John was explicit about the spiritual benefits he received from corresponding with laywomen, the benefits are not always obvious in his interactions with laymen in more secular matters. Certainly, there are moments where John's interactions with laymen had a direct spiritual purpose, which was to enable layfolks' souls to be saved through donations or letters of advice. However, the majority of John's relations with and ministrations to the secular sphere have more hidden spiritual benefits. What were the benefits of John's negotiating Fécamp's exemption, for example, beyond political autonomy from the interference of bishops? How were his confirmation of donations and land rights in accordance with the contemplative focus of his *Confessio theologica*? While many scholars have studied these lay endowments from the nobleman's point of view, noting how, for example, monastic patronage was essential to ducal control of Normandy,[100] the monks' interpretation of these actions remains less frequently investigated. As a result, in the historiography, the common perception is that the monks' motives were identical to their lay correspondents', that is, contrary to monastic spiritual purpose:[101] if ducal patronage of monasteries was a manifestation of Norman 'predatory kinship',[102] or more about consolidating and projecting power than it was about religious feeling,[103] then surely the monks were also engaged in a 'politics of holiness'.[104] Here, I will take a different view and will piece together John's understanding of his handling of Fécamp's secular engagements, showing how, to him, these interactions eventually served pastoral (and, ultimately, devotional) purposes.

Even if John and his monks had wanted to imagine themselves hermits in the desert, myopically focused on spiritual exercises, they could not have done so at Fécamp: until the 1060s, the main Norman ducal palace was literally across the street from the monastery (see Map 2).[105] Though Sant'Apollinare and Saint-Bénigne de Dijon were located in or near towns, allowing for frequent lay visitations and interactions, never in John's life had he been so spatially confronted by the secular world.[106] Not only could the monks of Fécamp see the ducal palace from their windows; their scriptorium served as the ducal chancery from the time of Richard II until the Conquest;[107] Duke Richard I (932–96), Duke Richard II (978–1026), and Richard II's son William (d. c. 1087, monk at Fécamp) were buried at Fécamp;[108] the monks even incorporated the palace gate into their liturgies, stationing processions there.[109] Monks at Fécamp were thus forced to reconcile the world to their spiritual lives. Sometimes these interactions were direct spiritual exchanges, requests by laymen for prayer or for the monks to perform certain spiritual duties. But at other times the spiritual benefits of these exchanges were more indirect, connected with John's interpretation of a good pastor's material concerns for the sake of his flock's spiritual welfare.

Fécamp's most obvious duty to the outside world was its monks' obligations to pray for the members of their confraternity.[110] While some gifts were given to the monastery for diplomatic purposes, many lords were interested in donating to the monastery out of spiritual need or to feel an affinity with their kin, rather than out of political motivation.[111] Altar gifts especially were considered sacrifices aiming towards redemption, in direct parallel with the gifts of the bread and wine of the Eucharist.[112] There has been some debate over why and how monks responded to or elicited such donations – whether they did so out of a spiritual interest or from a more worldly political acumen.[113] But the Fécamp monks took their confraternity seriously as a means for both mutual survival and mutual salvation.[114] Monks were not merely hypocritically performing these prayers in exchange for donations; indeed, they remembered these patrons in their prayers for significantly longer than was socially necessary to cultivate their relationships.[115] They also enlarged their churches to accommodate more lay pilgrims and to increase the number of altars to accommodate their lay guests.[116] And they even used this language of gift-giving in their prayers and theological writings, allowing it to inform their indebtedness to God's mercy.[117]

Through their interactions with secular folk, one of the goals of Norman monks in this period was indeed 'imparting to the secular world the blessings and spiritual rhythms of monastic communities, those islands of '"realized eschatology" in a fallen world'.[118] The Fécamp monks in their own chronicles even characterised the Norman dukes *as* monks, further legitimising their interactions with such pious laymen: Richard I was a 'precious son of Christ dressed in the habit of a layman';[119] Richard II was 'constant in his worship of Christ, so that he was rightly called most devout father of clerks and indefatigable supporter of the poor';[120] and Rodulfus Glaber called the dukes of Normandy a 'clan or family united in unbroken faith ... the needy, the poor, and all pilgrims were treated with the constant care with which fathers treat sons'.[121] Richard II and his sons in fact served as monks at Fécamp every Easter:[122]

> The duke was in the habit of holding his Easter court almost every year at Fécamp, and, at a time of his choosing, he and his wife would carry a box full of books, thuribles, candlesticks, and other ornaments, covered with a beautiful cloth, up to the altar of the Holy Trinity, and she and he would offer it there to God for their sins. On Easter Day itself, after mass and before he would go to his palace and eat with his men, he came with his two sons Richard and Robert to the monk's refectory. The two sons would carry the dishes from the kitchen, as the monks usually did, and give them to the father. He would himself place the first course before the abbot and afterwards served the monks. When this was done, he would approach the abbot with great humility and when he had his permission would go happily and cheerily to his palace.[123]

Here, the author of the *Brevis relatio* not only makes Richard II monklike in his piety, but also depicts the duke subverting his own power to that of the monks of Fécamp in a gesture suited to his ultimate goal of salvation. This sanctification of the Norman dukes was perpetuated into the thirteenth century, when the bodies of Richard I and Richard II began to be treated as saints' bodies at the monastery. The Fécamp monks likely saw this sanctification as evidence of their effort and influence on the lay donors around them.[124]

The monks' participation in the secular world did not just benefit the dukes of Normandy; it also trickled out to the rest of the laymen in the region. In a rare instance, John bestowed a neighbourhood church upon a priest, allowing him to minister to the people in the area.[125] He promised that an abbot or monk from Fécamp would serve mass at a small priory on the feasts of the Nativity, the Purification of the Virgin, and the Assumption.[126] He provided the opportunity for the oblation of a son of one Wigrinus and one Adeliza, for the sake of their sins.[127] Under his watch, Fécamp might have even have continued to serve as a school for priests in the region.[128] And John's abbey, at ducal requests, sent its own monks to private monasteries to reform their foundations and implement right spiritual practices.[129] Fécamp, then, provided the manpower and locus for laypeople to perform penance and save their souls. As Richard II funded pilgrimages to Jerusalem for abbots and monks, providing the funds to enable the devotion (and increasing his own devoutness thereby),[130] so John provides the inverse: devotion in exchange for the goods, enabling the sacralisation of the secular world (and increasing his own devoutness thereby).

The religious benefits from empowering lay devotion were not only the abbot's, however: a monastery's interactions with the secular world (including an abbot's on behalf of his monastery) yielded a communal benefit for its monks in return. Most of John's declarations in charters specify that he speaks with the counsel and approval of the community. Personal friendships on an individual basis were discouraged among the monks in Norman communities; but, by emphasising the corporate religious body in its secular agreements, an abbot could join the whole community in friendship (or confraternity) with secular people.[131] As we have seen, John condemned monks who decided to defy these communal bonds and live as individual hermits; to John, a monk is not 'exceptional':[132] he is obedient. As Gregory the Great warns in the *Moralia*, individuality yields pride, and ultimately moves the individual away from his divine aspirations. The Fécamp monks' interactions with the wider world as a community, then, allowed for the group to make spiritual strides for their neighbours and for themselves, gaining the benefits of caring for others' souls without the risk of pridefulness and exceptionalism.[133]

The skilful acquisition of property by the monastery – and the resulting accumulation of land and material goods – was also considered a sign of spiritual prosperity by the monks at Fécamp.[134] To Rodulfus Glaber, the monastic acquisition of land across Europe was a much-needed sacralisation of the landscape: instead of land being in secular hands, 'the whole world [was] shaking itself free, shrugging off the burden of the past, and cladding itself everywhere in a white mantle of churches'.[135] Norman monks explicitly encouraged laity to donate resources that would support the work of this sacralisation:[136] the richer the monastery's resources, the more its monks' elementary needs became ancillary, the more focused they could be on their spiritual work.[137] But, more than that, Dominique Iogna-Prat has shown how, for Cluny, secular gifts would regenerate from *temporalia* into *spiritualia* (an experience described as a *conversio*). Peter the Venerable argued that once a castle was given to a religious house, 'it cease[d] to be a fortress and start[ed] being a place of prayer'.[138] Like the Eucharist's transformation from bread to the host, or a monk's movement from tepidity to warmth in prayer, the surrender involved in a lay person's gift caused a type of spiritual *conversio*. Fécamp's chronicles' treatment of Richard I and Richard II, discussed above, even reflect this belief: because of their donations, the Norman dukes themselves transformed from secular lords into holy monks. The resulting wealth of the abbey was just a side-effect – the dregs of the transformation process – and a sign of the spiritual success of a monastery in its respective landscape.[139] Even the wealth was a means for 'rousing' people into 'holy rejoicing':[140] Dudo of Saint-Quentin (c. 965–1043) describes Richard I's building and decoration of Fécamp as enabling the monastery to 'be the mother of wonderful regeneration through the bath of symbolic washing'.[141] Just as twelfth-century lords would grant land to allow for a literal road to be built for pilgrims to Fécamp,[142] so, too, did these eleventh-century donations provide a spiritual path for both its monks and the surrounding community. While it is naturally hard to ignore the real political significance of land (or the potential for wealth to cause laziness among its monastic recipients), it is also quite easy to forget that the monks saw their worldly prosperity as evidence of the efficacy of their spiritual project.[143]

Even without the idea of a sacralised landscape, however, material contentment and physical safety were essential to the monks' ability to perform their spiritual tasks. As quoted above, to Gregory the Great, pastors, 'in neglecting all care for what pertains to the body, by no means meet the needs of those who are put under them'. John was very invested in the preservation of his monks' safety, in part to ensure that they did not entangle themselves in the secular world more than necessary. For instance, John gave a viscount of Rouen estates that an earlier viscount had given the abbey, asking him to enrich and improve the estates during his lifetime, and then to entrust them back to Fécamp after his death.[144] In this way, John skilfully tended to the physical health of the lands that fed and funded the Fécamp of the present and of the future, while protecting his monks from distraction with the procurement of their bread. In a letter to Leo IX, whom John addresses as the ultimate pastor of sheep,[145] John advocates for the safety of all the Normans – laymen as well as religious – with whose souls he has been entrusted[146] and who are constantly threatened with violence when they are travelling in Italy 'even if [they] be on a devout pilgrimage'.[147] The safety of prosperity, material support, and political advocacy enabled obedience and devotion.[148]

But John did not only feed and clothe his monks to ensure and protect the more physical and material aspects of his monks' lives. More often than not, John's secular-world dealings aimed at allowing his monks to have the freedom to follow the rules and regulations that their spiritual livelihood required – a freedom that, even with all of the material comforts of the world, could not always be guaranteed. For instance, by fighting against William the Conqueror's violation of monastic abbatial elections,[149] John worked to preserve his monks' ability to fully follow the *RB* by electing their abbot without ducal interference.[150] By fighting for Fécamp's exemption against the interference of bishops, John cleared the way for his monks to be *solus Deus colitur* as much as possible, keeping them from being distracted by conflicts with bishops or secular lords and allowing them to be more focused on their own prayer.[151] As he says to the new abbot of the monastery of Saint-Berthe of Blagny, a dependency of Fécamp, there is a direct link between Christ as heavenly shepherd and abbots as the shepherds of the Christians with whom they are entrusted.[152] Like the martyr Christ, John's attention to the secular world was a sacrifice for his monks: his political dealings allowed them to have the secure space they needed to best devote themselves to God.

John's worldly action as enabling further devotional awakening

John himself, it seems, was keenly aware of the sacrifices he was making on behalf of others' spiritual needs. In a short work called the *Lamentation for Lost Solitude* (hereafter *Lamentation*), written later in his life,[153] John mourns the burdensome duties of the abbacy that prevented him from engaging with contemplation as he should have done:

> It shames and sickens me to appear in public assemblies, to enter the city, to speak with the powerful, to look at women, to be concerned with the chattering masses and to endure many such things as the world does.[154]

Speaking here in his role as an abbot, John observes that the outside world encroaches on the world of the monastery and robs him of the otherworldly solitude he has prescribed in his own writings. Scholars have understood John's *Lamentation* solely as a yearning for the solitude of the cloister, as a sign that the secular duties of an abbot had no bearing on an abbot's spiritual life.[155] But, if we listen closely to how John mourns the loss of solitude, we see that he builds up the stakes of his grief about its loss expressly so that he can turn (in a *conversio*, *temporalia* to *spiritualia*), exasperated, back towards God. As he explicitly expressed in his letter to Agnes, John actually sees his interactions with the secular world to be a means for genuinely redirecting him with reawakened desire towards a deep hunger for the divine. After pages of mourning about the distractions of the world, John concludes his *Lamentation* with passages in this vein:

> Have mercy on me just as you began [to do], free me from this malignant age and do not allow me, your servant, to be implicated in it on any occasion ... from these tumults of instigations and the manifold noises of advances, from this great age which I suffer in the monastery (among this concourse of brothers who daily I offend in many things), and give me that recess of solitude and the spiritual leisure of freedom suited to you, as well as purity of heart and jubilation of mind, so that I may most sweetly merit to love [you] perfectly and to praise [you] worthily all the days of my life.[156]

It is this recognition of the 'malignant age' with its 'tumult of instigations' that makes John long for the time and space to 'love' God 'perfectly'. Without the sufferings of this world, John's desire for God would not be nearly so fervent. John identifies the need for such adversity in his *CT* when he credits those tribulations as inspiration for prayer. John says there that 'placed in the midst of snares ... [human beings] easily grow cold in our heavenly longing'. His *CT* is written in hopes 'that [the reader] might always have a short and handy word about God with [him], and from the fire of reading it, as many times as [he] grow[s] cool, [he] may be reignited in [God's] love'. But John notes that one needs to be inspired to seek reignition through adversity, 'a constant defence, so that, after being roused, we run back to [God], our true and highest good, whenever we slide away'.[157] It is only with a burning heart that the soul is ready to embark on its contemplative task, and one must be reminded of that burning need by hardships. If one contemplated all day, every day, the contemplation would become rote;

and what could be more reviving than the opposite of that contemplation, the *vita activa*?

The tension between opposing ideas (or, in this case, lifestyles) is a popular discourse in the Middle Ages. Dialectics are often proposed to stimulate genuine responses in medieval readers and thinkers.[158] Monastic and lay culture are therefore interdependent – each uses the other to define itself.[159] One effect of John's pastoral obligation to worldly affairs is that he has the distance and frustration that he needs to effect a genuine desire for the contemplative life; his secular experiences enrich his contemplation. As he asks in the *Lamentation*: 'Who was giving me swift feathers and quick wings in order that I may fly back to [God] and rest in you as before?'[160] It is a *revolem ad* God that John desires, and his worldly affairs enable and foster this contemplative hunger.[161]

This interdependence of worldly and spiritual duties is why most of the extant medieval manuscript copies of John's *Lamentation* are paired with his *CT*.[162] By bemoaning worldly distractions, the *Lamentation* serves to rekindle desire for God in its reader, creating an emotional base that is then ripe to engage with John's longer work. The *Lamentation* essentially prescribes reading works like the *CT* as the antidote for such a lamentable predicament: 'It is pleasing to read repeatedly of your peace and rest and to review frequently the things read in my heart, so that any repose between these whorls is accompanied by your memory.'[163] John's shorter *Lamentation* is filled with images that appear in the *CT* as well – talk of the heart,[164] internal contrition and connection to God,[165] and images of fountains and rivers of tears flowing from the eyes of the speaker[166] abound. Medieval compilers, therefore, did not simply bind the two texts together because they share an author; the *Lamentation* served to preview and hook the reader into developing a need for the *CT*, or to recall and revive in the reader the devotional emotion of the *CT*, just as John's secular duties worked in part to rekindle his true emotional desire for God.

Conclusion

It is worth noting, in conclusion, that these observations reveal an important insight for historians of the 'monastic reform' of the eleventh and twelfth centuries. The historiography of monastic reform is in the midst of a re-examination. Traditional studies have often insisted that a separation between the clerical and secular worlds was an essential facet of Gregorian reform.[167] To scholars of the past, 'reform monasticism' also often signified a concern for the proper remission of sins[168] and the proper rule and customs by which to live.[169] In looking at John's interactions with the larger world, we could cast him in the light of an abbot operating as a 'reformer' in what scholars have heretofore considered the Gregorian style: implementing and enforcing the *RB* (cf. the disobedient monks), opposing lay investiture (cf. his chastisement of William the Conqueror's appointment of abbots), writing against heresy (cf. Berengar of Tours), asserting autonomy against encroaching bishops (cf. his letter to the bishop of Evreux with Maurilius of Rouen).

But it is important to note that John's most important reform prerogative as defined by the *Confessio theologica* – emotional reform of the individual contemplative – is *enabled* by these secular interactions. Perhaps, then, we can complicate our understanding of monastic rhetoric that seems to desire the eradication of secular influence. The ideal is not a monastic *rejection* of the secular, but rather a monastic *tension* with the secular in order to cultivate genuine devotional emotion. Giles Constable has noted that medieval monks and clerics often used 'rekindle' (*recalescere*) or 'recoup' (*recuperari*) or 'conversion' (*conversione*) as reform vocabulary when hoping to limit secular interference.[170] But these are words also employed by John in his descriptions of emotional devotion, as reheating or returning or reconfessing or reprofessing love of God, and such secular involvement was essential to the achievement of that desired emotional devotion. We may be making it harder to understand monastic reform in the eleventh and twelfth centuries by insisting that monks desired seclusion and autonomy and by neglecting the ways that the monastery's involvement in the world was actually useful to its emotional, interior, devotional reform goals.[171] Right contemplation and true connection with God did not require a retreat to the 'desert', as later Cistercians might write[172] – for John and his monastic contemporaries, the world outside the monastery could be used to the benefit of such heartfelt prayer.

John of Fécamp has by and large been studied by historians of spirituality. Showing up in works by scholars like Jean Leclercq, Thomas Bestul, Rachel Fulton, Duncan Robertson, and Bernard McGinn, John's *Confessio theologica* and *Lamentation* have been interpreted for their spiritual desires in isolation from the wider responsibilities of monastic life. But when reinserted into the wider context of John's life and duties, the *CT* and *Lamentation* are seen in a more medieval light: a genuine commitment to contemplation that required a little worldly knowledge for practical purposes, certainly, but also in order to rekindle a true desire for God. John's whole *CT* is about the difficulties of maintaining the right emotional awareness for interior contemplation. By exploring his commitments to the world outside of his monastery, we can truly appreciate how he used those difficulties and distractions to achieve his deepest desire: an affective, prayerful focus on God.

Notes

1 Italics my emphasis. '*Sed quia oportet nos et recte credere et bene vivere (unum enim sine altero nihil perfectionis habet), ideo*' (*CT*, p. 121).
2 See Chapter 2. A copy of *Pastoral Care* was in Fécamp's library in John's time; now lost, the manuscript was no. 35 on the monastery's eleventh-century library list (Branch, 'Inventories').
3 *Pastoral Care* was read more often by monks than by bishops in the eleventh century, see Jestice, *Wayward Monks*, p. 68. The pastoral role of the abbot dated as far back as Basil of Caesarea at least; see Dilley, *Monasteries and the Care of Souls*, pp. 227–32.
4 Philip Schaff and Henry Wace (eds), *The Book of Pastoral Rule and Selected Epistles of Gregory the Great*, trans. James Barmby (Buffalo, NY: Christian Literature Publishing Company, 1895), Part II, ch. 7; as cited by Neslihan Şenocak in *Care of Souls in Medieval Italy, 600–1300* (Ithaca, NY: Cornell University Press, forthcoming).
5 In his *CT*, John actively describes Christ in this way: 'You give me salvation and rest of body and soul' ('*Das mihi salutem et quietem corporis et animae*'), *CT*, p. 130. One can imagine, then, that the abbot, in the footsteps of Christ, would need to care for both the body and soul of his monks.
6 As quoted in Steven Vanderputten, 'The Mind as Cell and the Body as Cloister: Abbatial Leadership and the Issue of Stability in the Early Eleventh Century', *Innovationen durch Deuten und Gestalten: Klöster im Mittelalter zwischen Jenseits und Welt* (Regensburg: Schnell & Steiner, 2014), p. 109. See also Jestice, *Wayward Monks*, pp. 190–1.
7 Jean-Hervé Foulon discusses the actions of the abbots of Bec as 'pastoral' in 'Les investitures abbatiales en Normandie: Quelques réflexions autour du cas de l'abbaye Bec-Hellouin', *Anglo-Norman Studies* 35 (2012), 204–5.
8 Musset, 'La vie économique de l'abbaye de Fécamp'.
9 On the separation between political and religious duties, see, for instance, John Nightingale, *Monasteries and Patrons in the Gorze Reform* (New York: Oxford University Press, 2001), pp. 4, 14–15, 30–8; Melville, *The World of Medieval Monasticism*, pp. 189–91, 316, 350, 361; Jean Truax, *Aelred the Peacemaker: The Public Life of a Cistercian Abbot* (Kalamazoo, MI: Cistercian Publications, 2017), pp. 2–3; License, *Hermits and Recluses in English Society*, pp. 7–8; Constable, 'The Cross in Medieval Monastic Life', p. 236; Romig, *Be a Perfect Man*, pp. 30, 133–4, 149–51, 154; Vanommeslaeghe, 'Wandering Abbots', pp. 6, 7, 22–3.
10 This idea contrasts with the idealised picture painted by George Duby in *The Three Orders: Feudal Society Reimagined* (Chicago: University of Chicago Press,

1982), p. 179 and Alexis Wilkin, 'Communautés bénédictines et environnement économique IXe–XIIe siècles. Réflexions sur les tendances historiographiques de l'analyse du temporel monastique', in Steven Vanderputten and Brigitte Meijns (eds), *Ecclesia in Medio Nationis: Reflections on the Study of Monasticism in the Central Middle Ages* (Leuven: Leuven University Press), pp. 101–50.

11 John Howe, *Church Reform and Social Change in Eleventh-Century Italy* (Philadelphia: University of Pennsylvania Press, 1997), p. 90; Truax, *Aelred the Peacemaker*, p. 231. See also *RB* 7: 99–115.

12 Van Engen, 'The "Crisis of Coenobitism" Reconsidered', pp. 269–304.

13 More often than not, scholars limit their analyses of the spiritual use of worldly engagement to the idea that a conscientious abbot would live his life according to religious principles, therefore supporting charity in the world or caring for the poor (see, for instance, Truax, *Aelred the Peacemaker*, pp. 33, 138). There are certain exceptions. Romig's *Be a Perfect Man*, especially his discussion of Gregory the Great on pp. 16–30, accounts for less distinction between spiritual and worldly behaviour. On p. 3 of Constance B. Bouchard, *Holy Entrepreneurs: Cistercians, Knights, and Economic Exchange in Twelfth-Century Burgundy* (Ithaca, NY: Cornell University Press, 1991), Bouchard argues against the idea that 'spirituality and economics are and were antithetical'. John Van Engen asserts that Rupert of Deutz believed that 'those who soar aloft in contemplation can expect to have their material needs provided', in *Rupert of Deutz* (Los Angeles: University of California Press, 1983), p. 302. Still, with the exception of Romig, these authors do not dwell on how economic and worldly activity may have *heightened* spiritual practice, instead simply noting how providing for worldly needs enabled and sustained monastic livelihoods.

14 The 'stone' here refers to the pillow that gave way to Jacob's revelatory dreams. As quoted by Choy, *Intercessory Prayer*, p. 186. The quotation is from *Mor* 5.55.

15 Lecouteux, 'Réseaux', I, pp. 477–9. Lecouteux notes only five such lavish manuscripts that survive from Fécamp: a copy of the *Moralia in Job*, now lost; Augustine's *De Trinitate* (important perhaps because Fécamp was dedicated to the Trinity); a Gospel book; and a collection of Ambrose's writings.

16 See Chapter 2.

17 Jehangir Malegam, *The Sleep of Behemoth: Disputing Peace and Violence in Medieval Europe, 1000–1200* (Ithaca, NY: Cornell University Press, 2013), p. 291.

18 Choy, *Intercessory Prayer*, p. 141.

19 J.N. Hilgarth, 'L'influence de la *Cité de Dieu* de saint Augustin au Haut Moyen Âge', *Sacris Erudiri: A Journal of Late Antique and Medieval Christianity* 28 (1985), 7–8.

20 Note that these annotations were copied from Mont Saint-Michel's copy of *De civitate dei*; Lecouteux, 'Réseaux', I, pp. 477–8.

21 The notes on fol. 150v highlight the last line of *City of God* 15.7: 'But Cain received that counsel of God in the spirit of one who did not wish to amend. In fact, the vice of envy grew stronger in him; and, having entrapped his brother, he slew him. Such was the founder of the earthly city. He was also a figure of the Jews

who slew Christ the Shepherd (*pastor*) of the flock of men, prefigured by Abel the shepherd (*pastor*) of sheep.'

22 Katherine O'Brien O'Keeffe notes that Abraham and Melchisedech are also good examples of obedience to monastic readers in *Stealing Obedience*, p. 29. A book of sermons from Fécamp, Paris, BnF, ms. lat. 989, also has a sermon with an extensive encomium to Melchisedech (starting on fol. 82v), where his example is discussed as a paradigm of obedience. The prominence of Melchisedech is seen in several other Fécamp manuscripts; he is highlighted in Paris, BnF, ms. lat. 564, ms. lat. 989, ms. lat. 2055, and ms. lat. 2628; and in Rouen, BM, ms. 546 (A301), ms. 477 (A191), ms. 532 (A395), ms. 553 (A452).

23 *De civitate dei* 16.22: 'He was then openly blessed by Melchisedech, who was of God most high, about whom many and great things are written in the epistle which is inscribed to the Hebrews ... For then first appeared the sacrifice which is now offered to God by Christians in the whole wide world, and that is fulfilled which long after the event was said by the prophet to Christ, who was yet to come in the flesh, "*You are a priest for ever after the order of Melchisedech*" – that is to say, not after the order of Aaron, for that order was to be taken away when the things shone forth which were intimated beforehand by these shadows.'

24 An abbot's spiritual care of the souls is also discussed by Brian Patrick McGuire, 'Taking Responsibility: Medieval Cistercian Abbots as Their Brothers' Keepers', *Cîteaux: Commentarii Cistercienses* 39 (1988), 249–68.

25 Melchisedech also appears in the sixth-century mosaic in San Vitale in Ravenna (albeit not with Abraham and Isaac). Melchisedech was associated with Abraham and Abel in the eleventh century as well, such as in a portable altar from Fulda, Germany, in the Musée National du Moyen Âge (i.e. Musée Cluny) in Paris; see Deborah Mauskopf Deliyannis, *Ravenna in Late Antiquity* (New York: Cambridge University Press, 2010), p. 273.

26 Jestice, *Wayward Monks*, pp. 76–86, 133, 141, 151–60, 216; Constable, *Reformation of the Twelfth Century*, p. 235; Giles Constable, 'Monasteries, Rural Churches, and the *Cura animarum*', in *Settimane di studio del Centro italiano di studi sull'Alto Medieoevo* (Spoleto: Centro italiano di studi sull'Alto Medioevo, 1982), pp. 367, 373; Kathleen G. Cushing, *Reform and Papacy in the Eleventh Century: Spirituality and Social Change* (Manchester: Manchester University Press, 2005), pp. 34, 95, 131–2.

27 Glaber's *Life of William of Volpiano* in *Rodulfi Glabri opera* (Oxford: Clarendon Press, 1989), pp. 280–1, ch. 10: '*patrem atque pastorem*'; Jestice, *Wayward Monks*, pp. 141, 174–8, 186–9; Mark Hagger, *Norman Rule in Normandy, 911–1144* (Woodbridge: Boydell Press, 2017), p. 213.

28 'For when the care of the souls is placed upon an abbot by a bishop, the pastoral care of the sheep of Christ handed over by him is entirely entrusted to [the abbot]. For unless the bishop should be invited by the abbot for the sake of any sort of business, the bishop is determined to have no right in [the abbot's] monastery; and if, however, anyone attempts to oppose these things which we

are asserting, we set forth to him the Rule of St Benedict.' ('*Quando enim abbati cura animarum imponitur ab episcopo, pastoralitas ovium Christi sibi traditarum ei commendatur omnimodo. Nisi enim ab abbate episcopus invitetur pro qualicumque negotio, nullum jus episcopus habere decernitur in eius monasterio; si autem contra haec quae dicimus aliquis repugnare tentaverit, regulam sancti benedicti sibi proponimus.*') Latin taken from the *Thesaurus novus anecdotorum: complectens regum ac principum* (Paris: Gregg, 1717), vol. I, pp. 206–7. Translation my own.

29 *CT*, p. 121: 'How have you loved us, O good shepherd (*pastor*)! How much have you cherished us, O holy creator, who also did not spare your own Son, but handed him over to the wicked for us? That one, having subjected himself to you unto death, even death on a cross, bore the bond of our sins and, fixing it to the cross, crucified sin and death ... For us he is both, victor and victim, and for you he is victor because the victim. For you he is both priest and sacrifice, and therefore for you he is priest because of his sacrifice.' ('*Quomodo nos amasti, pastor bone? Quantum nos dilexisti, pie conditor, qui etiam proprio Filio tuo non pepercisti, sed pro nobis impiis tradidisti illum? Subditus ille tibi usque ad mortem, mortem autem crucis, tulit chirographum peccatorum nostrorum et affigens illud cruci, peccatum crucifixit et mortem ... Pro nobis tibi victor et victima, et ideo victor quia victima. Pro nobis tibi sacerdos et sacrificium, et ideo sacerdos quia sacrificium.*') Note that, as in the mosaics, Christ is priest and victor, victim, sufferer and sacrifice.

30 '*ab originalibus vinculis expedistit et inter adoptionis filios aggregasti ... Gratias tibi ago qui me a vano huius mundi consortio separasti et das mihi servorum tuorum caritate et societate perfrui: das mihi salutem et quietem corporis et animae et opportunam ad tuum sanctum servilium vacationem, liberas me a vanissimis istius saeculi implicationibus ad profectum animae meae propter solam misericordiam tuam*' (*CT*, p. 130).

31 *RB*, ch. 2.

32 Jestice, *Wayward Monks*, p. 194. This parallel between pastor-abbots and Christ is also firmly made by Aelred of Rievaulx in his *Pastoral Prayer*; Aelred of Rievaulx, 'The Pastoral Prayer', in *Treatises and Pastoral Prayer*, trans. R. Penelope Lawson (Collegeville, MN: Liturgical Press, 1971), pp. 103–18.

33 Charles M. Radding and Francis Newton, *Theology, Rhetoric, and Politics in the Eucharistic Controversy, 1078–1079: Alberic of Monte Cassino against Berengar of Tours* (New York: Columbia University Press, 2003), p. 15; Jean de Montclos, *Lanfranc et Bérenger: La controverse eucharistique du XIe siècle* (Leuven: Spicilegium Sacrum Lovaniense, 1971), pp. 448–51.

34 Van Houts, 'Qui étaient les Normands?', p. 144. The letter from Leo IX summoning John is preserved in *PL* 143, col. 647B, letter 38.

35 This treatise may have been written by someone on Lanfranc's behalf; see Toivo J. Holopainen, '"Lanfranc of Bec" and Berengar of Tours', *Anglo-Norman Studies* 34 (2012), 105–22.

36 *Gazeau*, p. 372. Durandus's work is best preserved in a Fécamp manuscript from the late eleventh century, Paris, BnF, ms. lat. 2720; see *PL* 149, cols 1418–21. On Durandus as cross-bearer, see Ordericus Vitalis, *The Ecclesiastical History of*

England and Normandy, trans. Thomas Forester (London: Henry G. Bohn, 1856), ch. II, line 298.

37 Wilmart, *Auteurs spirituels*, pp. 128–30; Toivo J. Holopainen, *Dialectic and Theology in the Eleventh Century* (New York: E.J. Brill, 1996), p. 116; Brian Stock, *The Implications of Literacy: Written Language and Models of Interpretation in the Eleventh and Twelfth Centuries* (Princeton, NJ: Princeton University Press, 1983), p. 283; Leclercq and Bonnes, *Un maître*, pp. 31, 72–6. In 'Étude comparée', Serralda has claimed that the *Confessio fidei* was not written by John. Warren Pezé makes a more convincing argument that large parts of the *Confessio fidei* might pre-date John of Fécamp's *Confessio theologica* and might have served as inspiration to John in the way that Augustine's *Confessions* also did (in 'Aux origines').

38 Martineau, 'Envisioning Heaven', p. 121.

39 See *Confessio fidei*, *PL* 101, col. 1087.

40 See *Confessio fidei*, *PL* 101, col. 1088.

41 Piroska Nagy, 'Larmes et eucharistie. Formes du sacrifice en Occident au moyen âge central', in Nicole Bériou, Béatrice Caseau, and Dominique Rigaux (eds), *Pratiques de l'eucharistie* (Paris: Études augustiniennes, 2005), pp. 1073–109.

42 Jestice, *Wayward Monks*, p. 140.

43 Hagger, *Norman Rule in Normandy*, p. 209.

44 Straw, *Gregory the Great*, p. 105. Scholars have located the Eucharist's connection to the larger medieval narrative of affective piety some years after John's death, with Baldwin of Ford (c. 1125–90); see Constable, *Three Studies in Medieval Religious and Social Thought*, p. 192. John's passionate defence of the Eucharist within his early affective text contradicts that assumption.

45 'Panis sancte, panis vive, panis pulcher, panis munde qui descendisti de caelo et das vitam mundo, veni in cor meum et munda me ab omni inquinamento carnis et Spiritus, intra in animam meam, et sanctifica me interius et exterius' (*Confessio fidei* as quoted by Cottier, *Anima mea*, p. 110). This quotation is not found in the *CT*, but is often excerpted as the so-called *Summe sacerdos* prayer, contained in Metz, Mediathèque de Metz, ms. 245. For more on the medieval life of this prayer, see Cottier, *Anima mea*, pp. 101–11; Wilmart, *Auteurs spirituels*, pp. 101–25.

46 '*Magnum quippe et ineffabile constat esse sacramentum, in quo tua caro in veritate editur, et sanguis tuus in veritate bibitur. O pauendum reverendumque mysterium, ad cuius intuendam altitudinem humanus reverberatur intuitus. Per ipsum sacrosanctum et vivificum mysterium corporis et sanguinis tui ... resplende mihi, accende me, illumina et sanctifica vas tuum, de malitia evacua, imple de gratia et plenum conserva, ut ad salutem animae meae manducem cibum carnis tuae: quaetenus manducando te, vivam de te, vadam per te, perveniam ad te, repausem in te. Qui enim manducat te, ipse vivit propter te*' (*CT*, pp. 173–4).

47 See *Confessio fidei*, *PL* 101, col. 1087B.

48 Cf. Chapter 1.

49 '*dulcis cibus cordis mei*' (*CT*, p. 135).

50 Cf. Chapter 1.

51 Nagy, 'Larmes et eucharistie'.
52 Michal Kobialka, *This is My Body: Representational Practices in the Early Middle Ages* (Ann Arbor: University of Michigan Press, 2003), pp. 106–7, 115.
53 Noreen Hunt, *Cluny under Saint Hugh, 1049–1109* (Notre Dame, IN: University of Notre Dame Press, 1967), pp. 111–12.
54 De Montclos, *Bérenger et Lanfranc*, pp. 91–4.
55 Herbert Edward John Cowdrey, 'The Papacy and the Berengarian Controversy', in Peter Felix Ganz, Robert Burchard Huygens, and Friedrich Niewöhner (eds), *Auctoritas und Ratio: Studien zu Berengar von Tours* (Wiesbaden: Harrassowitz, 1990), pp. 135, 138; Lecouteux, 'Réseaux', I, pp. 463, 543, 546.
56 See n. 45 above.
57 Note that John was simultaneously abbot of Fécamp and of Saint-Bénigne de Dijon during these years.
58 My attribution here comes in part from provenance, and in part from an examination of script. In terms of provenance, the manuscript is part of Jean Bouhier III's collection at the École de Médicine in Montpellier, and Bouhier's manuscripts were for the most part from upper Champagne and lower Burgundy, where Saint-Bénigne de Dijon was located; several of Bouhier's manuscripts are even from Saint-Bénigne itself. The manuscript's script also compares with that of two manuscripts confirmed to be from Saint-Bénigne, Paris, BnF, ms. lat. 13370 and Montpellier, Bibliothèque interuniversitaire de Montpellier, H159. Note that another manuscript from Saint-Bénigne, Troyes, BM, ms. 2142, also contains in fols 180v–189r the first nine pages of the text of John's *Confessio fidei*. For more on this Troyes manuscript, see Gazeau, *Guillaume de Volpiano*, pp. 40–1.
59 Glastonbury's copy is in a catalogue of the thirteenth century; see J.P. Carley, R. Sharpe, R.M. Thomson, and A.G. Watson (eds), *English Benedictine Libraries: The Shorter Catalogues* (London: British Library, 1996), p. 198. The abbot of Glastonbury was uncle to Henry Sully, abbot of Fécamp in the twelfth century, and it is said that both Glastonbury and Fécamp had blood relics in the late eleventh and twelfth centuries because they were so closely linked (see Robert Jaffray, 'Glastonbury and Fécamp', in John Matthews (ed.), *Sources of the Grail* (Hudson, NY: Lindisfarne Press, 1996), pp. 347–55; and Chapter 5).
60 See Chapter 1.
61 Sweeney, *Anselm of Canterbury and the Desire for the Word*, p. 3.
62 Arne-Dannenberg, 'Charity and Law', pp. 13, 18–19, 23.
63 See Chapter 2; Bougaud and Garnier, *Chronique de l'abbaye de Saint-Bénigne de Dijon*, pp. 156–60.
64 See Chapter 1.
65 For John's entry in the Saint-Arnoul de Metz necrology, see M. Müller, *Am Schnittpunkt von Stadt und Land. Die Benediktinerabtei St. Arnulf zu Metz im hohen und späten Mittelalter* (Trier: Kliomedia, 1993), p. 22. For his entry in the necrologies of Saint-Bénigne de Dijon, Saint-Germain des Prés, Saint-Faron de Meaux, and Mont Saint-Michel, see Stéphane Lecouteux, 'Deux fragments d'un nécrologe

de la Trinité de Fécamp (XIe–XIIe siècles). Étude et édition critique d'un document mémoriel exceptionnel', *Tabularia* 16 (2016), 6–7.
66 See John's letter to Abbot Vital of Bernay (*PL* 147, col. 464D) or to the new abbot at Saint-Berthe de Blangy (*PL* 147, cols 474D–475C).
67 See Chapter 3.
68 See *CT* manuscript copies Paris, BnF, ms. lat. 3088 and Zwettl, ms. 164. Niskanen notes that introductory or dedicatory letters were often copied into medieval editions from the original manuscript, likely preserved either as a kind of preface or because they had import for the monastery copying the larger work; see Samu Niskanen, *The Letter Collections of Anselm of Canterbury* (Turnhout: Brepols, 2011), p. 63.
69 Brian Patrick McGuire, *Friendship and Community: The Monastic Experience, 350–1250* (Ithaca, NY: Cornell University Press, 1993), p. 195.
70 *CT*, p. 204; Jean Leclercq, *Otia monastica: Études sur le vocabulaire de la contemplation au moyen âge* (Rome: Orbis Catholicus, 1963), pp. 96–102.
71 See Chapter 3.
72 *CT*, p. 199. Note that Maiolus's name was rubbed out in Paris, BnF, ms. lat. 3088; Leclercq speculates that another name – perhaps William of Volpiano's or that of another abbot more closely connected to the recipient of ms. lat. 3088 – might have been written there to better customise John's point for the manuscript's audience.
73 *CT*, p. 204.
74 Medieval letters, after all, were not written solely for the eyes of the addressed recipient (Niskanen, *The Letter Collections*, p. 63).
75 'Be silent, dogs of Scylla; with my ears stopped, I shall transcend the obstreperous rage of your lacerations. In your assemblies, as they say, this letter resounds from the canine nostril: "When you acknowledge that it is proper for a monk of the monastic religion to be silent, why do you then speak to women? Where do you get the authority to sit in a master's chair and without blushing teach those women with writings?"' (*CT*, pp. 211–17; translation from Joan Ferrante's *Epistolae* project: https://epistolae.ccnmtl.columbia.edu/letter/129.html).
76 'Be quiet, wretches. You say these things because you are blind, and leaders of the blind. Go back, you evaders, to your heart and diligently consider where you lie down shamefully. If only your malicious mind would come to its senses and strive somewhat to imitate the pious works of honourable women' (*CT*, pp. 211–17).
77 *CT*, pp. 211–17.
78 Olson, 'Did Medieval English Women Read Augustine's *Confessiones*?', p. 84.
79 Agnes appointed John abbot of Saint-Bénigne de Dijon in 1052 (till 1054), a contact that likely precipitated this correspondence; Wilmart, 'Deux préfaces spirituelles', p. 35.
80 Albrecht Diem, 'The Gender of the Religious: Wo/Men and the Invention of Monasticism', in Judith M. Bennett and Ruth Mazo Karras (eds), *The Oxford*

Handbook of Women and Gender in Medieval Europe (New York: Oxford University Press, 2013), pp. 432–46.

81 This is the only female house in the Norman monastic network where John is also commemorated in the necrology; Véronique Gazeau, 'Femmes en religion, personnes d'authorité: Les abbesses normandes (XIe–XIIe siècles)', *Anglo-Norman Studies* 35 (2012), 30.

82 For instance, the twelfth-century Zwettl ms. 164 circulates with the letter to the Empress Agnes.

83 McNamer, *Affective Meditation*, pp. 58–85.

84 McNamer, *Affective Meditation*, p. 73. Others also have credited women with introducing monastic piety to wider lay culture: Richard Southern, *Saint Anselm and His Biographer: A Study of Monastic Life and Thought* (New York: Cambridge University Press, 1963), p. 37; S.G. Bell, 'Medieval Women Book Owners: Arbiters of Lay Piety and Ambassadors of Culture', in J.M. Bennett (ed.), *Sisters and Workers in the Middle Ages* (Chicago: University of Chicago Press, 1989), p. 136; Kathleen Quirk, 'Men, Women, and Miracles in Normandy, 1050–1150', in Elisabeth van Houts (ed.), *Medieval Memories: Men, Women, and the Past: 700–1300* (New York: Longman, 2001), pp. 53–71.

85 'I learned from friends that you also desire and request what I have uttered about the divine contemplation and love of Christ and about that supernal Jerusalem, the mother of all the faithful' (*CT*, 211–17); unfortunately, it seems that John's *CT* edition for Agnes has not survived. In the letter, John promises to send Agnes a copy of excerpted writings from the Fathers (likely akin to those at the beginning of BnF, ms. lat. 13593, see Mancia, 'Praying with an Eleventh-Century Manuscript') and a sermon about the life and customs of virgins along with a copy of his *CT*. While the letter to Agnes does circulate with other copies of John's *Libellus* recension (cf. Chapter 1), no manuscript circulates with a sermon about the life and customs of virgins.

86 'I ask your love that if you find any who want to have this little book, admonish them to transcribe it diligently and reread it frequently, so that they allow nothing to be added or subtracted or changed in it. We say this because of the carelessness of scribes, who not only corrupt the truth but also add lies to lies' (*CT*, 211–17).

87 Compare John with Augustine, William of St. Thierry (1085–1148), Adam of Dryburgh (1140–1212), Goscelin of Saint-Bertin (b. c. 1040), Aelred of Rievaulx (1110–67), and Anselm of Canterbury, who also thought to share their devotional practices with women and men alike. Olson, 'Did Medieval English Women Read Augustine's *Confessiones*?', pp. 72–3.

88 The nun 'do[es] not allow [her] mind to be darkened by carnal desires and earthly longings' ('*mentes suas carnalibus desideriis et terrenis concupiscentiis obtenebrari non sinunt*'). She also 'avoids outward business as much as she is able, provided obedience be preserved' ('*Forinseca negotia quantum valet, salva oboedientia, devitat*') (*CT*, p. 206).

89 'Sacris vigiliis et psalmodiae, non somnolenta sed intenta, studet interesse' (*CT*, p. 206).
90 'Solitudinem in oratione, quantum licet, pro deliciis habet' (*CT*, p. 206).
91 'Dulce est ei frequentius flere' (*CT*, p. 206).
92 'Nisi exteriorum desideria a se repellat, interna non penetrat, quia tanto subtilius invisibilia conspicit, quanto perfectius visibilia contemnit' (*CT*, p. 206).
93 'Tunc mitis lector ipso cordis palato sapit quid dulcendinis intus lateat' (*CT*, p. 206).
94 'Optimam partem semper, quantum licet sibi, cum vera Maria eligit' (*CT*, p. 206).
95 Fiona Griffiths has shown that men's pastoral care of women was often viewed by the men themselves as the one of the tools for their own redemption: Fiona Griffiths, 'Men's Duty to Provide for Women's Needs: Abelard, Heloise, and Their Negotiation of the *Cura monialium*', *Journal of Medieval History* 30 (2004), 1–24.
96 'Iustum namque est ut qui in actuali vita bene conversatus est contemplationis pennas assumat' (*CT*, p. 206).
97 Cf. Chapter 1 on John's *Confessio theologica*'s notions of spiritual warming.
98 'Utinam ille in me igniculus foret, qui vaporatae menti aliquid incrementi adolere posset' (*CT*, pp. 213–14).
99 Italics my emphasis. '*Praeclarum sanctae viduitatis exemplar, accipe, quaeso, pervigili mente illud quod expetis meae per Christi gratiam deflorationis opusculum*' (*CT*, p. 214).
100 Potts, *Monastic Revival and Regional Identity*, p. 42.
101 This is the position of, for instance, Isabelle Rosé, who believes tenth-century abbots were primarily interested in gaining and cultivating an 'aristocratic lordship', in 'Circulation abbatiale et pouvoir monastique de l'époque carolingienne au premier âge féodal (IXe–XIe siècles)', in *Des sociétés en mouvement. Migrations et mobilité au moyen âge. XLe Congrès de la SHMESP (Nice, 4–7 juin 2009)* (Paris: Publications de la Sorbonne, 2010), pp. 260–6. Such duplicity seems antithetical to the monastic project of sincere intercessory prayer; see Giles Constable, 'The Concern for Sincerity and Understanding in Liturgical Prayer, Especially in the Twelfth Century', in Irene Vaslef and Helmut Buschhausen (eds), *Classica et Mediaevalia: Studies in Honor of Joseph Szöverffy* (Washington, DC: Classical Folia, 1986), pp. 17–30.
102 Searle, *Predatory Kinship*.
103 Brooke, 'Princes and Kings as Patrons of Monasteries'.
104 Lucile Tran-Duc, 'Le culte des saints dans la Normandie médiévale (IXe–XIIe siècle). Enjeux de pouvoir dans les établissements bénédictins du diocèse de Rouen' (PhD dissertation, Université de Caen Basse-Normandie, 2015).
105 After the Conquest, William the Conqueror's primary residence was in Caen, but the palace was still often occupied by ducal associates if not the dukes themselves. Richard I, founder of the monastery of Fécamp, could see the monastic buildings from the entrance to his palace: 'While [Richard I] was standing on the raised platform at the entrance to his own house, he noticed that the house itself was taller and more capacious than the basilica dedicated in honour of

the deific Trinity. He summoned a stonemason who was skilled in the art of architecture, and said to him: "It is right and fitting that the house of God and prayer should be roofed superlatively well, with particular beauty and appropriate height, to be super-eminent over all the buildings of the city"' (Dudo of Saint-Quentin, *History of the Normans*, trans. Eric Christiansen (Rochester, NY: Boydell Press, 1998), Book 4, lines 290–1, pp. 165–6). Once the dukes abandoned the palace, it became a *palais de Dieu*, with the abbey assuming some of the buildings, according to Renoux, *Du palais ducale*.

106 Some Fécamp monks could not stand the proximity: an English monk named Clement left Fécamp for Saint-Bénigne because his contemplative peace was constantly being disturbed by visitors; Bates, *Normandy before 1066*, p. 220.

107 Cassandra Potts. 'The Early Norman Charters: A New Perspective on an Old Debate', in Carola Hicks (ed.), *England in the Eleventh Century: Proceedings of the 1990 Harlaxton Symposium* (Stamford: Paul Watkins, 1992), pp. 33–4.

108 Richard II's wife Judith is buried at Bernay, a dependency of Fécamp. Lucien Musset, 'Sepulutres des souverains normands: Un aspect de l'idéologie du pouvoir', in Jean-Michel Bouvris and Jean-Marie Maillefer (eds), *Autour du pouvoir ducal normand, Xe–XIIe siècles* (Caen: Centre d'études normandes, 1985), p. 30. Musset asserts that Richard III (c. 997–1027) and Robert the Magnificent (1000–35) would have been buried at Fécamp as well, had they not both died under special circumstances requiring burial elsewhere (Richard III was mysteriously murdered near Caen, and Robert died while returning from Jerusalem). See also B. Golding, 'Anglo-Norman Knightly Burials', in C. Harper-Bill and R. Harvey (eds), *The Ideals and Practice of Medieval Knighthood* (Woodbridge: Boydell & Brewer, 1986), pp. 35–48.

109 *Chadd* I, pp. 212–13. Constable, *Reformation of the Twelfth Century*, p. 235.

110 See, for instance, John's acceptance of a priest named Mainard into the community of Fécamp in exchange for all of his goods after his death; see Bloche, 'Le chartrier', charter no. 49, p. 352.

111 In charters, the Norman dukes explain that they give donations expecting salvation from God and prayers and intercession on their behalf (see, for example, *Faur* nos. 4, 9, 31, 34) or because the donations are good works required of all Christians (see *Faur* nos. 9, 25, 86). Additionally, Richard II demonstrated the spiritual motivations behind his gift-giving by making occasional gifts that had no potential for political implications or worldly results at all, which were instead simply gifts to ensure the benefit of his soul. For instance, Cassandra Potts describes an unpublished document in the Musée de la Bénédictine de Fécamp where Richard asks the monks to feed one poor man in his name in return for exemption of tolls on the ships of the abbey. Richard does not gain anything from exempting the monks of Fécamp from tolls except their favour and his own salvation, and such a donation shows a true commitment on Richard's part to giving in order to achieve heavenly rewards (Potts, *Monastic Revival and Regional Identity*, p. 49.) See also C. Harper-Bill, 'The Piety of the

Anglo-Norman Knightly Class', *Anglo-Norman Studies* 2 (1979), 66–7; Julie Ann Potter, 'The Friendship Network of the Abbey of Le Bec-Hellouin in the Eleventh and Twelfth Centuries' (PhD dissertation, University of Cambridge, 2014), pp. 68, 241–68.

112 David Ganz, 'Giving to God in the Mass: The Experience of the Offertory', in Wendy Davies and Paul Fouracre (eds), *The Languages of Gift in the Early Middle Ages* (New York: Cambridge University Press, 2010), p. 31.

113 The most infamous debate on this subject took place between Richard Southern and Sally Vaughn in the 1990s. Vaughn, in *Anselm of Bec and Robert of Meulan* (Berkeley: University of California Press, 1987), challenged Southern's interpretation of Anselm as a good spiritual leader (and bad administrator) in *Saint Anselm and His Biographer*. Southern then replied to her in 'Sally Vaughn's Anselm: An Examination of the Foundations', *Albion* 20 (1988), 181–204 and also in *Saint Anselm: A Portrait in a Landscape* (New York: Cambridge University Press, 1992). Vaughn persisted, representing her views of Anselm again in 'Anselm: Saint and Statesman', *Albion* 20 (1988), 205–20; in 'Anselm of Bec', p. 111; and in *Archbishop Anselm, 1093–1109: Bec Missionary, Canterbury Primate, Patriarch of Another World* (Burlington, VT: Ashgate, 2012).

114 Potter, *The Friendship Network*, pp. 89–91. See also Anselm of Canterbury, *The Letters of Saint Anselm of Canterbury*, trans. Walter Fröhlich (Kalamazoo, MI: Cistercian Publications, 1990), letters 3 and 45.

115 Stéphane Lecouteux, 'Associations de prières et confraternités spirituelles: Des unions éphémères ou pérennes? Enquête autour du réseau de confraternité de l'abbaye de la Trinité de Fécamp (XIe–XVe siècle)', in Nicole Lemaitre (ed.), *Réseaux religieux et spirituels: Du moyen âge à nos jours* (Paris: CTHS, 2016), pp. 75–92; *Chadd* I, pp. 692–5.

116 Carolyn Malone discusses this when characterising the reform of Saint-Bénigne de Dijon, 'Saint-Bénigne in Dijon as *Exemplum* of Rodulf Glaber's Metaphoric "White Mantle"', in Nigel Hiscock (ed.), *The White Mantle of Churches: Architecture, Liturgy, and Art around the Millennium* (Turnhout: Brepols, 2003), pp. 160–79.

117 Fulton, *From Judgment to Passion*, pp. 185–7.

118 Richard Landes, 'The White Mantle of Churches, Millennial Dynamics, and the Written and Architectural Record', in Nigel Hiscock (ed.), *The White Mantle of Churches: Architecture, Liturgy, and Art around the Millennium* (Turnhout: Brepols, 2003), pp. 249–64.

119 William of Jumièges, Orderic Vitalis, and Robert of Torigni, *The Gesta Normannorum Ducum of William of Jumièges, Orderic Vitalis, and Robert of Torigni*, ed. and trans. Elisabeth van Houts (Oxford: Clarendon Press, 1992), pp. 130–5. The above excerpt is from William of Jumièges's original text from 1050.

120 *Gesta Normannorum Ducum*, pp. 38–41. The excerpt is from William of Jumièges's original text from 1050.

121 *Glaber*, p. 37.

122 William the Conqueror also spent Easter at Fécamp in 1067, 1075, and 1083; see H.W.C. Davis and R.J. Whitwell (eds), *Regesta Regum Anglo-Normannorum* (Oxford, 1913), pp. xxi–xxii. In 1066, he likely celebrated his triumphant Conquest, especially since he had launched his ships bound for England from Fécamp; see van Houts, 'The Ship List of William the Conqueror', pp. 159–83. William issued several ducal charters from those meetings (including *Faur* no. 230); see Elisabeth van Houts, 'The Political Relations between Normandy and England before 1066 According to the *Gesta Normannorum Ducum*', in Raymonde Foreville (ed.), *Les mutations socio-culturelles au tournant des XIe–XIIe siècles* (Paris: CNRS, 1984), pp. 85–97.

123 From the *Brevis relatio*, in *Chronology, Conquest, and Conflict in Medieval England*. Camden Miscellany 34 (New York: Cambridge University Press, 1997), p. 46. Excerpt and translation from Potts, *Monastic Revival and Regional Identity*, p. 40. This story also shows up in Robert of Torigini's revision of the *Gesta Normannorum Ducum*, pp. 288–9.

124 The translation of the dukes' bones was celebrated in the liturgy of Fécamp in the years to come; *Chadd* I, fols 196v–199r. Miracles were even recorded as having happened at the tombs of the dukes Richard I and Richard II, and the ducal tombs became a popular stop for pilgrims visiting the blood relic (see Chapter 5).

125 See Bloche, 'Le chartrier', charter no. 49, p. 352. For the location of Saint-Léger, see Map 2.

126 See Bloche, 'Le chartrier', charter no. 51, p. 355. Constable discusses monks occasionally serving such pastoral needs in Constable, 'Monasteries, Rural Churches, and the *Cura animarum*', p. 351. Constable notes on p. 364 that at William of Volpiano's monastery at Fruttuaria, 70 per cent of the monks were ordained and 30 per cent were not.

127 See Bloche, 'Le chartrier', charter no. 52, p. 356.

128 Bates, *Normandy before 1066*, p. 193. An eleventh-century charter mentions a priest who was trained at the Fécamp school, *Faur* no. 29; Rouen, Archives départementales de Seine-Maritime, 7H, 2143. This is the lone mention of a school at Fécamp in the charter evidence; the remaining proof is from the chronicles of the abbey. For monks' duties at the comparative example schools at Bec and (perhaps) Caen, see Herbert Edward John Cowdrey, *Lanfranc: Scholar, Monk, and Archbishop* (New York: Oxford, 2003), pp. 19–22; Kuhl, 'Education and Schooling at Le Bec'; David S. Spear, 'The School of Caen Revisited', *Haskins Society Journal* 4 (1992), 55–66; and Mia Münster-Swendsen, 'Regimens of Schooling', in R.J. Hexter and D. Townsend (eds), *The Oxford Handbook of Medieval Latin Literature* (New York: Oxford University Press, 2012), pp. 403–22.

129 *Faur* nos. 70, 117. The Council of Rouen (1072), for instance, made it mandatory for monasteries to observe the *RB* (Lackner, *The Eleventh-Century Background of Cîteaux*, pp. 119–23) – this is the kind of 'reform' that the monks were providing.

130 Dom Hubert Dauphin, *Le bienheureux Richard, abbé de Saint-Vanne de Verdun* (Leuven: Peeters, 1946), pp. 56–7.
131 Potter, *The Friendship Network*, p. 89. See also Anselm's letter 20 as proof of this transference of *amicitia* to the corporate body. On the corporate body shielding its monks from the sin of uniqueness or personal wealth, see Bouchard, *Holy Entrepreneurs*, p. 189; Van Engen, *Rupert of Deutz*, pp. 302–3, 322.
132 See Chapter 3.
133 This idea of group versus individual is also shared by Caroline Walker Bynum, 'Did the Twelfth Century Discover the Individual?', in *Jesus as Mother: Studies in the Spirituality of the High Middle Ages* (Berkeley: University of California Press, 1982), pp. 82–109.
134 John Nightingale has spoken about this for Gorze, another of William of Volpaino's monasteries, in Nightingale, *Gorze Reform*, p. 235.
135 *Glaber*, pp. 100–5.
136 Sheila Bonde, Clark Maines, and Alba Serino, 'Mastering the Landscape: A Comparative Analysis of Monastic Domain Formation', conference paper, Medieval Academy of America Annual Meeting, Knoxville, TN, April 2013; Potter, *The Friendship Network*, p. 88; Vaughn, *Archbishop Anselm, 1093–1109*, p. 29.
137 Anne Müller, 'Presenting Identity in the Cloister: Remarks on Benedictine and Mendicant Concepts of Space', in Anne Müller and Karen Stöber (eds), *Self-Representation of Medieval Religious Communities: The British Isles in Context* (Berlin: Lit Verlag, 2009), p. 169.
138 Dominique Iogna-Prat, *Order and Exclusion: Cluny and Christendom Face Heresy, Judaism, and Islam (1000–1150)*, trans. Graham Robert Edwards (Ithaca, NY: Cornell University Press, 2003), pp. 215–16.
139 Constable, *Reformation of the Twelfth Century*, p. 30. Emphyteotic contracts, which were particularly popular among Fécamp's land transactions, could even have been seen as rental behaviour that was more spiritually advantageous than economically savvy: Jean-Claude Hélas sees these transactions as more beneficial to the lessee than to the landlord (i.e. than to Fécamp), and as the establishment of communal wealth. Such contracts, then, would have been made in opposition to the monastery's own economic interests, and would have allowed the monastery to reassert itself as a community (rather than a collection of sinful individuals), thereby prioritising spiritual considerations over economic ones. See Jean-Claude Hélas, 'Emphyteusis Tenure: Its Role in the Economy and in the Rural Society of Eastern Languedoc', in Kathryn L. Reyerson and J. Drendel (eds), *Urban and Rural Communities in Medieval France: Provence and Languedoc, 1000–1500* (Leuven: Brill, 1998), pp. 193–208, especially 206.
140 Dudo of Saint-Quentin, *History of the Normans*, Book 4, line 220, p. 96.
141 Dudo of Saint-Quentin, *History of the Normans*, Book 4, lines 290–1, pp. 165–6.
142 Leroux De Lincy, *L'abbaye de Fécamp*, p. 214; Soulignac, *Fécamp et sa campagne*, p. 130.

143 A masterful analysis of how monks saw their material property as an allegory for their spiritual purpose is Peter Fergusson, 'Canterbury Cathedral Priory's Bath House and Fish Pond', *Anglo-Norman Studies* 37 (2014), 115–30.
144 Potter, *The Friendship Network*, pp. 54–5.
145 *PL* 143, col. 797C.
146 *PL* 143, col. 799A.
147 *PL* 143, col. 798C.
148 O'Keeffe, *Stealing Obedience*, p. 26.
149 *PL* 147, cols 463C–464D, 476A–476C. In one letter to William, John claims to only *moleste acciperem* (to accept, in a vexed manner) and accuses William of acting *sine licentia nostra* (without the rightful consent of the abbot).
150 Barbara Rosenwien, Thomas Head, and Sharon Farmer, 'Monks and Their Enemies: A Comparative Approach', *Speculum* 66.4 (1991), 792; Foulon, 'Les investitures abbatiales en Normandie', p. 191.
151 The claim that Fécamp had been granted an exemption in 1006 by Duke Richard II seems to have been invented by the abbey sometime between the 1050s and 1080s. On Fécamp's assertions about exemption in the monastery's chronicles and elsewhere, see Mathieu Arnoux, 'Les premières chroniques de Fécamp: De l'hagiographie à l'histoire', in Pierre Boulet and François Neveux (eds), *Les saints dans le Normandie médiévale* (Caen: Presses universitaires de Caen, 1996), pp. 71–82, and Mathieu Arnoux, 'La fortune du *Libellus de revelatione, edificatione, et auctoritate Fiscannensis monsterii*', *Revue d'histoire des textes* 21 (1991), 135–58; Pohl and Vanderputten, 'Fécamp, Cluny, and the Invention of Traditions'.
152 *PL* 147, cols 475A–475B.
153 *CT*, p. 35; Wilmart, *Auteurs spirituels*, p. 128, n. 2.
154 '*Pudet me ac piget publicis conventibus repraesentari, urbem ingredi, potentes alloqui, feminas intueri, verbosae multitudini interesse et talia multa pati qualia mundus agit*' (*CT*, p. 195).
155 Jestice, *Wayward Monks*, pp. 66–7; Bernard McGinn, *The Growth of Mysticism* (New York: Crossroad, 1991), p. 130; C.H. Laurence, *Medieval Monasticism* (New York: Routledge, 2000), p. 149; Feiss, 'John of Fécamp's Longing for Heaven', p. 66. Similar complaints are noted from many of John's contemporaries, including Lanfranc (see Watkins, 'Lanfranc at Caen', p. 75).
156 '*Miserere mei sicut coepisti, libera me ab hoc maligno saeculo et ne sinas me famulum tuum ulla occasione implicari in eo ... ab his causarum tumultibus et multiplici adventantium strepitu, ab hoc multo saeculo quod patior in monasterio, inter hanc frequentiam fratrum ubi cotidie in multis offendo, et da mihi illud solitudinis secretum et spiritale oportunae ad te vacationis otium, necnon et cordis puritatem et mentis iubilationem, ut perfecte diligere et digne laudare merear dulcissime cunctis diebus vitae meae*' (*CT*, p. 195).
157 Cf. Chapter 1; *CT*, p. 182.
158 Cf. *Sic et non*, or God and man (Christ). 'Discourse of opposites' is a term taken from Constance B. Bouchard, *Every Valley Shall Be Exalted: The Discourse*

of *Opposites in Twelfth-Century Thought* (Ithaca, NY: Cornell University Press, 2003), p. 4. Barbara Newman recasts this as 'Both/And' in Barbara Newman, *Medieval Crossover: Reading the Secular against the Sacred* (Notre Dame, IN: Notre Dame University Press, 2013), p. 9.

159 Maureen Miller, 'Religion Makes a Difference: Clerical and Lay Cultures in the Courts of Northern Italy, 1000–1300', *American Historical Review* (2000), 1129.

160 '*Quis mihi dabat pennas praepetes et celeres alas, ut revolem ad te et sicut prius requiescam in te?*' (*CT*, p. 188).

161 This compares with a like complaint from one of John's contemporaries, Richard of Préaux (b. c. 1000), who 'amidst the stresses and the great disorder of mind' seeks and longs for the 'consolation ... that I may return to the streams of sacred scripture by which the filth may be cleansed from my feet and that in gazing upon them my troubled mind may be quieted, made calm, and become itself again'. William L. North notes that, while Richard constantly harped on the 'deleterious effects of his pastoral office on his contemplative abilities, he spoke with equal conviction about the redemptive power of the sacred text'. Here, I take this one step further: that indeed Richard (and John like him) craves that redemptive conversion from the 'filth' of this world to the 'calm' of an escape to contemplation. William L. North, 'St. Anselm's Forgotten Student: Richard of Préaux and the Interpretation of Scripture in Early Twelfth-Century Normandy', in Sally N. Vaughn and Jay Rubenstein (eds), *Teaching and Learning in Northern Europe, 1000–1200* (Turnhout: Brepols, 2006), p. 186.

162 See Paris, BnF, ms. lat. 1919; fragment Paris, BnF, ms. lat. 3088; and fragment Paris, BnF, ms. lat. 152, fols 47–47v. The sole manuscript (unplaced, from late eleventh century) containing John's *Lamentation* without his *CT*, Cambridge, Fitzwilliam Museum, McClean College, no.7, puts it at the back of a manuscript with the biblical books of Job, Wisdom, and Ecclesiastes, and with Cassiodorus's *De ecclesiastico.*

163 '*Libet ... de tua pace et requie cotidie lectitare et lecta frequenter sub corde revolvere, ut tua memoria sit inter hos turbines aliqua repausatio mea*' (*CT*, p. 187).

164 For example, *CT*, p. 186.

165 For example, *CT*, p. 196.

166 For example, *CT*, p. 187.

167 Constable, *Reformation of the Twelfth Century*, p. 210; Vanderputten, 'The Mind as Cell and the Body as Cloister', pp. 106–7; and Florian Mazel, 'Amitié et rupture de l'amitié: Moines et grands laïcs provençeaux au temps de la crise grégorienne (milieu XI–milieu XII siècle)', *Revue historique* 307 (2005), 53–96.

168 Herbert Edward John Cowdrey, *The Cluniacs and the Gregorian Reform* (Oxford: Clarendon Press, 1970), p. 122; Cushing, *Reform and the Papacy*, p. 156.

169 Constable, *The Reformation of the Twelfth Century*, p. 176, Cowdrey, *Cluniacs and Gregorian Reform*, pp. 134–5.

170 Constable, *The Reformation of the Twelfth Century*, p. 44.
171 Charles West has also questioned the 'fundamental antagonism between' monks and the laity in his article 'Monks, Aristocrats, and Justice: Monastic Advocacy in a European Perspective', *Speculum* 92.2 (2017), 403.
172 Melville, *The World of Medieval Monasticism*, pp. 351, 360.

5

John's medieval legacy: the monastic roots of affective piety

John's *Confessio theologica* and its ideas about monastic prayerful emotion were alive and well at Fécamp during the years of John's abbacy, from 1028 to 1078. But did they die with the abbot who authored them, or did they live on? This chapter will detail how John's ideas were embraced, built upon, and transformed by those who came after him: his students, the generations of monks that succeeded him at Fécamp, the Norman monks who were his younger contemporaries, and a wider audience of late medieval Christians. I will first examine John's immediate sphere of influence, looking at the writings of his students. I will then discuss Fécamp's cult of the Precious Blood of Christ, an extension of John's devotional practices that developed at Fécamp soon after his death. Next I will look at the work of John's younger, more famous contemporaries Anselm of Bec (1033–1109) and Guibert of Nogent (c. 1055–1124), showing how Anselm's affectivity and Guibert's use of Augustine's *Confessions* were both indebted to and also distinct from John's work. I will then discuss how John's ideas were transformed in the hands of his Cistercian readers. I will conclude by tracing the dissemination of John's *CT* in manuscripts after his death, from the twelfth century to the end of the Middle Ages, showing how John's ideas helped to shape late medieval devotional exercises. The reader will see a particular emphasis here on two topics in particular: understanding John's influence on his inheritors, from the lesser-known Gerbert of Saint-Wandrille (d. 1089) to the more famous Anselm of Bec; and understanding just how foundational John's work was for later medieval Christian affective piety.

John's legacy among his own students (from 1063 to 1089)

John was mentor to several monks at Fécamp who went on to write devotional works themselves, some even during John's lifetime. One was

Durandus (c. 1012–89), John's cross-bearer (later abbot of the monastery of Troarn), who, in the vein of John's *Confessio fidei*, wrote a treatise about the Eucharist against Berengar of Tours.[1] John of Reims (fl. c. 1100), later a monk at Saint-Evroult, composed a treatise, now lost, on the life of Christ; one can imagine that such a work might have included a focus on Christ's model suffering, perhaps in a tone akin to John's own.[2] Anastasius the Venetian (d. c. 1085), an Italian like John who first was as a hermit on Tomblaine, then at Fécamp under John, and ultimately abbot at Mont Saint-Michel, wrote a treatise on the body and blood of Christ. His *De veritate corpore et sanguine domini* (On the True Body and Blood of the Lord) was a sort of confession-credo letter, comparable with John's *Confessio fidei* in tone.[3] Maurilius, later bishop of Rouen (fl. 1055–67), maintained close connections with Abbot John throughout his life[4] and wrote contemplative prayers in a style similar to John's.[5] Maurilius's most popular devotional work, an *Oratio ad sanctam Mariam* (Prayer to Saint Mary), adopts the penitential tone of John's *CT*, painting the sinner as unworthy of intercession in his depravity.[6] Both Anastasius and Maurilius seem to have been heavily affected by the tone of John's *CT*, imitating his Augustinian self-loathing and desperation for connection with God.

Above all, the monk whose work was most akin to John's *Confessio theologica* was Gerbert of Saint-Wandrille (d. 1089), who left Fécamp to become abbot of Saint-Wandrille from 1063 until 1089.[7] A contemporary of Maurilius, and, like Maurilius, an occasional hermit, Gerbert is the author of *Scriptura* (Writing), an affective meditation on the passion and resurrection of Christ that is only preserved in one late-eleventh-century manuscript from Fécamp.[8] Tellingly, there is evidence of extensive reading of this manuscript at John's monastery: there are *lectio* marks all over the manuscript of Gerbert's work, and, by the thirteenth-century at least, Gerbert's words were read aloud by the abbot of Fécamp to his monks at mealtimes during Easter celebrations, inviting them to recall the events of the Passion that they had just celebrated in the liturgical calendar.[9]

Gerbert's *Scriptura* has elements indicating its composition imitated certain aspects of the *CT*.[10] Gerbert focuses primarily on the scene of the Passion of Christ, and, like John, uses Christ as a trigger to allow the onlooker to recall in his heart (*corde rememorans*) the sacrifice made by Jesus so that he may elicit proper devotional emotion.[11] That emotion is primarily sorrow: the sun and the moon cry over the scene, modelling appropriate feeling for the reader.[12] Like John, Gerbert's goal is also tears for his readers, tears that will parallel the 'gushing fountain' of *caritas* signified by Christ's merciful blood,[13] and these are best modelled by Mary Magdalene.[14] Also like John, Gerbert takes the reader step by step through the flagellation of Jesus and the deposition of his body from the cross, and, perhaps inspired by Fécamp's blood relic, includes details about the collection of Christ's blood by Joseph and Nicodemus.[15] The enumeration of Jesus's torments sounds very much like John's own. Gerbert says:

> And surely you, O good Jesus, did not at all merit thus, who, placed in agony, pray for those to the point of bloody sweat, with drops running to the ground. For soon you are interrogated by the criminal cohort with torments and mockery in examination of [your] reverence. Moreover, stripped of your white woollen robe, you are clothed with a scarlet cloak. That head, which the trembling hand of the Baptist feared, is punctured by the thorn of a wild crown. In your benedictional right hand rustles a reed for a sceptre. Gloria! Hence false adorers with bended knee, with haughty hearts, offer to the king of the Jews the hail of the Caesars ... but the font of mercy saturates with an overflow of love.[16]

John, similarly, says:

> He was tested so that we might be freed from under the yoke of demonic servitude. He was captured so that he might carry us captive from the hand of the enemy. He was sold, so that he might redeem us by his own blood. He was despoiled, so that he might clothe us with the robe of immortality. He was mocked so that he might keep us from the taunts of demons. He was crowned with thorns so that he might pluck from us completely the thorns and thistles of original sin. He was humiliated so that he might lift us up. He was lifted up on the cross in order that he might draw us up to himself. He was made drunk with gall and vinegar so that we could enter into a land of constant joy. He was sacrificed as a lamb without blemish on the altar of the cross so that he might remove the sins of the world. For all these things I give you thanks and magnify your name, O holy Father, by whose marvellous dispensation providence was done, so that only the lion of the tribe of Judah might loose and open the book which no one was able to open.[17]

In the passages above, Gerbert and John both dwell on the torments that Christ endured on his way to the crucifixion. But Gerbert notably does not imitate John's tone. While John details the ultimate importance of each torment in the third person, finally ending with a praiseful first-person prayer, Gerbert observes with disbelief the torments in the second person, using his immediate, dramatic observations to elicit an emotional response in the viewer. Despite the parallels with John's *CT*, Gerbert has ultimately evolved beyond his former abbot, eliminating the anagogical and tropological explanations of Christ's suffering and the prayerful thanks from the reader, and allowing the scene of the Passion to stand on its own and the reader to directly address God in the second person. This is one of the chief ways in which later writers embracing 'affective piety' differed from John. While John's pairing of strife-filled tone and Passion vignettes was an attempt to inspire true emotional *conversio* in his reader, later authors like Gerbert merely presented tableaus of Christ's suffering to the reader without explanation. What John had to explain in his *CT* about the parallels between Christ's suffering and the reader's proper devotional emotions had become self-evident in the later periods of the Middle Ages.

John's material legacy at Fécamp

The cult of the Precious Blood (from 1064 to 1171 and beyond)

One of the most significant elaborations on John's devotional ideals at his own monastery was Fécamp's cult of the Precious Blood of Christ. The story of Fécamp's relic of the Precious Blood was not widely popular until the late twelfth century, about a century after John's death. The relic itself was not officially 'discovered' at the abbey until 1171, when Abbot Henry of Sully (1140–87) found the relic in a church wall during a renovation campaign; yet, thirteenth-century *jongleurs* at Fécamp claimed that the relic was in fact 'rediscovered' by Henry, and that it had an earlier life dating back to Duke Richard I.[18] Indeed, there is significant evidence of the relic dating to at least the late eleventh century. Baudril of Bourgueil (c. 1050–1130), bishop of Dol, mentions the relic in a letter to the monks of Fécamp composed between 1107 and 1120.[19] Three miracles surrounding a relic of the Precious Blood were recorded in a miracle collection at Fécamp between 1089 and 1107.[20] The Fécamp chronicle, dated between 1079 and 1094, mentions a blood relic and its role in the foundation of the monastery.[21] Archaeological evidence of pilgrimage to Fécamp – perhaps to the blood relic – dates from as early as 1064.[22] A few scholars even suggest that the relic was in continuous use from 996 onwards.[23] These hints of an eleventh-century relic in the Fécamp source record at least suggest that a relic of the Precious Blood became increasingly part of the culture at Fécamp from the late eleventh century on, in the period when John of Fécamp's memory may have been freshest in the minds of his monks.

A late-eleventh-century relic of the blood of Christ is not a very common occurrence – only ten in Europe originate before the year 1100. Their incidence increased thereafter: twenty such relics existed in Europe by the end of the twelfth century, and by the end of the fifteenth century, there were twenty blood relics in Germany alone.[24] Furthermore, Fécamp's relic was the first of its kind in the north of France, a pioneer for the Anglo-Norman world and its neighbouring regions. What, then, is the explanation for this relatively precocious medieval materialisation at Fécamp? Several scholars have answered this question by considering the political context for the Fécamp relic, the use of such a relic in combating the Berengar of Tours Eucharistic heresy, and Fécamp's contact with blood relic stories from around medieval Europe.[25] These studies have concluded that the blood cult at Fécamp was imposed by outsiders on the monastery: they claim that the dukes gave the blood relic to the monastery to increase their power, or that the pope worked to clamp down on the Berengarian heresy by disseminating blood relics to reassert the real presence[26]; or that *jongleurs* composed the relic's legend to increase their fame. But no scholar has yet considered how the relic might have been an acquisition initiated by the monks at Fécamp – how the procurement of a blood relic might have been a natural extension of the devotional practices already present at the monastery, established by John in the eleventh century. Certainly the relic had political efficacy for the dukes, anti-heretical power for the pope, and entertainment value for the *jongleurs*; but when we examine the relic in the light of the devotional culture practised by the monks of Fécamp in the eleventh century, the meaning of the blood relic is much enriched, gaining a religious significance beyond the political, the anti-heretical, and the commercial, instead becoming a materialisation of John's devotional ideas.

The legend of Fécamp's relic of the Precious Blood starts in the time of Christ. After handling Jesus's body during the crucifixion, Joseph of Arimathea (or, depending on the account, Nicodemus[27]) gave a vial of the blood of Christ to his son Isaac for safe-keeping.[28] Isaac, fearful that his Roman countrymen would accuse him of performing Christian idolatry, decided to remove the vial from his house and concealed it in the trunk of a fig tree, which he then placed in the Mediterranean Sea. With the help of God, the fig tree floated to safety from the eastern Mediterranean to the coast of Normandy, where it implanted on the shore in the town of Fécamp. After many years, in the late tenth century, the relic was finally discovered by Richard I, duke of Normandy, who immediately erected an abbey in the field of the fig tree. He appropriately named the abbey *Fiscampus* (fig tree; in French, Fécamp), and buried the relic in the altar of the new abbey church. The relic was then lost for a while, and ceremoniously reclaimed in 1171 when Abbot Henry found it in the abbey church's wall.

Despite the relic's widespread popularity after its rediscovery in the late twelfth century, sources suggest that there was an increased veneration of the relic among monks at Fécamp after John's death specifically. We know this in part from the miracle collections, letters, and chronicles from Fécamp mentioned above, created in the years after John's death in 1079. But we also know this because of John's student, Herbert Losinga (d. 1119), who was briefly prior of Fécamp under John before leaving the monastery, eventually becoming bishop of Norwich in 1091.[29] Upon arriving at Norwich, Herbert sent a letter to Fécamp, asking the monastery to send two monks to England so that Herbert, with their help, could better implement Fécamp's customs for Norwich's cathedral canons.[30] Among Norwich's late-eleventh-century liturgical imports from Fécamp in that moment were an Easter sepulchre drama,[31] a blood relic, and a special mass to the Precious Blood (implying that the latter two were present at Fécamp by 1091).[32] Twelve years after John's death, then, a blood relic was exported from his monastery to that of his former student.

Herbert was not the only one of John's students who was interested in the blood: Maurilius of Rouen and Gerbert of Saint-Wandrille had made a pilgrimage to a blood relic in Lucca soon after leaving Fécamp but before taking up their other Norman posts.[33] Furthermore, two monasteries in Fécamp's network during John's time, Glastonbury and Bec, also acquired blood relics by the early twelfth century.[34] This increased veneration in the late eleventh century by monks and houses connected closely with John strongly suggest that the blood relic at Fécamp was somehow linked to the devotional programme developed by John of Fécamp.

As we have seen in proceeding chapters, blood figures prominently in John's *Confessio theologica*'s prescriptions for how its reader might move beyond exterior practices of devotion and cultivate the right 'interior sense of [his] soul'.[35] For John, the blood of Christ is the key point of divine access for the sinner: 'It is by [Christ's] blood that we have access to [God], both in one spirit.'[36] John believes that the blood of Christ grants the sinner access to God in three different ways. First, the blood of Christ promises the sinner access to heaven – Christ sheds his blood for the sinner, so that the sinner may be saved.[37] Second, to John, the blood of Christ is an emblem of the sinner's communion with God and a promise that God will grant the sinner the necessary grace for salvation.[38] John's third and most innovative use for Christ's blood is that he sees it as essential in fostering proper contrition in the sinner. By calling the bloody wounds of Christ to mind, John believes one can inspire proper lamentation in oneself.[39] In John's conception, the image of Christ's wounds in turn wound the sinner's own heart, making the sinner suffer in parallel with Christ: as blood flows from Christ's wounds on the cross, tears inspired by the scene of the crucifixion should flow from the repentant sinner's heart, putting him in a state of lamentation worthy enough for God.[40]

Christ's bloody body was also promoted as a tool for instigating this process elsewhere in Fécamp's devotional culture, as has been discussed.[41] Texts beyond the *CT* in the Fécamp library and liturgy referred to the suffering and blood of the crucified body, often using them as tools for prayer in the way that John prescribed. Most dramatically, the Easter play's Good Friday *depositio* drama featured the bloody body of Christ.[42] In the *depositio*, the celebrant (who was, at Fécamp, the abbot) imitated the events after the crucifixion, taking the cross down from the altar, cradling and kissing the body of Christ on the cross, and then burying the cross in a sepulchre.[43] With the blood cult, the abbot's deposition of Christ on Good Friday would have had special resonance: it depicted the moment when the blood relic was obtained from the body of Jesus. The abbot, taking down Jesus's body, would have been identified with Joseph of Arimathea or Nicodemus, deposer of the body of the suffering Christ *and* the procurer of the precious blood for Fécamp. Right after the dramatic burial of Christ's cross during the *depositio* drama, the abbot chanted the line 'Pilate said: I am innocent of the blood of this just man; you see to it.'[44] This text comes from Matthew 27:24, when Pilate washes his own hands, and it may have seemed to the monks that the abbot actually had some of Jesus's blood on his hands, and needed to wash them.[45]

While the *CT* would have been a prescription of John's devotional method, and the *depositio* drama would have been a performance of that method, the blood relic would have been a manifestation of the method into the material.[46] The majority of scholarly studies of medieval materiality – like the majority of studies about medieval Passion devotion – focus primarily on the Late Middle Ages. Holy matter, like Christ's suffering crucified body, is associated with practices and anxieties of that late period. But what we see here is that the *roots* of these materialisations – like the roots of medieval devotion to the crucified Christ – may have had their origin in earlier medieval devotional practices. While there is no evidence of widespread obsession with material in eleventh-century Fécamp, as in the European centuries to follow, there was a focus on Christ's blood, first in John's writings and then in the form of a relic. The *thing* of Christ's blood at Fécamp that existed into the Late Middle Ages grew from a contemplative *purpose* developed in the eleventh century.

John's legacy among younger Norman contemporaries (from 1072 to 1115)

Anselm of Bec and Guibert of Nogent

Like his students, John's younger contemporaries outside of Fécamp were inspired by John's contemplative method, building on his work in their own contexts in the later eleventh and early twelfth centuries. Robert of Tomblaine (fl. 1063–82), for instance, wrote a commentary on the Song of Songs, incorporating themes also embraced by John in his *CT*.[47] But the two most famous Norman followers of John are Anselm of Bec and Guibert of Nogent. Anselm, prior at Bec in 1063 before becoming abbot there in 1078, wrote his prayers and meditations while John was still alive, and likely after Bec had received an excerpted copy of John's own *CT*.[48] Guibert was a young monk at the monastery of Saint-Germer-de-Fly, a monastery in Fécamp's network, and went on to study with Anselm before becoming abbot of Nogent-sous-Coucy and writing his *Monodies*.[49] By reflecting on how the works of these two more famous medieval figures were indebted to John's influence, we can both secure John's importance as a contributor to the development of medieval devotion and reflect on how John's piety, affectivity, and confessional stances differ from these later Norman iterations.

Despite running in the same Norman monastic circles, there is no hard evidence that Anselm knew John personally, though some hopeful scholars have suggested that Anselm studied with John before settling down as Lanfranc's student in 1059.[50] This is possible, given the strength of the Italian monks' network in Normandy, but there is no proof: though letters exist between Anselm and other Italians recruited by William of Volpiano, no letters between the two monks survive; Anselm writes only to John's successor at Fécamp.[51] It is also hard to prove that Anselm had read the entirety of John's *CT*, especially since Anselm does not use any of John's phrases directly in his writings.[52] There is, however, a very strong possibility that Anselm encountered at least pieces of John's *CT*: I have argued elsewhere that an eleventh-century manuscript containing John's prayers to the crucified Christ was at Bec in Anselm's time.[53] Moreover, the argument that Anselm was aware of John's work in one way or another is only strengthened by comparisons between their writings.[54] Certainly those compiling Anselmian prayers in the later Middle Ages saw John and Anselm (and even others like Maurilius of Rouen) as part of the same tradition.[55]

Anselm composed his *Prayers and Meditations* piecemeal before he was elevated to the abbacy of Bec in 1078, sending them out individually to his friends at the request of laywomen and fellow monks before ultimately compiling the entire collection for Countess Matilda of Tuscany in 1104. Unlike his later more polemical and theological works, Anselm's prayers were not intended to be read for arguments, but instead for 'the sake of the emotions that they were intended to stir'.[56] The intention behind both Anselm's prayers and John's *CT* was therefore the same: both authors spoke of their works as devices for (in Anselm's words) 'stir[ring] up the mind of the reader into the love or fear of God, or to self-examination'.[57] Much as John wanted a 'little compilation of readings for your praise, in order that I might always have a short and handy word about God with me, and from the fire of reading it, as many times as I grow cool, I may be reignited in your love',[58] Anselm hopes that God will 'turn my lukewarmness into a fervent love of you'.[59] Both authors use language of warming and cooling to describe their prayer.[60] Both Anselm's prayers and John's *CT* are intended to be affective – they are tools to affect 'heat' and to affect a love of and emotional closeness to God. As the abbot of La Chaise-Dieu says in a letter to Anselm after receiving his prayers:

> [These prayers are] where you [Anselm] uttered and wrote very conscientiously about your contrite spirit and about the devotion of your contrite heart: these works show us your devoted tears when we read them and bring forth ours so that we marvel at both ... The devotion of your written prayer arouses in us the devotion of slumbering compunction to such an extent that we rejoice with you, as if by a leap of the mind, by loving those things in you, or rather you in them, and more than them and through them we love God and you.[61]

Much has been made of Anselm's prayers and the 'discovery' of the individual. To Southern, the prayers are the first to provide 'a complete programme of spiritual life in solitude' that make the 'sinner stand alone before God'.[62] But what Southern sees as radical individuation in Anselm also exists for the reader of John's *CT*. Both speakers use a performative first-person pronoun, writing what Bestul has described as a 'text ... [that] does not so much express the inner thoughts of the author, but functions rhetorically by constructing a speaking *exemplum* that an audience can respond to or even model its conduct upon'.[63] The introspection that both authors encourage in their readers is modelled after that of Augustine's *Confessions*,[64] as seen in the extensive self-revulsion, the embarrassed contrasting of the depraved sinner and his gracious God,[65] and the desperate, flailing, obsessively questioning rhetoric ('What shall I say? What shall I do? Whither shall I go? Where shall I seek him? Where and when shall I find him? Whom shall I ask? Who will tell me of my beloved?'[66]). Neither Anselm nor John allows his readers to rest, because, in Augustine's words, 'our hearts are restless until they rest in you [God]'.[67] Still, neither Augustine nor John nor Anselm is interested in seeking a *particular* self in his writings; rather, the performative 'I' of their texts serves every audience member, since all humans, they each argue, require a continual *conversio*.[68] Like John, Anselm asks in his *Prayer to Mary* for her to avert her face so that the speaker can make a *conversionem*,[69] and he asks Saint Benedict for a 'continual turning' and a *sanctae conversationis*.[70] Both Anselm and John fill their works with weepy, ceaseless desire, hopeful for at least a partial turning through the mercy of God.[71]

But there are features that distinguish Anselm's work from John's. In most of his prayers, Anselm chiefly embraces one technique of John's *CT*: the use of highly emotional scenes and dramatic images of biblical figures, particularly the scenes proximate to the crucified Christ. Anselm says that 'by remembering and meditating on the good things you have done I may be enkindled with your love';[72] he constantly asks his reader to 'recall', 'consider', 'ponder', or 'remember' certain scenes. While there were *moments* in the *CT* when John created an atmosphere that allowed the reader to imagine a biblical scene,[73] Anselm *regularly* envisions scenes from the Bible and of biblical exemplars for his readers. In his *Prayer to Mary Magdalene*, for instance, Anselm, like John, highlights the Magdalene's emotional response and the virtue of her grief; but John does not ask his readers to bear witness to her actions as if she was standing right in front of them, as Anselm does: 'See how she anxiously burns with desire for you, searching, questioning, but nowhere does that which she seeks appear.'[74] Like John's student Gerbert of Saint-Wandrille, Anselm takes his vision of the crucifixion beyond that of John, focusing on the scene's atmospheric details without explanation, and he goes even farther than Gerbert does in immersing the reader in the emotion of the scene.

John paves the way for Anselm: he explains the emotional mechanisms at work in devotion in his *CT*, drawing parallels between the sinner's body and Christ's to elicit suffering, occasionally bombarding the reader with images to elicit compassion and proper contrition. Ultimately, though, John's *CT*'s chief goal is to *explain* how the reader must embark on an emotional journey in order to achieve the mental and emotional excitation necessary and, through explanation, agitate the reader towards practising devotional emotion. Anselm, in contrast, is more incisive: he creates tightly packaged prayers, favouring 'memory-sized pieces'[75] of biblical scenes, focusing John's meandering desire to draw parallels between the suffering Christ and the sinner by dropping the reader into the scene – into the very shoes of a witness. Anselm directly talks the reader through the process of emotional empathy, asking: 'Would that I with happy Joseph, might have taken down my Lord from the cross, wrapped him in spiced grave-clothes and laid him in the tomb ... would that with the blessed band of women I might have trembled at the vision of angels and have heard the news of the Lord's Resurrection, news of my consolation, so much looked for, so much desired.'[76] Less exposition about the interior journey and its pitfalls is required for Anselm. Taking the need for introspection and the futility of a sinner's aspirations as a given, Anselm performs and makes physical the emotions required through the scenes of his prayers in a way more akin to John's abbatial performance of the *depositio* drama than to John's *CT*. Anselm's prayers therefore effect the same 'revolution in sentiment' that John does;[77] they breach the distance between God and the sinner, as the *CT* does;[78] but they do so more through vision than exposition.

There is another difference between Anselm and John: Anselm's prayers evidence a confidence in potential union with the divine that is not in John's writing: Anselm 'loses God ... [but] God does not lose him'.[79] John's self-debasement and insecurity is final, hopeless, permanent – he feels that such humility is necessary to effect the desired actions in his readers and himself. John is a theorist of emotion. He is fascinated by how these devotional emotions work, how to elicit them, how easily they are lost, how impermanent they are when fleetingly found; but he remains anxious about whether they will be well received by God. Anselm, in contrast, is ultimately interested in the logic of atonement, and the potential for union of God through that cleansing. To Anselm, 'the sinner can make a giant leap from the depths of hellish despair to a sense of entitlement to heavenly communion. The entitlement, however, is grounded in the addressee's greatness and mercy rather than in the sinner's merits or even lack of demerits.'[80] Because of Anselm's assurance in the absolute greatness and goodness of God, the absolute depravity of the sinner does not stand in his way. As he confidently says in his *Prayer to Saint Stephen*: 'Your merits are great, great Stephen, so that they can suffice for you and me.'[81] Such sufficiency and self-assuredness is foreign to John; but it appears to be the logical conclusion for Anselm (and his student Guibert of Nogent). It creates the possibility of the mystical union that inspired so many later medieval readers and writers.

At the heart of John's connection to Guibert of Nogent, besides that which was transmitted through Anselm, lies John's unique interest in Augustine's *Confessions* and his likely dissemination of the work around Normandy.[82] By the twelfth century, Fécamp's copy of *Confessions* had been passed around the Norman network.[83] Several medieval authors famous for drawing extensively from the *Confessions* were likely inspired by these Norman copies: Gilbert Crespin's (1055–1117) *vita* of Herluin of Bec (1034–78) is structured around the theme of the *conversio*[84] to the monastic life, drawing from motifs present in Augustine's *Confessions*;[85] Ivo of Chartres (1040–1115, and a former monk of Bec) and Robert of Saint-Quentin (d. c. 1134) both quoted the *Confessions* extensively in their writings;[86] Baudril of Bourgueil, bishop of Dol and a correspondent of the monks of Fécamp, wrote a letter to prior Peter of Jumièges (fl. 1154–1169) modelled in the style of the *Confessions*;[87] and Goscelin of Saint-Bertin's (d. c. 1107) *Liber confortatorius* was written at the Flemish abbey of Saint-Bertin (a house which exchanged manuscripts with Norman monasteries), and recommends Augustine's *Confessions* as a model for meditation.[88] But no example is more famous than that of Guibert of Nogent's *Monodies*.

Guibert's *Monodies* had an extremely small circulation in the Middle Ages, surviving in no medieval copies and in only a few post-medieval ones.[89] Jay Rubenstein has observed that Guibert's notoriety as a medieval author is actually a modern construction, as more recent historians have embraced him as a 'modern' medieval who displayed his psychology and neuroses in a way that made him a man before his time.[90] Rubenstein has worked to demonstrate how Guibert was a product of the medieval context; Guibert's affinity for the *Confessions* seems to make him more specifically a product of his *Norman* medieval context, resulting from his time at Fly and his tutelage by Anselm.[91]

Like John's *Confessio theologica*, the *Monodies* showcases a medieval monk's conception of his own inner life. In his autobiography, Guibert, reminiscent of John, begins by listing his 'relentless depravities' caused in part by his 'hardened heart'.[92] Like John, Anselm, and Augustine before him, Guibert knows that because he 'always sin[s]', a 'return' (i.e. a *conversio*) to God is always required.[93] In a way akin to John and Augustine, he reflects: '[I]sn't it more salubrious to struggle towards you [God] for a while, to find rest in you even for a moment, than to forget the remedy completely and despair of your grace?'[94] Like John in his *CT*, the challenge that comes up again and again in Guibert's life is being 'placed by God face to face with ourselves, [so] we [can] look into our consciences'.[95] Humans, Guibert acknowledges, despite their depravities, can always recognise their failings as a first step in an effort 'coming to recognise [God] after [episodes of] inner drunkenness'.[96] John would agree.

Though John and Guibert both use Augustine as a model for repetitive attempts at returning to God through self-reflective prayer, theirs are very different books, perhaps reflective of the changes that had occurred in the century between their composition. While Guibert begins his *Monodies* with the word *confiteor* (I confess) – an explicit allusion to Augustine's text[97] – this particular choice immediately reveals the key difference between Guibert and the abbot of Fécamp. Neither Augustine's *Confessions* nor John's *CT* begins immediately with a first-person confession; instead, both begin with extensive prayers praising the greatness of God.[98] In contrast, Guibert upholds *himself* as an ethical example for his readers (much as his contemporary Abelard did).[99] The object of Guibert's text is not to praise God – it is to chronicle the events of his life. While Book 1 of *Monodies* contains prayerful addresses to the divine, they die out steadily until, by Books 3 and 4, they are completely absent, overtaken by his details of events around his world. God serves merely as one of the witnesses to Guibert's tales, almost like any other onlooker. Occasionally, Guibert interrupts the narrative to tell God directly how he wants his readers to understand his book, saying, for instance, 'I am telling this, my God, not to brand such a good friend with a mark of disgrace, but to make every reader understand that I do not want them to take everything I say for certain.'[100] At other times, Guibert casually reflects on how God has provided for him, without the effusive thanks or gratitude that would have been given by John: 'I remember well the inestimable generosity you displayed to me then.'[101] But this still sharply contrasts with John and Augustine, for whom God is the chief witness and constant addressee in their works. One explanation for this distinction is that Guibert is writing an autobiography about an individual (himself), rather than writing a more universal treatise that anyone could adopt for himself (like John).[102] Yet, this also reflects a difference between John's and Guibert's interpretation of Augustine's *Confessions*. John holds onto Augustine's relapsing–remitting piety as universal, acknowledging the limits of self-knowledge despite its necessity, and addressing God with the humble awareness of his limitations. Distinctively, Guibert adopts Augustine's autobiographical exposition of an individual life, indulging a self-assurance and a self-promotion that John's ideal reader would never dare to assume.[103] While John uses a performative first-person pronoun in his *CT* to allow his reader to better adopt the actions prescribed, he tempers that 'I' with many second-person addresses and prostrations before God; yet, for Guibert, the 'I' is what confidently dominates his text. In the early eleventh century, John attempts an intervention among his readers, teaching them that they (like Augustine) barely know themselves, and urging them to perform introspective prayer in order to attempt to pay God his due; by the early twelfth century, Guibert acknowledges his inadequacy as a sinner quickly, and then moves on to the task of introspection to assert his confidence in eventual union with God (like Anselm) and his righteous analyses of the events around him (like Abelard).

John's legacy among Cistercian readers (from 1100 onwards)

Caritas *and the suffering Christ in Cistercian affective piety*

In scholarship on affective devotion, Cistercians are the second most widely promoted originators of such piety after Anselm. Bernard of Clairvaux and

Aelred of Rievaulx have 'long been recognized' as emotive contemplators of the Passion, who believed that such contemplation was the 'starting place' for the love of God.[104] John's *Confessio theologica* has in fact survived in several copies from Cistercian houses, suggesting that, at certain places, John's work helped to fuel the Cistercian propensity to dwell on the physicality of Christ and to cry over his wounds.[105] I would argue, however, that, equal to John's Passion devotion, Cistercians may have found John's embrace of *caritas* as a salutary emotion particularly resonant with their own approach.[106] More than the traditional monks who had come before, the Cistercian order, formed in 1098, believed that *caritas* – a suffering love for God – was the *chief* Christian concern. As individual monks living in community with others, and as advisers to clerics, aristocrats, knights, and rulers in the outside world, Cistercians regularly gave advice laced with *caritas*, often correcting others harshly in order to save them. Following the mission statement of their order contained in the *carta caritatis* (the Charter of Charity),[107] Cistercian monks would often invoke *caritas* when counselling others on their Christian behaviour, and their *caritas* would often adopt an aggressive valence, as a kind of enforced brotherly love for the good of the morality of Christendom.[108] Like John's advice to the disobedient monks living as hermits or to the abbot Warin of Metz, Cistercians like Bernard of Clairvaux often antagonised (or verbally harmed) fellow Christians in order to help them ultimately achieve salvation.[109]

As Cistercian philosophy developed over the course of the twelfth century, however, the Cistercian ideal of *caritas* gradually became less corrective (as John of Fécamp's was) and closer to a more modern idea of 'charity'.[110] In the later twelfth century, Aelred of Rievaulx (1110–67) redefined *caritas* as a way to recognise the suffering of other human beings and to extend oneself towards the less fortunate.[111] Because Cistercians were joining the monastery as adult converts of their own free will, their charity towards others was also about regularly engaging their will to do what was difficult,[112] often engaging, for instance, in a penitential practice of caring for the poor or the sick.[113] After the Third Lateran Council (1179) required monks to actively participate in tending to the growing population of urban poor, a revolution in institutionalised charity took place in medieval Europe,[114] one that was solidified with the dawn of the Franciscan order's spiritual poverty.[115] John's notion of *caritas* therefore reinforced and perhaps augmented the initial Cistercian conceptions of charity, but, by the thirteenth century, John's notion of *caritas* was no longer embraced by medieval Cistercians.

This transformation in the Cistercian conception of *caritas* also aligns with a transformation in the Cistercian explication of Passion meditation.

Aelred of Rievaulx paired his changing conception of *caritas* (now about empathising with the less fortunate) with a new empathy with the suffering of the crucified Christ, who Aelred suggested was exemplary for his empathy to the point of self-sacrifice.[116] To Aelred, just as Jesus chose to be crucified in commiseration with the needs of humankind, so too did humans need to imagine themselves next to the foot of the cross, filled with compassion for Christ's suffering.[117] *Caritas* was godly love to Aelred not because tearful suffering directed Christians towards godly emotion (as in John's *Confessio theologica*), but instead because tearful suffering was a kind of charitable empathy for Christ. The definition of *caritas* and the interpretation of Passion devotion's use went hand in hand – as *caritas* became more about empathy with the suffering of others, so too did Passion devotion. As with the medieval conception of *caritas*, once the Franciscan conception of Passion devotion (the *imitatio Christi*) dominated the medieval scene in the thirteenth century, John's definitions of *caritas* and Passion devotion became vestigial, no longer accurate to medieval Christian practice. So while Cistercian medieval ideas of *caritas* and devotion to the suffering Christ were supplemented and encouraged by John's writings early on, by the thirteenth century, these two concepts had been so altered by later Cistercians and Franciscans that they would have been unrecognisable to John.

John's reception in the Late Middle Ages (from 1100 to 1500)

By just a generation after John's death, his *Confessio theologica*'s attitudes might have read as old-fashioned, overly insecure or overly expository. Why, then, was such an outdated text read *hundreds* of years after John's death, in the later Middle Ages? John's *CT* indeed circulated widely over the course of the Middle Ages, but it quickly took a different form from that initially composed by John in the eleventh century, precisely to suit a newer, more confident audience.

In the eleventh and twelfth centuries, John's *Confessio theologica* usually circulated in its entirety in its several recensions among a primarily monastic readership. But, from the late twelfth century onwards, it exclusively circulated in reorganised and reattributed fragments, often appended to collections of meditations and prayers credited to Augustine, Anselm, or Bernard of Clairvaux, and read by both religious and lay people alike. In its later medieval circulation, John's work was still read for devotional edification, but with different emphases. When read in the monastery in the eleventh and twelfth centuries, John's *CT* served as a *lectio divina*-style advice manual for monks and nuns pursuing contemplative ends, a prefatory warm-up to rekindle the heart and the mind before praying. When collected and read in fragments in the later Middle Ages, John's work transformed into a series of focused, short, confessional meditations on Christ. What began its medieval life as a lengthy treatise explaining and modelling a particular devotional technique, with a clear message about the value of tears and the emotions appropriate to prayer, had evolved into a series of brief meditations, sometimes in the confessional style of Augustine and sometimes sounding more like the experiential writings of Anselm and later medieval 'affective' writers. In these excerpts, the original message of John's *CT* was often lost: the focus on the technique of prayer was eliminated, and a new confidence in mystical union could be read into John's work. John's writing, in the later Middle Ages, became another tool for feeling close to God, like Anselm's prayers; but, when fragmented, it lost the full effect of its frenzied uncertainty and emotional methodology. Below, I will examine the *CT*'s reception during that period. First, I will detail how John's work came to mean something different to its later medieval readers than it did for its eleventh-century ones. Then I will show how John's work was an anonymous force behind more famous later medieval affective texts and images, making an important and specific contribution to the medieval devotion practised after John's time.

Late in John's life and immediately after his death, the *Confessio theologica* circulated primarily to monasteries in Fécamp's network. The manuscripts that survive from the late eleventh century were made for Saint-Bénigne de Dijon, Bec, Saint-Arnoul de Metz, and other houses closely affiliated with Fécamp.[118] While the majority of these manuscripts were complete versions of the *CT*, *Libellus*, or *Confessio fidei* recensions, the one exception to this is the version of the *CT* sent to Bec, which excerpted pieces of John's *CT* dealing with the crucified Christ, creating four prayers that later became an essential piece of the *Meditations of St Augustine*.[119] This edition, likely made in the last years of John's life or just after his death, was a taste of what was to come: John's future circulation would most often be in the form of shortened prayers, and the most successful excerpts of John's work to survive would be those depicting and reflecting on the image of the crucified Christ.

By the twelfth century, John's *Confessio theologica* still circulated in its entirety to monasteries rather than in excerpts, and its reach began to extend to houses beyond John's personal network.[120] Two manuscripts from present-day Austria, Vienna, Österreichische Nationalbibliothek, Cods 1580 and 1582,[121] paired the *CT* with Smaragdus's *Diadema monastica* and Ephraem's *De compunctione cordis*, placing John's work alongside others aiming to fortify monastic practices of compunction and contemplation.[122] These twelfth-century codices reveal how John's writing was still considered useful to monastic audiences in a way akin to its original usage: like Smaragdus's and Ephraem's works, John's work was seen as effective in instructing monks in contemplative practice.[123] A reader of Vienna, Österreichische Nationalbibliothek, Cod. 1580 even wrote anonymous prayers in an unprofessional hand in the margins of fols 66v–67r and 78v–79r, elaborating on the very themes that John himself adopted from these earlier texts, like the gift of tears. John's intention to 'reignite' love of God to inspire engagement in prayer seems to have still been apt for at least two houses among his twelfth-century monastic readers.

Another twelfth-century manuscript of John's *Confessio theologica* also collects the text in its entirety, adding a prefatory illumination which serves as a gloss, hinting at its contemporaries' interpretations of John's work. Barcelona, Archivo de la Corona de Aragón, Ripoll ms. 214 is a manuscript made for Santa Maria de Ripoll in Catalonia, a monastery strongly connected with William of Volpiano, if not with John himself.[124] Fol. 6v of Ripoll ms. 214 depicts a tonsured monk, kneeling in adoration of an enthroned Christ who presents himself to the viewer and adoring monk in a mandorla (Figure 6).[125] Christ is here seated on a heavenly throne, holding a book in one hand and making a gesture of blessing with the other, surrounded by the symbols of the four evangelists, who are all in turn holding their own Gospel books and looking confidently and directly at Jesus. The monk, in contrast, does not look directly at Jesus; he instead turns his head towards the viewer so that we can see his expression of uncertainty and contrition; his humble, pathetic visage is paired with his gesture of humility and obedience, as he kneels with his knees together, crouching with his back rounded, his eyes straining upwards, and his hands lifted to God.[126] The posture of the monk suggests he is almost embarrassed, in contrast with the assured, adoring stares of the evangelists surrounding Christ, their books serving as badges of merit that they present to Christ proudly. Their hands are full, but the monk's hands are empty, which only further emphasises the unworthiness of the monk as he kneels before God. The image of the monk in Ripoll, ms. 214 instructs the manuscript's reader that God should be approached with the same amount of pathetic self-regard that the monk has here (and that John's text insists upon). Such a prefatory illumination was therefore quite faithful to its author's prescriptions a century after his death.[127]

An image preceding another twelfth-century manuscript, Zwettl, Stiftsbibliothek, Cod. 164, hints at how John's text began to be reinterpreted

Figure 6 Tonsured monk before an enthroned Christ in a twelfth-century *Confessio theologica*

in the twelfth century and beyond (Figure 7).[128] On the one hand, prayer is again a goal for *Zwettl* 164's compilers: as in earlier manuscripts, Anselm's and Bernard's prayers follow after John's *Confessio theologica* in the manuscript, relying on John's words to prepare the reader for prayer.[129] But *Zwettl* 164's opening image directs readers to what *later* medieval Christians will *most* value about the *CT*: its meditations on the crucified Christ. *Zwettl* 164's prefatory illumination is a quintessential *Christus patiens* image: the cross is a simple outline in red; Jesus's body, outlined in black, is that of a dead man, with head slumped and eyes closed, with wounds that bleed simple red lines of blood from hands, feet, and side. While John's other *exempla* (the crying Mary Magdalene and Hannah, for instance) were equally useful in John's *CT*, *Zwettl* 164 solely highlights the crucified Christ for the later medieval reader. In the fourteenth century, this Zwettl image was further annotated with texts directing the reader to the image and to meditate on the Passion. Such a focus on the Passion would become a mainstay in later medieval devotion, and also in the ways that later medieval people read John of Fécamp.

After the twelfth century, John's work was chiefly read as Augustine's, reattributed because it was included in two compilations of short meditations: the *Manuale* and the *Meditations* of Pseudo-Augustine. Both the *Manuale* and the *Meditations* were predominantly composed of texts taken directly from John's *Confessio theologica*, excerpted and repurposed as short meditations (in a way similar to those found in the eleventh-century Bec manuscript[130]). Cédric Giraud has observed that these selections drew chiefly from passages in John's *CT* that either praised or longed for God directly (i.e. the passages that are the most prayerlike and the most reminiscent of Augustine's *Confessions*) or that depicted the crucified Christ.[131] This focus on John's most prayerful passages makes sense, since both of these pseudo-Augustinian texts were filled exclusively with prayers (repackaged from Anselm, Hugh of Saint-Victor, Bernard of Clairvaux, and others as well as John). And yet, several essential aspects of John's work are lost in these collections: the emphasis on the depravity of the sinner is lessened; the teachings on tears are severely diminished; the instructive purpose and emotional focus are lost; the *exempla* of Mary Magdalene and Hannah are omitted; and, absent continuous prose, John's flailing narrative is missing, diminishing the effect of the *CT*'s original *Confessions*-like air of desperation. In these pseudo-Augustinian editions, John's *CT* is forced into a mould that is more like Anselm's prayers than Ephraem's, Smaragdus's or Gregory's prose manuals for prayer.

Still, these pseudo-Augustinian prayer collections were extremely influential in later medieval devotional practice, circulating extensively in

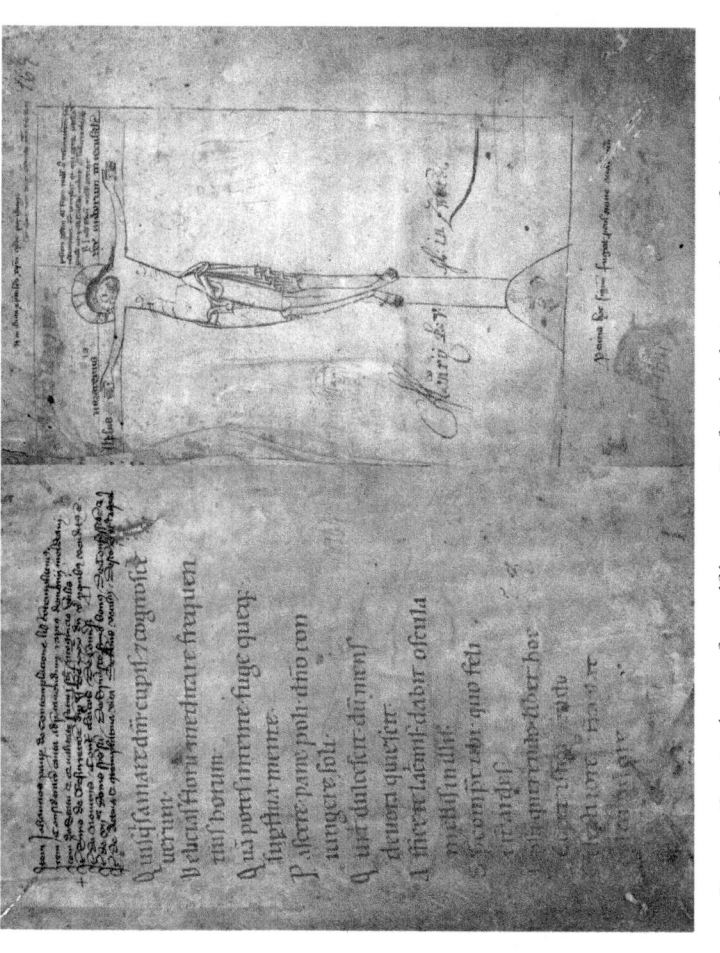

Figure 7 Opening leaves of a twelfth-century *Confessio theologica*, with crucifix dating from twelfth century on the right and fourteenth-century Passion meditations on the left

the Late Middle Ages in small books intended for individual reading.[132] The *Manuale*, a compilation of short meditations, circulated in over 450 manuscripts between the thirteenth and fifteenth centuries, for monastic and lay readers alike.[133] The *Meditations*, for which Metz, Médiathèque, ms. 245 and *Paris* 13593 are the oldest (albeit partial) witnesses, circulated in 115 Latin manuscripts before the sixteenth century, and in even more vernacular manuscripts after it was translated for lay devotees.[134] Jean Gerson, Thomas à Kempis, and the writers of the *Devotio moderna* were all heavily influenced by the confessional tone and emotional attitude of the prayers of the *Manuale* and *Meditations*, and therefore were directly (though unknowingly) indebted to John of Fécamp, the first medieval writer to embrace the voice of Augustine's *Confessions* and to model this particular prayerful attitude.[135] Even Fécamp had a copy of the *Manuale* in the thirteenth century, one that was likely used in the practice of confessional prayer in the monastery, since several short confessions were haphazardly transcribed on its final folios in an amateur hand.[136] Therefore, in its late medieval incarnations, even absent its original emotional devotional instruction, John's *CT* had a robust life and influence, although a different influence from that which it exerted in John's own eleventh-century moment.

Perhaps the most famous late medieval manuscript containing John's work is the Rothschild Canticles (New Haven, Yale University, Beinecke Rare Book and Manuscript Library, MS 404), a small devotional manuscript that was illuminated in northern France around 1300 (Figure 8). Inspired by (but not a direct copy of) pseudo-Augustinian texts like the *Manuale* and *Meditations*, the Canticles provides its reader with a series of short meditations on a variety of contemplative subjects.[137] Fragments of John's *Confessio theologica* are scattered throughout the enigmatic collection in a unique excerpt found in no other medieval manuscript. Jeffrey Hamburger has shown that it is likely that the compiler of the Canticles even paraphrased some of John's texts from memory rather than transcribing them.[138] It is also likely that the compiler's quotations from both Augustine's *Confessions* and the Song of Songs came by way of John's *CT*, since much of the spirit and focus of the Canticles' collection, and many of the Canticles' quotations from Augustine are also included by John.[139] Hamburger argues that, though John quotes the 'words of the Fathers' extensively, his particular recombination of quotations created a unique product in his *CT* that was then replicated by the Canticles' compiler.[140]

It is not just the words of the Rothschild Canticles that transmit John's ideas, however; it is also the images of the manuscript. The compiler of the manuscript likely designed (if not executed) the celebrated and mysterious

Figure 8 Christ wounded by the Sponsa in the fourteenth-century Rothschild Canticles, fols 18v–19r

miniatures in the Canticles.[141] In fact, Hamburger claims that 'in order to understand the miniatures, the [medieval] viewer had to recognize not only the explicit connection between text and image but also a penumbral area of implicit connections between image and an unspecified range of uncited texts'.[142] Hamburger uses John's uncited *CT* five separate times to tease out the meaning of five different images from the Canticles, claiming that knowledge of John's *CT* would have also helped the medieval reader decipher the meaning of the images. For instance, the idiosyncratic image of the *fons vitae* on fol. 34r is inspired by John's texts describing Christ as the fountain of life from the *CT*, passages which themselves do not appear in the Rothschild Canticles.[143]

The most important example of John's influence on the images from the Canticles is one of the most famous and 'startlingly unconventional' images from the book: that of Christ being wounded by the Sponsa (the bride from the Song of Songs) on fols 18v and 19r (Figure 8).[144] In the image, the Sponsa on fol. 18v thrusts a long lance towards a standing Christ on fol. 19r, peeling back her veil from her face so that she can better guide the lance and see Christ's wound on the opposite page. Christ, in turn, has twisted his head so that he can meet the gaze of the Sponsa, despite being nailed to a cross with his left hand and tied to a pillar with his left foot (many of the *arma Christi*, including the crown of thorns and the whips used by Christ's torturers, also grace the page). In addition to meeting the Sponsa's gaze, he points to his side wound with his right hand, a gesture that both focuses the Sponsa's gaze and also seems to direct the point of her lance to his wound. Several texts have been cited as sources for this inventive image, which has no precedent elsewhere in medieval art: Bonaventure's (1221–74) *De perfectione vitae ad sorores*, which invites women to touch and see the wounds of Christ in order to truly know his love; Bernard's sermon 29 on the Song of Songs, which asks for the wound of Christ's love; Caesarius of Heisterbach's (1180–1240) *Dialogus miraculorum*, which proclaims that the body of a monk must be fastened to a 'cross' by the rigour of the Rule of St Benedict;[145] and John's *Confessio theologica*, whose passage on wounding the sinner and 'piercing' the tough shield of the human heart is akin to the Canticles image.[146] Hamburger claims that, as in John's *CT*, this *ostentatio vulnerum* is a reference to Christ's victory over death[147] and his love and compassion for all Christians, and is intended to inspire visionary experiences in its reader (cf. the Sponsa's gaze).[148] But I would add that the Canticles image also embraces the *reciprocal* wounding desired by the *CT*'s passage – that the Sponsa must pull back her veil to watch the wounding so that her own heart might be wounded. Recall that John summons an image of Christ's wounds not to elicit mystical vision in his readers but rather so that the *sight* of the wounds might effect a wounding of the sinner's own hard heart, so that the image might effect *caritas* in the reader. Jesus guides the Sponsa's gaze to that wounding and redemptive sight – his own wound. Such wounding is parallel to the imagery of Fécamp's 'harming to help' images (Figures 3 and 4): the lance of the Rothschild Canticles recalls the 'darts of compassion' and 'wounds of love' thrust into the heretics by correcting Church Fathers.[149] But, importantly, in the Rothschild Canticles' image, the wounding is desired, but not accomplished: the lance does not touch Christ's wound, rather a distance of two whole page margins and the gully of the book's binding stand between the two. In a gesture more like John than like Anselm or other later medieval writers, union is *not* achieved, and the Sponsa's heart remains unwounded; like the desire expressed in the *CT*, the Sponsa's gaze in the Rothschild Canticles image expresses longing, not a vision fulfilled.

In examining the Rothschild Canticles, we see how John's text served as one of the foundation points for the affective iconographies of the later Middle Ages. In his discussion of the iconography of this Sponsa/Christ lance image, Hamburger cites an image from a late medieval devotional compendium where Christ shoots a 'dart of love' into the hearts of Bernard of Clairvaux and Augustine (Figure 9), arguing that these two medieval saints are chosen as Christ's recipients of such 'darts' because they are the most famous and quintessential emotional devotees from medieval Christianity.[150] In consideration of the role John's work likely played in the creation of the Rothschild Canticles and his work's dissemination alongside Augustine's and Bernard's, however, it seems the compendium's author was remiss in not including John of Fécamp in his illumination. John's *Confessio theologica* – in its entirety, in fragments, or in the 'penumbral area of implicit connections' – was explicitly and implicitly part of the fabric of the devotional prayers and images that constituted the (wounded) heart of late medieval 'affective piety'.

Conclusion

Over the course of this chapter, we have seen how John's *Confessio theologica* and his programme for prayer at Fécamp inspired the writings of Norman monks like Gerbert of Saint-Wandrille, Anselm of Bec, and Guibert of Nogent. We have seen how John's ideas also precipitated a new devotional practice in later medieval Fécamp, namely the devotion to the relic of the Precious Blood of Christ. And we have seen just how flexible John's

Folz est qui scet la droite voie.
Et a son ensaent foruoie.
Cest la lamentation. S. bernart
Et comant il prollec de la gce
nre signour Et. S. augustins
meismes enprollec comāt il se
tort la grace nre signour.

ins ber
nars dit
que la
grace
nostre
signour
Est de
tres grāt
subtillite. Car elle uient subti
lement. Car alz meismes an cui
elle descent ne puer cognostre q͑t
elle uient. ne cant elle en uuit. ne
ne scet dont elle uient ne ou elle
uait. En aucune maniere puet

Figure 9 Bernard and Augustine with Christ's 'darts of love' (thirteenth century)

CT was, allowing later medieval people to excerpt John's work, recasting, reinterpreting, and even silencing it in the light of their own contemporary devotional styles.

John's *Confessio theologica* in its complete eleventh-century form could never have been mistaken as a later medieval work – it was too much in the *lectio divina* style; its scenes of the crucifixion were relatively few and represented just as often as scenes of Mary Magdalene and Hannah; it was explicitly pessimistic about a possible union with Christ in this life; its use of *caritas* was antiquated; and it was unnecessarily expository, not experiential enough for the late medieval audience. This is likely why John's complete *CT* stopped circulating in its entirety by the end of the twelfth century. It is also why medievalists, reading John's *CT* as excerpted by its later medieval editions instead of its more complete, original eleventh-century ones, have mischaracterised John's devotional ideas as wholly analogous to late medieval affective piety. It has been the work of this chapter to instead distinguish John's ideas from those of his later medieval inheritors, while acknowledging how indebted those inheritors may have been to John's work.

Notes

1 See Chapters 3 and 4.
2 Ordericus Vitalis tells us of this work, as quoted in Constable, *Three Studies in Medieval Religious and Social Thought*, p. 180.
3 Arnoux, 'Un Vénitien au Mont-Saint-Michel', pp. 62–4. See also *PL* 149, cols 423–32 (Anastasius's *vita*) and *PL* 149, cols 433–6 (*De veritate corporis et sanguinis Christi Domini*).
4 Maurilius wrote a letter to Bishop William of Evreux with John, see *PL* 143, cols 1387–90, which was collected in a Fécamp manuscript Paris, BnF, ms. lat. 2403, fol. 165; cf. Chapter 4.
5 For more on Maurilius of Rouen, see Louis Violette, 'Une étape décisive dans l'éveil des activités historiographiques au service du siège de Rouen: l'épiscopat de Maurille, moine de Fécamp', *Tabularia* 3 (2003), 57–67; Lucien Musset, 'Observations sur la formation intellectuelle du haut clergé normand (v. 1050–v.1150)', in C.E. Viola (ed.), *Mediaevalia christiana, XIe–XIIIe siècles (hommage à Raymonde Foreville)* (Paris: Éditions universitaires, 1989), pp. 279–89; Monique Dosdat, 'Les évêques normands de 985 à 1150', in Pierre Bouet and François Neveux (eds), *Les évêques normands du XIe siècle* (Caen: Presses universitaires de Caen, 1995), pp. 19–37; Monique Dosdat, Les évêques de la province de Rouen et la vie intellectuelle au XIe siècle', in Pierre Bouet and François Neveux (eds), *Les évêques normands du XIe siècle* (Caen: Presses universitaires de Caen, 1995),

Emotional monasticism

pp. 241–43; Michel de Boüard, 'Notes et hypothèses sur Maurille, moine de Fécamp, et son élection au siège métropolitain de Rouen', in *L'abbaye bénédictine de Fécamp: Ouvrage scientifique du XIIIe centenaire (658–1958)* (Fécamp: EMTN, 1959), vol. I, pp. 81–92; David Douglas, 'The Norman Episcopate before the Norman Conquest', *Cambridge Historical Journal* 13.2 (1957), pp. 106–7.

6 See Bestul (ed.), *A Durham Book of Devotions*, 59–60.
7 *Gazeau*, pp. 338–40. According to chronicles, Gerbert and Maurilius of Rouen were both from Italy and both were temporarily hermits.
8 The manuscript, Paris, BnF, ms. lat. 2628, is detailed in François Dolbeau, 'Passion et résurrection du Christ, selon Gerbert, abbé de Saint-Wandrille (d. 1089)', in Michael W. Herren, C.J. McDonough, and Ross G. Arthur (eds), *Latin Culture in the Eleventh Century* (Turnhout: Brepols, 2002), pp. 223–49. Dolbeau's chapter also contains the only published transcription of Gerbert's *Scriptura*.
9 *Scriptura*, pp. 234–5; 'Lectiones ad prandium', ed. Grémont, p. 21.
10 In his chapter, Dolbeau cites other sources for Gerbert, see especially *Scriptura*, pp. 230–4.
11 *Scriptura*, stanza 3.
12 *Scriptura*, stanza 9.
13 *Scriptura*, stanza 7. This is reminiscent of John's own desire for fountains of tears in his *CT* (see Chapter 1).
14 *Scriptura*, stanza 12. Dolbeau notes on *Scriptura*, p. 241, that Mary's behaviour is here significantly inspired by what Gerbert might have witnessed in the Easter drama (cf. Chapter 3).
15 *Scriptura*, stanza 10.
16 'Et certe tu, o bone Jesu, haud sic meritus, qui in agonia positus oras pro illis usque ad sudorem sanguinis, ad terram currentibus guttis. Nam mox a cohorte sceleris ad scrutinium reverentaie tormentis interrogaris et illusione. Porro exutus candida agnei velleris stola, amphibularis clamide coccinea. Verticem illum, quem expauit Baptistae tremula manus, incultae pungit spina coronae. In dextera benedictionaria stridet arundo pro sceptri Gloria. Hinc falsi adoratores poplite flexo, corde supercilioso, aue Caesarum regi offerunt Judeorum ... Verum fons misericordiae caritatis exuberantia saturiens' (*Scriptura*, stanzas 4–5).
17 'Tentus est, ut nos dimitteremur de sub iugo daemoniacae servitutis. Captus est, ut nos de manu hostis captivos auferet. Venumdatus est, ut nos suo sanguine compararet. Exspoliatus est ut nos stola immortalitatis indueret. Irrisus est, ut nos ab irrisione daemonum tolleret. Spinis coronatus est, ut spinas ac tribulos primae maledictionis prorsus de nobis evelleret. Humiliatus est, ut nos exaltaret. Exaltatus in cruce est, ut nos ad se traheret. Felle potatus est et aceto, ut nos faceret in terram perennis laetitiae intrare. Sacrificatus est in ara crucis agnus immaculatus, ut peccata mundi tolleret. Pro his omnibus tibi gratias ago et magnifico nomen tuum, Pater sancte, cuius providentiae mira dispensatione actum est, ut librum quem nemo poterat aperire solus leo de tribu Iuda solveret et aperiret' (*CT*, p. 140).
18 Henri Omont, 'L'invention du Précieux Sang dans l'église de l'abbaye de Fécamp au XIIe siècle', *Bulletin de la Société de l'histoire de Normandie* 12 (1913),

John's medieval legacy

52–66; Oskari Kajava, *Études sur deux poèmes français relatifs a l'abbaye de Fécamp* (Helsinki: Imprimerie de la Société de littérature finnoise, 1928), pp. 24–35. An edition of the text originally published by Omont is found in Jean-Guy Gouttebroze, *Le Précieux Sang de Fécamp, origine et développement d'un mythe chrétien* (Paris: Honoré Champion, 2000), pp. 68–78. The legend is also retold in Leroux De Lincy, *L'abbaye de Fécamp*, pp. 204–10. For more on *jongleurs* in thirteenth-century France, see John Baldwin, 'The Image of the Jongleur in Northern France around 1200', *Speculum* 72 (1997), 635–63.

19 Arthur Du Monstier, *Neustria Pia, seu de omnibus et singulis abbatiis et prioratibus totius Normaniae* (Rouen: J. Berthelin, 1663), p. 227; *PL* 166, cols 1173–82.

20 L'abbé Sauvage (ed.), 'Des miracles advenus en l'église de Fécamp', *Mélanges: Société de l'histoire de Normandie*, 2nd ser. (1893), no. 5.

21 *Libellus de revelacione*, *PL* 151, col. 717D, ch. 16. Matthieu Arnoux dates the chronicle to the period between 1079 and 1094 because he believes the work engages with the debates about Fécamp's exemption that were raging in that period: Arnoux, 'Les premières chroniques de Fécamp', p. 75; Arnoux, 'La fortune du *Libellus de revelatione*', pp. 136, 150.

22 Abbé Sauvage's miracle collection provides the date of 1064 given above. Archaeology indicates both a rebuilding campaign of the choir in the eleventh century and an influx of pilgrims, perhaps to see a blood relic; see Renoux, *Du palais ducal*, pp. 318, 503–6; Karin Brockhaus, 'Form Follows Function? De la corrélation entre pèlerinage et architecture dans l'abbatiale de Fécamp à la fin du XIe siècle', in *Pèlerinages et lieux de pèlerinage en Normandie* (Fécamp: Fédération des Sociétés Historiques et Archéologiques de Normandie, 2010), pp. 195–205. Even earlier archaeological evidence of pilgrimage to the monastery has been used to make an argument for the blood relic to have been in continuous use from Duke Richard I's founding of the monastery in 996, though this argument remains somewhat unsubstantiated; see Le Maho, 'Aux sources d'un grand pèlerinage normand', p. 100.

23 A fountain of some sort (perhaps even of the precious blood) is alluded to in earlier texts, describing the first Norman Duke Rollo's founding of the monastery (Colette Beaune, 'Les ducs, le roi et le saint sang', in Françoise Autrand, Claude Gauvard, and Jean-Marie Moeglin (eds), *Saint Denis et la royauté: Études offertes à Bernard Guenée* (Paris: Éditions de la Sorbonne, 1999), p. 717). Arnoux believes that the blood relic was actually at Fécamp as early as 996 as part of William's initial reform of the monastery, as part of the assertion of Fécamp's abbot's supremacy over the old cultures of the monks (Mathieu Arnoux, 'Before the *Gesta Normannorum* and beyond Dudo: Some Evidence on Early Norman Historiography', *Anglo-Norman Studies* 22 (1999), 34). The absence of such a relic at William's other reformed monasteries, or in other sources from Fécamp from the period, however, makes this argument questionable.

24 These ten include: Gaudix, seventh century; Einbeck and Weingarten, eleventh century; Mantua, 804/eleventh century; Reichenau, 923/925; Lucca Volto Santo, eleventh century; and Charroux, 1080; see Nicholas Vincent, *The Holy Blood: King*

Henry III and the Westminster Blood Relic (New York: Cambridge University Press, 2001).

25 Brigitte Cazelles, 'Le Précieux Sang de Fécamp: Origine et développement d'un mythe chrétien by Jean-Guy Gouttebroze' [review], *Speculum* 78.2 (2003), 504–6; Gouttebroze, *Le Précieux Sang de Fécamp*; Jean-Guy Gouttebroze, 'À l'origine du culte du Précieux Sang de Fécamp, le Saint Voult de Lucques', *Tabularia* (2002), 1–8; René Herval, 'En marge de la légende du Précieux-Sang: Lucques, Fécamp, Glastonbury', in *L'abbaye bénédictine de Fécamp: Ouvrage scientifique du XIIIe centenaire(658–1958)* (Fécamp: EMTN, 1959), vol. I, pp. 105–25; Tran-Duc, 'De l'usage politique du Précieux Sang'; André Vauchez, 'Du culte des reliques à celui du Précieux Sang', *Tabularia* (2008), 81–8; Marc Venard, 'Le sang du Christ: Sang eucharistique ou sang relique?' *Tabularia* 9 (2009), 1–12

26 Norbert Kruse has noted that Pope Leo IX distributed pieces of an existing blood relic from Mantua when he condemned Berengar of Tours at councils in Rome and Vercelli in 1054 in 'Weg des Heiligen Blutes von Mantua nach Altdorf-Weingarten', in Norbert Kruse and Hans Ulrich Rudolf (eds), *900 Jahre Heilig Blut Verehrung in Weingarten, 1094–1994* (Sigmaringen: Jan Thorbecke Verlag, 1994), p. 59. It is possible, then, that John got the relic from Leo IX when he went to Rome. See also Beaune, 'Les ducs, le roi et le saint sang', p. 723; Arnoux, 'Before the *Gesta Normannorum*', p. 34; Vincent, *The Holy Blood*, pp. 57–8; Bates, *Normandy before 1066*, pp. 203–4.

27 Legends using Nicodemus might have been used to combat Berengar. John of Avranches, bishop in Normandy from 1060 to 1067, composed a *Libellus divinorum officiorum* in which he proved the real presence of the Eucharist by elevating the role of Nicodemus, who, by collecting the blood of Christ during the deposition, was a proto-priest of sorts, and a witness to the 'realness' of the body and blood; see *PL* 147, cols 35–6. Gerbert of Saint-Wandrille's *Scriptura* also details both Joseph's and Nicodemus's presence at the deposition.

28 This recounting combines the many different iterations of the story as told at Fécamp. There are some variations not included here: in the miracle collection from 1064, for instance, Issac is a priest; in the twelfth- and thirteenth-century iterations, Nicodemus puts the relic into the sea. But the basic contours of each version of the myth align with what is told here.

29 Edward Meyrick and Henry Symonds Goulburn (eds), *The Life, Letters, and Sermons of Bishop Herbert de Losinga (ca. 1050–1119)* (Oxford: James Parker and Co., 1878), p. 62; Munns, *Cross and Culture*, pp. 52–4.

30 Meyrick and Goulburn (eds), *The Life, Letters, and Sermons of Bishop Herbert de Losinga*, letters 5 and 34, pp. 64–5. For more on Herbert's reforms, see B. Dodwell, 'The Foundation of Norwich Cathedral', *Transactions of the Royal Historical Society* 7 (1957), 1–18; Tim Pestell, 'Monastic Foundation Strategies in the Early Norman Diocese of Norwich', *Anglo-Norman Studies* 23 (2001), 199–229; N.R. Ker, 'Medieval Manuscripts from Norwich Cathedral Priory', *Transactions of the Cambridge Bibliographical Society* 1 (1949), 1–28.

31 See Chapter 3.
32 See Tolhurst (ed.), *The Customary of the Cathedral Priory Church*; James Alexander, 'Herbert of Norwich, 1091–1119: Studies in the History of Norman England', *Studies in Medieval and Renaissance History* 6 (1969), 115–233. Leroux de Lincy also details the liturgy for a certain Mass of the Precious Blood (in *L'abbaye de Fécamp*, pp. 177–87), the text for which does not appear in any extant early medieval sources at Fécamp, so his claim remains uncertain.
33 The legend of Lucca's blood was known in Normandy in the second half of the eleventh century by historians such as Ordericus Vitalis and Wace; Gerbert of Saint-Wandrille also refers to Joseph of Arimathea and Nicodemus, and, in describing Christ on the cross, calls him a 'true fountain' of 'sweating blood' (*Scriptura*, p. 236).
34 Bec adopted both Fécamp's customs and their idea of a blood relic, which, at Bec, according to Eadmer, became a relic of the Virgin's blood (Vincent, *The Holy Blood*, p. 58.). On Glastonbury, see Jaffray, 'Glastonbury and Fécamp', p. 347; Herval, 'En marge de la légende'.
35 '*in interioribus sensibus animae meae*' (*CT*, p. 179).
36 '*Per eius sanguinem habemus accessum ad te, ambo in uno spiritu*' (*CT*, p. 140).
37 *CT*, p. 173.
38 *CT*, p. 128.
39 *CT*, pp. 180–1; cf. Chapter 1.
40 John likely was exposed to the eleventh-century relic of Christ's tears at the abbey of La Trinité, Vendôme. This relic was possibly given to the abbey by the Empress Agnes, who, as we saw in Chapter 4, was a correspondent of John's. Additionally, the monastery of Orléans had a sculpture that miraculously cried in the eleventh century known to Rodulfus Glaber (*Glaber*, pp. 64–6). There is possibly a parallel between the relic of tears and the relic of blood, in the same way that there is a parallel between tears and blood in John's *CT* and elsewhere: Elina Gertsman, 'Introduction: "Going They Went and Wept": Tears in Medieval Discourse', in Elina Gertsman (ed.), *Crying in the Middle Ages: Tears of History* (New York: Routledge, 2011), pp. xi, xiii; René Crozet, 'Le monument de la Sainte Larme à la Trinité de Vendôme', *Bulletin Monumental* 121 (1963), 171–80; Katja Boertjes, 'Pilgrim Ampullae from Vendôme: Souvenirs from a Pilgrimage to the Holy Tear of Christ', in Sarah Blick and Rita Tekippe (eds), *Art and Architecture of Late Medieval Pilgrimage in Northern Europe and the British Isles* (Boston: Brill, 2005), pp. 443–72.
41 Cf. Chapter 3.
42 For more on the *depositio* drama, see Chapter 3 and Sheingorn, *The Easter Sepulchre in England*; Morris, *The Sepulchre of Christ*; Parker, 'The Descent from the Cross'; Sticca, 'The Montecassino Passion', p. 211; Smoldon, 'The Easter Sepulchre Music-Drama', p. 2; Young, *The Drama of the Medieval Church*, p. 13; Corbin, *La deposition liturgique du Christ au Vendredi Saint*.
43 Cf. Chapter 3.

44 'Ait Pilatus innocens ego sum a sanguine iusti huius vos videritis'; cf. Matthew 27:24; Chadd I, p. 231.
45 Nicholas Vincent says that one of the origins of Fécamp's blood relic legend might have been the Acts of Pontius Pilate from the Gospel of Nicodemus (Vincent, *The Holy Blood*, p. 61). Fécamp had a copy of the Gospel of Nicodemus by the twelfth century at least (Lecouteux, 'Réseaux', I, p. 656). Colum Hourihane notes that Pilate's washing of the hands would have been associated with Jesus's washing of the feet of the Apostles; that the abbot would perform both gestures over the course of two days (Holy Thursday and Good Friday), thus only further strengthening the image of the Christlike abbot in the Fécamp liturgy (Colum Hourihane, *Pontius Pilate, Anti-Semitism, and the Passion in Medieval Art* (Princeton, NJ: Princeton University Press, 2009), pp. 69, 76, 178). There is also a parallel here to John's comment in his letter to the disobedient monks: 'Truly, your inner eye has not rightly discerned that I [John] am shedding innocent blood or that I am cruel in the death of our sons' (cf. Chapter 3).
46 The majority of scholarly studies of medieval materiality – like the majority of studies about medieval passion devotion – focus primarily on the Late Middle Ages. Holy matter, like Christ's suffering crucified body, is increasingly associated with practices and anxieties of late medieval piety in scholarship. See, for instance, Caroline Walker Bynum, *Christian Materiality* (New York: Zone Books, 2011); Sara Ritchey, *Holy Matter: Changing Perceptions of the Material World in Late Medieval Christianity* (Ithaca, NY: Cornell University Press, 2014).
47 Paul Quivy and Joseph Thiron, 'Robert de Tomblaine et son commentaire sur le Cantique des Cantiques', in Raymonde Foreville (ed.), *Millénaire monastique du Mont Saint-Michel* (Paris: Paul Lethielleux, 1967), vol. II, pp. 347–56. William North notes that John knew Robert in 'St. Anselm's Forgotten Student', pp. 174–5, 183.
48 Mancia, 'Praying with an Eleventh-Century Manuscript', pp. 161–85.
49 Lecouteux, 'Deux fragments d'un nécrologe'. Guibert of Nogent's work on the body and blood of Christ existed at twelfth-century Fécamp in Paris, BnF, ms. lat 2446 and ms. lat. 2501. On Guibert as Anselm's student, see Vaughn, 'The Pattern of his Teaching', p. 118.
50 Wilmart, 'Deux préfaces spirituelles', p. 43; Radding, 'The Geography of Learning'; Leclercq, *Un maître*, pp. 72–6; Gillian Evans, 'Mens devota: The Literary Community of the Devotional Works of John of Fécamp and St. Anselm', *Medium Aevum* 43.2 (1974), 105–15; Southern, *Portrait in a Landscape*, pp. xxvi, 92.
51 Anselm became abbot of Bec the year that John died, so he only corresponds with John's successor, William of Ros. Anselm writes to Anastasius of Venice, Suppo of Rome, Bernard of Etrurie, and Hauteville du Cotentin, all of whom were recruited by William of Volpiano; Maurilius of Rouen is also an adviser to Anselm (see Vaughn, 'Anselm of Le Bec and Canterbury', p. 69).
52 McGuire, 'John of Fécamp and Anselm of Bec', pp. 156, 163.
53 Mancia, 'Praying with an Eleventh-Century Manuscript', pp. 178–81.

John's medieval legacy

54 Interestingly, though he is far overshadowed by Anselm's reputation in scholarship today, John was reclaimed as the 'greatest medieval thinker between St. Gregory and St. Bernard' by Wilmart in 1937, about thirty years before Anselm was more extensively studied by F.S. Schmitt and R.W. Southern (McGuire, 'John of Fécamp and Anselm of Bec', p. 164).
55 Fulton, *From Judgment to Passion*, pp. 146–50, 189–91.
56 Fulton, *From Judgment to Passion*, p. 173.
57 *Anselm*, p. 89.
58 'huic defloratiunculae ad laudem tuam operam dedi, ut breve et manuale verbum de Deo mecum semper haberem, ex cuius lectionis igne, quoties tepefio, in tuum reaccendar amorem' (*CT*, p. 182).
59 *Anselm*, p. 93.
60 Compare with John's '*facile a caelesti desiderio frigescimus*' ('we easily grow cold in our heavenly longing'; *CT*, p. 182).
61 *Letters of Saint Anselm of Canterbury*, vol. I, p. 193.
62 Southern, *Making of the Middle Ages*, p. 227; Southern, *Portrait in a Landscape*, p. 100.
63 See Chapter 1; Bestul, 'Self and Subjectivity', p. 151.
64 On the *Confessions* and Anselm, see Brian Stock, *Augustine the Reader: Meditation, Self-Knowledge, and the Ethics of Interpretation* (Cambridge, MA: Harvard University Press, 1998), pp. 277–8; M.B. Pranger, *The Artificiality of Christianity: Essays on the Poetics of Monasticism* (Stanford, CA: Stanford University Press, 2002), pp. 162–4; Sweeney, *Anselm of Canterbury and the Desire for the Word*, p. 119; Thomas H. Bestul, 'St. Augustine and the *Orationes sive meditations* of St. Anselm', *Anselm Studies* 2 (1988), 597–606.
65 Morrison, 'Framing the Subject', p. 10.
66 *Anselm*, p. 97.
67 Augustine, *Confessions* 1.1; *CT*, p. 142; *Anselm*, p. 98.
68 Bynum, 'Did the Twelfth Century Discover the Individual?', p. 87.
69 *Anselm*, p. 107.
70 *Anselm*, p. 196.
71 *Anselm*, p. 95.
72 *Anselm*, p. 94.
73 Cf. Chapter 1.
74 *Anselm*, p. 204.
75 Carruthers, *The Craft of Thought*, pp. 101–3.
76 *Anselm*, p. 96.
77 McGuire, 'John of Fécamp and Anselm of Bec', p. 165.
78 Fulton, *From Judgment to Passion*, p. 153.
79 Sweeney, *Anselm of Canterbury and the Desire for the Word*, p. 39.
80 Sweeney, *Anselm of Canterbury and the Desire for the Word*, p. 17.
81 *Anselm*, p. 177.
82 Cf. Chapter 2; Mancia, 'Reading Augustine's *Confessions*', Part II.

83 See Chapter 2.
84 Lucile Trân-Duc, 'Herluin, fondateur de l'abbaye du Bec: La fabrique d'un saint à l'époque de la réforme de l'église', in Julia Barrow, Fabrice Delivré, and Véronique Gazeau (eds), *Autour de Lanfranc (1010–2010): Réforme et réformateurs dans l'Europe du Nord-Ouest (XIe–XII siècles)* (Caen: Presses universitaires de Caen, 2015), pp. 228, 231–3.
85 Vaughn, 'The Pattern of his Teaching', p. 121.
86 Courcelle, *Les Confessions de saint Augustine*, pp. 265–6 and 270.
87 Jean-Yves Tilliette, 'Une lettre inédite sur le mépris du monde et la compunction du coeur adressé par Baudri de Bourgeuil à Pierre de Jumièges', *Révue des études augustiniennes* 28.3/4 (1982), 271–8.
88 On Goscelin, see Olson, 'Did Medieval English Women Read Augustine's *Confessiones*?'; Monika Otter, 'Interpretive Essay', in *Goscelin of St. Bertin: The Book of Encouragement and Consolation*, trans. Monika Otter (Cambridge: D.S. Brewer, 2004), pp. 152, 155.
89 Jay Rubenstein, *Guibert of Nogent: Portrait of a Medieval Mind* (New York: Routledge, 2002), pp. 61–3.
90 Rubenstein, *Guibert of Nogent*, p. 2.
91 Parallels between Guibert's theology and Anselm's is discussed in Jaroslov Pelikan, 'A First Generation Anselmian: Guibert de Nogent', in F. Forrester Church and Timothy George (eds), *Continuity and Discontinuity in Church History: Essays Presented to George Huntston Williams on the Occassion of His 65th Birthday* (Leiden: Brill, 1979), pp. 71–82.
92 Guibert of Nogent, *Monodies and On the Relics of Saints: The Autobiography and a Manifesto of a French Monk from the Time of the Crusades*, trans. Joseph McAlhany and Jay Rubentein (New York: Penguin Books, 2011), p. 3. Latin edition is in Guibert de Nogent, *Autobiographie*, trans. Edmond-René Labande (Paris: Les Belles Lettres, 1981).
93 Guibert of Nogent, *Monodies*, p. 4. Here Guibert uses the word *rediens*. Cf. Chapter 1.
94 Guibert of Nogent, *Monodies*, p. 4. Cf. Chapter 1.
95 Guibert of Nogent, *Monodies*, p. 73. Cf. Chapter 1.
96 Guibert of Nogent, *Monodies*, p. 4. Cf. Chapter 1.
97 Frederick Amory, 'The Confessional Superstructure of Guibert de Nogent's Vita', *Classica et mediaevalia* 25 (1964), pp. 235–6.
98 Mancia, 'Reading Augustine's *Confessions*', pp. 203–4.
99 Rubenstein, *Guibert of Nogent*, p. 78.
100 Guibert of Nogent, *Monodies*, p. 16.
101 Guibert of Nogent, *Monodies*, p. 45.
102 He in fact uses the word 'individual' (*singulis*) as distinct from the group several times; for example: 'If you can reach everyone altogether (*generalissime*), then couldn't you provide for an individual (*singulis*)?' (Guibert of Nogent, *Monodies*, p. 3) Here, therefore, he almost characterises himself as exceptional, a risk that

Gregory the Great, for instance (cf. Chapters 2 and 4), would have condemned alongside John (cf. Chapters 3 and 4).
103 Augustine's parallel acknowledgement of the limitations of self-knowledge is discussed by Amory, 'The Confessional Superstructure', p. 237.
104 Quotations taken from Bestul, *Texts of the Passion*, pp. 38–40. See also Reilly, *The Cistercian Reform and the Art of the Book*, p. 17; Fulton, *From Judgment to Passion*, pp. 417–28.
105 Among the few placed manuscripts of John's work, BnF, ms. lat. 1919, a twelfth-century manuscript of *Confessio theologica* (which served as the basis for Leclercq's 1946 edition of the *CT*), is likely from a Cistercian abbey in Champagne, perhaps around Troyes; Zwettl, Stiftsbibliothek, Cod. 225 is also likely Cistercian. See Chapter 1, n. 8 on Stéphane Lecouteux's ideas about Fécamp's influence on the Cistercian houses of Champagne; see also Reilly, *The Cistercian Reform and the Art of the Book*, pp. 104–6, on the connection between the manuscripts of Saint-Bénigne de Dijon and those of other Cistercian houses.
106 Cf. Chapter 3.
107 Arne-Dannenberg, 'Charity and Law', pp. 13–23.
108 Martha Newman, *The Boundaries of Charity: Cistercian Culture and Ecclesiastical Reform* (Stanford, CA: Stanford University Press, 1996), pp. 219, 239.
109 Bernard invokes *caritas*, for instance, during his famous condemnation of Abelard; see Constant Mews, 'Bernard of Clairvaux, Peter Abelard and Heloise on the Definition of Love', *Revista Portuguesa de Filosofia* 60.3 (2004), 633–60. Bernard also cites *caritas* when interfering in politics; see Henry Mayr-Harting, 'Two Abbots in Politics: Wala of Corbie and Bernard of Clairvaux', *Transactions of the Royal Historical Society* 40 (1990), 217–37.
110 Lauren Mancia, '*Caritas* avant qu'elle ne devienne 'charité'', *Sensibilités* 5 (2018), 128–32.
111 Julia Bourke, 'An Experiment in "Neurohistory": Reading Emotions in Aelred's *De institutione inclusarum* (Rule for a Recluse)', *Journal of Medieval Religious Cultures* 42.1 (2016), 130.
112 Mirko Breitenstein, 'Is There a Cistercian Love? Some Considerations on the Virtue of Charity', in Gert Melville (ed.), *Aspects of Charity: Concern for One's Neighbor in Medieval Vita Religiosa* (Berlin: Lit Verlag, 2011), p. 72.
113 Anne Lester, *Creating Cistercian Nuns: The Women's Religious Movement and Its Reform in Thirteenth-Century Champagne* (Ithaca, NY: Cornell University Press, 2011), p. 119.
114 André Vauchez, 'Assistance et charité en occident, XIIIe–XVe siècles', in Vera Barbagli Bagnoli (ed.), *Domanda e consumi: Livelli e strutture (nei secoli XIII–XVIII)* (Florence: Olschki, 1978), pp. 151–62.
115 Gert Melville, 'What Role Did Charity Play in Francis of Assisi's Attitude towards the Poor?', in Gert Melville (ed.), *Aspects of Charity: Concern for One's Neighbor in Medieval Vita Religiosa* (Berlin: Lit Verlag, 2011), p. 107.
116 Morrison, 'Framing the Subject', p. 22.

117 Bestul, *Texts of the Passion*, p. 39.
118 Cf. Chapter 2 (Paris, BnF, ms. lat. 13593, ms. lat. 3088; Metz, Médiathèque, ms. 245) and Chapter 4 (Montpellier, Bibliothèque interuniversitaire de Montpellier, H309). These manuscripts include one copy of the *Confessio fidei*, one fragment of the *Confessio theologica*, and several copies of the *Libellus* recension.
119 John's excerpts in Paris, BnF, ms. lat. 13593 are: fols 43v–47r, *Liber meditationum*, c. XXXV, *PL* 40, cols 928–30; fol. 47r, *Liber meditationum*, c. XXXVI, *PL* 40, cols 930–2; fols 47r–49v, *Liber meditationum*, c. XXXVII, *PL* 40, cols 933–4; fols 49v–51v, *Liber meditationum*, c. XXXVII, *PL* 40, cols 934–6. See also Wilmart, 'Deux préfaces spirituelles', pp. 38–41; Mancia, 'Praying with an Eleventh-Century Manuscript'.
120 Paris, BnF, ms. lat. 1919, a twelfth-century manuscript (*Confessio theologica* recension) that served as the basis for Leclercq's 1946 edition of the *CT*, is from a Cistercian or Premonstratensian abbey in Champagne, perhaps around Troyes. That John's work potentially circulated throughout the Cistercian world makes sense, as his work and Bernard of Clairvaux's have a similar affect. For more on this comparison, see Pierre Courcelle, *Connais-toi toi-même, de Socrate à saint Bernard* (Paris: Études augustiniennes, 1974); Christoph Benke, 'Gottesliebe im 11. Jahrhundert. Johannes von Fécamp – ein Wegbereiter Bernhards von Clairvaux', *Studia Monastica* 39.2 (1997), 339–63.
121 Vienna, Österreichische Nationalbibliothek, Cod. 1580 is almost identical to Vienna, Österreichische Nationalbibliothek, Cod. 1582, and is thus likely part of the same recension if not copied from Cod. 1582 – 1580 possesses a later script, but the same text and even similar dimensions (Cod. 1580 measures 54.84 × 74.19 cm; Cod. 1582 measures 58.06 cm × 70.97 cm).
122 Vienna, Cod. 1580 has Smaragdus's work on fols 1–58r; Vienna, Cod. 1582 on fols 1–64r; Vienna, Cod. 1580 has Ephraem's work on fols 99r ff.; Vienna, Cod. 1582 on fols 105v ff.
123 The binding of both books is late medieval, so it is hard to ascertain whether or not their collected texts were originally bound together, especially since there are many different hands throughout each manuscript; however, since the two manuscripts seem to mirror each other, their texts were likely bound together in the Middle Ages as they are today. Still, even if the texts were bound at a later moment in history, their identical compilation suggests that, at least at the time each book was rebound, John's *CT* was widely considered to be a text just like Smaragdus's: affective prose directing the reader towards the contemplation of God.
124 Stéphane Lecouteux has shown that William of Volpiano is listed in the necrology of Ripoll (in 'Deux fragments d'un nécrologe'), and he reasons that this was due to the Italian connection between William, several disciples of Romualdus of Ravenna (who had spent some time at Cuxa, according to Romualdus's *vita*), Doge Pietro I Orseolo of Venice (who retired as monk-hermit at the abbey of Saint-Michel de Cuxa), and Abbot Oliga of Ripoll and Saint-Michel de Cuxa. There is also a similarity between the rotunda of

John's medieval legacy

     Cuxa's church (near Ripoll) and William's church of Saint-Bénigne (see Baker, '"The Whole World a Hermitage"', p. 207). Therefore, the influence of William of Volpiano in Catalonia was strong. There is no direct evidence of John's connection with Catalonia, though we could imagine that John, also Italian and William's protégé, maintained William's network in the region.

125 The mandorla, highlighted in reddish-orange, could read as a large wound to a late medieval audience, much like the wounds present in later Middle English devotional manuscripts (cf. Hamburger, 'The Visual and the Visionary').

126 This type of *Devotionsbild* is common in Ottonian manuscripts in the tenth century; cf. Joachim Prochno, *Das Schreiber- und Dedikationsbild in der deutschen Buchmalerei. 1. Teil bis zum Ende des 11. Jahrhunderts (800–1100)* (Leipzig: B.G. Teubner, 1929); Klaus Gereon Beuckers, 'Das Ottonische Stifterbild. Bildtypen, Handlungsmotiven und Stifterstatus in ottonischen und fruehsalischen Stifterdarstellungen', in Klaus Gereon Beuckers, Johannes Cramer, and Michael Imhof (eds), *Die Ottonen: Kunst – Architektur – Geschichte* (Petersburg: Imhof, 2006), pp. 63–102.

127 Several of the earliest manuscripts of Anselm's prayers circulated with John's *CT*: Bestul, 'The Collection of Private Prayers', p. 359. Metz, Médiatheque, ms. 245, for instance, is the earliest manuscript of Anselm's collected prayers and meditations. There is also a twelfth-century manuscript of John's *CT*, Zwettl, Stiftsbibliothek, Cod. 225, which collects John's work along with Smaragdus's and several prayers attributed to Anselm of Canterbury.

128 *Zwettl* 164 can be traced as far back as the fourteenth century to the Carthusian abbey of Gaming, in Austria. Its whereabouts before that are unknown. It is from a unique recension of John's work, prefaced with the only extant copy of the letter written to the anonymous nun; see Hurlbut, *The Picture of the Heavenly Jerusalem*, pp. v, 18.

129 Often, these pseudo-Anselmian collections of prayers contained prayers from the school of John of Fécamp, including Maurilius of Rouen's prayer to the Virgin. See Bestul, 'The Collection of Private Prayers', p. 361; Cottier, *Anima Mea*, pp. 159–81.

130 Cf. *Paris* 13593, discussed above.

131 Cédric Giraud, *Spiritualité et histoire des textes entre moyen âge et époque moderne: Genèse et fortune d'un corpus pseudépigraphe de méditations* (Paris: Institut d'études augustiniennes, 2016), pp. 131–3 and 207–13.

132 Giraud, *Spiritualité et histoire des textes*, pp. 185–96.

133 The *Manuale* can be found in *PL* 40, cols 951–68. Chapters 1–13 are taken from John's *CT*. For more on which pieces of John's text are taken, see Giraud, *Spiritualité et histoire des textes*, pp. 37, 131–3.

134 Chapters 12–25, 27–33, 35–8 of the *Meditations* are pieces of John's *CT*; the full *Meditations* are in *PL* 40, cols 901–42; see Wilmart, *Auteurs spirituels*, pp. 127–8, 420; Leclercq and Bonnes, *Un maître*, pp. 39–40; Wilmart, 'Deux préfaces spirituelles', pp. 35–41; Giraud, *Spiritualité et histoire des textes*, pp. 185–212.

Emotional monasticism

For more on the transmission of monastic texts to the laity, see Mary Agnes Edsall, 'From "Companion to the Novitiate" to "Companion to the Devout Life": San Marino, Huntington Library, ms HM 744 and Monastic Anthologies of the Twelfth-Century Reform', in Nicole R. Rice (ed.), *Middle English Religious Writing in Practice: Texts, Readers, and Transformations* (Turnhout: Brepols, 2013), pp. 115–48.

135 Giraud, *Spiritualité et histoire des textes*, pp. 227–79, 471–2.
136 The manuscript contains only chapters 1–24 of the *Manuale*; see Rouen, BM, ms. A528 (555), fols 40vb–48vb. Giraud, *Spiritualité et histoire des textes*, pp. 123, 128, 202, 222, 230, 254.
137 Jeffery Hamburger, *The Rothschild Canticles: Art and Mysticism in Flanders and the Rhineland ca. 1300* (New Haven, CT: Yale University Press, 1990), p. 22.
138 Hamburger, *The Rothschild Canticles*, pp. 23–4.
139 Hamburger, *The Rothschild Canticles*, pp. 23–4.
140 Hamburger, *The Rothschild Canticles*, p. 24. On the creativity of the compiler(s), see also Barbara Newman, 'Contemplating the Trinity: Text, Image, and the Origins of the Rothschild Canticles', *Gesta* 52.2 (2013), 147.
141 Newman, 'Contemplating the Trinity', p. 140; Michael Camille, '"Him whom you have ardently desired you may see": Cistercian Exegesis and the Prefatory Pictures in a French Apocalypse', in M.P. Lillich (ed.), *Studies in Cistercian Art and Architecture* (Kalamazoo, MI: Cistercian Publications, 1987), p. 141.
142 Hamburger, *The Rothschild Canticles*, p. 33.
143 Hamburger cites *CT*, p. 215: 'For it is just that you who are well versed in the current life of contemplation take up wings and, flying upwards, drink from the font of supernal sweetness, saying with the prophet, "for with thee is the font of life"' (*'Iustum namque est ut tu quae in actuali bene conversaris vita contemplationis pennas assumas et sursum volitans de fonte supernae dulcedinis haurias, dicens cum Propheta: "Quoniam apud te est fons vitae"'*). I would go a step further, however, and propose that this image may also have alluded to John's consideration of a contemplative's eyes being a fountain of tears (cf. Chapter 1). Hamburger several times elsewhere cites John's *CT* to be an inspiration for inexplicable images in the manuscript, quoting John on the Heavenly Jerusalem to justify an image of the Sponsa and Christ in the Song of Songs (*The Rothschild Canticles*, p. 56), and elsewhere citing John's desire to participate in Christ's Resurrection (*The Rothschild Canticles*, pp. 67–8), and John's use of wing imagery and John's request for a wound of charity (*The Rothschild Canticles*, p. 68).
144 Hamburger, *The Rothschild Canticles*, p. 72.
145 Cf. Chapter 3.
146 *CT*, pp. 180–1; cf. Chapter 1 and Chapter 3.
147 Despite the presence of the *arma christi*, Christ here is very much alive; while his right foot is bound, his left hand has successfully removed his nails.
148 Hamburger, *The Rothschild Canticles*, p. 74.
149 Cf. Chapter 3.
150 Hamburger, *The Rothschild Canticles*, p. 74.

Conclusion

Ever since André Wilmart published his study of John of Fécamp in the 1930s, medievalists have slowly begun to acknowledge that so-called 'Anselmian spirituality' did not, in fact, originate with Anselm, and that 'affective piety' was not an invention of the later Middle Ages. My study of John of Fécamp builds on that trend, both by giving the details of his full-length *Confessio theologica* and by placing John's devotional method in his wider monastic context, showing just how proper to eleventh-century Benedictine monasticism affective piety was. Devotional interiority was indeed felt while living in monastic community – no solitary retreat into the wilderness was needed. Heartfelt tears and the suffering Christ were in fact tools valued by monks in the early eleventh century. Prayer was felt even more deeply by Benedictine abbots when it was an active, regular escape from the distractions of the secular world. Emotional devotion was undeniably practised and even modelled by men and male authors, not just by compassionate women. Affective devotions were performed with the words and phrases of the authoritative and early Church Fathers (John's *dicta patrum*). And John's strategies for emotional implementation and self-investigation were, to him, the best preparation for prayer to God.[1]

In this book I have presented John of Fécamp as a case study to the reader, hoping to use the particulars of his writing, influences, context, and legacy to illuminate the realities of emotional devotion in the Benedictine monastery of the eleventh century. In the first chapter, I worked to define the contours of John's own particular devotional philosophy, elucidating the *Confessio theologica* in its entirety for the first time since 1946. I showed how that text, written initially for the personal use of the monks at Fécamp and in John's monastic network, plotted out a plan for keeping praying monks ardently awake to their task and desirous of their God. I showed how John's method prescribed a kind of emotional reform at the site of the interior heart of its readers, exposing the frailties and sinfulness of every hard-hearted devotee and naming *caritas*, a wounded, suffering love, as the most productive devotional emotion in prayer. Through his models of Hannah, Mary Magdalene, and the crucified Christ, John urged his readers to engage in tearful, penitent, persistent, and passionate prayer. His treatise strove to effect an emotional reform of how his monks felt when they prayed, attempting to metaphorically crucify his obedient, sinful readers alongside Christ, the affective exemplar *par excellence* for devout emotion.

Having defined John's brand of affective piety on his own terms, I provided a foundation on which I built the rest of my study. Chapter 2 showed that many of John's ideas about emotional devotion were not *sui generis* or revolutionary, but instead stemmed from the ideas of earlier Christian authors, some of whom were widely known, while others were primarily read in the monastic contexts where John came of age. Additionally, I highlighted which of John's ideas were largely new, particularly his use of Augustine's *Confessions*, a text that he likely introduced to the Anglo-Norman world. Chapters 3 and 4 exposed how John's *Confessio theologica*'s methodology was present throughout the devotional culture at Fécamp, serving as the core of many of his devotional and disciplinary actions inside the monastery and in his secular and religious activities around the wider world. These chapters proved that John's *Confessio theologica*'s ideology were of a piece with the monastic devotional, liturgical, homiletic, educational, and visual culture at Fécamp, and that his ideology motivated John's engagement with anti-heretical movements and religious and lay people outside Fécamp seeking devotional advice. I showed how even John's abbatial administration of the property and economy of Fécamp in part served his devotional purpose, these more secular activities creating a tension with John's devotional aspirations and thereby motivating his deeper emotional engagement in prayer. Chapter 5 outlined how John's students, Norman peers, and subsequent monks and Christian devotees built upon and elaborated his affective devotional programme and concepts; and I concluded by showing how John's *Confessio theologica* was excerpted and read in the Late Middle Ages in a way distinct from its complete eleventh-century version.

As a monograph focused on a single monk and his abbey, this book first and foremost serves to elucidate our understanding of Abbot John, a medieval individual largely unexamined by scholars in the decades since Jean Leclercq and Jean-Paul Bonnes published the first full-length study on him. This study has, I hope, fortified our understanding of John of Fécamp and of the devotional dimensions of Norman monasticism, providing important background on the atmosphere that nurtured Anselm of Canterbury and Guibert of Nogent, among other later, well-known medieval figures.

Yet, my hope is that this book goes beyond a simple case study. John of Fécamp and his monastery provide us with unique windows into early monastic devotional praxis: they show us that Benedictine monks were not rote liturgical machines with primarily political or economic motivations, but were rather passionately engaged devotional innovators, striving to forge profound connections to God through deeply felt prayer centuries before the advent of Cistercian, Franciscan, and late medieval mystical piety. John of Fécamp's *Confessio theologica*, the intellectual inheritance it evidences, and the application of its devotional principles in John's monastic context reveal how 'Gregorian' monastic reform went far beyond correcting monastic behaviours through rules or customs. Abbots at reformed monasteries like Fécamp also made improvements to interior devotional behaviours through a process I have here called emotional reform. Moreover, the systematic study of John's ideas in their eleventh-century context and thereafter has confirmed that affective piety was practised in the earlier medieval period, yet it also has uncovered how its eleventh-century monastic iteration was notably different from the type practised by later lay, Cistercian, mendicant, or mystical Christians. I have not here claimed John of Fécamp to be a point of *origin* for affective devotion, or even to be a *unique* practitioner of this emotional-devotional methodology; rather, through the lens of a single monk's work and monastic context, I have shown how *distinctive* the practice of affective piety was in the eleventh-century monastery and how essential its study is to our understanding of this historical narrative of medieval religious practice and belief.

In this book, I have recast early medieval monks as instrumental players in the story of affective piety; in so doing, I hope to have troubled the scholarly understanding of that phrase. Scholars have historically used 'affective piety' as a catch-all term, one vaguely referring to the highly emotional and experiential late medieval devotion to the humanity of Jesus and the sorrow of Mary.[2] This study of John of Fécamp has shown how insufficient and narrow those generalised associations actually are, especially for the eleventh-century monastic context. This book does not just claim that affective piety was practised earlier in the Middle Ages; it redefines what affective piety was to monks like John, in order to expose just how much is lost in its more general definition.

Something about affective piety – particularly the widely accepted variety hyper-focused on the humanity of the crucified Christ – has fascinated medievalists for decades. The changing depiction of the crucified Christ from triumphant to suffering, or the extreme emotional practices of medieval mystics, are always popular paper topics for my medieval history students, undergraduate and graduate alike. The International Medieval Bibliography lists hundreds of articles and books dealing with topics pertaining to 'affective spirituality'. What is it that fascinates contemporary scholars so much about this devotional trend? It could be the strangeness of these devotional experiences, the intensity of the medieval desire for a connection with Christ that appears so wholly different from the kinds of experiences we regularly seek in our modern, secular world. It could be the digestibility of this narrative, a story that tracks the progress of medieval devotion over the course of time, evolving from a moment when medievals cowered before a domineering God to one where they confidently claimed a connection with a more empathetic, personal one. It could be how, with affective piety, scholars have identified a proto-Renaissance humanism in the Middle Ages, revealing how medieval souls were less dark age than otherwise thought, how they were longing to see their individual human frailties reflected in the image of their God, taking the first step towards the 'Renaissance idea' that man was the measure of all things.

In my opinion, this last idea – affective piety's ability to locate a 'renaissance' in the Middle Ages – is the most fruitful path to ascertaining why scholars have hesitated to explore John of Fécamp or to study the early monastic practices of affective devotion. By attributing the trend of affective piety to a medieval desire to connect with Jesus's humanity or to elicit compassion from an omnipotent God, scholars made medieval religion more palatable to an American academy that came of age during and after the anti-establishment, secular, anti-conformist revolution of the 1960s.[3] The form of affective piety that emphasises Jesus's humanity and favours lay devotees promotes an 'expressive individualism' among late medieval people that many claim is only found outside the reach of religious institutions.[4] This version rejects the possibility that an individual could find his religious self in community, upholding the notion that it is only a free, autonomous individual who can find interiority and introspection.[5] This casts the monastic vow of obedience as a kind of brain-washing that negates the possibility for an individual's independence.[6] It privileges the modern idea that emotional authenticity is divorced from institutions and from cognition and intellect, instead being 'pure feeling, sensation, or experience [that is] easily separable from subsequent acts of thinking, loving, and deciding'.[7]

Conclusion

In contrast, the monastic form of affective piety embraced by John and examined in this book requires modern scholars to understand that a medieval religious person could be capable of connecting, thinking, and acting of his own volition within the confines of a religious institution.[8] The monastic context does not rob the individual of emotional and devotional agency by 'demand[ing] a radical submission to something external to oneself'.[9] At eleventh-century Fécamp under John, affective prayer became a 'process of human intentionality and self-presence';[10] it was not coerced by a hegemonic institution, but was rather enabled by it.[11] To John of Fécamp, the authority of the Fathers, the discipline of monastic life, the arrangement of the liturgy, the pastoral duties expected of the abbot, and the very structure of coenobitic monasticism *allowed* for the rigorous cultivation of affective and efficacious prayer.

This study of John of Fécamp asks scholars to understand 'affective piety' in a way that acknowledges its many varieties, each adapted for the complex spectrum of medieval contexts in which it was practised. We do a disservice to the evolution of medieval devotion when we see late medieval trends as innovative *ex nihilo*, instead of tracing their roots to earlier epochs and contexts. The obsession with humanism that still persists in today's world ignores the strife and beauty that is found in the central medieval monastic communities' very human devotional efforts.[12] To neglect medieval monastic lived religious emotional experience is to adopt the Reformation's distrust of the institutions of the medieval Church. We must attend to the affective piety evidenced at the eleventh-century monastery of Fécamp because it shows us the numerous, inventive, surprising, and fascinating ways in which eleventh-century monks strove to commune with their God: through interior prayer and through communal liturgy, through material and through text, through thought and through feeling, through secular undertakings and religious performances, and through the words and deeds of one very important abbot – John of Fécamp.

Notes

1 Emotional belief as consciously wrought, and not spontaneously felt, is discussed by Steven Justice in 'Did the Middle Ages Believe in Their Miracles?', *Representations* 103 (2008), 1–28. Amy Hollywood agrees, saying that 'submission must always be submission freely given' in 'Spiritual but Not Religious: The Vital Interplay between Submission and Freedom', *Harvard Divinity Bulletin* 38.1/2 (2010), https://bulletin.hds.harvard.edu/articles/winterspring2010/spiritual-not-religious.

Emotional monasticism

2 Thomas H. Bestul, 'Meditation/*Meditatio*', in Amy Hollywood and Patricia Z. Beckman (eds), *The Cambridge Companion to Christian Mysticism* (New York: Cambridge University Press, 2012), pp. 157–66.
3 Or apparently secular. For more on this, see Kathleen Davis, *Periodization and Sovereignty: How Ideas of Feudalism and Secularization Govern the Politics of Time* (Philadelphia: University of Pennsylvania Press, 2008), pp. 77–102; Brad S. Gregory, *The Unintended Reformation: How a Religious Revolution Secularized Society* (Cambridge, MA: Harvard University Press, 2012), pp. 365–87.
4 Charles Taylor, *A Secular Age* (Cambridge, MA: Harvard University Press, 2007), p. 473.
5 Susan Boynton writes against this in 'Prayer as Liturgical Performance'; but even medieval people sometimes thought individual piety was better than communal piety, as in Kathryn L. Jasper, 'Reforming the Monastic Landscape: Peter Damian's Design for Personal and Communal Devotion', in Albrecht Classen (ed.), *Rural Space in the Middle Ages and Early Modern Age: The Spatial Turn in Premodern Studies* (Boston: De Gruyter, 2012), pp. 193–207.
6 Isabelle Cochelin writes against this in 'Obedience or Agency?'.
7 Bernard McGinn, 'Mystical Consciousness: A Proposal', *Spiritus* 8 (2008), 46.
8 Hollywood, 'Spiritual but Not Religious'.
9 Hollywood, 'Spiritual but Not Religious'.
10 McGinn, 'Mystical Consciousness', 46.
11 Andrea Sterk and Nina Caputo (eds), *Faithful Narratives: Historians, Religion, and the Challenge of Objectivity* (Ithaca, NY: Cornell University Press, 2014), p. 6.
12 Steven Pinker, *Enlightenment Now: The Case for Reason, Science, Humanism, and Progress* (New York: Viking, 2018); Anthony Pagden, *The Enlightenment: And Why it Still Matters* (New York: Random House, 2013); Stephen Greenblatt, *The Swerve: How the World Became Modern* (New York: Norton, 2012).

Bibliography

Manuscript sources

Angers, Bibliothèque municipale

ms. 14

Avranches, Bibliothèque municipale

ms. 50
ms. 57
ms. 72
ms. 76
ms. 90

Barcelona, Archivo de la Corona de Aragón

Ripoll 214

Berlin, Staatsbibliothek

Phillips, ms. 1866

Bern, Burgerbibliothek

Bongars ms. 162

Bibliography

Cambridge, Fitzwilliam Museum

McClean ms. no. 7

Fécamp, Musée de la Bénédictine

ms. 186

Hanover, Kestner-Museum

WM XXIa 36

Le Havre, Bibliothèque municipale

ms. 332

Metz, Médiathèque

ms. 134
ms. 232
ms. 245

Montpellier, Bibliothèque interuniversitaire, section de médecine

BISM ms. H159
BISM ms. H309

Munich, Bayerische Staatsbibliothek

Clm. 11352
Clm. 12607

New Haven, Beinecke Rare Book and Manuscript Library, Yale University

Beinecke ms. 404 (*Rothschild Canticles*)

New York, Morgan Library and Museum

ms. 641

Bibliography

Paris, Bibliothèque nationale de France

Dupuy 651
ms. lat. 152
ms. lat. 188
ms. lat. 258
ms. lat. 281
ms. lat. 298
ms. lat. 437
ms. lat. 465
ms. lat. 524
ms. lat. 528
ms. lat. 564
ms. lat. 989
ms. lat. 1201
ms. lat. 1535
ms. lat. 1632
ms. lat. 1684
ms. lat. 1713
ms. lat. 1714
ms. lat. 1805
ms. lat. 1843
ms. lat. 1872
ms. lat. 1919
ms. lat. 1928
ms. lat. 1939
ms. lat. 1970
ms. lat. 2019
ms. lat. 2055
ms. lat. 2079
ms. lat. 2101
ms. lat. 2253
ms. lat. 2331
ms. lat. 2401
ms. lat. 2403
ms. lat. 2446
ms. lat. 2501
ms. lat. 2531
ms. lat. 2628

Bibliography

ms. lat. 2639
ms. lat. 2707
ms. lat. 2712
ms. lat. 2720
ms. lat. 2771
ms. lat. 2801
ms. lat. 2821
ms. lat. 2899
ms. lat. 2976
ms. lat. 2994
ms. lat. 3088
ms. lat. 3314
ms. lat. 3330
ms. lat. 3501
ms. lat. 3503
ms. lat. 3711
ms. lat. 3776
ms. lat. 3858A
ms. lat. 4210
ms. lat. 4339
ms. lat. 5080
ms. lat. 5318
ms. lat. 5329
ms. lat. 5359
ms. lat. 5390
ms. lat. 11902
ms. lat. 13070
ms. lat. 13370
ms. lat. 13953
ms. lat. 18095

Perugia, Biblioteca Comunale Augusta

MS I 17

Rouen, Archives départementales de la Seine-Maritime

7H49
7H2143
14H17

Bibliography

Rouen, Bibliothèque municipale

ms. 25 (A110)
ms. 29 (A165)
ms. 82 (U103)
ms. 86 (A351)
ms. 106 (A332)
ms. 116 (A310)
ms. 118 (A317)
ms. 238 (A328)
ms. 244 (A261)
ms. 245 (A190)
ms. 253 (A538)
ms. 290 (A313)
ms. 313 (A279)
ms. 424 (A133)
ms. 425 (A178)
ms. 427 (A143)
ms. 437 (A318)
ms. 440 (A298)
ms. 444 (A321)
ms. 448 (A371)
ms. 464 (A47)
ms. 471 (A271)
ms. 477 (A191)
ms. 478 (A71)
ms. 489 (A254)
ms. 491 (A8)
ms. 492 (A105)
ms. 524 (I49)
ms. 526 (A275)
ms. 528 (A362)
ms. 532 (A395)
ms. 537 (A438)
ms. 540 (U148)
ms. 546 (A301)
ms. 553 (A452)
ms. 555 (A528)
ms. 978 (I57)

ms. 1132 (Y15)
ms. 1388 (U32)
ms. 1400 (U3)
ms. 1404 (U20)
ms. 1406 (Y41)
ms. 1417 (U45)
ms. 1470 (O32)

Troyes, Bibliothèque municipale

ms. 2142

Vatican City, Biblioteca Apostolica Vaticana

Chig. DV 77
Ottob. lat. 120
Reg. lat. 107
Reg. lat. 633
Reg. lat. 755

Vienna, Österreichische Nationalbibliothek

Cod. 1580
Cod. 1582

Zwettl, Zisterzienserstift Zwettl

Cod. 164
Cod. 225

Primary sources

Aelred of Rievaulx, 'The Pastoral Prayer', in *Treatises and Pastoral Prayer*, trans. R. Penelope Lawson. Collegeville, MN: Liturgical Press, 1971, pp. 103–18.

'Anciens inventaires du trésor de l'abbaye de Fécamp', ed. Charles de Beaurepaire. *Bibliothèque de l'école des chartes* 20.1 (1859): 153–70.

Anselm of Canterbury, *The Letters of Saint Anselm of Canterbury*, trans. Walter Fröhlich. Kalamazoo, MI: Cistercian Publications, 1990.

Bibliography

Anselm of Canterbury, *The Prayers and Meditations of Saint Anselm with the Proslogion*, trans. Benedicta Ward. New York: Penguin Books, 1973.

Assemani, J.S., ed. *Ephraemi Syri opera omnia*, vol. III. Rome: Ex typographia Vaticana, 1746.

Augustine of Hippo, *Confessions*, trans. Henry Chadwick. New York: Oxford University Press, 1991.

Augustine of Hippo, *Retractionum libri II*, Corpus Christianorum Series Latina 57, ed. Almut Mutzenbecher. Turnhout: Brepols, 1984.

Augustine of Hippo, *Sermones*. PL 38, col. 195.

Augustine of Hippo, *St. Augustine: The Writings against the Manichaeans and against the Donatists*, ed. and trans. Philip Schaff. Select Library of the Nicene and Post-Nicene Fathers of the Christian Church 4. Buffalo, NY: Christian Literature Company, 1974.

Pseudo-Augustine, *Meditations of Saint Augustine*, trans. Matthew J. O'Connell. Villanova, PN: Augustinian Press, 1995.

Baudril of Bourgueil, Letter to the Monks of Fécamp. PL 166, cols 1173–82.

Benedict of Nursia, *Rule of St. Benedict*, trans. Bruce Venarde. Cambridge, MA: Harvard University Press, 2011.

Berengar of Tours, *Beringerius Turonensis Rescriptum contra Lanfrannum*, ed. Wolfgang Milde. Turnhout: Brepols, 1988.

Berengar of Tours, *De sacra coena adversus Lanfrancum*, ed. W.H. Beekenkamp. The Hague: Martinus Nijhoff, 1942.

Bibliothèques de manuscrits médiévaux en France: Relevé des inventaires du VIIIe au XVIIIe siècle, ed. A.-M. Genevois, J.-F. Genest, and A. Chalandon. Paris: Éditions du CNRS, 1987.

Caesarius of Arles, *Sermones, nunc primum in unum collecti et ad leges artis criticae ex innumeris mss. recogniti*, ed. Dom G. Morin. Turnhout: Brepols, 1953.

Cassian, John. *Sermones*. PL 49, cols 0053–0475B.

Catalogi bibliothecarum antiqui, ed. Gustavus Becker. Bonn: Max Cohen et Filium, 1935.

Catalogus codicum latinorum Bibliothecae Regiae Monacensis, ed. Carolus Halm, Thomas Georgius, and Gulielmus Meyer. Wiesbaden: Harrassowitz, 1968. Vols III; IV.1; IV.2.

Un censier normand du XIIIe siècle: Le livre des jurés de l'abbaye Saint-Ouen de Rouen, ed. Henri Dubois. Paris: CNRS, 2001.

Chartes et documents de Saint-Bénigne de Dijon: Prieurés et dépendances des origines à 1300, ed. Georges Chevrier and Maurice Chaume. Dijon: Imprimerie Bernigaud et Privat, 1933.

Bibliography

'Le chartrier de l'abbaye de la Trinité de Fécamp: Étude et édition critique, 928/929–1190', ed. Michaël Bloche. PhD dissertation, École nationale des chartes, 2012.

The Chronicle of Hugh of Flavigny, ed. Patrick Healy. Burlington, VT: Ashgate, 2006.

Chronique de l'abbaye de Saint-Bénigne de Dijon, ed. E. Garnier and J. Bougaud. Dijon: Darantiere, 1875.

Consuetudines Beccenses, ed. Marie Pascal Dickson. *Corpus consuetudinum monasticarum*, vol. IV. Siegburg: Franciscum Schmitt, 1967.

Consuetudines Cluniacensium antiquiores cum redactionibus derivatis, ed. Kassius Hallinger. *Corpus consuetudinum monasticarum*, vol. VII.2. Siegburg: Franciscum Schmitt, 1983.

Consuetudines Fructuarienses-Sanblasianae, ed. Luchesius G. Spätling and Petrus Dinter. *Corpus consuetudinum monasticarum*, vol. XII.1. Siegburg: Franciscum Schmitt Success., 1985.

The Customary of the Cathedral Priory Church of Norwich, ed. J.B.L. Tolhurst. London: Henry Bradshaw Society, 1948.

Damian, Peter, *Peter Damian Letters*. The Fathers of the Church: Mediaeval Continuation. Washington, DC: Catholic University of America Press, 1990.

Damian, Peter, *Selected Writings on the Spiritual Life*, trans. Patricia McNulty. London: Faber and Faber, 1959.

Damian, Peter, *Vita Beati Romualdi*. Rome: Istituto Palazzo Borromini, 1957.

De admonitio ad filium spiritualem. PL CIII, cols 683–700.

'Des miracles advenus en l'église de Fécamp', ed. L'abbé Sauvage. *Mélanges: Société de l'histoire de Normandie*, 2nd series (1893): 9–49.

Dudo of Saint-Quentin, *History of the Normans*, trans. Eric Christiansen. Rochester, NY: Boydell Press, 1998.

Durandus of Troarn, *De corpore et sanguine domini*. PL 149, cols 1375–1424B.

A Durham Book of Devotions, ed. Thomas Bestul. Toronto: Pontifical Institute of Mediaeval Studies, 1987.

Eadmer, *The Life of Anselm*, trans. R.W. Southern. New York: Thomas Nelson and Sons, 1962.

English Benedictine Libraries: The Shorter Catalogues, vol. IV, ed. R. Sharpe, J.P. Carley, R.M. Thomson, and A.G. Watson. London: British Library, 1996.

Ephraem the Syrian, *S. Ephraem Syri opera: textum Syriacum Graecum Latinum ad fidem codicum recensuit*, ed. Joseph Mercati. Rome: Sumptibus Pontificii Instituti Biblici, 1915.

L'eremo e la Cattedra: Vita di san Pier Damiani, ed. Ruggero Benericetti. Florence: Ancora, 2007.

Bibliography

Geoffrey of Vendôme, *Geoffrey de Vendôme, Oeuvres*, ed. and trans. G. Giordanengo, Sources d'histoire médiévale 26. Paris: Éditions du CNRS, 1996.

Glaber, Rodulfus, *Rodulfi Glabri opera*, trans. John France and Paul Reynolds. Oxford: Clarendon Press, 1989.

Gregory the Great, *The Book of Pastoral Rule and Selected Epistles of Gregory the Great*, ed. Philip Schaff and Henry Wace, trans. James Barmby. Nicene and Post Nicean Fathers 12, 2nd ser. Buffalo, NY: Christian Literature Publishing Company, 1895.

Gregory the Great, *Moralia in Job*. South Bend, IN: Ex Fontibus Company, 2012.

Guibert of Nogent, *Autobiographie*, ed. and trans. Edmond-René Labande. Paris: Les Belles Lettres, 1981.

Guibert of Nogent, *Monodies and On the Relics of Saints: The Autobiography and a Manifesto of a French Monk from the Time of the Crusades*, trans. Joseph McAlhany and Jay Rubenstein. New York: Penguin Books, 2011.

Guigo II, *Guigo II: Ladder of Monks and Twelve Meditations*, ed. James Walsh and Edmund Colledge. Kalamazoo, MI: Cistercian Publications, 1997.

H 159 Montpellier: *Tonary of Saint-Bénigne of Dijon*, ed. Finn Egeland Hansen. Copenhagen: Dan Fog Musikforlag, 1974.

Herbert de Losinga, *The Life, Letters, and Sermons of Bishop Herbert de Losinga (ca. 1050–1119)*, ed. Edward Meyrick Goulburn and Henry Symonds. 2 vols. Oxford: James Parker and Co., 1878.

Hugh of Lincoln, 'Bishop Hugh of Lincoln's Devotion to Relics', in *Medieval Popular Religion, 1000–1200: A Reader*, ed. John Shinners. Toronto: Toronto University Press, 2007, pp. 181–3.

Jean d'Avranches, *Le De officiis ecclesiasticis*, ed. R. Delamare. Paris: Librarie Auguste Picard, 1922.

Jean d'Avranches, *Libellus divinorum officiorum*. PL 147, cols 35–6.

John of Fécamp, *Confessio Fidei* of Pseudo-Alcuin, PL 101, cols 1027–1098D.

John of Fécamp, *Confessio theologica tribus partibus absoluta*. Paris: M. Vascovanum, 1539.

John of Fécamp, *La Confession théologique*, trans. Philippe de Vial. Paris: Les Éditions du Cerf, 1992.

John of Fécamp, Letter to Abbot of St. Berthe of Blagny. PL 147, cols 474D–475C.

John of Fécamp, Letter to Abbot Vital of Bernay. PL 147, cols 464D–465A.

John of Fécamp, Letter to Abbot Warin of Metz. PL 147, cols 465C–D.

Bibliography

John of Fécamp, Letter to Empress Agnes. *Epistolae* project, ed. Joan Ferrante. https://epistolae.ccnmtl.columbia.edu/letter/129.html.

John of Fécamp, Letter to *monachos dyscolos*. *PL* 147, cols 473B–474C.

John of Fécamp, Letter to Pope Leo IX. *PL* 143, cols 797–800B.

John of Fécamp, Letters to William the Conquerer. *PL* 147 cols 463C–464D, 476A–476C.

John of Fécamp, *Libellus de scripturis et verbis patrum collectus*, *PL* 147, cols 445–460C.

John of Fécamp, *Liber meditationem*. *PL* 40, cols 928–36.

John of Fécamp, *Un maître de la vie spirituelle au XI siècle: Jean de Fécamp*, ed. Jean Leclercq and Jean-Paul Bonnes. Paris: Vrin, 1946.

John of Fécamp, *Manuale* of Pseudo-Augustine. *PL* 40, cols 951–68.

John of Fécamp, *Meditationes* of Pseudo-Augustine. *PL* 40, cols 901–42.

John of Fécamp and Maurilius of Rouen, Letter to Bishop William of Evreux. *PL* 143, cols 1387–90.

John of Salerno, *St. Odo of Cluny: Being the Life of St. Odo of Cluny by John of Salerno*, ed. Gerard Sitwell. New York: Sheed and Ward, 1958.

Lanfranc of Canterbury, *The Monastic Constitutions of Lanfranc*, ed. David Knowles. Oxford: Clarendon Press, 2002.

Lanfranc of Canterbury and Guitmund of Aversa, *Lanfranc of Canterbury's On the Body and Blood of the Lord; Guitmund of Aversa's On the Truth of the Body and Blood of Christ in the Eucharist*, trans. Mark G. Vaillancourt. The Fathers of the Church: Medieval Continuation. Washington, DC: Catholic University of America Press, 2009.

'Lectiones ad prandium à l'abbaye de Fécamp au XIIIe siècle', ed. Denis-Bernard Grémont. *Cahiers Léopold Deslisle* 20 (1971): 3–41.

Leo IX, *Letters*. *PL* 143, col. 647B, letter 38.

Libellus de revelatione, aedificatione, et auctoritate Fiscannensis monasterii. *PL* 151, cols 701–24.

Liber tramitis aevi odilonis abbatis, ed. Petrus Dinter. *Corpus consuetudinum monasticarum*, vol. X. Siegburg: Franciscum Schmitt 1980.

Mabillon, Jean, ed., *Vetera analecta*. Paris: Montalant, 1723.

Martene, Edmond, and Ursin Durand, eds., *Thesaurus novus anecdotorum: Complectens regum ac principum*, vol. I. Paris: Gregg, 1717.

Odilo of Cluny, 'Un opuscule inédit de saint Odilon de Cluny', *Revue bénédictine* 16 (1899): 477–8.

Odonis abbatis Cluniacensis Occupatio, ed. Antonius Swoboda. Leipzig: B.G. Teubner, 1900.

Ordericus Vitalis, *The Ecclesiastical History of England and Normandy*, trans. Thomas Forester. London: Henry G. Bohn, 1856.

Ordinaire et coutumier de l'église cathédrale de Bayeux (XIIIe siècle), ed. Ulysse Chevalier. Paris: Alphonse Picard et Fils, 1902.
The Ordinal and Customary of the Abbey of Saint Mary, York, ed. Abbess of Stanbrook and J.B.L. Tolhurst. London: Henry Bradshaw Society, 1937.
The Ordinal of the Abbey of the Holy Trinity Fécamp (Fécamp, Musée de la Bénédictine, Ms 186), ed. David Chadd. 2 vols. London: Henry Bradshaw Society, 1999.
Recueil des actes des ducs de Normandie (911–1066), ed. Marie Fauroux. Caen: Société d'Impressions CARON, 1961.
Regesta Regum Anglo-Normannorum, ed. H.W.C. Davis and R.J. Whitwell. New York: Oxford University Press, 1913.
Registrum Anglie de Libris Doctorum et Auctorum Veterum, ed. Richard H. and Mary A. Rouse. London: British Library in association with the British Academy, 1991.
Robert de Torigni, *Chronique de Robert de Torigni*. Rouen: Librarie de la société de l'histoire de Normandie, 1873.
Sigebert of Gembloux, *Chronicon*, ed. Ludwig Conrad Bethmann. *MGH* Scriptores 6. Hanover, 1844.
Smaragdus of Saint-Mihiel, *Commentary on the Rule of Saint Benedict*, trans. David Barry. Cistercian Studies 212. Kalamazoo, MI: Cistercian Publications, 2007.
Smaragdus of Saint-Mihiel, *Diadema monastica*. PL 102, cols 593B–689A.
Le très ancien coutumier, ed. A. Lestringant. Rouen: Librarie de la société de l'histoire de Normandie, 1903.
Warin of Metz, Letter to John of Fécamp. PL 147, cols 466A–473A.
William of Jumièges, Orderic Vitalis, and Robert of Torigni, *The Gesta Normannorum Ducum of William of Jumièges, Orderic Vitalis, and Robert of Torigni*, ed. and trans. Elisabeth M.C. van Houts. Oxford: Clarendon Press, 1992.

Secondary sources

Adamo, Philip C. *New Monks in Old Habits: The Formation of the Caulite Monastic Order, 1193–1267*. Toronto: Pontifical Institute of Mediaeval Studies, 2014.
Albu, Emily. *The Normans in their Histories: Propaganda, Myth, and Subversion*. Woodbridge: Boydell Press, 2001.
Alexander, James. 'Herbert of Norwich, 1091–1119: Studies in the History of Norman England', *Studies in Medieval and Renaissance History* 6 (1969): 115–233.

Bibliography

Alexander, J.J.G. *Norman Illumination at Mont St. Michel*. Oxford: Clarendon Press, 1970.

Althoff, Gert, 'The Variability of Rituals in the Middle Ages', in *Medieval Concepts of the Past: Ritual, Memory, Historiography*, ed. Gerd Althoff, Johannes Fried, and Parick J. Geary. Cambridge: Cambridge University Press, 2002, pp. 71–87.

Altvater, Fran, 'Barren Mother, Dutiful Wife, Church Triumphant: Representations of Hannah in 1 Kings Illuminations', *Different Visions: A Journal of New Perspectives on Medieval Art* 3 (2011): 1–29.

Amory, Frederick, 'The Confessional Superstructure of Guibert de Nogent's Vita', *Classica et mediaevalia* 25 (1964): 224–40.

Arne-Dannenberg, Lars. 'Charity and Law. The Juristic Implementation of a Core Monastic Principle', in *Aspects of Charity: Concern for One's Neighbor in Medieval Vita Religiosa*, ed. Gert Melville. Berlin: Lit Verlag, 2011, pp. 11–28.

Arnoux, Mathieu. 'A.D. MI: Willelmus abbas Fiscannensis efficitur année de seigneur 1001: Guillaume devient abbé de Fécamp', in *De l'histoire à la légende, la broderie du Précieux-Sang*. Fécamp: Musée des Terre-Neuvas, 2001, p. 8.

Arnoux, Mathieu. 'Before the *Gesta Normannorum* and beyond Dudo: Some Evidence on Early Norman Historiography', *Anglo-Norman Studies* 22 (1999): 29–48.

Arnoux, Mathieu. 'Classe agricole, pouvoir seigneurial et autorité ducale: L'évolution de la Normandie féodale d'après le témoignage des chroniqueurs (Xe–XIIe siècles)', *Le Moyen Age* 97.1 (1992): 34–60.

Arnoux, Mathieu. *Des clercs au service de la réforme*. Turnhout: Brepols, 2000.

Arnoux, Mathieu. 'Disparition ou conservation des sources et abandon de l'acte écrit: Quelques observations sur les actes de Jumièges', *Tabularia* 1 (2001): 1–10.

Arnoux, Mathieu. 'Ermites et ermitages en Normandie (XI–XII siècles)', in *Ermites de France et d'Italie (XIe–Xve siècle)*, ed. André Vauchez. Rome: École française de Rome, 2003, pp. 115–35.

Arnoux, Mathieu. 'La fortune du *Libellus de revelatione, edificatione, et auctoritate Fiscannensis monsterii*', *Revue d'histoire des textes* 21 (1991): 135–58.

Arnoux, Mathieu. 'Le pays normand. Paysages et peuplement (IXe–XIIIe siècles)', *Tabularia* 3 (2003): 1–27.

Arnoux, Mathieu. 'Les premières chroniques de Fécamp: De l'hagiographie à l'histoire', in *Les saints dans le Normandie médiévale*, ed. Pierre Bouet and François Neveux. Caen: Presses universitaires de Caen, 1996, pp. 71–82.

Arnoux, Mathieu. 'Un Vénitien au Mont-Saint-Michel: Anastase, moine, ermite, et confesseur (d. vers 1085)', *Médiévales* 28 (1995): 55–78.

Bibliography

Asad, Talal. 'On Discipline and Humility in Medieval Christian Monasticism', in *Genealogies of Religion: Discipline and Reasons of Power in Christianity and Islam*. Baltimore, MD: Johns Hopkins University Press, 1993, pp. 125–67.

Augier, Marie-Françoise. 'La bibliothèque de Saint-Bénigne de Dijon au XVIIe siècle: Le témoignage de Dom Hugues Lanthenas', *Scriptorium* 39.2 (1985): 234–64.

Avril, François. *Manuscrits normands XI–XIIeme siècles*. Rouen: Musée des Beaux Arts, 1975.

Avril, François. 'Notes sur quelques manuscrits Bénédictins Normands du XIe et du XIIe siècle', *Mélanges d'archéologie et d'histoire* 76 (1964): 491–525.

Baert, Barbara. 'Heraclius, l'exaltion de la croix et le Mont-Saint-Michel au XIe s.: Une lecture attentive du ms. 641 de la Pierpont Morgan Library à New York', *Cahiers de civilisation médiévale* 51 (2008): 3–20.

Baker, Derek. '"The Whole World a Hermitage": Ascetic Renewal and the Crisis of Western Monasticism', in *The Culture of Christendom*, ed. Marc Anthony Meyer. London: Hambledon Press, 1993, pp. 207–23.

Banniard, Michel. 'Vrais aveux et fausses confessions du IXe au XIe siècle: Vers une écriture autobiographique?' in *L'aveu. Antiquité et moyen-âge*, ed. Jean-Claude Marie Vigueur. Rome: École française de Rome, 1984, pp. 215–41.

Bannister, Emily A. '"From Nitria to Sitria": The Construction of Peter Damian's *Vita Beati Romualdi*', *European Review of History* 18.4 (2011): 499–522.

Bardy, G. 'Le souvenir de S. Ephrem dans le haut moyen-âge latin', *Revue du moyen âge latin* 2 (1946): 297–300.

Barrau, Julie. 'Did Medieval Monks Actually Speak Latin?', in *Understanding Practices of Oral Communication (Western Europe, Tenth–Thirteenth Centuries)*, ed. Steven Vanderputten. Turnhout: Brepols, 2011, pp. 293–317.

Barret, Sébastien. 'Cluny et les Ottoniens', in *Ottone III e Romualdo di Ravenna: Impero, monasteri e santi asceti*. Fonte Avellana: Gabrielli, 2002, pp. 179–213.

Barret, Sébastien. 'L'individu en action: Quelques réflexions autour des coutumes et statuts clunisiens (XIe–XIIIe siècles)', in *Das Eigene und das Ganze. Zum individuellen im mittelalterlichen Religiosentum*, ed. Gert Melville and Markus Schürer. Münster: Lit Verlag, 2002, pp. 531–62.

Barrow, Julia. 'Ideas and Applications of Reform', in *The Cambridge History of Christianity*, vol. III, ed. Thomas F.X. Noble and Julia M.H. Smith. New York: Cambridge University Press, 2008, pp. 345–62.

Bates, David. 'The Earliest Norman Writs', *English Historical Review* 100.395 (1985): 266–84.

Bibliography

Bates, David. *Normandy before 1066*. New York: Longman, 1982.
Bates, David. 'Rouen from 900 to 1204: From Scandanavian Settlement to Angevin "Capital"', in *Medieval Art, Architecture, and Archaeology at Rouen*, ed. Jenny Stratford. London: British Archaeological Association, 1986, pp. 1–8.
Bauduin, Pierre. *La première Normandie (Xe–XIe siècles)*. Caen: Presses universitaires de Caen, 2004.
Bauduin, Pierre. 'Les sources de l'histoire du duché: Publications et inventaires récents', *Tabularia* 3 (2003): 29–55.
Baylé, Maylis. 'Architecture et enluminure dans le monde normand', in *Manuscrits et enluminures dans le monde normand (Xe–XVe siècles)*, ed. Pierre Bouet and Monique Dosdat. Caen: Office universitaire d'études normandes, 1999, pp. 51–69.
Baylé, Maylis. 'L'influence des Italiens sur l'art roman de Normandie: Légende ou réalité?', *Cahier des Annales de Normandie* 29 (2000): 45–64.
Baylé, Maylis. 'Norman Architecture around the Year 1000: Its Place in the Art of Northwestern Europe', *Anglo-Norman Studies* 22 (2000): 1–25.
Beaune, Colette. 'Les ducs, le roi et le saint sang', in *Saint-Denis et la royauté: Études offertes à Bernard Guenée*, ed. Françoise Autrand, Claude Gauvard, and Jean-Marie Moeglin. Paris: Éditions de la Sorbonne, 1999, pp. 711–32.
Beaurepaire, M.F. de. 'Essai sur le Pays de Caux au temps de la première abbaye de Fécamp', in *L'abbaye bénédictine de Fécamp: Ouvrage scientifique du XIIIe centenaire (658–1958)*, vol. I. Fécamp: EMTN, 1959, pp. 3–21.
Beckwith, Sarah. *Christ's Body: Identity, Culture, and Society in Later Medieval Writings*. London: Routledge, 1993.
Bell, S.G. 'Medieval Women Book Owners: Arbiters of Lay Piety and Ambassadors of Culture', in *Sisters and Workers in the Middle Ages*, ed. J.M. Bennett. Chicago: University of Chicago Press, 1989, pp. 135–61.
Belting, Hans. *The Image and Its Public in the Middle Ages: Form and Function of Early Paintings of the Passion*. New Rochelle, NY: Caratzas, 1990.
Benke, Christoph. 'Gottesliebe im 11. Jahrhundert. Johannes von Fécamp –ein Wegbereiter Bernhards von Clairvaux', *Studia Monastica* 39.2 (1997): 339–63.
Bennett, J.A.W. *Poetry of the Passion*. Oxford: Clarendon Press, 1982.
Benton, John F. 'Consciousness of Self and of Individuality', in *Renaissance and Renewal in the Twelfth Century*, ed. Robert L. Benson, and Giles Constable. Cambridge, MA: Harvard University Press, 1982, pp. 263–98.
Berger, Blandine-Dominique. *Le drame liturgique de Paques du Xe au XIIIe siècle: Liturgie et théâtre*. Théologie historique 37. Paris: Éditions Beauchesne, 1976.

Berger, Samuel. 'Confession des péchés attribuée à Saint Patrice', *Revue celtique* 15 (1894): 155–9.

Bériou, Nicole, ed. *Prier au moyen âge: Pratiques et expériences (Ve–XVe siècles)*. Turnhout: Brepols, 1991.

Bestul, Thomas H. 'The Collection of Private Prayers in the "Portiforium" of Wulfstan of Worcester and the "Orationes Sive Meditationes" of Anselm of Canterbury', in *Les mutations socio-culturelles au tournant des XIe–XIIe siècles*, ed. Raymonde Foreville. Paris: CNRS, 1984, pp. 355–64.

Bestul, Thomas H. 'Meditation/*Meditatio*', in *The Cambridge Companion to Christian Mysticism*, ed. Amy Hollywood and Patricia Z. Beckman. New York: Cambridge University Press, 2012, pp. 157–66.

Bestul, Thomas H. 'Self and Subjectivity in the *Prayers and Meditations* of Anselm of Canterbury', in *Saint Anselm, Bishop and Thinker*, ed. Roman Majeran and Edward Iwo Zielinski. Lublin: Catholic University of Lublin Press, 1996, pp. 147–56.

Bestul, Thomas H. 'St. Augustine and the *Orationes side meditations* of St. Anselm', *Anselm Studies* 2 (1988): 597–606.

Bestul, Thomas H. *Texts of the Passion: Latin Devotional Literature and Medieval Society*. Philadelphia: University of Pennsylvania Press, 1996.

Beuckers, Klaus Gereon. 'Das Ottonische Stifterbild. Bildtypen, Handlungsmotiven und Stifterstatus in ottonischen und frühsalischen Stifterdarstellungen', in *Die Ottonen: Kunst – Architektur – Geschichte*, ed. Klaus Gereon Beuckers, Johannes Cramer, and Michael Imhof. Petersburg: Imhof, 2006, pp. 63–102.

Bischoff, Bernhard. *Mittelalterliche Schatzverzeichnisse: von der Zeit Karls des Großen bis zur Mitte des 13. Jahrhunderts*. Munich: Prestel-Verlag, 1967.

Bisson, Thomas N. *The Crisis of the Twelfth Century*. Princeton, NJ: Princeton University Press, 2009.

Bjork, David A. 'On the Dissemination of the *Quem quaeritis* and the *Visitatio sepulchri* and the Chronology of their Early Sources', in *The Drama of the Middle Ages: Comparative and Critical Essays*, ed. Clifford Davidson, C.J. Gianakaris, and John H. Stroupe. New York: AMC Press, 1982, pp. 1–24.

Blacker, Jean. 'Monastic History in a Courtly Mode? Author and Audience in Guillaume de Saint-Pair's *Roman du Mont-Saint-Michel* and the Anonymous *Histoire de l'Abbaye de Fécamp*', in *Literary Aspects of Courtly Culture*, ed. Donald Maddox and Susan Strum-Maddox. Cambridge: D.S. Brewer, 1992, pp. 291–9.

Bligny, Bernard. 'L'église et le siècle de l'an mil au début du XIIe siècle', *Cahiers de civilisation médiévale* 27 (1984): 5–33.

Bloche, Michaël. 'Le chartrier de l'abbaye de la Trinité de Fécamp: Etude et édition critique, 928/929–1190'. PhD dissertation, École nationale des chartes, 2012.

Bloche, Michaël. 'Le chartrier de l'abbaye de la Trinité de Fécamp (929–1190): Une source importante pour l'histoire anglo-normande', *Études normandes* 12.2 (2012).

Bloche, Michaël. 'La souscription dans les actes des abbés de Fécamp (XIe–début du XIVe siècle)', *Tabularia* 12 (2012): 1–28.

Boertjes, Katja. 'Pilgrim Ampullae from Vendôme: Souvenirs from a Pilgrimage to the Holy Tear of Christ', in *Art and Architecture of Late Medieval Pilgrimage in Northern Europe and the British Isles*, ed. Sarah Blick and Rita Tekippe. Boston: Brill, 2005, pp. 443–72.

Bolotte, Pierre and Paul Feuilloley. *Trésors des abbayes normandes*. Rouen: Musée des Antiquités, 1979.

Bonde, Sheila, Clark Maines, and Alba Serino. 'Mastering the Landscape: A Comparative Analysis of Monastic Domain Formation', conference paper, Medieval Academy of America Annual Meeting, Knoxville, TN, April 2013.

Bonnes, Jean-Paul and Jean Leclercq. *Un maître de la vie spirituelle au XIe siècle*. Paris: Vrin, 1946.

Boquet, Damien. 'Affectivity in the Spiritual Writings of Aelred of Rievaulx', in *A Companion to Aelred of Rievaulx (1110–1167)*, ed. Marsha L. Dutton. Boston: Brill, 2017, pp. 167–96.

Boquet, Damien. *L'ordre de l'affect au moyen âge: Autour de l'anthropologie affective d'Aelred de Rievaulx*. Caen: CRAHM, 2005.

Boquet, Damien, and Piroska Nagy. *Medieval Sensibilities: A History of Emotions in the Middle Ages*. New York: Polity, 2018.

Boquet, Damien, and Piroska Nagy. *Sensible moyen âge: Une histoire des émotions dans l'Occident médiéval*. Paris: Seuil, 2015.

Boquet, Damien, and Piroska Nagy. *Le sujet des émotions au moyen âge*. Paris: Beauchesne, 2008.

Bouchard, Constance B. *Every Valley Shall Be Exalted: The Discourse of Opposites in Twelfth-Century Thought*. Ithaca, NY: Cornell University Press, 2003.

Bouchard, Constance B. *Holy Entrepreneurs: Cistercians, Knights, and Economic Exchange in Twelfth-Century Burgundy*. Ithaca, NY: Cornell University Press, 1991.

Bouchard, Constance B. 'Monastic Cartularies: Organizing Eternity', in *Charters, Cartularies, and Archives: The Preservation and Transmission of Documents in the Medieval West*, ed. Anders Winroth and Adam J. Kosto. New York: Pontifical Institute of Mediaeval Studies, 2002, pp. 22–32.

Bouet, Pierre. 'Dudon de Saint-Quentin et Fécamp', *Tabularia* 2 (2002): 57–70.

Bouet, Pierre, and Monique Dosdat. *Manuscrits et enluminures dans le monde normand (Xe–XVe siècles)*. Caen: Office universitaire d'études normandes, 1999.

Bourke, Julia. 'An Experiment in "Neurohistory": Reading Emotions in Aelred's *De institutione inclusarum* (Rule for a Recluse)', *Journal of Medieval Religious Cultures* 42.1 (2016): 124–42.

Bouvris, Jean-Michel. 'Contribution à une étude de l'institution vicomtale en Normandie au XIe siècle. L'exemple de la partie orientale du Duché: Les vicomtes de Rouen et de Fécamp', in *Autour du pouvoir ducal normand Xe–XIIe siècles*, ed. Lucien Musset. Caen: Centre d'études normandes de l'Université de Caen, 1985, pp. 148–74.

Boynton, Susan. '*Libelli Precum* in the Central Middle Ages', in *A History of Prayer*, ed. Roy Hammerling. Leiden: Brill, 2008, pp. 255–318.

Boynton, Susan. 'Oral Transmission of Liturgical Practice in the Eleventh-Century Customaries of Cluny', in *Understanding Monastic Practices of Oral Communication (Western Europe, Tenth–Thirteenth Centuries)*, ed. Steven Vanderputten. Turnhout: Brepols, 2011, pp. 67–85.

Boynton, Susan. 'Prayer as Liturgical Performance in Eleventh- and Twelfth-Century Monastic Psalters', *Speculum* 82 (2007): 895–931.

Boynton, Susan. *Shaping a Monastic Identity: Liturgy and History at the Imperial Abbey of Farfa, 1000–1125*. Ithaca, NY: Cornell University Press, 2006.

Bozoky, Edina. 'Les romans du Graal et le culte du Précieux Sang', *Tabularia* 9 (2009): 13–25.

Branch, Betty. 'The Development of Script in Eleventh- and Twelfth-Century Manuscripts of the Norman Abbey of Fécamp'. PhD dissertation, Duke University, 1974.

Branch, Betty. 'Inventories of the Library of Fécamp from the Eleventh and Twelfth Centuries', *Manuscripta* 23 (1979): 159–72.

Branch, Betty. 'William Peccator et les manuscrits de Fécamp 1100–1150', *Cahiers de civilisation médiévale* 26 (1983): 195–201.

Brantley, Jessica. *Reading in the Wilderness*. Chicago: University of Chicago Press, 2007.

Brasington, Bruce C. 'From Charitable Sentiments to Amicable Settlements: A Note on the Terminology of Twelfth-Century Canon Law', in *Aspects of Charity: Concern for One's Neighbor in Medieval Vita Religiosa*, ed. Gert Melville. Berlin: Lit Verlag, 2011, pp. 1–10.

Bréhier, Louis. 'L'église abbatiale de Fécamp', *Journal des savants* June/July (1930): 225–60, 307–15.

Breitenstein, Mirko. 'Is There a Cistercian Love? Some Considerations on the Virtue of Charity', in *Aspects of Charity: Concern for One's Neighbor in Medieval Vita Religiosa*, ed. Gert Melville. Berlin: Lit Verlag, 2011, pp. 55–98.

Brockhaus, Karin. *L'abbatiale de la Trinité de Fécamp et l'architecture normande au moyen âge*. Caen: Société des Antiquaires de Normandie, 2009.

Brockhaus, Karin. 'Form Follows Function? De la corrélation entre pèlerinage et architecture dans l'abbatiale de Fécamp à la fin du XIe siècle', in *Pèlerinages et lieux de pèlerinage en Normandie*. Fécamp: Fédération des Sociétés Historiques et Archéologiques de Normandie, 2010, pp. 195–205.

Brockhaus, Karin. 'La genèse architecturale de l'église de la Trinité de Fécamp', *Tabularia* 2 (2002): 71–82.

Brooke, Christopher. *Europe in the Central Middle Ages: 962–1154*. Harlow: Longman, 1995.

Brooke, Christopher. 'Princes and Kings as Patrons of Monasteries: Normandy and England', in *Il monachesimo e la riforma ecclesiastica (1049–1122)*. Milan: Vita e Pensiero, 1971, pp. 125–52.

Brown, Peter. *Augustine of Hippo: A Biography*. Berkeley: University of California Press, 1967.

Bruce, Scott. 'The Lost Patriarchs Project: Recovering the Greek Fathers in the Medieval Latin Tradition', *Religion Compass* 12 (forthcoming).

Bryan, Jennifer. *Looking Inward: Devotional Reading and the Private Self in Late Medieval England*. Philadelphia: University of Pennsylvania Press, 2008.

Bull, Marcus. *Knightly Piety and the Lay Response to the First Crusade: The Limousin and Gascony, c. 970–c. 1130*. Oxford: Clarendon Press, 1993.

Bulst, Neithard. 'La réforme monastique en Normandie: Étude prosopographique sur la diffusion et l'implantation de la réforme de Guillaume de Dijon', in *Les mutations socio-culturelles au tournant des XIe–XIIe siècles*, ed. Raymonde Foreville. Paris: CNRS, 1984, pp. 317–30.

Bulst, Neithard. *Untersuchungen zu den Klosterreformen Wilhelms von Dijon (962–1031)*. Bonn: Ludwig Röhrscheid Verlag, 1973.

Bultot, R. *La doctrine du mépris du monde*. Louvain: Nauwelaerts, 1963–64.

Burton, Janet, and Julie Kerr. *The Cistercians in the Middle Ages*. Woodbridge: Boydell & Brewer, 2011.

Bynum, Caroline Walker. *Christian Materiality*. New York: Zone Books, 2011.

Bynum, Caroline Walker. *Docere verbo et exemplo: An Aspect of Twelfth-Century Spirituality*. Cambridge, MA: Harvard University Press, 1979.

Bynum, Caroline Walker. *Fragmentation and Redemption: Essays on Gender and the Human Body in Medieval Religion*. New York: Zone Books, 1991.

Bynum, Caroline Walker. *Jesus as Mother: Studies in the Spirituality of the High Middle Ages*. Berkeley: University of California Press, 1982.

Bibliography

Bynum, Caroline Walker. *Wonderful Blood: Theology and Practice in Late Medieval Northern Germany and Beyond*. Philadelphia: University of Pennsylvania Press, 2007.

Cadiou-Delabos, Yannique. 'Un abbé réformateur face aux ducs de Normandie: Jean de Fécamp (1028–1078)', *Annales du patriomoine de Fécamp* 2 (1995): 42–51.

Callahan, Daniel. *Jerusalem and the Cross in the Life and Writings of Ademar of Chabannes*. Turnhout: Brill, 2016.

Camille, Michael. '"Him whom you have ardently desired you may see": Cistercian Exegesis and the Prefatory Pictures in a French Apocalypse', in *Studies in Cistercian Art and Architecture*, ed. M.P. Lillich. Kalamazoo, MI: Cistercian Publications, 1987, pp. 137–60.

Cantor, Norman F. 'The Crisis of Western Monasticism, 1050–1130', *American Historical Review* 66 (1960): 47–67.

Carment-Lanfry, Anne-Marie. 'Les églises Romanes dans les anciens archidiaconés du grand et du petit caux au diocèse de Rouen: Fécamp', *Annales du patriomoine de Fécamp* 2 (1995): 72–9.

Carruthers, Mary. *The Book of Memory: A Study of Memory in Medieval Culture*. New York: Cambridge University Press, 1990.

Carruthers, Mary. 'The Concept of *Ductus*, or Journeying through a Work of Art', in *Rhetoric beyond Words: Delight and Persuasion in the Arts of the Middle Ages*, ed. Mary Carruthers. New York: Cambridge University Press, 2010, pp. 190–213.

Carruthers, Mary. *The Craft of Thought: Meditation, Rhetoric, and the Making of Images, 400–1200*. New York: Cambridge University Press, 1998.

Cary, Phillip. *Augustine's Invention of the Inner Self: The Legacy of a Christian Platonist*. New York: Oxford University Press, 2000.

Cazelles, Brigitte. '*Le Précieux Sang de Fécamp: Origine et développement d'un mythe chrétien* by Jean-Guy Gouttebroze' [review], *Speculum* 78.2 (2003): 504–6.

Chadd, David. 'The Medieval Customary of the Cathedral Priory', in *Norwich Cathedral: Church, City, and Diocese*, ed. Ian Atherton, Eric Fernie, Christopher Harper-Bill, and Hassell Smith. London: Hambleton Press, 1996, pp. 314–24.

Chaplais, M. Pierre. 'Une charte originale de Guillaume le Conquerant pour l'abbaye de Fécamp: La donation de Steyning et de Bury (1085)', in *L'abbaye bénédictine de Fécamp: Ouvrage scientifique du XIIIe centenaire (658–1958)*, vol. I. Fécamp: EMTN, 1959, pp. 355–7.

Chaussy, Yves. 'Les Mauristes et l'édition de saint Augustin', in *Troisième centenaire de l'édition Mauriste de saint Augustin*. Collection des Études augustiniennes. Turnhout: Brepols, 1990, pp. 29–35.

Bibliography

Chazelle, Celia. *The Crucified God in the Carolingian Era: Theology and Art of Christ's Passion*. Cambridge: Cambridge University Press, 2001.

Chenu, Marie-Dominique. *Nature, Man, and Society in the Twelfth Century: Essays on New Theological Perspectives in the Latin West*. Toronto: University of Toronto Press, 1997.

Chiailley, Jacques. 'Jumièges et les séquences aquitaines', in *Jumièges: Congrès scientifique du XIIIe centenaire*, vol. II. Rouen: Lecerf, 1954, pp. 937–41.

Chibnall, Marjorie. 'The Empress Matilda and Bec-Hellouin', in *Piety, Power, and History in Medieval England and Normandy*. Brookfield, VT: Ashgate, 2000, pp. 35–48.

Chibnall, Marjorie. 'The Empress Matilda and Church Reform', in *Piety, Power, and History in Medieval England and Normandy*. Brookfield, VT: Ashgate, 2000, pp. 107–30.

Chibnall, Marjorie. 'Fécamp and England', in *L'abbaye bénédictine de Fécamp: Ouvrage scientifique du XIIIe centenaire (658–1958)*, vol. I. Fécamp: EMTN, 1959, pp. 363–6.

Chibnall, Marjorie. 'From Bec to Canterbury: Anselm and Monastic Privilege', in *Piety, Power, and History in Medieval England and Normandy*. Brookfield, VT: Ashgate, 2000, pp. 23–44.

Chibnall, Marjorie. *The Normans*. Malden, MA: Blackwell, 2000.

Chibnall, Marjorie. *The World of Orderic Vitalis: Norman Monks and Norman Knights*. Woodbridge: Boydell & Brewer, 1984.

Choy, Renie S. '"The Brother Who May Wish to Pray by Himself": Sense of Self in Carolingian Prayers of Private Devotion', in *Prayer and Thought in Monastic Tradition: Essays in Honour of Benedicta Ward, SLG*, ed. Santha Bhattacharji, Rowan Williams, and Dominic Mattos. New York: Bloomsbury, 2014, pp. 101–20.

Choy, Renie S. *Intercessory Prayer and the Monastic Ideal in the Time of the Carolingian Reforms*. New York: Oxford University Press, 2017.

Christ, Karl. *The Handbook of Medieval Library History*, trans. Theophil M. Otto. Metuchen, NJ: Scarecrow Press, 1984.

Christ, Karl. 'In Caput Quadragesimae', *Zentralblatt für Bibliothekswesen* 60 (1943): 33–59.

Clark, James G. *The Benedictines in the Middle Ages*. Woodbridge: Boydell Press, 2011.

Cochelin, Isabelle. 'Besides the Book: Using the Body to Mould the Mind: Cluny in the Tenth and Eleventh Centuries', in *Medieval Monastic Education*, ed. George Ferzoco and Carolyn Muessig. New York: Leicester University Press, 2000, pp. 21–35.

Cochelin, Isabelle. 'Étude sur les hiérarchies monastiques: Le prestige de l'ancienneté et son éclipse à Cluny au XIe siècle', *Revue Mabillon* 11 (2000): 5–37.

Cochelin, Isabelle. 'Évolution des coutumiers monastiques dessinée à partir de l'étude de Bernard', in *From Dead of Night to End of Day: The Medieval Customs of Cluny*, ed. Susan Boynton and Isabelle Cochelin. Turnhout: Brepols, 2005, pp. 29–66.

Cochelin, Isabelle. 'Obedience or Agency?', in *Oboedientia: zu Formen und Grenzen von Macht und Unterordnung im mittelalterlichen Religiosentum*, ed. Sébastien Baret and Gert Melville. Münster: Lit Verlag, 2005, pp. 229–53.

Cochelin, Isabelle. 'Peut-on parler de noviciat à Cluny pour les Xe–XIe siècles?', *Revue Mabillon* 70 (1998): 17–52.

Cohen, Adam. 'Art, Exegesis, and Affective Piety in Twelfth-Century German Manuscripts', in *Manuscripts and Monastic Culture: Reform and Renewal in Twelfth-Century Germany*, ed. Alison I. Beach. Turnhout: Brepols, 2002, pp. 45–68.

Cohen, Adam. *The Uta Codex: Art, Philosophy, and Reform in the Eleventh-Century*. Philadelphia: Pennsylvania State University Press, 2000.

Collamore, Lila. 'Charting the Divine Office', in *The Divine Office in the Latin Middle Ages*, ed. Margot Fassler and Richard Baltzer. New York: Oxford University Press, 2000, pp. 3–11.

Conant, Kenneth John. 'Cluny II and Saint-Bénigne at Dijon', *Archaeologia* 99 (1965): 179–94.

Constable, Giles. 'The Authority of Superiors in the Religious Communities', in *La notion d'autorité au moyen âge. Islam, Byzance, Occident*, ed. George Makdisi, Dominique Sourdel, and Janine Sourdel-Thomine. Paris: Presses universitaires de France, 1982, pp. 189–210.

Constable, Giles. 'The Concern for Sincerity and Understanding in Liturgical Prayer, Especially in the Twelfth Century', in *Classica et Mediaevalia: Studies in Honor of Joseph Szöverffy*, ed. Irene Vaslef and Helmut Buschhausen. Washington, DC: Classical Folia, 1986, pp. 17–30.

Constable, Giles. 'The Cross in Medieval Monastic Life', in *Christianity and Culture in the Middle Ages: Essays to Honor John Van Engen*, ed. David C. Mengel and Lisa Wolverton. Notre Dame, IN: University of Notre Dame Press, 2014, pp. 236–50.

Constable, Giles. *Letters and Letter Collections*. Typologie des sources du moyen âge occidental 17. Turnhout: Brepols, 1976.

Constable, Giles. 'Monasteries, Rural Churches, and the *Cura animarum*', in *Settimane di studio del Centro italiano di studi sull'Alto Medioevo*. Spoleto: Centro italiano di studi sull'Alto Medioevo, 1982, pp. 349–95.

Bibliography

Constable, Giles. 'Monastic Possession of Churches and "Spiritualia" in the Age of Reform', in *Il monachesimo e la riforma ecclesiastica (1049–1122)*. Milan: Vita e Pensiero, 1971, pp. 304–31.

Constable, Giles. *The Reformation of the Twelfth Century*. New York: Cambridge University Press, 1996.

Constable, Giles. 'Renewal and Reform in Religious Life: Concepts and Realities', in *Renaissance and Renewal in the Twelfth Century*, ed. Robert L. Benson and Giles Constable. Toronto: Medieval Academy Reprints for Teaching, 1991, pp. 37–67.

Constable, Giles. *Three Studies in Medieval Religious and Social Thought*. New York: Cambridge University Press, 1995.

Copeland, Rita. 'The Middle English "Candet nudatum pectus" and the Norms of Early Vernacular Translation Practice', *Leeds Studies in English* 15 (1984): 57–81.

Corbin, Solange. *La deposition liturgique du Christ au Vendredi Saint: Sa place dans l'histoire des rites et du théâtre religieux (analyse de documents portugais)*. Paris: Les Belles Lettres, 1960.

Cottier, Jean-François. *Anima mea: Prières privées et textes de dévotion du moyen âge latin*. Turnhout: Brepols, 2001.

Cottier, Jean-François. 'Le recueil apocryphe des *Orationes sive meditationes* de saint Anselme: Sa formation et sa réception en Angleterre et en France au XIIe siècle', in *Anselm: Aosta, Bec, and Canterbury*, ed. D.E. Luscombe and G.R. Evans. Sheffield: Sheffield Academic Press, 1996, pp. 282–96.

Cottier, Jean-François, ed. *La prière en latin de l'antiquité au XVIe siècle: Formes, évolutions, significations*. Turnhout: Brepols, 2006.

Coupry, Claude. 'Les pigments utilisés pour l'enluminure à Fécamp aux XIe et XIIe siècles', in *Manuscrits et enluminures dans le monde normand (Xe–XVe siècles)*, ed. Pierre Bouet and Monique Dosdat. Caen: Office universitaire d'études normandes, 1999, pp. 69–81.

Courcelle, Pierre. *Les Confessions de saint Augustin dans la tradition littéraire: Antécédents et postérité*. Paris: Études augustiniennes, 1963.

Courcelle, Pierre. *Connais-toi toi-même, de Socrate à saint Bernard*. Paris: Études augustiniennes, 1974.

Courcelle, Pierre. 'Quelques illustrations du *Contra Faustum* de saint Augustin', in *Oikoumene*, ed. Jeanne Courcelle-Ladmirant. Catania: VDM Publishing, 1964, pp. 1–9.

Cousin, Patrice. 'Le monastère de Fécamp des origines à la destruction par les Normands', in *L'abbaye bénédictine de Fécamp*, vol. I. Fécamp: EMTN, 1959, pp. 23–5.

Cousins, Ewert. 'The Humanity and Passion of Christ', in *Christian Spirituality: High Middle Ages and Reformation*, ed. Jill Raitt, Bernard McGuinn, and John Meyendorff. New York: Crossroad, 1987, pp. 380–4.

Cowdrey, Herbert Edward John. *The Cluniacs and the Gregorian Reform.* Oxford: Clarendon Press, 1970.

Cowdrey, Herbert Edward John. *Lanfranc: Scholar, Monk, and Archbishop.* New York: Oxford University Press, 2003.

Cowdrey, Herbert Edward John. 'The Papacy and the Berengarian Controversy', in *Auctoritas und Ratio: Studien zu Berengar von Tours*, ed. Peter Felix Ganz, Robert Burchard Huygens, and Friedrich Niewöhner. Wiesbaden: Harrassowitz, 1990, pp. 109–36.

Cownie, Emma. *Religious Patronage in Anglo-Norman England 1066–1135.* Woodbridge: Boydell Press, 1998.

Crozet, René. 'Le monument de la Sainte Larme à la Trinité de Vendôme', *Bulletin Monumental* 121 (1963): 171–80.

Cushing, Kathleen. *Reform and Papacy in the Eleventh Century: Spirituality and Social Change.* New York: Manchester University Press, 2005.

D'Acunto, Nicolangelo. *L'età dell'obbedienza. Papato, impero, e poteri locali nel secolo XI.* Naples: Liguori Editore, 2007.

Dauphin, Dom Hubert. *Le bienheureux Richard, abbé de Saint-Vanne de Verdun.* Leuven: Peeters, 1946.

Dauphin, Dom Hubert. 'Monastic Reforms from the Tenth Century to the Twelfth', *Downside Review* 70 (1952): 62–75.

Davis, Kathleen. *Periodization and Sovereignty: How Ideas of Feudalism and Secularization Govern the Politics of Time.* Philadelphia: University of Pennsylvania Press, 2008.

Davis, Robert Glenn. *The Weight of Love: Affect, Ecstacy, and Union in the Theology of Bonaventure.* New York: Fordham University Press, 2017.

de Boüard, Michel. 'Notes et hypothèses sur Maurille, moine de Fécamp, et son élection au siège métropolitain de Rouen', in *L'abbaye bénédictine de Fécamp: Ouvrage scientifique du XIIIe centenaire (658–1958)*, vol. I. Fécamp: EMTN, 1959, pp. 81–92.

de Genouillac, Gourdon. *Histoire de l'abbaye de Fécamp et ses abbés.* Fécamp: A. Marinier, 1875.

de Jong, Mayke. 'From Scholastici to Scioli: Alcuin and the Formation of an Intellectual Elite', in *Alcuin of York*, ed. L.A.J.R. Houwen and A.A. MacDonald. Groningen: Egbert Forsten, 1998, pp. 45–57.

de Jong, Mayke. *In Samuel's Image: Child Oblation in the Early Medieval West.* Leiden: E.J. Brill, 1996.

Bibliography

de Jong, Mayke. *The Penitential State: Authority and Atonement in the Age of Louis the Pious, 814–840*. New York: Cambridge University Press, 2009.

de Montclos, Jean. *Lanfranc et Bérenger: La controverse eucharistique du XIe siècle*. Leuven: Spicilegium Sacrum Lovaniense, 1971.

Debiais, Vincent. 'L'écrit sur la tombe: Entre nécessité pratique, souci pour le salut et élaboration doctrinale. À travers la documentation épigraphique de la Normandie médiévale', *Tabularia* 7 (2007): 179–202.

DeGregorio, Scott. 'Affective Spirituality: Theory and Practice in Bede and Alfred the Great', *Essays in Medieval Studies* 22 (2005): 129–39.

Dekkers, Eligius. 'Sur la diffusion au moyen âge des oeuvres moins connues de saint Augustin', in *Homo Spiritalis: Festgabe für Luc Verheijen OSA*, ed. Cornelius Mayer. Würzburg: Augustinus-Verlag, 1987, pp. 446–59.

Delaporte, Yves. 'L'office Fécampois de Saint Taurin', in *L'abbaye bénédictine de Fécamp: Ouvrage scientifique du XIIIe centenaire (658–1958)*, vol. I. Fécamp: EMTN, 1959, pp. 171–89.

Delaporte, Yves. 'Les ordinaires de Jumièges', in *Jumièges: Congrès scientifique du XIIIe centenaire*, vol. II. Rouen: Lecerf, 1954, pp. 873–82.

Delhaye, Philippe. 'Un dossier eucharistique d'Anselme de Laon à l'abbaye de Fécamp au XIIe siècle', in *L'abbaye bénédictine de Fécamp: Ouvrage scientifique du XIIIe centenaire (658–1958)*, vol. II. Fécamp: EMTN, 1959, pp. 153–61.

Deliyannis, Deborah Mauskopf. *Ravenna in Late Antiquity*. New York: Cambridge University Press, 2010.

Derbes, Anne. *Picturing the Passion in Late Medieval Italy*. New York: Cambridge University Press, 1996.

Derolez, Albert. *Les catalogues de bibliothèques*. Turnhout: Brepols, 1979.

Deslile, Léopold. *Inventaire des manuscrits de la Bibliothèque nationale: Fonds de Cluni*. Paris: Librarie H. Champion, 1924.

Deuffic, Jean-Luc. 'La production manuscrite des scriptoria Bretons (VIIIe–XIe siècles)', in *Landévennec et le monachisme breton dans le haut moyen âge*, ed. Marc Simon. Bannalec: Association Landévennec, 1985, pp. 289–321.

Diard, Olivier. 'Histoire et chant liturgique en Normandie au XIe siècle: Les offices propres particuliers des diocèses d'Évreux et de Rouen', *Annales de Normandie* 53.3 (2003): 195–223.

Diard, Olivier. *Répertoire des manuscrits liturgiques en Haute-Normandie*. Rouen: Presses universitaires de Rouen et du Havre, 2011.

Diehl, Jay. 'From Piety to Parchment: Monastic Spirituality and the Formation of Literate Cultures, 1050–1200'. PhD dissertation, New York University, 2011.

Diem, Albrecht. 'The Gender of the Religious: Wo/Men and the Invention of Monasticism', in *The Oxford Handbook of Women and Gender in Medieval Europe*, ed. Judith M. Bennett and Ruth Mazo Karras. New York: Oxford University Press, 2013, pp. 432–46.

Diem, Albrecht. 'The Stolen Glove: On the Hierachy and Power of Objects in Columbanian Monasteries', in *Shaping Stability: The Normation and Formation of Religious Life in the Middle Ages*, ed. K. Pansters and A. Plunkett-Latimer. Turnhout: Brepols, 2016, pp. 51–67.

Dilley, Paul C., *Monasteries and the Care of Souls in Late Antique Christianity*. New York: Cambridge University Press, 2017.

Dixon, Thomas M. *From Pasions to Emotions: The Creation of a Secular Psychological Category*. New York: Cambridge University Press, 2003.

Dodwell, B. 'The Foundation of Norwich Cathedral', *Transactions of the Royal Historical Society* 7 (1957): 1–18.

Dolan, Diane. *Le drame liturgique de Pâques en Normandie et en Angleterre au moyen-âge*. Paris: Presses universitaires de France, 1975.

Dolbeau, François. 'Passion et résurrection du Christ, selon Gerbert, abbé de Saint-Wandrille (d. 1089)', in *Latin Culture in the Eleventh Century*, ed. Michael W. Herren, C.J. McDonough, and Ross G. Arthur. Turnhout: Brepols, 2002, pp. 223–49.

Dolbeau, François. 'Prier avec les mots des saints dans l'occident médiéval', in *La prière en latin de l'antiquité au XVIe siècle*, ed. Jean-François Cottier. Turnhout: Brepols, 2006, pp. 419–40.

Dolley, Michael and Jacques Yvon. 'A Group of Tenth-Century Coins Found at Mont-Saint-Michel', *British Numismatic Journal* 40 (1971): 1–16.

Dosdat, Monique. *L'enluminure romane au Mont Saint-Michel*. Rennes: Ouest-France, 2006.

Dosdat, Monique. 'Les évêques de la province de Rouen et la vie intellectuelle au XIe siècle', in *Les évêques normands du XIe siècle*, ed. Pierre Bouet and François Neveux. Caen: Presses universitaires de Caen, 1995, pp. 241–3.

Dosdat, Monique. 'Les évêques normands de 985 à 1150', in *Les évêques normands du XIe siècle*, ed. Pierre Bouet and François Neveux. Caen: Presses universitaires de Caen, 1995, pp. 19–37.

Douglas, David. 'The First Ducal Charter for Fécamp', in *L'abbaye bénédictine de Fécamp: Ouvrage scientifique du XIIIe centenaire (658–1958)*, vol. I. Fécamp: EMTN, 1959, pp. 45–56.

Douglas, David. 'The Norman Episcopate before the Norman Conquest', *Cambridge Historical Journal* 13.2 (1957): 101–15.

Du Monstier, Arthur. *Neustria pia, seu de omnibus et singuilis abbatiis et prioratibus totius normaniae*. Rouen: Joannem Berthelin, 1663.

Dubuc, André, ed. *Les abbayes de Normandie*. Rouen: Lecerf, 1979.
Duby, George. *The Three Orders: Feudal Society Reimagined*. Chicago: University of Chicago Press, 1982.
Duffy, Eamon. *The Stripping of the Altars: Traditional Religion in England, c. 1400–1580*. New Haven, CT: Yale University Press, 1992.
Dunn, E. Catherine. 'Voice Structure in the Liturgical Drama: Sepet Reconsidered', in *Medieval English Drama*, ed. Jerome Taylor and Alan H. Nelson. Chicago: University of Chicago Press, 1972, pp. 44–64.
Dyer, Joseph. 'The Psalms in Monastic Prayer', in *The Place of the Psalms in the Intellectual Culture of the Middle Ages*, ed. Nancy Van Deusen. Albany: State University of New York Press, 1999, pp. 59–76.
Ebersole, Gary L. 'The Function of Ritual Weeping Revisited: Affective Expression and Moral Discourse', in *Religion and Emotion: Approaches and Interpretations*, ed. John Corrigan. New York: Oxford University Press, 2004, pp. 211–46.
Edsall, Mary Agnes. 'From "Companion to the Novitiate" to "Companion to the Devout Life": San Marino, Huntington Library, ms HM 744 and Monastic Anthologies of the Twelfth-Century Reform', in *Middle English Religious Writing in Practice: Texts, Readers, and Transformations*, ed. Nicole R. Rice. Turnhout: Brepols, 2013, pp. 115–48.
Edsall, Mary Agnes. 'Reading Like a Monk: *Lectio Divina*, Religious Literature, and Lay Devotion'. PhD dissertation, Columbia University, 2000.
Ehrstine, Glenn. 'Passion Spectatorship between Private and Public Devotion', in *Thresholds of Medieval Visual Culture: Liminal Spaces*, ed. Elina Gertsman and Jill Stevenson. Woodbridge: Boydell Press, 2012, pp. 302–20.
Elliot, Dyan. *The Bride of Christ Goes to Hell: Metaphor and Embodiment in the Lives of Pious Women, 200–1500*. Philadelphia: University of Pennsylvania Press, 2012.
Engh, L.C. *Gendered Identities in Bernard of Clairvaux's Sermons on the* Song of Songs: *Performing the Bride*. Turnhout: Brepols, 2014.
Esnos, G. 'Les traductions médiévales françaises et italiennes des *Soliloques* attribués à saint Augustin', *Mélanges d'archéologie et d'histoire* 79 (1976): 299–370.
Evans, Gillian. '*Mens devota*: The Literary Community of the Devotional Works of John of Fécamp and St. Anselm', *Medium Aevum* 43.2 (1974): 105–15.
Fassler, Margot. 'The Office of the Cantor in Early Western Monastic Rules and Customaries: A Preliminary Investigation', *Early Music History* 5 (1985): 29–51.

Bibliography

Fassler, Margot. *The Virgin of Chartres: Making History through Liturgy and the Arts*. New York: Cambridge University Press, 2010.

Feiss, Hugh. 'John of Fécamp's Longing for Heaven', in *Imagining Heaven in the Middle Ages*, ed. Hugh Feiss and Jan Swango Emerson. New York: Garland Publishing, 2000.

Fergusson, Peter. 'Canterbury Cathedral Priory's Bath House and Fish Pond', *Anglo-Norman Studies* 37 (2014): 115–30.

Fillastre, Guillaume. *Mémoire sur la musique à l'abbaye de Fécamp*. Rouen: Henry Boissel, 1878.

Fischer, Annika Elisabeth. 'Cross, Altar, and Crucifix in Ottonian Germany: Past Narrative, Present Ritual, Future Resurrection', in *Decorating the Lord's Table: On the Dynamics between Image and Altar in the Middle Ages*, ed. Søren Kaspersen and Erik Thunø. Copenhagen: Museum Tusculanum Press, 2006, pp. 43–62.

Flanigan, C. Clifford. 'The Liturgical Context of the *Quem Queritis* Trope', *Trope* 8.1 (1974): 45–62.

Flanigan, C. Clifford. 'Medieval Liturgy and the Arts: Visitatio Sepulchri as Paradigm', in *Liturgy and the Arts in the Middle Ages*, ed. Eva Louise Lillie and Nils Holger Petersen. Copenhagen: Museum Tusculanum Press, 1996, pp. 9–35.

Foreville, Raymonde. 'The Synod of the Province of Rouen in the Eleventh and Twelfth Centuries', in *Church and Government in the Middle Ages: Essays Presented to C.R. Cheney on his Seventieth Birthday*, ed. C.N.L. Brooke. Cambridge: Cambridge University Press, 1976, pp. 19–39.

Foreville, Raymonde, ed. *Millénaire monastique du Mont Saint-Michel*. Paris: Paul Lethielleux, 1962.

Fornasari, Giuseppe. *Medioevo riformato del secolo XI: Pier Damiani e Gregorio VII*. Naples: Liguori Editore, 1996.

Foulon, Jean-Hervé. *Église et réforme au môyen age: Papauté, milieu réformateurs et ecclésiologie dans les Pays de la Loire au tournant des XIe–XIIe siècles*. Brussels: De Boeck, 2008.

Foulon, Jean-Hervé. 'Les investitures abbatiales en Normandie: Quelques réflexions autour du cas de l'abbaye Bec-Hellouin', *Anglo-Norman Studies* 35 (2012): 181–212.

Fournée, Jean. 'L'abbaye de Fécamp et les origines du culte de l'Immaculée Conception en Normandie', in *L'abbaye bénédictine de Fécamp: Ouvrage scientifique du XIIIe centenaire (658–1958)*, vol. II. Fécamp: EMTN, 1959, pp. 163–70.

Bibliography

Fournée, Jean. 'Le culte popularie des saints fondateurs d'abbayes pré-Normandes', in *Les abbayes de Normandie*, ed. André Dubuc. Rouen: Lecerf, 1979, pp. 59–81.

Fournié, Madeleine. 'L'unum necessarium à Jumièges: Le culte de sainte Marie-Madeleine', in *Jumièges: Congrès scientifique du XIIIe centenaire*, vol. II. Rouen: Lecerf, 1954, pp. 991–6.

Franke, Walter. *Romuald von Camaldoli und seine Reformtätigkeit zur Zeit Ottos III*. Berlin: Verlag von Emil Ebering, 1913.

Frassetto, Michael, ed. *Medieval Purity and Piety: Essays on Medieval Clerical Celibacy and Religious Reform*. New York: Garland Publishing, 1998.

Fulton, Rachel. 'Anselm and Praying with the Saints', in *Studies on Medieval Empathies*, ed. Karl F. and Rudolph M. Bell. Turnhout: Brepols, 2013, pp. 115–38.

Fulton, Rachel. *From Judgment to Passion: Devotion to Christ and the Virgin Mary, 800–1200*. New York: Columbia University Press, 2002.

Fulton, Rachel. 'Praying with Anselm at Admont: A Meditation on Practice', *Speculum* 81.3 (2006): 700–13.

Fulton, Rachel. '"Taste and See That the Lord is Sweet" (Ps. 33:9): The Flavor of God in the Monastic West', *Journal of Religion* 86.2 (2006): 169–204.

Fulton, Rachel. 'What's in a Psalm? British Library MS Arundel 60 and the Stuff of Prayer', in *Rome and Religion in the Medieval World: Studies in Honor of Thomas F.X. Noble*, ed. Valerie Garver and Owne Phelan. New York: Routledge, 2014, pp. 235–52.

Gameson, Richard. *The Manuscripts of Early Normand England (c. 1066–1130)*. New York: Oxford University Press, 1999.

Gameson, Richard. 'La Normandie et l'Angleterre au XIe siècle: Le témoignage des manuscrits', in *La Normandie et l'Angleterre au moyen âge*, ed. Véronique Gazeau and Pierre Bouet. Caen: CRAHN, 2003, pp. 129–76.

Ganz, David. 'Giving to God in the Mass: The Experience of the Offertory', in *The Languages of Gift in the Early Middle Ages*, ed. Wendy Davies and Paul Fouracre. New York: Cambridge University Press, 2010, pp. 18–32.

Ganz, David. 'Knowledge of Ephraim's Writings in the Merovingian and Carolingian Age', *Hugoye: Journal of Syriac Studies* 2.1 (1999): 32–46.

Ganze, Ronald J. 'The Medieval Sense of Self', in *Misconceptions about the Middle Ages*, ed. Stephen J. Harris and Bryon L. Grigsby. New York: Routledge, 2008, pp. 103–16.

Garrec, René, ed. *Richesses des bibliothèques et archives de Basse-Normandie*. Caen: Co. RAIL, 1991.

Bibliography

Gasper, Giles E.M. *Anselm of Canterbury and His Theological Inheritance*. Burlington, VT: Ashgate, 2004.

Gazeau, Véronique. 'Les abbés bénédictins dans la Normandie ducale: Des abbés etrangers?', in *L'étranger au moyen âge*. Paris: Publications de la Sorbonne, 2000, pp. 245–57.

Gazeau, Véronique. 'Les abbés bénédictins de la Normandie ducale', *Anglo-Norman Studies* 26 (2003): 75–86.

Gazeau, Véronique. 'The Effect of the Conquest of 1066 on Monasticism in Normandy: The Abbeys of the Risle Valley', in *England and Normandy in the Middle Ages*, ed. David Bates and Anne Curry. London: Hambledon Press, 1994, pp. 131–42.

Gazeau, Véronique. 'Femmes en religion, personnes d'authorité: Les abbesses normandes (XIe–XIIe siècles)', *Anglo-Norman Studies* 35 (2012): 17–33.

Gazeau, Véronique. 'From Bec to Canterbury: Between Cloister and World, the Legacy of Anselm, a *personne d'autorité*', in *Saint Anselm of Canterbury and His Legacy*, ed. Giles E.M. Gasper and Ian Logan. Durham: Institute of Medieval and Renaissance Studies, 2012, pp. 61–72.

Gazeau, Véronique. 'Guillaume de Volpiano en Normandie: État des questions', *Tabularia* 2 (2002): 35–46.

Gazeau, Véronique. *Normannia monastica: Prosopographie des abbés bénédictines*. Caen: CRAHM, 2007.

Gazeau, Véronique. 'Note sur l'orgue de Fécamp. Extrait de la lettre de Baudri de Bourgueil aux moines de Fécamp', in *De part et d'autre de la Normandie médiévale: Recueil d'études en hommage à François Neveux*, ed. Pierre Bouet, Catherine Bougy, Bernard Garnier, and Christophe Maneuvrier. Caen: Cahier des annales de Normandie, 2009, pp. 347–51.

Gazeau, Véronique and Monique Goullet. *Guillaume de Volpiano: Un réformateur en son temps (962–1031)*. Caen: CRAHM, 2008.

Geary, Patrick. 'Exchange and Interaction between the Living and the Dead in Early Medieval Society', in *Living with the Dead in the Middle Ages*. Ithaca, NY: Cornell University Press, 1994, pp. 77–92.

Gehl, Paul F. '"Comptens silentium": Varieties of Monastic Silence in the Medieval West', *Viator* 18 (1987): 125–60.

Genevois, A.-M., J.-F. Genest, and A. Chalandon, eds. *Bibliothèques de manuscrits médiévaux en France: Relevé des inventaires du VIIIe au XVIIIe siècle*. Paris: CNRS, 1987.

Gertsman, Elina. 'Introduction: "Going They Went and Wept": Tears in Medieval Discourse', in *Crying in the Middle Ages: Tears of History*, ed. Elina Gertsman. New York: Routledge, 2011, pp. xi–xx.

Gibson, Margaret. *Lanfranc of Bec*. Oxford: Oxford University Press, 1978.

Bibliography

Giraud, Cédric. *Spiritualité et histoire des textes entre moyen âge et époque moderne: Genèse et fortune d'un corpus pseudépigraphe de méditations.* Paris: Institut d'études augustiniennes, 2016.

Golding, Brian. 'Anglo-Norman Knightly Burials', in *The Ideals and Practice of Medieval Knighthood*, ed. C. Harper-Bill and R. Harvey. Woodbridge: Boydell & Brewer, 1986, pp. 35–48.

Golding, Brian. 'The Coming of the Cluniacs', *Proceedings of the Battle Conference* 3 (1980): 65–77.

Gordon, Olga Koseleff, 'The Calendar Cycle of the Fécamp Psalter', in *Studien zur Buchmalerei und Goldschmiedekunst des Mittelalters: Festschrift zür Karl Hermann Usener zum 60. Geburtstag am 19. August 1965.* Marburg an der Lahn: Verlag des Kunstgeschichtlichen Seminars der Universität Marburg an der Lahn, 1967, pp. 209–24.

Gourdon de Genouillac, Henri. *Histoire de l'abbaye de Fécamp et ses abbés.* Fécamp: A. Marinier, 1875.

Gouttebroze, Jean-Guy. 'À l'origine du culte du Précieux Sang de Fécamp, le Saint Voult de Lucques', *Tabularia* (2009): 1–8.

Gouttebroze, Jean-Guy. *Le Précieux Sang de Fécamp, origine et développement d'un mythe chrétien.* Paris: Honoré Champion, 2000.

Grandjean, Michel. *Laïcs dans l'église: Regards de Pierre Damien, Anselme de Cantorbéry, Yves de Chartres.* Paris: Beauchesne, 1994.

Grant, Lindy. *Architecture and Society in Normandy, 1120–1270.* New Haven, CT: Yale University Press, 2005.

Grant, Lindy. 'Fécamp et l'architecture en Normandie', *Tabularia* 2 (2002): 83–94.

Green, Judith Ann. 'Fécamp et les rois Anglo-Normands', *Tabularia* 2 (2002): 9–18.

Greenblatt, Stephen. *The Swerve: How the World Became Modern.* New York: Norton, 2012.

Gregory, Brad S. *The Unintended Reformation: How a Religious Revolution Secularized Society.* Cambridge, MA: Harvard University Press, 2012.

Griffiths, Fiona. *The Garden of Delights: Reform and Renaissance for Women in the Twelfth Century.* Philadelphia: University of Pennsylvania Press, 2007.

Griffiths, Fiona. 'Men's Duty to Provide for Women's Needs: Abelard, Heloise, and Their Negotiation of the *Cura monialium*', *Journal of Medieval History* 30 (2004): 1–24.

Griffiths, Fiona. *Nuns' Priests' Tales: Men and Salvation in Medieval Women's Monastic Life.* Philadelphia: University of Pennsylvania Press, 2017.

Hagen, Hermannus. *Catalogus Codicum Bernensium (Bibliotheca Bongarsiana).* Bern: B.F. Haller, 1874.

Hagger, Mark. *Norman Rule in Normandy, 911–1144*. Woodbridge: Boydell Press, 2017.

Hale, R. '"Taste and See, for God is Sweet": Sensory Perception and Memory in Medieval Christian Mystical Experience', in *Vox Mystica: Essays on Medieval Mysticism in Honor of Professor Valerie M. Lagorio*, ed. Ann Clarke Bartlett. Rochester, NY: D.S. Brewer, 1995, pp. 3–14.

Halkin, F. 'À la recherche de l'état primitif du martyrologie d'Usuard: Le manuscrit de Fécamp', *Analecta Bollandiana: Revue critique d'hagiographie* 95 (1977): 42–74.

Hallinger, Kassius. 'The Spiritual Life of Cluny in the Early Days', in *Cluniac Monasticism in the Central Middle Ages*, ed. Noreen Hunt. New York: Macmillan, 1971, pp. 29–55.

Hamburger, Jeffrey. *The Rothschild Canticles: Art and Mysticism in Flanders and the Rhineland ca. 1300*. New Haven, CT: Yale University Press, 1990.

Hamburger, Jeffrey. 'The Visual and the Visionary: The Image in Late Medieval Monastic Devotions', in *The Visual and the Visionary: Art and Female Spirituality in Late Medieval Germany*. New York: Zone Books, 1998, pp. 111–48.

Hamburger, Jeffrey and Hildegard Elisabeth Keller. 'A Battle for Hearts and Minds: The Heart in Reformation Polemic', in *Mysticism and Reform: 1400–1750*. Notre Dame, IN: University of Notre Dame Press, 2015, pp. 321–44.

Hamilton, Louis I. *A Sacred City: Consecrating Churches and Reforming Society in Eleventh-Century Italy*. Manchester: Manchester University Press, 2010.

Hamilton, Sarah. *The Practice of Penance, 900–1050*. London: Royal Historical Society/Boydell Press, 2001.

Hardison, O.B. *Christian Rite and Christian Drama in the Middle Ages*. Baltimore, MD: Johns Hopkins Press, 1969.

Harper-Bill, Christopher. 'The Piety of the Anglo-Norman Knightly Class', *Anglo-Norman Studies* 2 (1979): 63–77.

Harper-Bill, Christopher and Elisabeth van Houts, eds. *A Companion to the Anglo-Norman World*. Rochester, NY: Boydell Press, 2003.

Harris, Jennifer A. 'Building Heaven on Earth: Cluny as *Locus Sanctissimus* in the Eleventh Century', in *From Dead of Night to End of Day: The Medieval Customs of Cluny*, ed. Susan Boynton and Isabelle Cochelin. Turnhout: Brepols, 2005, pp. 131–51.

Harris, Jennifer A. 'Peter Damian and the Architecture of the Self', in *Das Eigene und das Ganze. Zum individuellen im mittelalterlichen Religiosentum*, ed. Gert Melville and Markus Schürer. Münster: Lit Verlag, 2002, pp. 131–57.

Bibliography

Harrison, Madeline. 'A Life of St. Edward the Confessor in Early Fourteenth-Century Stained Glass at Fécamp in Normandy', *Journal of the Wartburg and Courtauld Institutes* 26.1 (1963): 22–37.

Haskins, Charles Homer. 'A Charter of Canute for Fécamp', *English Historical Review* 33.131 (1918): 342–4.

Haskins, Charles Homer. 'The Materials for the Reign of Robert I of Normandy', *English Historical Review* 31.122 (1916): 257–68.

Haskins, Charles Homer. *Norman Institutions*. New York: Frederick Ungar Publishing, 1967.

Haskins, Charles Homer. *The Renaissance of the Twelfth Century*. Cambridge, MA: Harvard University Press, 1955.

Hasseldine, Julian, ed. *Friendship in Medieval Europe*. Stroud: Sutton Publishing, 1999.

Head, Thomas and Richard Landes, eds. *The Peace of God: Social Violence and Religious Response in France around the Year 1000*. Ithaca, NY: Cornell University Press, 1992.

Heinzelmann, Martin. *L'hagiographie du haut moyen âge en Gaule du Nord: Manuscrits, textes, et centres de production*. Stuttgart: Jan Thorbecke Verlag, 2001.

Heitz, Carol. *Recherches sur les rapports entre architecture et liturgie à l'époque Carolingienne*. Paris: SEVPEN, 1963.

Hélas, Jean-Claude. 'Emphyteusis Tenure: Its Role in the Economy and in the Rural Society of Eastern Languedoc', in *Urban and Rural Communities in Medieval France: Provence and Languedoc, 1000–1500*, ed. Kathryn L. Reyerson and J. Drendel. Leuven: Brill, 1998, pp. 193–208.

Hennessy, Marlene Villalobos. 'Passion Devotion, Penitential Reading, and the Manuscript Page: "The Hours of the Cross" in London, British Library Additional 37049', *Mediaeval Studies* 66 (2004): 213–52.

Henriet, Patrick. *La parole et la prière au moyen âge*. Brussels: DeBoeck Université, 2000.

Henriet, Patrick and Anne Wagner. 'Les moines du XIe siècle entre érémitisme et cénobisme', in *Les saints et l'histoire*, ed. Anne Wagner. Rosny-sous-Bois: Bréal, 2008, pp. 231–5.

Herrick, Samantha Kahn. *Imagining the Sacred Past: Hagiography and Power in Early Normandy*. Cambridge, MA: Harvard University Press, 2007.

Herval, René. 'En marge de la légende du Précieux-Sang: Lucques, Fécamp, Glastonbury', in *L'abbaye bénédictine de Fécamp: Ouvrage scientifique du XIIIe centenaire(658–1958)*, vol. I. Fécamp: EMTN, 1959, pp. 105–25.

Herval, René. 'Un moine de l'an mille: Guillaume de Volpiano, 1er abbé de Fécamp (962–1031)', in *L'abbaye bénédictine de Fécamp: Ouvrage scientifique du XIIIe centenaire (658–1958)*, vol. I. Fécamp: EMTN, 1959, pp. 27–43.

Hesbert, René-Jean. 'Les manuscrits liturgiques de Jumièges', in *Jumièges: Congrès scientifique du XIIIe centenaire*, vol. II. Rouen: Lecerf, 1954, pp. 856–72.

Hesbert, René-Jean. 'Les manuscrits musicaux de Jumièges', in *Jumièges: Congrès scientifique du XIIIe centenaire*, vol. II. Rouen: Lecerf, 1954, pp. 901–14.

Hesbert, René-Jean. 'Les séquences de Jumièges', in *Jumièges: Congrès scientifique du XIIIe centenaire*, vol. II. Rouen: Lecerf, 1954, pp. 943–58.

Hesbert, René-Jean. 'Les tropes de Jumièges', in *Jumièges: Congrès scientifique du XIIIe centenaire*, vol. II. Rouen: Lecerf, 1954, pp. 959–76.

Heurtevent, Raoul. *Durand de Troarn et les origines de l'hérésie Bérengarienne*. Paris: Gabriel Beauchesne, 1912.

Hicks, Leonie V. *Religious Life in Normandy, 1050–1300*. Woodbridge: Boydell Press, 2007.

Hildebrandt, M.M. *The External School in Carolingian Society*. New York: E.J. Brill, 1992.

Hiley, David. 'The Norman Chant Traditions: Normandy, Britain, Sicily', *Proceedings of the Royal Musical Association* 107 (1980–81): 1–33.

Hiley, David. *Thurstan of Caen and Plainchant at Glastonbury: Musicological Reflections on the Norman Conquest*. London: British Academy, 1986.

Hiley, David. *Western Plainchant: A Handbook*. Oxford: Clarendon Press, 1993.

Hilgarth, J.N. 'L'influence de la *Cité de Dieu* de saint Augustin au Haut Moyen Âge', *Sacris Erudiri: A Journal of Late Antique and Medieval Christianity* 28 (1985): 5–34.

Hill, Robert C. 'St. John Chrysostom's Homilies on Hannah', *St. Vladimir's Theological Quarterly* 45.4 (2001): 319–38.

Hingst, Amanda Jane. *The Written Word: The Past and its Place in the Work of Orderic Vitalis*. Notre Dame, IN: University of Notre Dame Press, 2009.

Hiscock, Nigel. 'The Ottonian Revival: Church Expansion and Monastic Reform', in *The White Mantle of Churches: Architecture, Liturgy, and Art around the Millennium*, ed. Nigel Hiscock. Turnhout: Brepols, 2003, pp. 1–28.

Høgel, Christian and Elisabetta Bartoli, eds. *Medieval Letters: Between Fiction and Document*. Turnhout: Brepols, 2015.

Hollister, C. Warren. 'Anglo-Norman Political Culture and the Twelfth-Century Renaissance', in *Anglo-Norman Political Culture and the*

Twelfth-Century Renaissance, ed. C. Warren Hollister. Woodbridge: Boydell Press, 1997, pp. 1–16.

Hollywood, Amy. 'Song, Experience, and the Book in Benedictine Monasticism', in *The Cambridge Companion to Christian Mysticism*, ed. Amy Hollywood and Patricia Z. Beckman. New York: Cambridge University Press, 2012, pp. 59–79.

Hollywood, Amy. 'Spiritual but Not Religious: The Vital Interplay between Submission and Freedom', *Harvard Divinity Bulletin* 38.1/2 (2010), https://bulletin.hds.harvard.edu/articles/winterspring2010/spiritual-not-religious.

Holopainen, Toivo J. *Dialectic and Theology in the Eleventh Century*. New York: E.J. Brill, 1996.

Holopainen, Toivo J. '"Lanfranc of Bec" and Berengar of Tours', *Anglo-Norman Studies* 34 (2012): 105–22.

Hotchin, Julie. 'Women's Reading and Monastic Reform in Twelfth-Century Germany: The Library of the Nuns of Lippoldberg', in *Manuscripts and Monastic Culture: Reform and Renewal in Twelfth-Century Germany*, ed. Alison I. Beach. Turnhout: Brepols, 2007, pp. 138–89.

Hourihane, Colum. *Pontius Pilate, Anti-Semitism, and the Passion in Medieval Art*. Princeton, NJ: Princeton University Press, 2009.

Hourlier, Jacques. *Saint Odilon: Abbé de Cluny*. Louvain: Bibliothèque de l'université, 1964.

Howe, John. *Church Reform and Social Change in Eleventh-Century Italy*. Philadelphia: University of Pennsylvania Press, 1997.

Huglo, Michel. 'Un nouveau manuscrit du "Dialogue sur la Musique" du Pseudo-Odon (Troyes, Bibliothèque Municipale 2142)', *Revue d'histoire des textes* 9 (1979): 299–314.

Hurlbut, Stephen A. *The Picture of the Heavenly Jerusalem in the Writings of Johannes of Fécamp, De Contemplativa Vita, and in the Elizabethan Hymns*. Washington, DC: St. Alban's Press, 1943.

Hunt, Hannah. 'The Reforming Abbot and his Tears: Penthos in Late Byzantium', in *Spirituality in Late Byzantium: Essays Presenting New Research by International Scholars*, ed. Eugenia Russell. Newcastle: Cambridge Scholars Publishing, 2009, pp. 13–21.

Hunt, Noreen. *Cluny under Saint Hugh, 1049–1109*. Notre Dame, IN: University of Notre Dame Press, 1967.

Hunt, R.W. 'The Library of the Abbey of Saint Albans', in *Medieval Scribes, Manuscripts, and Libraries*, ed. M.B. Parkes and Andrew G. Watson. London: Scolar Press, 1978, pp. 251–78.

Hunt, Tony. 'Fécamp and Vernacular Historiography', *Medium Aevum* 72.2 (2003): 189–207.

Illich, Ivan. *In the Vineyard of the Text: A Commentary to Hugh's Didascalicon*. Chicago: University of Chicago Press, 1993.

Innes-Parker, Catherine. 'The Middle English Doctrine of the Hert and its Manuscript Context', in *A Companion to the Doctrine of the Hert: The Middle English Translation and its Latin and European Contexts*, ed. Denis Renevey and Christiana Whitehead. Exeter: University of Exeter Press, 2009, pp. 159–82.

Iogna-Prat, Dominique. *Agni immaculati: Recherches sur les sources hagiographiques relatives à saint Maieul de Cluny*. Paris: Cerf, 1988.

Iogna-Prat, Dominique. 'La croix, le moine, et l'empereur: Dévotion à la Croix et théologie politique à Cluny autour de l'an mil', in *Haut moyen âge: Culture, éducation, société. Études offertes à Pierre Riché*, ed. Michel Sot. Paris: Publidix/Éditions européennes de Erasme, 1990, pp. 449–75.

Iogna-Prat, Dominique. 'La Madeleine du *Sermo in veneratione sanctae Mariae Magdalenae* attribué à Odon de Cluny', *Mélanges de l'École française de Rome* 104.1 (1992): 37–70.

Iogna-Prat, Dominique. *La Maison Dieu: Une histoire monumentale de l'église au moyen âge*. Paris: Éditions du Seuil, 2006.

Iogna-Prat, Dominique. *Order and Exclusion: Cluny and Christendom Face Heresy, Judaism, and Islam (1000–1150)*, trans. Graham Robert Edwards. Ithaca, NY: Cornell University Press, 2003.

Iogna-Prat, Dominique. 'Panorama de l'hagiographie abbatiale clunisienne (v. 940–v.1140)', in *Manuscrits hagiographiques et travail des hagiographes*, ed. Martin Heinzelmann. Sigmaringen: Thorbecke, 1992, pp. 77–119.

Jaeger, C. Stephen. *The Envy of Angels: Cathedral Schools and Social Ideals in Medieval Europe, 950–1200*. Philadelphia: University of Pennsylvania Press, 2000.

Jaffray, Robert. 'Glastonbury and Fécamp', in *Sources of the Grail*, ed. John Matthews. Hudson, NY: Lindisfarne Press, 1996, pp. 347–55.

James, Montague Rhodes. *A Descriptive Catalogue of the McClean Collection of Manuscripts in the Fitzwilliam Museum*. Cambridge: Cambridge University Press, 1912.

Jansen, Katherine Ludwig. *The Making of the Magdalen: Preaching and Popular Devotion in the Later Middle Ages*. Princeton, NJ: Princeton University Press, 2000.

Jasper, Kathryn L., 'Reforming the Monastic Landscape: Peter Damian's Design for Personal and Communal Devotion', in *Rural Space in the*

Middle Ages and Early Modern Age: The Spatial Turn in Premodern Studies, ed. Albrecht Classen. Boston: De Gruyter, 2012, pp. 193–207.

Jestice, Phyllis G. *Wayward Monks and the Religious Revolution of the Eleventh Century*. New York: Brill, 1997.

Johnson, Penelope. *Prayer, Patronage, and Power: The Abbey of la Trinité, Vendôme, 1032–1187*. New York: New York University Press, 1981.

Jones, C.A. 'Monastic Custom in Early Norman England: The Significance of Bodleian Ms. Wood Empt. 4', *Revue bénédictine* 113.1 (2003): 135–69.

Jones, Sara E. 'The Twelfth-Century Reliefs from Fécamp: New Evidence for their Dating and Original Purpose', *Journal of the British Archaeological Association* 138 (1985): 79–88.

Joyce, Ellen. 'Speaking of Spiritual Matters: Visions and the Rhetoric of Reform in the *Liber Visionum* of Otloh of St. Emmeram', in *Manuscripts and Monastic Culture: Reform and Renewal in Twelfth-Century Germany*, ed. Alison I. Beach. Turnhout: Brepols, 2007.

Justice, Steven. 'Did the Middle Ages Believe in Their Miracles?', *Representations* 103 (2008): 1–28.

Kajava, Oskari. *Études sur deux poèmes français relatifs a l'abbaye de Fécamp*. Helsinki: Imprimerie de la Société de littérature finnoise, 1928.

Kaminsky, H. 'Zur Gründung von Fruttuaria durch den Abt Wilhelm von Dijon', *Zeitschrift für Kirchengeschichte* 77 (1966): 238–67.

Karat-Nunn, Susan. *The Reformation of Feeling*. New York: Oxford University Press, 2010.

Karras, Ruth Mazo. 'Holy Harlots: Prostitute Saints in Medieval Legend', *Journal of the History of Sexuality* 1.1 (1990): 3–32.

Ker, N.R. 'Medieval Manuscripts from Norwich Cathedral Priory', *Transactions of the Cambridge Bibliographical Society* 1 (1949): 1–28.

Kessler, Herbert L. 'A Sanctifying Serpent: Crucifix as Cure', in *Studies on Medieval Empathies*, ed. Karl F. Morrison and Rudolph M. Bell. Turnhout: Brepols, 2013, pp. 161–85.

King, Edward B. and Jacqueline T. Schaefer, eds. *Saint Augustine and his Influence in the Middle Ages*. Sewanee, TN: Press of the University of the South, 1988.

Knowles, David. *The Monastic Order in England: A History of Its Development from the Times of St Dunstan to the Fourth Lateran Council, 943–1216*. New York: Cambridge University Press, 1963.

Kobialka, Michal. *This is My Body: Representational Practices in the Early Middle Ages*. Ann Arbor: University of Michigan Press, 2003.

Bibliography

Kottje, Raymund. 'Klosterbibliotheken und Monastische Kultur in der zweiten Häfte des 11. Jahrhunderts', in *Il monachesimo e la riforma ecclesiastica (1049–1122)*. Milan: Vita e Pensiero, 1971, pp. 145–62.

Krawiec, Rebecca. *Shenoute and the Women of the White Monastery: Egyptian Monasticism in Late Antiquity*. New York: Oxford University Press, 2002.

Kramer, Susan. *Sin, Interior, and Selfhood in the Twelfth-Century West*. Toronto: Pontifical Institute of Mediaeval Studies, 2015.

Kramer, Susan R. and Caroline W. Bynum. 'Revisiting the Twelfth-Century Individual: The Inner Self and the Christian Community', in *Das Eigene und das Ganze. Zum individuellen im mittelalterlichen Religiosentum*, ed. Gert Melville and Markus Schürer. Münster: Lit Verlag, 2002, pp. 57–85.

Krüger, Kristina. 'Monastic Customs and Liturgy in the Light of the Architectural Evidence: A Case Study on Processions (Eleventh–Twelfth Centuries)', in *From Dead of Night to End of Day: The Medieval Customs of Cluny*, ed. Susan Boynton and Isabelle Cochelin. Turnhout: Brepols, 2005, pp. 191–220.

Kruse, Norbert. 'Weg des Heiligen Blutes von Mantua nach Altdorf-Weingarten', in *900 Jahre Heilig Blut Verehrung in Weingarten, 1094–1994*, ed. Norbert Kruse and Hans Ulrich Rudolf. Sigmaringen: Jan Thorbecke Verlag, 1994, pp. 57–76.

Kuhl, Elizabeth. 'Education and Schooling at Le Bec: A Case Study of Le Bec's Florilegia', in *A Companion to the Abbey of Le Bec in the Central Middle Ages (11th–13th Centuries)*, ed. Benjamin Pohl and Laura Gathagan. Leiden: Brill, 2017, pp. 248–77.

Kumler, Aden. 'Handling the Letter', in *St. Albans and the Markyate Psalter: Seeing and Reading in the Twelfth Century*, ed. Kristen Collins and Matthew Fischer. Kalamazoo, MI: Medieval Institute Publications, 2017, pp. 69–100.

Kupfer, Marcia, ed. *The Passion Story: From Visual Representation to Social Drama*. University Park: Pennsylvania State University Press, 2008.

Lackner, Bede K. *The Eleventh-Century Background of Cîteaux*. Washington, DC: Cistercian Publications, 1972.

Ladner, Gerhart B. *The Idea of Reform: Its Impact on Christian Thought and Action in the Age of the Fathers*. New York: Harper Torchbooks, 1967.

Lambert, Jean. 'Les calendriers de Jumièges', in *Jumièges: Congrès scientifique du XIIIe centenaire*, vol. II. Rouen: Lecerf, 1954, pp. 883–8.

Landes, Richard. 'The White Mantle of Churches, Millennial Dynamics, and the Written and Architectural Record', in *The White Mantle of Churches: Architecture, Liturgy, and Art around the Millennium*, ed. Nigel Hiscock. Turnhout: Brepols, 2003, pp. 249–64.

Bibliography

Långfors, Arthur. 'Histoire de l'abbaye de Fécamp: En vers français du XIIIe siècle', *Annales academiae scientiarum Fennicae* B 22 (1928): 7–208.

Laporte, J. 'Les associations spirituelles entre monastères. L'exemple de trois abbayes bénédictines normandes', *Cahiers Léopold Deslisle* 22 (July–September 1963): 29–45.

Laporte, J. 'Epistulae fiscannenses: Lettres d'amitié, de gouvernement et d'affaires (XIe–XIIe siècles)', *Revue Mabillon* 43 (1953): 5–36.

Laporte, J. 'Influences intellectuelles sur la Normandie des dixième et onzième siècles', in *La Normandie bénédictine au temps de Guillaume le Conquérant (XIe siècle)*. Lille: Facultés catholiques, 1967, pp. 443–51.

Laporte, J. 'Quelques documents sur Fécamp au temps d'Henri de Sully (1140–1189)', *Analecta Monastica* (1962): 23–33.

Largier, Niklaus. 'Inner Senses–Outer Senses: The Practice of Emotions in Medieval Mysticism', in *Codierung von Emotionen im Mittelalter/Emotions and Sensibilities in the Middle Ages*, ed. Stephen Jaeger and Ingrid Kasten. New York: De Gruyter, 2003, pp. 3–15.

Lassus, Louis-Albert. *Saint Pierre Damien: L'homme des déserts de dieu*. Paris: OEIL, 1986.

Lauer, Philippe. *Catalogue général des manuscrits latins*. Paris: Bibliothèque nationale, 1939. Vols I; II; III; IV; V; VI.

Laurence, C.H. *Medieval Monasticism: Forms of Religious Life in Western Europe in the Middle Ages*. New York: Routledge, 2000.

Lauwers, Michel. 'La prière comme fonction sociale dans l'occident médiéval (Ve–XIIIe siècle)', in *La prière en latin de l'antiquité au XVIe siècle*, ed. Jean-François Cottier. Turnhout: Brepols, 2006, pp. 209–27.

Lawrence, Anne. 'Anglo-Norman Book Production', in *England and Normandy in the Middle Ages*, ed. David Bates and Anne Curry. London: Hambledon Press, 1994, pp. 79–93.

Lazikani, A.S. *Cultivating the Heart: Feeling and Emotion in Twelfth- and Thirteenth-Century Religious Texts*. Cardiff: University of Wales Press, 2015.

Le Hule, Guillaume. *Le thresor ou abbrégé de l'histoire de la noble et royalle abbaye de Fescamp*. Fécamp: Banse Fils, 1684.

Le Maho, Jacques. 'Aux sources d'un grand pèlerinage normand: L'origine des reliques fécampoises du Précieux Sang', in *Identités pèlerines*, ed. Catherine Vincent. Rouen: Publications de l'Université de Caen, 2004, pp. 93–106.

Le Maho, Jacques. 'La dispersion des bibliothèques du diocèse de Rouen au temps des invasions normandes: Autour d'un manuscrit carolingien anciennement conservé à la Sainte-Trinité de Fécamp', *Tabularia* 4 (2004): 61–78.

Bibliography

Le Pree, James Francis. 'Pseudo-Basil's *De admonitio ad filium spiritualem*: A New English Translation', *The Heroic Age: A Journal of Early Medieval Northwestern Europe* 13 (2010), www.heroicage.org/issues/13/lepree2.php.

Leblond, Bernard. *L'accession des Normands de Neustrie à la culture occidentale (X–XIème siècles)*. Paris: A.G. Nizet, 1966.

Leclercq, Jean. 'Écrits spirituels de l'école de Jean de Fécamp', in *Analecta monastica*, vol. I, ed. Jean Leclercq. Vatican City: Vatican Library, 1948, pp. 108–14.

Leclercq, Jean. 'Un écrivan très lu et peu connu: Jean de Fécamp (d. 1078)', *Annales du Patriomoine de Fécamp* 2 (1995): 27–33.

Leclercq, Jean. *The Love of Learning and the Desire for God: A Study of Monastic Culture*. New York: Fordham University Press, 1982.

Leclercq, Jean. 'The Monastic Crisis of the Eleventh and Twelfth Centuries', in *Cluniac Monasticism in the Central Middle Ages*, ed. Noreen Hunt. New York: Macmillan, 1971, pp. 217–37.

Leclercq, Jean. *Otia monastica: Études sur le vocabulaire de la contemplation au moyen âge*. Rome: Orbis Catholicus, 1963.

Leclercq, Jean. 'La prière au sujet des vices et des virtues', in *Analecta monastica*, vol. I, ed. Jean Leclercq. Vatican City: Vatican Library, 1948, pp. 3–17.

Leclercq, Jean. 'Prières attribuables à Guillaume et à Jean de Fruttuaria', in *Monasteri in alta Italia dopo le invasioni saracene e magiare (sec. X–XII)*. Turin: Deputazione Subalpina di Storia Patria, 1966, pp. 157–66.

Leclercq, Jean. 'Recherches sur d'anciens sermons monastiques', *Revue Mabillon* 36 (1946): 1–14.

Leclercq, Jean. *Regards monastiques sur le Christ au moyen âge*. Paris: Mame-Desclée, 2010.

Leclercq, Jean. *Saint Pierre Damien: Ermite et homme d'église*. Rome: Edizioni di storia e letteratura, 1960.

Leclercq, Jean. 'Textes sur la vocation et la formation des moines au moyen âge', in *Corona Gratiarum: Miscellanea Patristica, Historica, et Liturgica Eligio Dekkers O.S.B. XII Lustra Complenti Oblata*, vol. II. Bruges: Sint Pietersabde, 1975, 169–94.

Leclercq, Jean, François Vandenbroucke, and Louis Bouyer, eds. *The Spirituality of the Middle Ages. A History of Christian Spirituality* 2. New York: Seabury Press, 1961.

Lecouteux, Stéphane. 'Associations de prières et confraternités spirituelles: Des unions éphémères ou pérennes? Enquête autour du réseau de confraternité de l'abbaye de la Trinité de Fécamp (XIe–XVe siècle)', in *Réseaux religieux et spirituels: Du moyen âge à nos jours*, ed. Nicole Lemaitre. Paris: CTHS, 2016, pp. 75–92.

Bibliography

Lecouteux, Stéphane. 'Deux fragments d'un nécrologe de la Trinité de Fécamp (XIe–XIIe siècles). Étude et édition critique d'un document mémoriel exceptionnel', *Tabularia* 16 (2016): 1–89.

Lecouteux, Stéphane. 'Une reconstitution hypothétique du cheminement des *Annales* de Flodard, depuis Reims jusqu'à Fécamp', *Tabularia* 4 (2004): 1–38.

Lecouteux, Stéphane. 'Réseaux de confraternité et histoire des bibliothèques: L'exemple de l'abbaye bénédictine de la Trinité de Fécamp'. PhD dissertation, Université de Caen Normandie/École Pratique des Hautes Études, 2015.

Lecouteux, Stéphane. 'Sur la dispersion de la bibliothèque bénédictine de Fécamp. Partie 1: Identification des principales vagues de démembrement des fonds', *Tabularia* 7 (2007): 1–50.

Lecroq, Dom Gaston. 'Les manuscrits liturgiques de Fécamp', *Bulletin de l'Association des Amis du Vieux-Fécamp* 1934 (1934): 53–111.

LeMarignier, Jean-François. 'L'exemption de Fécamp au début du XIe siècle', in *Étude sur les privilèges d'exemption et de juridiction ecclésiastique des abbayes Normandes depuis les origines jusqu'en 1140*. Paris: Archives de la France monastique, 1937, pp. 288–340.

LeMarignier, Jean-François. 'Paix et réforme monastique en Flandre et en Normandie autour de l'année 1023', in *Droit privé et institutions régionales: Etudes historiques offertes à Jean Yver*. Paris: Presses universitaires de France, 1976, pp. 443–68.

LeMarignier, Jean-François. 'Political and Monastic Structures in France at the End of the Tenth and the Beginning of the Eleventh Century', in *Lordship and Community in Medieval Europe*, ed. Frederic L. Cheyette. New York: Holt, Rinehart and Winston, 1968, pp. 100–27.

Leroux de Lincy, A.-J.-V. *Essai historique et littéraire sur l'abbaye de Fécamp*. Rouen: Librarie de la Bibliothèque de la Ville, 1840.

Lesne, Émile. *Histoire de la propriété ecclésiastique en France: Les livres, scriptoria, et bibliothèques*, vol. IV. Lille: Facultés catholiques, 1938.

Lester, Anne. *Creating Cistercian Nuns: The Women's Religious Movement and Its Reform in Thirteenth-Century Champagne*. Ithaca, NY: Cornell University Press, 2011.

Leys, Ruth. 'The Turn to Affect: A Critique', *Critical Inquiry* 37.3 (2011): 434–72.

Leyser, Conrad. '*Lectio divina, oratio pura*: Rhetoric and the Techniques of Asceticism in the *Conferences* of John Cassian', in *Modelli di santità e modelli di comportamento: contrasti, intersezioni, complementarità*, ed. Giulia Barone, Marina Caffiero, and Francesco Scorza Barcellona. Turin: Rosenberg & Sellier, 1994, pp. 79–105.

Leyser, Henrietta. *Hermits and the New Monasticism: A Study of Religious Communities in Western Europe, 1000–1150*. New York: St. Martin's Press, 1984.

Licence, Tom. *Hermits and Recluses in English Society, 950–1200*. New York: Oxford University Press, 2011.

Licence, Tom. 'History and Hagiography in the Late Eleventh Century: The Life and Work of Herman the Archdeacon, Monk of Bury St. Edmunds', *English Historical Review* 124.508 (2009): 516–44.

Lifshitz, Felice. *The Norman Conquest of Pious Neustria*. Toronto: Pontifical Institute of Mediaeval Studies, 1995.

Lipphardt, Walther. *Die Weisen der Lateinischen Osterspiele des 12. und 13. Jahrhunderts*. Kassel: Bärenreiter-Verlag, 1948.

Lipphardt, Walther, ed. *Lateinische Osterfeien und Osterspiele*. New York: De Gruyter, 1990. Vols V; VIII; IX.

Lohmer, Christian. *Heremi conversatio: Studien zu den monastischen Vorschriften des Petrus Damiani*. Münster: Aschendorff, 1991.

Loprete, Kimberly A. *Adela of Blois: Countess and Lord (c.1067–1137)*. Dublin: Four Courts Press, 2007.

Lutter, Christina. *Geschlecht und Wissen, Norm und Praxis, Lesen und Schreiben: Monastische Reformgemeinschaften im 12. Jahrhundert*. Vienna: R. Oldenbourg, 2005.

Lutz, Catherine. 'Emotion, Thought, and Estrangement: Emotion as a Cultural Category', *Cultural Anthropology* 1.3 (1986): 287–309.

MacDonald, A.A., H.N.B. Ridderbos, and R.M. Schlusemann, eds. *The Broken Body: Passion Devotion in Late Medieval Culture*. Groningen: Egbert Forsten, 1998.

Macy, Gary. 'Theology of the Eucharist in the High Middle Ages', in *A Companion to the Eucharist in the Middle Ages*, ed. Ian Christopher Levy, Gary Macy, and Kristen Van Ausdall. Boston: E.J. Brill, 2012, pp. 365–98.

Malegam, Jehangir. *The Sleep of Behemoth: Disputing Peace and Violence in Medieval Europe, 1000–1200*. Ithaca, NY: Cornell University Press, 2013.

Malone, Carolyn M. 'Interprétation des pratiques liturgiques à Saint-Bénigne de Dijon d'après ses coutumiers d'inspiration clunisienne', in *From Dead of Night to End of Day: The Medieval Customs of Cluny*, ed. Susan Boynton and Isabelle Cochelin. Turnhout: Brepols, 2005, pp. 221–50.

Malone, Carolyn M. 'The Rotunda of Sancta Maria in Dijon as "Ostwerk"', *Speculum* 75.2 (2000): 285–317.

Malone, Carolyn M. *Saint-Bénigne de Dijon en l'an mil, 'totius Gallie basilicis mirabilior': Interprétation politique, liturgique et théologique*. Turnhout: Brepols, 2009.

Malone, Carolyn M. *Saint-Bénigne et sa rotonde: Archéologie d'une église bourguignonne de l'an mil.* Dijon: Éditions universitaires de Dijon, 2008.

Malone, Carolyn M. 'Saint-Bénigne in Dijon as *Exemplum* of Rodulf Glaber's Metaphoric "White Mantle"', in *The White Mantle of Churches: Architecture, Liturgy, and Art around the Millennium*, ed. Nigel Hiscock. Turnhout: Brepols, 2003, pp. 161–79.

Mancia, Lauren. 'Affective Devotion and Emotional Reform at the Eleventh-Century Monastery of John of Fécamp'. PhD dissertation, Yale University, 2013.

Mancia, Lauren. '*Caritas* avant qu'elle ne devienne 'charité'', *Sensibilités* 5 (2018): 128–32.

Mancia, Lauren. 'John of Fécamp and Affective Reform in Eleventh-Century Normandy', *Anglo-Norman Studies* 37 (2015): 161–80.

Mancia, Lauren. 'Praying with an Eleventh-Century Manuscript: A Case Study of Paris, BnF, MS lat. 13593', in *Boundaries in the Medieval and Wider World: Essays in Honour of Paul Freedman*, ed. Thomas Barton, Susan McDonough, Sara McDougall, and Matthew Wranovix. Turnhout: Brepols, 2017, pp. 161–85.

Mancia, Lauren. 'Reading Augustine's *Confessions* in Normandy in the Eleventh and Twelfth Centuries', *Tabularia* 14 (2014): 195–233.

Marett-Crosby, Anthony. 'The Norman Reinvigoration', in *Monks of England*, ed. Daniel Rees. London: Society for Promoting Christian Knowledge, 1997, pp. 84–99.

Marrow, James H. *Passion Iconography in Northern European Art of the Late Middle Ages and Early Renaissance.* Kortrijk, Belgium: Van Ghemmert, 1979.

Martin, John Jeffries. *Myths of Renaissance Individualism.* New York: Palgrave Macmillan, 2004.

Martineau, Fay Anne. 'Envisioning Heaven with Faith, Imagination, and Historical Relevance: Selected Writings from Early and Medieval Christianity'. PhD dissertation, Harvard University, 2007.

Massumi, Brian. *Parables for the Virtual: Movement, Affect, Sensation.* Durham, NC: Duke University Press, 2002.

Mathon, Gérard. 'Jean de Fécamp, théologien monastique?', in *La Normandie bnédictine au temps de Guillaume le Conquérant (XIe siècle).* Lille: Facultés catholiques, 1967, pp. 485–500.

Matronola, D. Martino. *Un testo inedito di Berengario di Tours e il Concilio Romano del 1079.* Milan: Vita e Pensiero, 1936.

Matthew, Donald. *Norman Monasteries and their English Possessions.* Oxford: Clarendon Press, 1962.

Bibliography

Matthews, John, ed. *Sources of the Grail*. Hudson, NY: Lindisfarne Press, 1996.

Mayr-Harting, Henry. 'Two Abbots in Politics: Wala of Corbie and Bernard of Clairvaux', *Transactions of the Royal Historical Society* 40 (1990): 217–37.

Mazel, Florian. 'Amitié et rupture de l'amitié: Moines et grands laïcs provençeaux au temps de la crise grégorienne (milieu XI–milieu XII siècle)', *Revue historique* 307 (2005): 53–96.

McCormack, Frances. 'Those Bloody Trees: The Affectivity of Christ', in *Anglo-Saxon Emotions: Reading the Heart in Old English Language, Literature, and Culture*, ed. Alice Jorgensen, Frances McCormack, and Jonathan Wilcox. New York: Ashgate, 2015, pp. 143–61.

McEntire, Sandra J. *The Doctrine of Compunction in Medieval England: Holy Tears*. Lewiston, NY: Edwin Mellen Press, 1991.

McGinn, Bernard. *The Growth of Mysticism*. New York: Crossroad, 1991.

McGinn, Bernard. 'Mystical Consciousness: A Proposal', *Spiritus* 8 (2008): 44–63.

McGuire, Brian Patrick. 'Aelred's Attachments: Individual Growth in Community Life', in *Das Eigene und das Ganze. Zum individuellen im mittelalterlichen Religiosentum*, ed. Gert Melville and Markus Schürer. Münster: Lit Verlag, 2002, pp. 439–65.

McGuire, Brian Patrick. *Friendship and Community: The Monastic Experience, 350–1250*. Ithaca, NY: Cornell University Press, 1993.

McGuire, Brian Patrick. 'John of Fécamp and Anselm of Bec: A New Language of Prayer', in *Prayer and Thought in Monastic Tradition: Essays in Honour of Benedicta Ward SLG*, ed. Santha Bhattacharji, Rowan Williams, and Dominic Mattos. New York: Bloomsbury, 2014, pp. 153–66.

McGuire, Brian Patrick. 'Taking Responsibility: Medieval Cistercian Abbots as Their Brothers' Keepers', *Cîteaux: Commentarii Cistercienses* 39 (1988): 249–68.

McLaughlin, Megan. *Sex, Gender, and Episcopal Authority in an Age of Reform, 1000–1122*. New York: Cambridge University Press, 2010.

McNamer, Sarah. *Affective Meditation and the Invention of Medieval Compassion*. Philadelphia: University of Pennsylvania Press, 2010.

Melville, Gert. 'Der Mönch als Rebell gegen gesatzte Ordnung und religiöse Tugend. Beobachtungen zu Quellen des 12. und 13. Jahrhunderts', in *De ordine vitae. Zu Normvorstellungen, Organisationsformen und Schriftlichkeit im mittelalterlichen Ordenswesen*, ed. Gert Melville. Munster: Lit Verlag, 1996, pp. 153–86.

Melville, Gert. 'What Role Did Charity Play in Francis of Assisi's Attitude towards the Poor?', in *Aspects of Charity: Concern for One's Neighbor in Medieval Vita Religiosa*, ed. Gert Melville. Berlin: Lit Verlag, 2011, pp. 99–122.

Bibliography

Melville, Gert. *The World of Medieval Monasticism: Its History and Forms of Life*. Collegeville, MN: Liturgical Press, 2016.

Mews, Constant. 'Bernard of Clairvaux, Peter Abelard and Heloise on the Definition of Love', *Revista Portuguesa de Filosofia* 60.3 (2004): 633–60.

Miller, Maureen C. 'Reconsidering Reform: A Roman Example', in *Christianity and Culture in the Middle Ages: Essays to Honor John Van Engen*, ed. David C. Mengel and Lisa Wolverton. Notre Dame, IN: University of Notre Dame Press, 2015, pp. 123–40.

Miller, Maureen C. 'Religion Makes a Difference: Clerical and Lay Cultures in the Courts of Northern Italy, 1000–1300', *American Historical Review* 105.4 (2000): 1095–130.

Morelle, Laurent. 'Les mots de la "réforme" dans les sources diplomatiques du XIe siècle: Un premier bilan', in *Autour de Lanfranc (1010–2010): Réforme et réformateurs dans l'Europe du Nord-Ouest (XIe–XIIe siècles)*, ed. Julia Barrow, Fabrice Delivré, and Véronique Gazeau. Caen: Presses universitaires de Caen, 2015, pp. 33–55.

Morgan, Ben. *On Becoming God: Late Medieval Mysticism and the Modern Western Self*. New York: Fordham University Press, 2013.

Morin, Dom G., 'Le catalogue des manuscrits de l'abbaye de Gorze au XIe siècle', *Revue bénédictine* 22 (1905): 1–14.

Morris, Colin. *The Discovery of the Individual, 1050–1200*. Toronto: University of Toronto Press, 1987.

Morris, Colin. *The Sepulchre of Christ and the Medieval West*. New York: Oxford University Press, 2005.

Morrison, Karl Frederick. 'Framing the Subject: Humanity and the Wounds of Love', in *Studies on Medieval Empathies*, ed. Karl F. Morrison and Rudolph M. Bell. Turnhout: Brepols, 2013, pp. 1–58.

Morrison, Karl Frederick. *'I Am You': The Hermeneutics of Empathy in Western Literature, Theology, and Art*. Princeton, NJ: Princeton University Press, 1988.

Müller, Anne. 'Presenting Identity in the Cloister: Remarks on Benedictine and Mendicant Concepts of Space', in *Self-Representation of Medieval Religious Communities: The British Isles in Context*, ed. Anne Müller and Karen Stöber. Berlin: Lit Verlag, 2009, pp. 166–87.

Müller, Harald. *Päpstliche Delegationsgerichtsbarkeit in der Normandie*. 2 vols. Bonn: Bouvier, 1997.

Müller, Margit. *Am Schnittpunket van Stadt und Land: die Benediktinerabtei St. Arnulf zu Metz im hohen und späten Mittelalter*. Trier: Trierer Historische Forschungen, 1993.

Mullins, Juliet, Jenifer Ní Ghrádaigh, and Richard Hawtree, eds. *Envisioning Christ on the Cross: Ireland and the Early Medieval West*. Portland, OR: Four Courts Press, 2013.

Munns, John. *Cross and Culture in Anglo-Norman England: Theology, Imagery, Devotion*. Woodbridge: Boydell Press, 2016.

Münster-Swendsen, Mia. 'Regimens of Schooling', in *The Oxford Handbook of Medieval Latin Literature*, ed. R.J. Hexter and D. Townsend. New York: Oxford University Press, 2012, pp. 403–22.

Murray, Alexander. 'Confession before 1215', *Transactions of the Royal Historical Society* 3 (1993): 51–81.

Murray, Alexander. 'Counselling in Medieval Confession', in *Handling Sin: Confession in the Middle Ages*, ed. Peter Biller and A.J. Minnis. Woodbridge: York Medieval Press/Boydell & Brewer, 1998, pp. 63–77.

Musset, Lucien. 'Actes inédits du XIe siècle: II, une nouvelle charte de Robert le Magnifique pour Fécamp', *Bulletin de la Société des antiquaires de Normandie* 52 (1955): 142–53.

Musset, Lucien. 'La contribution de Fécamp à la reconquête monastique de la Basse-Normandie', in *L'abbaye bénédictine de Fécamp: Ouvrage scientifique du XIIIe centenaire (658–1958)*, vol. I. Fécamp: EMTN, 1959, pp. 76–9.

Musset, Lucien. 'Monachisme d'époque franque et monachisme d'époque ducale en Normandie: Le problème de la continuité', in *Aspects du monachisme en Normandie (IVe–XVIIIe siècles)*, ed. Lucien Musset. Paris: Vrin, 1982, pp. 55–74.

Musset, Lucien. 'Notules fécampoises', *Bulletin de la Société de l'histoire de Normandie* 54 (1959): 584–98.

Musset, Lucien. 'Observations sur la formation intellectuelle du haut clergé normand (v. 1050–v.1150)', in *Mediaevalia christiana, XIe–XIIIe siècles (hommage à Raymonde Foreville)*, ed. C.E. Viola. Paris: Éditions universitaires, 1989, pp. 279–89.

Musset, Lucien. 'Recherches sur les pèlerins et les pèlerinages de Normandie jusqu'à la Première Croisade', *Annales de Normandie* 12.3 (1962): 127–50.

Musset, Lucien. 'Les sepultures des souverains normands: Un aspect de l'idéologie du pouvoir', in *Autour du pouvoir ducal normand, Xe–XIIe siècles*, ed. Jean-Michel Bouvris and Jean-Marie Maillefer. Caen: Centre d'etudes normandes, 1985, pp. 19–44.

Musset, Lucien. 'La vie économique de l'abbaye de Fécamp sous l'abbatiat de Jean de Ravenne (1028–1078)', in *L'abbaye bénédictine de Fécamp: Ouvrage scientifique du XIIIe centenaire (658–1958)*, vol. I. Fécamp: EMTN, 1959, pp. 67–79, 345–9.

Nagy, Piroska. 'Au-delà du verbe: L'efficacité de la prière individuelle au moyen âge entre ame et corps', in *La prière en latin de l'antiquité au XVIe siècle*, ed. Jean-François Cottier. Turnhout: Brepols, 2006, pp. 441–71.

Nagy, Piroska. *Le don des larmes au moyen âge. Un instrument en quête d'institution (Ve–XIIIe siècle)*. Paris: Éditions Albin Michel, 2000.

Nagy, Piroska. 'Individualité et larmes monastiques: Une experience de soi ou de Dieu?', in *Das Eigene und das Ganze. Zum individuellen im mittelalterlichen Religiosentum*, ed. Gert Melville and Markus Schürer. Münster: Lit Verlag, 2002, pp. 107–29.

Nagy, Piroska. 'Larmes et eucharistie. Formes du sacrifice en Occident au moyen âge central', in *Pratiques de l'eucharistie*, ed. Nicole Bériou, Béatrice Caseau, and Dominique Rigaux. Paris: Études augustiniennes, 2005, pp. 1073–109.

Nagy, Piroska. 'Religious Weeping as Ritual in the Medieval West', *Social Analysis* 48.2 (2004): 119–37.

Nagy, Piroska, Véronique Frandon, David El Kenz, and Matthias Grässlin. 'Pour une histoire de la souffrance: Expressions, représentations, usages', *Médiévales* 27 (1994): 5–15.

Nagy, Piroska and Damien Boquet, eds. *Politiques des emotions au moyen âge*. Florence: Sismel Edizioni del Galluzzo, 2010.

Nebbiai-Dalla Guarda, D. 'Les listes médiévales de lectures monastiques. Contribution à la connaissance des anciennes bibliothèques bénédictines', *Revue bénédictine* (1930): 271–327.

Nees, Lawrence. 'On the Image of Christ Crucified in Early Medieval Art', in *Il Volto Santo in Europa: Culto e immagini del crocifisso nel Medioevo; Atti del Convegno internazionale di Engelberg (13–16 settembre 2000)*, ed. Michele Camillo Farrari and Andreas Meyer. Lucca: Istituto storico lucchese, 2005, pp. 239–304.

Newman, Barbara. 'Contemplating the Trinity: Text, Image, and the Origins of the Rothschild Canticles', *Gesta* 52.2 (2013): 133–59.

Newman, Barbara. *Medieval Crossover: Reading the Secular against the Sacred*. Notre Dame, IN: Notre Dame University Press, 2013.

Newman, Martha G. *The Boundaries of Charity: Cistercian Culture and Ecclesiastical Reform, 1098–1180*. Stanford, CA: Stanford University Press, 1996.

Nightingale, John. *Monasteries and Patrons in the Gorze Reform*. New York: Oxford University Press, 2001.

Niskanen, Samu. *The Letter Collections of Anselm of Canterbury*. Turnhout: Brepols, 2011.

North, William L. 'St. Anselm's Forgotten Student: Richard of Préaux and the Interpretation of Scripture in Twelfth-Century Normandy', in

Teaching and Learning in Northern Europe, 1000–1200, ed. Sally N. Vaughn and Jay Rubenstein. Turnhout: Brepols, 2006, pp. 170–215.

Nortier, Geneviève. *Les bibliothèques médiévales des abbayes bénédictines de Normandie: Fécamp, Le Bec, Le Mont Saint-Michel, Saint-Évroul, Jumièges, Saint-Wandrille, Saint-Ouen*. Paris: Paul Lethielleux, 1971.

Novikoff, Alex J. 'Toward a Cultural History of Scholastic Disputation', *American Historical Review* 117.2 (2012): 330–64.

O'Donnell, James J. 'Augustine: His Time and Lives', in *The Cambridge Companion to Augustine*, ed. Eleonore Stump and Norman Kretzmann. New York: Cambridge University Press, 2001, pp. 8–25.

O'Keeffe, Katherine O'Brien. *Stealing Obedience: Narratives of Agency and Identity in Later Anglo-Saxon England*. Toronto: University of Toronto Press, 2012.

Olson, Linda. 'Did Medieval English Women Read Augustine's *Confessiones*? Feminine Interiority and Literacy in the Eleventh and Twelfth Centuries', in *Learning and Literacy in Medieval England and Abroad*, ed. Sarah Rees Jones. Turnhout: Brepols, 2003, pp. 69–96.

Omont, Henri. 'Cartulaire-obituaire de la pitancerie de l'abbaye de Fécamp au XIIIe siècle', *Mélanges: Société de l'histoire de Normandie* 9 (1925): 271–80.

Omont, Henri. *Catalogue général des manuscrits – Départements*, Vols I, II. Paris: Librairie Plon, 1888.

Omont, Henri. 'L'invention du Précieux Sang dans l'église de l'Abbaye de Fécamp au XIIe siècle', *Bulletin de la Société de l'histoire de Normandie* 12 (1913): 52–66.

Otter, Monika. *Goscelin of St. Bertin: The Book of Encouragement and Consolation*, ed. and trans. Monika Otter. Cambridge: D.S. Brewer, 2004.

Oursel, M.C. 'La bibliothèque de l'abbaye de Saint-Bénigne et ses plus anciens manuscrits enluminés', *Mémoires de la Commission des Antiquités* 18 (1922–26): 112–40.

Pagden, Anthony. *The Enlightenment – And Why It Still Matters*. New York: Random House, 2013.

Parisse, Michel. *Religieux et religieuses en Empire du Xe au XIIe siècle*. Paris: Picard, 2011.

Parker, Elizabeth. 'The Descent from the Cross: Its Relation to the Extra-Liturgical Depositio Drama'. PhD dissertation, Institute of Fine Arts, New York University, 1975.

Parker, Elizabeth C. and Charles T. Little. *The Cloisters Cross: Its Art and Meaning*. New York: Abrams, 1994.

Parkes, M.B. 'Introduction', in *The Role of the Book in Medieval Culture*, ed. Peter Ganz, vol. I. Turnhout: Brepols, 1986, pp. 11–16.

Parkes, M.B. *Pause and Effect: An Introduction to the History of Punctuation in the West*. Berkeley: University of California Press, 1993.

Pastor, Martine. 'Jean de Fécamp, Un auteur sans amour-propre', *Annales du patrimoine de Fécamp* 2 (1995): 36–41.

Pattie, T.S. 'Ephraim the Syrian and the Latin Manuscripts of the *De Paenitentia*', *British Library Journal* 13 (1987): 1–27.

Paxton, Frederick. 'Performing Death and Dying at Cluny in the High Middle Ages', in *Practicing Catholic: Ritual, Body, and Contestation in Catholic Faith*, ed. Bruce T. Morrill, Susan Rodgers, and Joanna E. Ziegler. New York: Palgrave Macmillan, 2006, pp. 43–57.

Pelikan, Jaroslov. 'A First Generation Anselmian: Guibert de Nogent', in *Continuity and Discontinuity in Church History: Essays Presented to George Huntston Williams on the Occassion of His 65th Birthday*, ed. F. Forrester Church and Timothy George. Leiden: Brill, 1979, pp. 71–82.

Penco, Gregorio. 'Le "Consuetudines Fructuarienses"', in *Monasteri in alta Italia dopo le invasioni saracene e magiare (sec. X–XII)*. Turin: Deputazione Subalpina di Storia Patria, 1966, pp. 137–56.

Penco, Gregorio. 'Il movimento di Fruttuaria e la riforma Gregoriana', in *Il monachesimo e la riforma ecclesiastica (1049–1122)*. Milan: Vita e Pensiero, 1971, pp. 229–39.

Pestell, Tim. 'Monastic Foundation Strategies in the Early Norman Diocese of Norwich', *Anglo-Norman Studies* 23 (2001): 199–229.

Peters, Edward. *Heresy and Authority in Medieval Europe*. Philadelphia: University of Pennsylvania Press, 1980.

Petersen, Nils Holger. 'The Representational Liturgy of the *Regularis Concordia*', in *The White Mantle of Churches: Architecture, LIturgy, and Art around the Millennium*, ed. Nigel Hisock. Turnhout: Brepols, 2003, pp. 107–17.

Peterson, Herman. 'The Genesis of Monastic Libraries', *Libraries and the Cultural Record*. 45.3 (2010): 320–32.

Pezé, Warren. 'Aux origines de la Confession de Saint Martin', *Revue Mabillon* 86 (25 n.s.) (2014): 5–44.

Phipps, Colin. 'Romuald – Model Hermit: Eremitical Theory in Saint Peter Damian's *Vita Beati Romualdi*, Chapters 16–27', in *Monks, Hermits and the Ascetic Tradition: Papers Read at the 1984 Summer Meeting and the 1985 Winter Meeting of the Ecclesiastical History Society*, ed. W.J. Sheils. Oxford: Basil Blackwell, 1985, pp. 65–77.

Pinker, Steven. *Enlightenment Now: The Case for Reason, Science, Humanism, and Progress*. New York: Viking, 2018.

Plamper, Jan. *The History of Emotions: An Introduction*. New York: Oxford University Press, 2015.

Pohl, Benjamin and Steven Vanderputten. 'Fécamp, Cluny, and the Invention of Traditions in the Later Eleventh Century', *Journal of Medieval Monastic Studies* 5 (2016): 1–41.

Poor, Sara S. and Nigel Smith, eds. *Mysticism and Reform: 1400–1750*. Notre Dame, IN: University of Notre Dame Press, 2015.

Porée, Adolphe Andre. *Histoire de l'abbaye du Bec*. Évreux: Herissey, 1901.

Posset, Franz. 'The "Palate of the Heart" in St. Augustine and Medieval Spirituality', in *Augustine: Biblical Exegete*, ed. Frederick van Schnaubelt and Joseph C. Fleteren. New York: Peter Lang, 2001, pp. 254–7.

Potter, Julia Ann. 'The Friendship Network of the Abbey of Le Bec-Hellouin in the Eleventh and Twelfth Centuries'. PhD dissertation, University of Cambridge, 2014.

Potts, Cassandra. 'Les ducs normands et leurs nobles: Le patronage monastique avant la conquete de l'Angleterre', *Études normandes* 3 (1986): 29–37.

Potts, Cassandra. 'The Early Norman Charters: A New Perspective on an Old Debate', in *England in the Eleventh Century: Proceedings of the 1990 Harlaxton Symposium*, ed. Carola Hicks. Stamford: Paul Watkins, 1992, pp. 25–40.

Potts, Cassandra. *Monastic Revival and Regional Identity in Early Normandy*. Woodbridge: Boydell Press, 1997.

Potts, Cassandra. 'Normandy, 911–1144', in *A Companion to the Anglo-Norman World*, ed. Christopher Harper-Bill and Elisabeth van Houts. Rochester, NY: Boydell Press, 2003, pp. 19–42.

Potts, Cassandra. 'When the Saints Go Marching: Religious Connections and the Political Culture of Early Normandy', in *Anglo-Norman Political Culture and the Twelfth-Century Renaissance*, ed. C. Warren Hollister. Woodbridge: Boydell Press, 1995, pp. 15–31.

Pranger, M.B. *The Artificiality of Christianity: Essays on the Poetics of Monasticism*. Stanford, CA: Stanford University Press, 2002.

Pranger, M.B. *Bernard of Clairvaux and the Shape of Monastic Thought: Broken Dreams*. New York: E.J. Brill, 1994.

Pranger, M.B. 'Bernard the Writer', in *A Companion to Bernard of Clairvaux*, ed. Brian Patrick McGuire. Leiden: E.J. Brill, 2011, pp. 220–48.

Prentout, H. 'Le regne de Richard II duc de Normandie, 996–1027. Son importance dans l'histoire', *Mémoires de l'Academie nationale des sciences, arts et belles-lettres de Caen* 5(1929): 57–104.

Bibliography

Prochno, Joachim. *Das Schreiber- und Dedikationsbild in der deutschen Buchmalerei. 1. Teil bis zum Ende des 11. Jahrhunderts (800–1100)*. Leipzig: B.G. Teubner, 1929.

Prost, Bernard. *Le trésor de l'abbaye Saint-Bénigne de Dijon: Inventaires de 1395, 1519, 1789–1791*. Dijon: Darantière, 1894.

Quick, Kathleen. 'Men, Women, and Miracles in Normandy, 1050–1150', in *Medieval Memories: Men, Women, and the Past: 700–1300*, ed. Elisabeth van Houts. New York: Longman, 2001, pp. 53–71.

Quivy, Paul and Joseph Thiron. 'Robert de Tomblaine et son commentaire sur le Cantique des Cantiques', in *Millénaire monastique du Mont Saint-Michel*, ed. Raymonde Foreville, vol. II. Paris: Paul Lethielleux, 1967, pp. 347–56.

Radding, Charles M. 'The Geography of Learning in Early Eleventh-Century Europe: Lanfranc of Bec and Berengar of Tours Revisited', *Bullettino dell'Istituto storico italiano per il Medio Evo e archivio muratoriano* 99 (1992): 145–72.

Radding, Charles M. *A World Made by Men: Cognition and Society, 400–1200*. Chapel Hill: University of North Carolina Press, 1985.

Radding, Charles M. and Francis Newton. *Theology, Rhetoric, and Politics in the Eucharistic Controversy, 1078–1079: Alberic of Monte Cassino against Berengar of Tours*. New York: Columbia University Press, 2003.

Ramseyer, Valerie. *The Transformation of a Religious Landscape: Medieval Southern Italy, 850–1150*. Ithaca, NY: Cornell University Press, 2006.

Ranft, Patricia. *The Theology of Work: Peter Damian and the Medieval Religious Renewal Movement*. New York: Palgrave Macmillan, 2006.

Rauwel, Alain. 'Circulations liturgiques, circulations dévotes dans l'espace abbatial: Autour de Guillaume de Dijon', in *Monastères et espace social. Genèse et transformation d'un système de lieux dans l'Occident médiéval*, ed. Michael Lauwers. Turnout: Brepols, 2014, pp. 377–86.

Raw, Barbara C. *Anglo-Saxon Crucifixion Iconography and the Art of Monastic Revival*. New York: Cambridge University Press, 1990.

Reddy, William M. *The Navigation of Feeling: A Framework for the History of Emotions*. New York: Cambridge University Press, 2001.

Reilly, Diane J. *The Art of Reform in Eleventh-Century Flanders*. Boston: Brill, 2006.

Reilly, Diane J. *The Cistercian Reform and the Art of the Book in Twelfth-Century France*. Amsterdam: Amsterdam University Press, 2018.

Reilly, Diane J. 'The Cluniac Giant Bible', in *From Dead of Night to End of Day: The Medieval Customs of Cluny*, ed. Susan Boynton and Isabelle Cochelin. Turnhout: Brepols, 2005, pp. 163–89.

Reilly, Diane J. 'Education, Liturgy, and Practice in Early Citeaux', in *Understanding Monastic Practices of Oral Communication (Western Europe, Tenth–Thirteenth Centuries)*, ed. Steven Vanderputten. Turnhout: Brepols, 2011, pp. 85–115.

Reilly, Diane J. and Steven Vanderputten. 'Reconciliation and Record Keeping: Heresy, Secular Dissent, and the Exercise of Episcopal Authority in Eleventh-Century Cambrai', *Journal of Medieval History* 37 (2011): 343–57.

Renoux, Annie. *Fécamp: Du palais ducal au palais de dieu*. Paris: CNRS, 1991.

Renoux, Annie. 'Fouilles sur le site du chateau ducal de Fécamp (Xe–XIIe siècle)', *Proceedings of the Battle Conference* 4 (1981): 133–52.

Rice, Nicole. *Lay Piety and Religious Discipline in Middle English Literature*. New York: Cambridge University Press, 2008.

Riché, Pierre. 'La vie scholaire et la pédagogie au Bec au temps de Lanfranc et de Saint Anselme', in *Les mutations socio-culturelles au tournant des XIe–XIIe siècles*, ed. Raymonde Foreville. Paris: CNRS, 1984, pp. 213–27.

Ritchey, Sara. *Holy Matter: Changing Perceptions of the Material World in Late Medieval Christianity*. Ithaca, NY: Cornell University Press, 2014.

Robertson, Duncan. *Lectio Divina: The Medieval Experience of Reading*. Kalamazoo, MI: Cistercian Publications, 2011.

Robertson, Nicola. 'Dunstan and Monastic Reform: Tenth-Century Fact or Twelfth-Century Fiction', *Anglo-Norman Studies* 28 (2006): 153–67.

Rokseth, Yvonne. 'La liturgie de la passion vers la fin du Xe siècle', *Revue de Musicologie* 31.89/92 (1949): 1–58.

Romig, Andrew J. *Be a Perfect Man: Christian Masculinity and the Carolingian Aristocracy*. Philadelphia: University of Pennsylvania Press, 2017.

Rosé, Isabelle. 'Circulation abbatiale et pouvoir monastique de l'époque carolingienne au premier âge féodal (IXe–XIe siècles)', in *Des sociétés en mouvement. Migrations et mobilité au moyen âge. XLe Congrès de la SHMESP (Nice, 4–7 juin 2009)*. Paris: Publications de la Sorbonne, 2010, pp. 251–66.

Rosé, Isabelle. *Construire une société seigneuriale: Itinéraire et ecclésiologie de l'abbé Odon de Cluny (fin du IXe–milieu du Xe siècle)*. Turnhout: Brepols, 2008.

Rosé, Isabelle. 'La *Vita Gregorii Turonensis* d'Odon de Cluny. Un texte clunisien?', *Memini. Travaux et douments* 9–10 (2005–6): 191–277.

Rosenwein, Barbara. *Emotional Communities in the Early Middle Ages*. Ithaca, NY: Cornell University Press, 2006.

Rosenwein, Barbara. *Generations of Feeling: A History of Emotions, 600–1700*. New York: Cambridge University Press, 2016.

Rosenwein, Barbara. *Negotiating Space: Power, Restraint and Privileges of Immunity in Early Medieval Europe*. Ithaca, NY: Cornell University Press, 1999.

Rosenwein, Barbara. 'The Political Uses of an Emotional Community: Cluny and its Neighbors 833–965', in *Politiques des emotions au moyen âge*, ed. Piroska Nagy and Damien Boquet. Florence: Sismel Edizioni del Galluzzo, 2010, pp. 205–24.

Rosenwein, Barbara. *To Be the Neighbor of Saint Peter: The Social Meaning of Cluny's Property, 909–1049*. Ithaca, NY: Cornell University Press, 1989.

Rosenwein, Barbara. 'Worrying about Emotions in History', *American Historical Review* 107.3 (2002): 821–45.

Rosenwein, Barbara, Thomas Head, and Sharon Farmer. 'Monks and Their Enemies: A Comparative Approach', *Speculum* 66.4 (1991): 764–96.

Ross, Ellen. *The Grief of God: Images of the Suffering Jesus in Late Medieval England*. New York: Oxford University Press, 1997.

Rousseau, Dom. O. 'La rencontre de saint Ephrem et de saint Basile', *L'orient syrien: Revue trimestrielle d'études et de recherches sur les églises de langue syriaque* 2.1 (1960): 261–84.

Rubenstein, Jay. *Guibert of Nogent: Portrait of a Medieval Mind*. New York: Routledge, 2002.

Rubin, Miri. *Corpus Christi: The Eucharist in Late Medieval Culture*. New York: Cambridge University Press, 1991.

Rubin, Miri. *Mother of God: A History of the Virgin Mary*. New Haven, CT: Yale University Press, 2009.

Ruether, Rosemary Radford. *Gregory of Nazianzus: Rhetor and Philosopher*. Oxford: Clarendon Press, 1969.

Rudolph, Conrad. *Artistic Change at St-Denis: Abbot Suger's Program and the Early Twelfth-Century Controversy over Art*. Princeton, NJ: Princeton University Press, 1990.

Rudolph, Conrad. 'Bernard of Clairvaux's *Apologia* as a Description of Cluny, and the Controversy over Monastic Art', *Gesta* 27.1/2 (1988): 125–32.

Saenger, Paul. *Space between Words: The Origins of Silent Reading*. Stanford, CA: Stanford University Press, 1997.

Salmon, Pierre. *Analecta liturgica: Extraits des manuscrits liturgiques de la Bibliothèque vaticane*. Vatican City: Biblioteca Apostolica Vaticana, 1974.

Samaran, Charles and Robert Marichal, eds. *Catalogue des manuscrits en écriture latine*, vol. VII. Paris: Éditions du Centre National de la Recherche Scientifique, 1984.

Sanderson, Warren. 'Monastic Reform in Lorraine and the Architecture of the Outer Crypt, 950–1100', *Transactions of the American Philosophical Society* 61.6 (1971): 1–34.

Sansterre, Jean-Marie. 'Ermites de France et d'Italie, XIe–XVe siècle', in *Le monachisme bénédictin d'Italie et les bénédictins italiens en France face au renouveau de l'érémitisme à la fin du Xe et au XIe siècle*, ed. André Vauchez. Rome: École française de Rome, 2003, pp. 29–46.

Sansterre, Jean-Marie. 'Le moine et le miles exaltés par l'humilité du Crucifié: a propos de deux miracles racontés au XIe siècle', *Revue Belge de philologie et d'histoire* 77:4 (1999): 831–42.

Saurette, Marc Philip. 'Rhetorics of Reform: Abbot Peter the Venerable and the Twelfth-Century Rewriting of the Cluniac Monastic Project'. PhD dissertation, University of Toronto, 2005.

Scheer, Monique. 'Are Emotions a Kind of Practice (And is That What Makes Them Have a History)? A Bordieuian Approach to Understanding Emotion', *History and Theory* 51 (2012): 193–220.

Schenk, Susanne. 'Queen Matilda and Anselm's Mary Magdalene', in *Saint Anselm and His Legacy*, ed. Giles E.M. Gasper and Ian Logan. Durham: Institute of Medieval and Renaissance Studies, 2012, pp. 27–39.

Schmidt, Margot. 'Influence de saint Ephrem sur la littérature latine et allemande du début du moyen-age', *Parole de l'Orient: Revue semestrielle des études syriaques et arabes chrétiennes* 4.1 (1973): 325–41.

Schott, Gerhard. *Die Handscriften der Universitätsbibliothek München*. Wiesbaden: Harrassowitz, 2000.

Sciacca, Christine. 'The Gradual and Sacramentary of Hainricus Sacrista (Pierpont Morgan Library, M. 711): Liturgy, Devotion, and Patronage at Weingarten Abbey'. PhD dissertation, Columbia University, 2008.

Searle, Eleanor. *Predatory Kinship and the Creation of Norman Power, 840–1066*. Berkeley: University of California Press, 1988.

Şenocak, Neslihan. *Care of Souls in Medieval Italy, 600–1300*. Ithaca, NY: Cornell University Press, forthcoming.

Serralda, Vincent. 'Étude comparée de la "Confessio Fidei" attribuée à Alcuin et de la "Confessio Theologica" de Jean de Fécamp', in *Mittellatinisches Jahrbuch*, ed. Walter Beschin *et al*. Stuttgart: Anton Hiersemann, 1988, pp. 17–27.

Sharpe, Richard. 'Anselm as Author: Publishing in the Late Eleventh Century', *Journal of Medieval Latin* 19 (2009): 1–87.

Sheingorn, Pamela. *The Easter Sepulchre in England*. Kalamazoo, MI: Medieval Institute Publications, 1987.

Shoemaker, Stephen J. 'Mary at the Cross, East and West: Maternal Compassion and Affective Piety in the Earliest *Life of the Virgin* and the High Middle Ages', *Journal of Theological Studies* 62.2 (2011): 570–606.

Shopkow, Leah. *History and Community: Norman Historical Writing in the Eleventh and Twelfth Centuries*. Washington, DC: Catholic University of America Press, 1997.

Bibliography

Sicard, Patrice. *Diagrammes médiévaux et exégèse visuelle: Le 'Libellus de formation arche' de Hughes de Saint-Victor*. Paris: Brepols, 1993.

Siegmund, Albert. *Die Überlieferung der griechischen christlichen Literatur in der lateinischen Kirche bis zum zwölften Jahrhundert*. Munich: Filser-Verlag, 1949.

Sitwell, Gerard. *Spiritual Writers of the Middle Ages*. New York: Hawthorne Books, 1961.

Skutella, M. 'Der Handschriftenbestand der Confessiones S. Augustini', *Revue bénédictine* 42 (1930): 205–9.

Smith, Katherine Allan. 'Footprints in Stone: Saint Michael the Archangel as a Medieval Saint, 1000–1500'. PhD dissertation, New York University, 2004.

Smith, Katherine Allan. *War and the Making of Medieval Monastic Culture*. Woodbridge: Boydell Press, 2011.

Smoldon, Wm. L. 'The Easter Sepulchre Music-Drama', *Music and Letters* 27.1 (1946): 1–17.

Snijders, Tjamke. *Manuscript Communication: Visual and Textual Communication in Hagiographical Texts from the Southern Low Countries, 900–1200*. Turnhout: Brepols, 2015.

Somerville, Robert. 'The Case against Berengar of Tours: A New Text', in *Papacy, Councils, and Canon Law in the 11th–12th Centuries*. Aldershot: Variorum, 1990, pp. 55–75.

Sonntag, Jörg. 'Obedience in High Medieval Monastic Sources: Some Brief Remarks in Light of Ritual', in *Rules and Observance: Devising Forms of Communal Life*, ed. Mirko Breitenstein, Julia Burkhardt, Stefan Burkhardt, and Jens Röhrkasten. Berlin: Lit Verlag, 2014, pp. 253–63.

Sonntag, Jörg. 'On the Way to Heaven. Rituals of *Caritas* in High Medieval Monasteries', in *Aspects of Charity: Concern for One's Neighbor in Medieval Vita Religiosa*, ed. Gert Melville. Berlin: Lit Verlag, 2011, pp. 29–54.

Soulignac, Robert. *Fécamp et sa campagne à l'époque des ducs de Normandie: 911–1204*. Fécamp: EMTN, 1987.

Southern, Richard W. *The Making of the Middle Ages*. New Haven, CT: Yale University Press, 1953.

Southern, Richard W. *Saint Anselm and his Biographer: A Study of Monastic Life and Thought*. New York: Cambridge University Press, 1963.

Southern, Richard W. *Saint Anselm: A Portrait in a Landscape*. New York: Cambridge University Press, 1992.

Southern, Richard W. 'Sally Vaughn's Anselm: An Examination of the Foundations', *Albion* 20 (1988): 181–204.

Spear, David S. 'The Norman Empire and the Secular Clergy, 1066–1204', *Journal of British Studies* 21.2 (1982): 1–10.

Spear, David S. *The Personnel of the Norman Cathedrals during the Ducal Period*. London: Institute of Historical Research, 2006.

Spear, David S. 'The School of Caen Revisited', *Haskins Society Journal* 4 (1992): 55–66.

Spearing, A.C. *Medieval Autographies: The 'I' of the Text*. Notre Dame, IN: University of Notre Dame Press, 2012.

Spick, Louis-Marie. *Histoire de l'abbaye de St-Évroul-Notre-Dame-du-Bois*. L'Aigle: SNIEP, 1993.

Steiner, Emily. *Documentary Culture and the Making of Medieval English Literature*. New York: Cambridge University Press, 2003.

Sterk, Andrea and Nina Caputo, eds. *Faithful Narratives: Historians, Religion, and the Challenge of Objectivity*. Ithaca, NY: Cornell University Press, 2014.

Stevenson, Jane. 'The Holy Sinner: The Life of Mary of Egypt', in *The Legend of Mary of Egypt in Medieval Insular Hagiography*, ed. Erich Poppe and Bianca Ross. Portland, OR: Four Courts Press, 1996, pp. 19–50.

Sticca, Sandro. 'The Montecassino Passion and the Origin of the Late Passion Play', *Italica* 44.2 (1967): 209–19.

Stock, Brian. *After Augustine: The Meditative Reader and the Text*. Philadelphia: University of Pennsylvania Press, 2001.

Stock, Brian. *Augustine the Reader: Meditation, Self-Knowledge, and the Ethics of Interpretation*. Cambridge, MA: Harvard University Press, 1998.

Stock, Brian. *The Implications of Literacy: Written Language and Models of Interpretation in the Eleventh and Twelfth Centuries*. Princeton, NJ: Princeton University Press, 1983.

Stock, Brian. 'Reading, Writing, and the Self: Petrarch and His Forerunners', *New Literary History* 26 (1995): 717–30.

Stratford, Neil, ed. *Cluny 910–2012: Onze siècles de rayonnement*. Paris: Editions du patriomine/Centre des monuments nationaux, 2010.

Straw, Carol. *Gregory the Great: Perfection in Imperfection*. Los Angeles: University of California Press, 1991.

Straw, Carol. 'Job's Sin in the *Moralia* of Gregory the Great', in *A Companion to Job in the Middle Ages*, ed. Franklin T. Harkins and Aaron Canty. Turnhout: Brill, 2016, pp. 71–100.

Strieder, Leon. *The Promise of Obedience: A Ritual History*. Collegeville, MN: Liturgical Press, 2001.

Sullivan, Richard. 'What Was Carolingian Monasticism? The Plan of St. Gall and the History of Monasticism', in *After Rome's Fall: Narrators and Sources of Early Medieval History, Essays Presented to Walter Goffart*. Toronto: University of Toronto Press, 1998, pp. 251–87.

Sweeney, Eileen. *Anselm of Canterbury and the Desire for the Word*. Washington, DC: Catholic University of America Press, 2012.

Swift, Christopher. 'The Penitent Prepares: Affect, Contrition, and Tears', in *Crying in the Middle Ages: Tears of History*, ed. Elina Gertsman. New York: Routledge, 2011, pp. 79–101.

Szövérffy, Joseph. '"Crux Fidelis": Prolegomena to a History of the Holy Cross Hymns', *Traditio* 22 (1966): 1–41.

Taylor, Charles. *A Secular Age*. Cambridge, MA: Harvard University Press, 2007.

Thoby, Paul. *Le crucifix: Des origines au Concile de Trente*. Nantes: Bellanger, 1959.

Thomas, Owen C. 'Interiority and Christian Spirituality', *Journal of Religion* 80 (2000): 41–60.

Thompson, James Westfall. *The Medieval Library*. Chicago: University of Chicago Press, 1939.

Thompson, R.M. 'The Library of Bury St. Edmunds Abbey in the Eleventh and Twelfth Centuries', *Speculum* 47.4 (1972): 617–64.

Thompson, R.M. 'The Norman Conquest and English Libraries', in *The Role of the Book in Medieval Culture*, vol II, ed. Peter Ganz. Turnhout: Brepols, 1986, pp. 27–40.

Tilliette, Jean-Yves. 'Une lettre inédite sur le mépris du monde et la compunction du coeur adressé par Baudri de Bourgeuil à Pierre de Jumièges', *Révue des études augustiniennes* 28.3/4 (1982): 257–79.

Tock, Benoît-Michel. 'Les chartres originales de l'abbaye de Jumièges jusqu'en 1120', *Tabularia* 2 (2002): 1–19.

Tran-Duc, Lucile. 'Le culte des saints dans la Normandie médiévale (IXe–XIIe siècle). Enjeux de pouvoir dans les établissements bénédictins du diocèse de Rouen'. PhD dissertation, Université de Caen Basse-Normandie, 2015.

Tran-Duc, Lucile. 'De l'usage politique du Précieux Sang dans l'Europe médiévale', *Tabularia* 8 (2008): 89–106.

Tran-Duc, Lucile. 'Herluin, fondateur de l'abbaye du Bec: La fabrique d'un saint à l'époque de la réforme de l'église', in *Autour de Lanfranc (1010–2010): Réforme et réformateurs dans l'Europe du Nord-Ouest (XIe–XII siècles)*, ed. Julia Barrow, Fabrice Delivré, and Véronique Gazeau. Caen: Presses universitaires de Caen, 2015, pp. 227–40.

Tran-Duc, Lucile. 'Les princes normands et les reliques (Xe–XIe siècles): Contribution du culte des saints à la formation territoriale et identitaire d'une principauté', in *Reliques et sainteté dans l'espace médiéval*, ed. Jean-Luc Deuffie. Paris: PECIA, 2005, pp. 525–61.

Trocmé, Etienne. *The Passion as Liturgy: A Study in the Origin of the Passion Narratives in the Four Gospels*. London: SCM Press, 1983.

Bibliography

Truax, Jean. *Aelred the Peacemaker: The Public Life of a Cistercian Abbot*. Kalamazoo, MI: Cistercian Publications, 2017.

Turner, Denys. *The Darkness of God: Negativity in Christian Mysticism*. New York: Cambridge University Press, 1995.

Turner, Denys. *Eros and Allegory: Medieval Exegesis of the Song of Songs*. Kalamazoo, MI: Cistercian Publications, 1995.

Ugé, Karine. *Creating the Monastic Past in Medieval Flanders*. Woodbridge: York Medieval Press/Boydell & Brewer, 2005.

Unterkircher, Franz. *Inventar der illuminierten Handschriften, Inkunabeln und Frühdrucke der Österreichischen Nationalbibliothek*. Vienna: Georg Prachner Verlag, 1957.

van 't Spijker, Ineke. *Fictions of the Inner Life: Religious Literature and Formation of the Self in the Eleventh and Twelfth Centuries*. Turnhout: Brepols, 2004.

Van Engen, John. 'The "Crisis of Coenobitism" Reconsidered: Benedictine Monasticism n the Years 1050–1150'. *Speculum* 61.2 (1986): 269–305.

Van Engen, John. *Rupert of Deutz*. Los Angeles: University of California Press, 1983.

van Houts, Elisabeth. 'Edward and Normandy', in *Edward the Confessor: The Man and the Legend*, ed. Richard Mortimer. Woodbridge: Boydell Press, 2009, pp. 63–76.

van Houts, Elisabeth. *The Normans in Europe*. Manchester: Manchester University Press, 2000.

van Houts, Elisabeth. 'The Political Relations between Normandy and England before 1066 According to the *Gesta Normannorum Ducum*', in *Les mutations socio-culturelles au tournant des XIe–XIIe siècles*, ed. Raymonde Foreville. Paris: CNRS, 1984, pp. 85–98.

van Houts, Elisabeth. 'Qui étaient les Normands? Quelques observations sur des liens entre la Normandie, l'Angleterre, et l'Italie au début du XIe siècle', in *911–2011: Penser les mondes normands médiévaux. Actes du colloque international de Caen et Cerisy (29 septembre–2 octobre 2011)*, ed. David Bates and Pierre Bauduin. Caen: CRAHAM, 2016, pp. 129–46.

van Houts, Elisabeth. 'The Ship List of William the Conquerer', in *History and Family Traditions in England and the Continent, 1000–1200*. Brookfield, VT: Varorium, 1999, pp. 159–83.

van Tongeren, Louis. *Exaltation of the Cross: Toward the Origins of the Feast of the Cross and the Meaning of the Cross in the Early Medieval Liturgy*. Leuven: Peeters, 2000.

Vanderputten, Steven. 'Crises of Cenobitism: Abbatial Leadership and Monastic Competition in Late Eleventh-Century Flanders', *English Historical Review* 127.525 (2012): 259–84.

Vanderputten, Steven. *Imagining Religious Leadership in the Middle Ages: Richard of Saint-Vanne and the Politics of Reform*. Ithaca, NY: Cornell University Press, 2015.

Vanderputten, Steven. 'The Mind as Cell and the Body as Cloister: Abbatial Leadership and the Issue of Stability in the Early Eleventh Century', in *Innovationen durch Deuten und Gestalten: Klöster im Mittelalter zwischen Jenseits und Welt*. Regensburg: Schnell & Steiner, 2014, pp. 105–26.

Vanderputten, Steven. *Monastic Reform as Process: Realities and Representations in Medieval Flanders, 900–1100*. Ithaca, NY: Cornell University Press, 2013.

Vanderputten, Steven. 'Oboedientia: Réformes et discipline monastique au début du XI siècle', *Cahiers de civilisation médiévale* 53 (2010): 255–66.

Vanderputten, Steven and Tjamke Snijders. 'Echoes of Benedictine Reform in an Eleventh-Century Booklist from Marchiennes', *Scriptorium* 63.1 (2009): 77–88.

Vanommeslaeghe, Helena. 'Wandering Abbots: Abbatial Mobility and *stabilitas loci* in Eleventh-Century Lotharingia and Flanders', in *Medieval Liège at the Crossroads of Europe: Monastic Society and Culture, 1000–1300*, ed. Steven Vanderputten, Tjamke Snijders, and Jay Diehl. Turnhout: Brepols, 2017, pp. 1–28.

Vauchez, André. 'Assistance et charité en occident, XIIIe–XVe siècles', in *Domanda e consumi: Livelli e strutture (nei secoli XIII–XVIII)*, ed. Vera Barbagli Bagnoli. Florence: Olschki, 1978, pp. 151–62.

Vauchez, André. 'Du culte des reliques à celui du Précieux Sang', *Tabularia* 8 (2008): 81–8.

Vauchez, André. *La spiritualité au moyen âge occidental: VIIIe–XIIe siècles*. Paris: Presses universitaires de France, 1975.

Vaughn, Sally N. 'Anselm in Italy 1097–1100', *Anglo-Norman Studies* 16 (1987): 245–70.

Vaughn, Sally N. *Anselm of Bec and Robert of Meulan: The Innocence of the Dove and the Wisdom of the Serpent*. Berkeley: University of California Press, 1987.

Vaughn, Sally N. 'Anselm of Bec: The Pattern of His Teaching', in *Teaching and Learning in Northern Europe, 1000–1200*, ed. Sally N. Vaughn and Jay Rubenstein. Turnhout: Brepols, 2006, pp. 98–127.

Vaughn, Sally N. 'Anselm of Le Bec and Canterbury: Teacher by Word and Example, Following in the Footprints of His Ancestors', in *A Companion to the Abbey of Le Bec in the Central Middle Ages (11th–13th Centuries)*, ed. Benjamin Pohl and Laura Gathagan. Leiden: Brill, 2017, pp. 57–93.

Vaughn, Sally N. 'Anselm: Saint and Statesman', *Albion* 20 (1988): 205–20.

Vaughn, Sally N. *Archbishop Anselm, 1093–1109: Bec Missionary, Canterbury Primate, Patriarch of Another World*. Burlington, VT: Ashgate, 2012.

Vaughn, Sally N. 'Lanfranc, Anselm, and the School of Bec: In Search of the Students of Bec', in *The Culture of Christendom: Essays in Medieval History in Commemoration of Denis L.T. Bethell*, ed. Marc Anthony Meyer. London: Hambledom Press, 1993, pp. 151–81.

Vaughn, Sally N. *St. Anselm and the Handmaidens of God: A Study of Anselm's Correspondence with Women*. Turnhout: Brepols, 2002.

Vaughn, Sally N. 'The Students of Bec in England', in *Saint Anselm of Canterbury and His Legacy*, ed. Giles E.M. Gasper and Ian Logan. Durham: Institute of Medieval and Renaissance Studies, 2012, pp. 72–91.

Venard, Marc. 'Le sang du Christ: Sang eucharistique ou sang relique?' *Tabularia* 9 (2009): 1–12.

Verbender, Suzanne. *The Medieval Fold: Power, Repression, and the Emergence of the Individual*. New York: Palgrave Macmillan, 2013.

Vernet, André. *Histoire des bibliothèques françaises: Les bibliothèques médiévales du VIe siècle à 1530*. Paris: Promodis, 1988.

Vincent, Nicholas. *The Holy Blood: King Henry III and the Westminster Blood Relic*. New York: Cambridge University Press, 2001.

Viola, Coloman. 'Un célèbre prieur du XIe siècle: Saint Anselme. Contribution à l'histoire de la notion et de la fonction de prieur', in *Prieurs et prieurés dans l'occident médiéval*, ed. Jean-Loup Lemaitre. Geneva: Librarie Droz, 1987, pp. 29–47.

Violante, Cinzio. 'Le monachisme clunisien en Italie pendant l'abbatiat d'Hugues de Semur', in *Le gouvernement d'Hugues de Semur à Cluny: Actes du colloque scientifique international*. Cluny: Musée Ochier, 1988, pp. 133–48.

Violette, Louis. 'Une étape décisive dans l'éveil des activités historiographiques au service du siège de Rouen: L'episcopat de Maurille, moine de Fécamp', *Tabularia* 3 (2003): 57–67.

Von Büren, Veronika, 'Le grand catalogue de la bibliothèque de Cluny', in *Le gouvernement d'Hugues de Semur à Cluny: Actes du colloque scientifique international*. Cluny: Musée Ochier, 1988, pp. 259–60.

Vööbus, Arthur. *Literary Critical and Historical Studies in Ephrem the Syrian*. Stockholm: Etse, 1958.

Vregille, Bernard de. 'Aldewald the Scribe of Cluny and the Bible of Abbot William of Dijon', in *Cluniac Monasticism in the Central Middle Ages*, ed. Noreen Hunt. New York: Macmillan, 1971, pp. 85–97.

Wagner, Anne. 'De l'humilité de l'abbé Richard', in *Autour de la congrégation de Saint-Vanne et de Saint-Hydulphe: L'idée de réforme religieuse en Lorraine,* ed. Noëlle Cazin and Philippe Martin. Bar-le-duc: Société des lettres, sciences et arts, 2006, pp. 231–63.

Wagner, Anne. *Gorze au XIe siècle: Contribution à l'histoire du monachisme bénédictin dans l'Empire*. Turnhout: Brepols, 1996.

Waller, Katherine. 'Rochester Cathedral Library: An English Book Collection Based on Norman Models', in *Les mutations socio-culturelles au tournant des XIe–XIIe siècles*, ed. Raymonde Foreville. Paris: CNRS, 1984, pp. 237–50.

Walsh, Christine. 'The Role of the Normans in the Development of the Cult of St. Katherine', in *St. Katherine of Alexandria: Texts and Contexts in Western Medieval Europe*, ed. Jacqueline Jenkins and Katherine J. Lewis. Turnhout: Brepols, 2003, pp. 19–35.

Warren, Frederick Edward. *The Liturgy and Ritual of the Celtic Church*. Oxford: Clarendon Press, 1881.

Watkins, Priscilla D. 'Lanfranc at Caen: Teaching by Example', in *Teaching and Learning in Northern Europe, 1000–1200*, ed. Sally N. Vaughn and Jay Rubenstein. Turnhout: Brepols, 2006, pp. 70–97.

Webber, Teresa. 'Cantor, Sacrist, or Prior? The Provision of Books in Anglo-Norman England', in *Medieval Cantors and their Craft: Music, Liturgy, and the Shaping of History, 800–1500*, ed. Margot Fassler, A.B. Kraebel, and Katie Ann-Marie Bugyis. Woodbridge: York Medieval Press/Boydell & Brewer, 2017, pp. 172–89.

Webber, Teresa. 'The Diffusion of Augustine's *Confessions* in England during the Eleventh and Twelfth Centuries', in *The Cloister and the World: Essays in Medieval History in Honor of Barbara Harvey*, ed. John Blair and Brian Golding. Oxford: Clarendon Press, 1996, pp. 29–45.

Webber, Teresa. 'Monastic Space and the Use of Books in the Anglo-Norman Period', *Anglo-Norman Studies* 36 (2013): 221–40.

Webber, Teresa. 'The Patristic Content of English Book Collections in the Eleventh Century: Towards a Continental Perspective', in *Of the Making of Books: Medieval Manuscripts, Their Scribes and Readers*, ed. P.R. Robinson and Rivkah Zim. Aldershot: Scolar, 1997, pp. 191–205.

Webber, Teresa. *Scribes and Scholars at Salisbury Cathedral, c. 1075–c.1125*. Oxford: Clarendon Press, 1992.

West, Charles. 'Monks, Aristocrats, and Justice: Monastic Advocacy in a European Perspective', *Speculum* 92:2 (2017): 372–404.

White, Stephen D. *Custom, Kinship, and Gifts to the Saints: The Laudatio Parentum in Western France, 1050–1150*. Chapel Hill: University of North Carolina Press, 1988.

Williams, Watkin. 'William of Dijon: A Monastic Reformer of the Early XIth Century', *Downside Review* 52 (1944): 520–45.

Williamson, Beth. 'Sensory Experience in Medieval Devotion: Sound and Vision, Invisibility and Silence', *Speculum* 88.1 (2013): 1–43.

Wilkin, Alexis. 'Communautés bénédictines et environnement économique IXe–XIIe siècles. Réflexions sur les tendances historiographiques de l'analyse du temporel monastique', in *Ecclesia in Medio Nationis: Reflections on the Study of Monasticism in the Central Middle Ages*, ed. Steven Vanderputten and Brigitte Meijns. Leuven: Leuven University Press, pp. 101–50.

Wilmart, André. *Auteurs spirituels et textes dévots du moyen âge latin*. Paris: Librarie Bloud et Gay, 1932.

Wilmart, André. 'Le convent et la bibliothèque de Cluny vers le milieu du XIe siècle', *Revue Mabillon* 11 (1921): 87–124.

Wilmart, André. 'Deux préfaces spirituelles de Jean de Fécamp', *Revue d'ascétique et de mystique* 69 (1937): 3–44.

Wilmart, André. 'Formes successives ou parallèles des "Meditations de Saint Augustin"', *Revue d'ascétique et de mystique* 68 (1936): 337–57.

Wilmart, André. 'Jean l'homme de Dieu auteur d'un traité attribué à saint Bernard', *Revue Mabillon* 15 (1925): 5–29.

Wilmart, André. *Precum libelli quattuor aevi karolini*. Rome: Ephemerides Liturgicae, 1940.

Wilmart, André. 'Prières médiévales pour l'adoration de la croix', *Ephemerides liturgicae* 46 (1932): 22–65.

Wormald, Francis. 'The Monastic Library', in *Gatherings in Honor of Dorothy E. Miner*, ed. Ursula E. McCracken, Lilian M. C. Randall, and Richard H. Randall, Jr. Baltimore, MD: Walters Art Gallery, 1973, pp. 15–31.

Wormald, Francis and C.E. Wright, eds. *The English Library before 1700: Studies in Its History*. London: University of London, The Athlone Press, 1958.

Worthen, J.F. '"Dicta mea dicta sunt patrum": John of Fécamp's *Confessiones*', *Recherches de théologie ancienne et médiévale* 59 (1992): 111–24.

Wright, Georgia Sommers. 'A Tomb Program at Fécamp', *Zeitschrift für Kunstgeschichte* 47.2 (1984): 186–209.

Young, Karl. *The Drama of the Medieval Church*. Oxford: Clarendon Press, 1933.

Yvart, Maurice. 'Les possessions de l'abbaye de Fécamp en Angleterre', in *Les abbayes de Normandie*, ed. André Dubuc. Rouen: Lecerf, 1979, pp. 317–25.

Ziegler, Charlotte. *Liturgie und Buchkunst der Zisterzienser im 12. Jahrhundert: Katalogisierung von Handschriften der Zisterzienserbibliotheken*. New York: Peter Lang, 2000.

Bibliography

Ziegler, Charlotte and Joachim Rössl. *Zisterzienserstift Zwettl: Katalog der Handschriften des Mittelalters*. Vienna: Verlag Anton Schroll & Co., 1985. Vols I; II; III.

Zimmermann, Michel. *Écrire et lire en Catalogne (IXe–XIIe siècle)*. Madrid: Casa de Velázquez, 2003.

Zombory-Nagy, Piroska. 'Les larmes du Christ dans l'exégèse médiévale', *Médiévales* 27 (1994): 37–49.

Index

Abba Arsenius 106n.15
abbot 2-4, 10
   Anselm of Bec *see* Anselm of Bec
   authority of 85-7, 89-102
   depositio drama *see depositio* drama
   discipline 109n.52, 126, 195
   'harming to help' *see* 'harming to help'
   Lanfranc of Bec *see* Lanfranc of Bec
   lordship 92
   obedience 92, 89-102
   as pastor 116-23
   political acumen 117-18, 129-34
   second-generation reformers 61
   vicar of Christ 92, 109n.45
   William of Volpiano *see* William of Volpiano
Abelard, Peter 44, 146, 165-6, 187
Abraham and Issac 120-3, 140
Ademar of Chabannes 53
Aelred of Rievaulx 128, 138, 139, 141, 145, 167, 168, 187
affect vs. emotion 7-8
affect theory 7-8
affective devotion *see* affective piety
affective piety
   Anglo-Saxon 16n.47, 53
   Anselmian 1-8
   see also Anselm of Bec

Christus patiens see Passion of Christ
Cistercian 137, 154, 166-8
compassion 6, 93, 95-102, 110n.61, 163, 168, 176-7, 191, 194
empathy 30, 43n.93, 50, 163, 168
female 18, 31, 42n.91, 45n.114, 118, 126-9
Franciscan 167, 168, 193
gift of tears 35n.5, 52, 59, 70n.33, 170
historiography of 1-8
late medieval 154, 168-79
lay piety 133, 190n.134
Passion of Christ 29-32, 34, 48, 49-51, 53, 54, 56, 60, 61, 63, 64, 84, 85, 87, 91, 93-7, 104, 105n.5, 125, 155-7, 160-79
Southern, Richard W. 6, 15n.36, 17n.48, 145n.84, 148n.113
affectivity *see* affective piety
affectus 26-9
Agnes of Poitou 19, 20, 22, 127-9
Ambrose, Aurelius 25, 39n.51, 85, 105n.11, 106n.15, 112n.72, 139n.15
   De fuga saeculi 85
   De paradyso 106n.15
Anastasius the Venetian 72n.60, 155, 179n.3, 184n.51
   De veritate corpore et sanguine domini 155

Index

Anselm of Bec 86, 148n.113, 150n.131
  affective piety and 2–3, 6, 10, 18, 47, 53, 65
  John of Fécamp and 11n.9, 13n.23, 53, 160–4
  Prayers and Meditations 2, 20, 69n.16, 125, 160–4, 168–9, 172, 177
Arians 95–102
arma Christi 176
Arne-Dannenberg, Paul 126
Assumption 132
Athanasius of Alexandria (Saint) 52, 97–102
  Contra Arianos 97–102
Augustine of Hippo (Saint)
  Confessions
    Fécamp's copy of 66–7, 85, 103
    John's use of 23, 25, 39n.51, 40n.67, 42n.84, 47, 56, 65–7, 68n.10, 81n.174, 82n.177, 111n.70, 112n.72
    medieval reception of 52, 66–7, 126, 154, 162, 165, 172, 174
  Contra Faustum 97–102
  Contra Felicianum 100, 114n.91
  De civitate dei 105n.12, 112n.72, 115n.94
    Fécamp's copy of 85, 112n.72, 119–23, 140n.23
  Manuale of Pseudo-Augustine 172–7
    Fécamp's copy of 190n.136
  Meditations of Saint Augustine 1, 10, 172–7
  On the Correction of the Donatists 95
  Retractiones 65, 81n.172

Baudril of Bourgueil 157, 164
Bec 66, 70n.36, 72n.60, 86, 123, 126, 138n.7, 149n.128, 154, 161, 164, 169, 172, 177
  blood relic 159, 183n.40
Benedict of Aniane 46, 52
Benedict of Nursia 21, 101, 118, 162, 176
Benedictine reform *see* monastic reform
'Benedictines' 2, 4, 12n.11, 191, 192
  'blind', communal ritual 2, 92

Berengar of Tours 19, 96, 112n.72, 118, 123–6, 137, 155, 158, 182n.26
Bernard of Clairvaux 4, 10, 65, 166–8, 172, 176, 177, 178, 187n.109, 188n.120
Bestul, Thomas 137, 162
Bisson, Thomas 92, 109n.47
blood 1, 9, 29, 30, 43n.94, 49, 56, 61, 87, 89, 90, 91, 93, 94, 124, 143n.59, 172
  blood relic *see* relic of the Precious Blood of Christ
Bonaventure 176
  De perfectione vitae ad sorores 176
Bonnes, Jean-Paul 19–20, 192
Brevis relatio (Fécamp chronicle) 131, 149n.123
Brionne 125

Caesarius of Arles 59, 76n.109
Caesarius of Heisterbach 176
  Dialogus miraculorum 176
Cain and Abel 119, 139n.21
caritas 27–33, 40n.70, 41n.72, 42n.87, 83, 87, 89–96, 102, 104, 110n.61, 111n.67, 126, 155, 166–8, 177, 179, 187n.109, 192
Cassian, John 28, 41n.77, 104n.2, 106n.18
Cassiodorus, Flavius Magnus Aurelius 52, 152n.162
Choy, Renie 49
Christ *see* Jesus Christ
chronicles at Fécamp *see Brevis relatio*; Dudo of Saint-Quentin; *Libellus de revelacione*
Chrysostom, John 56, 59, 60, 73n.73, 78n.123
Cistercian piety 1, 10, 19, 35n.8, 36n.8, 137, 154, 166–8, 187n.105, 188n.120, 193
carta caritatis 167
Cluny *see also* Maiolus of Cluny; Odilo of Cluny; Odo of Cluny
  influence on John of Fécamp 62–5
  William of Volpiano and 62–5

260

Index

compassionate cruelty *see* 'harming to help'
compunction 51, 52, 56, 59, 64, 85, 106n.15, 162, 170
confessio 38n.33, 82n.178, 118
Confessio fidei (John of Fécamp) 3, 19, 20, 21, 35n.5, 36n.9, 123–6, 142n.37, 143n.58, 155, 169, 188n.118
  authenticity of 36n.9, 142n.37
Confessio theologica (John of Fécamp)
  Byzantine sources 47, 56, 72n.69, 114n.89
  Confessions of St Augustine and 10, 23, 25, 39n.43, 40n.67, 42n.84, 47, 51, 52, 56, 65–7, 81, 82, 85, 103, 106, 122, 126, 128, 154, 164–8, 172, 174, 192
  male monastic audience for 19–24
  manuscript at Bec 37n.19, 70n.36, 161, 174, 188n.118
  medicine of penance 48, 59
  medieval circulation 11n.3, 36n.15–17, 37n.19, 125, 143n.58, 152n.162, 168–77, 188n.119–122
  meditatio 52
  performative 'I' 22
  recensions of *see Confessio fidei*; *Libellus de scripturis et verbis patrum collectus ad eorum presertim utilitatem qui contemplativae vitae sunt amatores*
  wounding love *see* wounds
  see also compunction; contrition; *confessio*; *conversio*; 'dart of love'; emotional reform; Hannah; interiority; Jesus Christ; Mary Magdalene; palate of the heart; tears
Confessions see Augustine of Hippo
Constable, Giles 137
contrition 23, 38n.27, 43n.92, 51, 52, 60, 61, 63, 64, 65, 67, 85, 87, 107n.25, 118, 136, 159, 163, 170

conventio 92
conversio 18, 24, 38n.33, 66, 82n.178, 118, 133, 135, 137, 157, 162, 164, 165
Courcelle, Pierre 65
Crespin, Gilbert 164
cross *see also depositio* drama; Jesus Christ
  Adoration of the Cross 49
  devotion to 29–31, 83–5
  Exaltation of the Cross 56, 81n.167
  Invention of the Cross 56
Cuxa, Saint-Michel 37n.19

Damian, Peter 55–6, 71n.56
'dart of love' 30, 96, 102, 115n.95, 177
Davis, Robert Glenn 7
Deleuze, Gilles 7
depositio drama 86–9, 91, 106n.19, 109n.45, 160, 164, 183n.42
devotio moderna 174
discipline in the monastery 52, 63, 84, 89–102, 195
Dol 157, 164
Donatists 95–7, 111n.68, 112n.72
Dudo of Saint-Quentin 133, 147n.105, 150n.140–1
Durandus of Troarn 96, 112n.72, 123, 125, 141n.36, 155

Easter drama *see visitatio sepulchri*
Easter sepulchre 61, 86–9, 106n.19, 159, 160, 183n.42
Easter Sunday 80n.152, 86–9
emotion as an invention of the nineteenth century 17n.55
emotional reform 4, 9, 18, 23, 24, 29, 34, 46, 54, 58, 83, 89, 111n.70, 125, 137, 192, 193
Ephraem the Syrian 56, 59, 61, 67, 75n.94, 77n.118, 78n.120, 85, 119, 126, 172
  De compunctione cordis 60, 76n.105, 169–70, 188n.122
eremitic spirituality *see* hermits

261

Index

Eucharist 19, 23, 35n.7, 62, 64, 96, 113n.78, 118, 120, 123, 124, 125, 131, 133, 142n.44, 155, 158, 182n.27
   heresy of Berengar of Tours
   see Berengar of Tours
Evreux 122, 137, 179n.4

Faustus the Manichean 97-102, 115n.94
Fécamp abbey
   archaeology 4, 13n.22, 181n.22
   architecture xix, 4, 13n.22, 130, 146-7n.105
   blood relic 4, 143n.59, 149n.124, 156, 157-60, 177, 181-2n.19-30
   charters 3, 4, 57, 132, 147n.110, 149n.125-7
   chronicles *see Brevis relatio*; *Libellus de revelacione*
   donations to the abbey 129-34
   ducal palace and xix, 130
   economic holdings 12n.24, 129-34, 138n.9
   education at the monastery 47-54
   etymology of 158
   exemption for 4, 12n.18, 129, 134, 147n.111, 151n.151, 181n.21
   Norman conquest and 4, 12n.15, 149n.122
   Norman dukes and 3, 9, 53, 56, 57, 130, 129-34, 146n.105, 147n.108, 149n.122, 151n.151, 157, 181n.23
   pilgrimage to 122, 157, 181n.22
   relic to Mary Magdalene 33, 44n.108, 87, 108n.31
   school for priests 58, 122, 132, 149n.128
Franciscan piety 1, 167, 168, 193
Fruttuaria 61, 75n.89, 79n.131, 81n.161, 105n.7, 106n.19, 107n.26, 108n.33
Fulton, Rachel 31, 137

Gelduin of Mont Saint-Michel 100
Geoffrey of Vendôme 92

Gerbert of Saint Wandrille 9, 159, 163, 177, 180n.8
   Scriptura 154-7, 180n.8, 182n.27, 183n.33
Gerson, Jean 174
Glaber, Rodulfus 58, 74n.79, 75n.88, 122, 131, 133, 140n.27, 148n.116, 150n.135, 183n.40
Glastonbury 125, 143n.59
   blood relic 159, 182n.25, 183n.34
Good Friday drama *see depositio* drama
Gorze 2, 60, 77n.120, 106n.19, 107n.26, 138n.9, 150n.134
Goscelin of Saint Bertin 67, 128, 145n.87, 165, 186n.88
grace 8, 24, 28, 32, 52, 53, 54, 93, 124, 159, 165, 176
Gregorian reform *see* monastic reform
Gregory of Nazianzus 56
Gregory the Great 9, 124
   Moralia in Job 47, 51-2, 63, 70n.27, 82n.178, 116, 132
   Pastoral Care 116-23
Guibert of Nogent 154, 177, 184n.49, 193
   Monodies 160-6, 186n.89-96
Guitmund of Aversa 123

habitus 5, 86
Hallinger, Kassius 64
Hamburger, Jeffrey 174, 176, 177
Hannah 8, 24, 29, 31-4, 43, 44, 45, 47, 56, 68, 73n.76, 83, 85, 90, 102, 105n.12, 108n.38, 172, 179, 192
'harming to help' 89-102, 110n.61, 177
Henry of Sully 159
Herbert Losinga 159, 182n.30
heresy *see* Arians; Donatists
Herluin of Bec 72n.60, 164, 186n.84
hermits 12n.14, 47, 55, 56, 59, 71n.54, 72n.59-62, 78n.124, 89, 91, 93, 94, 95, 96, 102, 111, 122, 127, 130, 132, 155, 167, 180n.5, 188n.124
Hildebert of Lavardin 92

Index

Hilgarth, Jocelyn 119
history of emotions 7-8, 10, 14n.27, 15n.35, 16n.44-47, 17n.50-56, 18, 26-9, 38n.26, 41n.78, 161, 164, 169
Hollywood, Amy 23, 93
homilies at Fécamp 9, 42n.91, 56, 59, 60, 61, 62, 63, 73n.75, 76n.109, 77n.114, 78n.123, 79n.141, 80n.152, 81n.159, 84-5, 86, 88, 89, 92, 102, 104n.1, 108n.32, 112n.72, 113n.80, 140n.122, 145n.85, 176
Hugh of Saint-Victor 172

individual 2, 6, 22-5, 55, 59, 64, 132, 137, 166, 174, 186n.102
   'discovery of the individual' historiography 5-6, 15n.36-16n.39, 150n.133, 162, 194-6
   interiority 18, 24-6, 29, 31, 32, 47, 52, 53, 54, 55, 56, 59, 60, 63, 64, 67, 83, 89, 91, 102, 104, 109n.41, 111n.70, 118, 122, 124, 129, 137, 159, 163, 192, 193, 194, 195
Iogna-Prat, Dominique 133
Isidore of Seville 52, 59, 75n.94, 76n.98, 104n.3
Ivo of Chartres 164

Jerome (Saint), Eusebius Sophronius 24, 112n.72
Jerusalem, pilgrimage to 53, 132
Jesus Christ *see also* affective piety; *depositio* drama
   Christus Pastor 119, 120, 122
   crucified, suffering 1, 2, 6, 7, 8, 9, 10, 27, 29-31, 48, 49, 50, 51, 53, 54, 56, 60, 64, 68, 84, 85, 91, 92, 94, 102, 104, 117, 155, 156, 157, 159, 160, 163, 166-8, 169, 172, 176, 177
   deposition *see depositio* drama
   empathy 50, 64, 163, 168
   humanity 34, 94, 102, 104, 193, 194n.72
Job *see* Gregory the Great
John of Reims 155
John of Salerno 63
John the Evangelist 101, 170
jongleurs at Fécamp 157, 158, 181n.18
Joseph of Arimathea 158, 160, 183n.33
Jumièges 66, 80n.151, 82n.181, 148n.119, 165, 186n.87

La Chaise-Dieu 162
Lament for Lost Solitude (John of Fécamp) 35, 80n.7, 134-6, 137, 152n.162
Lanfranc of Bec 47, 56, 72n.58, 86, 106n.16, 123, 125, 141n.35, 143n.54, 149n.128, 151n.155, 161
Lazarus 63
Leclercq, Jean 19, 20, 64, 137, 192
Lecouteux, Stéphane 59
lectio divina 5, 35, 38n.25, 41n.77, 51, 69n.14, 168, 179
Lent 85, 103
Letter, *Ad monachos dyscolos* (John of Fécamp) 89-93
Letter, *Tuae Quidem* (John of Fécamp) 126-9
Letter to the abbot of Saint-Berthe of Blagny (John of Fécamp) 134
Letter to the anonymous nun (John of Fécamp) 19, 112n.76, 126-9, 189n.128
Letter to the bishop William of Evreux (John of Fécamp) 122, 137, 179n.4
Letter to the Empress Agnes (John of Fécamp) 19, 20, 22, 126-9, 135, 144n.79, 183n.40
letters in the Middle Ages 36n.15, 37n.20, 144n.68

Index

Leo IX (Pope) 123, 182
   John of Fécamp as papal legate 3, 122
   Letters between Leo IX and John 134, 141n.26
libelli precum 46, 47, 48–50, 69n.15, 70n.23
Libellus de revelacione 57, 74n.86, 75n.88, 151n.151, 181n.21
Libellus de scripturis et verbis patrum collectus ad eorum presertim utilitatem qui contemplativae vitae sunt amatores (John of Fécamp) 3, 19, 21, 22, 35n.5, 36n.15, 37n.22, 42n.90, 43n.96, 44n.109, 110n.56, 123, 145n.85, 169, 188n.118
liturgical customs at Fécamp
   comparable liturgies 86, 87, 106n.19, 106n.21
   liturgical manuscripts 107n.26
   William of Volpiano and 57, 61, 193
   see also Assumption; *depositio* drama; Easter sepulchre; Nativity; Purification of the Virgin; *Quem quaeritis*; *visitatio sepulchri*
longing for the divine 9, 13n.23, 21, 29, 32, 44n.104, 47, 48, 52, 60, 65, 68, 73n.78, 112n.76, 117, 129, 135, 145n.88, 151n.155, 177, 185n.60, 194
Lucca blood relic 159, 181n.24, 183n.33
Ludolfus of Saxony 2
Lyre 66, 82n.183

Maiolus of Cluny 55, 57, 62, 64, 74n.79, 75n.88, 79n.139, 81n.162, 127, 144
Manicheans 96, 98, 115n.94
Manuale of Pseudo-Augustine *see* Augustine of Hippo
manuscripts from Fécamp's library
   Barcelona, Ripoll ms. 214 viii, 36n.17, 37n.19, 170
   BnF ms. lat. 1684 viii, 97, 106n.15
   BnF ms. lat. 1714 58, 62, 63, 75n.94, 76n.106, 77n.118, 78n.120, 105n.13
   BnF ms. lat. 1919 19, 35n.3, 36n.17, 152n.162, 187n.105, 188n.120
   BnF ms. lat. 2055 105n.12, 112n.72, 119, 140n.22
   BnF ms. lat. 2079 73n.76, 97, 99, 100, 112n.72
   BnF ms. lat 3088 19, 21, 35n.7, 37n.19, 144n.68, 152n.162, 188n.118
   BnF ms. lat 5290 62, 79n.145
   BnF ms. lat. 13593, 36n.16, 37n.19, 70n.36, 145n.85, 174, 188n.118, 189n.130
   Metz, Médiathèque ms. 245, 36n.16, 37n.19, 61, 69n.16, 108n.31, 142n.45, 174, 188n.118, 189n.127
   Montpellier, Bibliothèque interuniversitaire, ms. H309 36n.16, 37n.19, 125, 188n.118
   paleography of 4
   Rouen, BM ms. 1400 62
   Rouen, BM ms. 1404 62, 79n.141, 81n.159
   Vienna, Österreichische Nationalbibliothek, Cod. 1580 36n.17, 169, 170n.105, 188n.121
   Vienna, Österreichische Nationalbibliothek, Cod. 1582 36n.17, 169, 170, 188n.121
   Zwettl, Stiftsbibliothek, Cod. 164, viii, 36n.17, 144n.68, 145n.82, 170, 172, 189n.128
Martha 32
Mary *see* Virgin Mary
Mary Magdalene 163, 172, 179, 192
   Confessio theologica 8, 24, 29, 31–4, 41n.74, 43n.106–45n.114, 56, 61–5, 68, 80n.148–156, 81n.159–161, 83, 87, 89, 102, 108n.134, 155, 163, 172, 179, 192
Mary of Egypt 59, 60, 63, 77n.114, 78n.125
Marys, at the tomb 87–9, 108n.31
Massumi, Brian 7, 17n.52
Matilda of Tuscany 161

Index

Maundy Thursday 89
Maurilius of Rouen 9, 122, 125, 137, 159, 161, 179, 180n.4, 184n.59, 189n.129
  Oratio ad sancta Mariam 155
McGinn, Bernard 137
McNamer, Sarah 11n.6, 17n.50, 36n.15, 38n.25, 145n.83-4
Meditations of Saint Augustine see Augustine of Hippo
Melchisedech 115n.94, 119, 120, 121, 122, 140n.22
mendicants *see* Franciscan piety
monachos dyscolos see letter, *Ad monachos dyscolos*
monastic discipline *see* discipline in the monastery
monastic reform *see also* Cistercian piety
  'crisis of coenobitism' 4, 14n.29, 71, 139n.12
  customs and rules 2, 3, 10, 46, 47, 55, 58-65, 67, 75n.95, 79n.129, 86, 106n.19, 107n.26, 118, 126, 132, 149n.124, 181n.22, 182n.30
  emotional reform 4, 9, 18, 22-9, 32, 33, 34, 54, 56, 83, 89, 91, 102, 103, 111n.70, 192-5
  historiography of 14n.25-6, 15n.32, 136-8
Mont Saint-Michel 71n.54, 72n.60, 73n.70, 100, 107n.26, 114n.89, 119, 139n.20, 143n.65, 155, 179n.3
Montivilliers 128
Morrison, Karl 93

Nativity 132
Nicodemus 156, 158, 160, 182n.27, 183n.33, 184n.45
Nogent-sous-Coucy 161
Norman dukes 9, 57, 131, 132, 133, 146n.105, 147n.108, 149n.149, 158
Norwich 107n.21, 159, 182n.30, 183n.32
Notre-Dame-aux-Nonnais 128
novices 46, 55, 62, 84-5, 92, 104n.1-2, 120

obedience in the monastery 55, 58, 62, 64, 89-95, 102, 103, 109n.52, 110n.52, 134, 140n.22, 145n.88, 151n.148, 170, 194, 196n.6
Odilo of Cluny 53, 62, 63, 64, 74n.85, 79n.139, 81n.163, 107n.21
Odo of Cluny 62-5, 67, 79n.139, 80n.146, 122
  Occupatio 63, 79n.144
Ordericus Vitalis 141n.36, 179, 183n.33

palate of the heart 23-6, 39n.53, 112n.76, 129
passiones 8
pastoral care 116-23, 126, 127, 128, 129, 130, 136, 138n.2, 140n.28, 141n.28, 146n.95, 149n.126, 152n.161, 195
Paul of Saint Père de Chartres 100
penance 5, 48, 49, 51, 53, 59, 60, 61, 63, 64, 81n.164, 85, 127, 132
Peter of Blois 64, 81n.165
Peter of Jumièges 165
Peter the Venerable 133
Phipps, Colin 55
Pilate, Pontius 160, 184n.45
Précieux-Sang, relic of *see* relic of the Precious Blood of Christ
Premonstratensian 19, 188n.120
prior 3, 11n.8, 18, 19, 20, 35n.3, 46, 55, 57, 59, 62, 67, 86, 115n.99, 159, 161, 165
psalms xv, 23, 41, 46, 47-50, 57, 68n.10, 69, 114n.89, 128
Purification of the Virgin 132

Quem quaeritis 79n.129, 87, 89, 107n.26

Ravenna 9, 23, 46, 47, 51, 54-7, 65, 67, 68, 71n.54, 96, 120-2, 140n.25, 188n.124, 192
Reddy, William 7, 17, 38n.26
reform, monastic *see* monastic reform

265

Index

relic of the Precious Blood of Christ 143n.59, 149n.124, 156–60, 177, 181n.20–184n.46
Renaissance humanism 194
Richard I of Normandy (Duke) 130–4, 146n.105, 149n.124, 157, 158, 181n.22
Richard II of Normandy (Duke) 3, 53, 56, 57, 58, 130–4, 147n.108, 149n.124, 151n.151
Richard of Saint Vanne 53, 54
Richard of Saint-Victor 24
Ripoll 37n.19, 170, 188n.124
Robert of Saint-Quentin 164
Robert of Tomblaine 161, 184n.47
Robert of Torigny 92
Robertson, Duncan 137
Romuald of Ravenna 55–7, 60, 67, 71n.54, 72n.57, 76n.102, 122, 188n.124
Rosenwein, Barbara 8, 14n.27, 15n.33, 17n.56, 38n.29, 40n.69
Rothschild Canticles 115n.95, 174–7, 190n.137–50
Rouen 9, 56, 134, 137, 155, 159
Rubenstein, Jay 165, 186n.89–90
Rule of Saint Basil 59, 60, 76n.107, 77n.120, 78n.124
Rule of Saint Benedict (RB) 20–1, 23, 28, 41n.76, 42n.92, 46, 55, 57, 58, 62, 75n.88, 90–3, 95–6, 102, 103, 105n.6, 109n.45, 110n.61, 115n.100, 122, 134, 137, 139n.11, 141n.31, 149n.129

Saenger, Paul 52
Saint-Arnoul in Metz 37n.37, 57, 60, 61, 77n.120, 79n.131, 143n.65, 169
Saint-Bénigne de Dijon 3, 9, 37n.19, 46, 51, 54, 55, 59, 61, 62, 67, 71n.53, 74n.79, 75n.89, 79n.127, 80n.146, 106n.19, 111n.63, 115n.99, 125, 126, 130, 143n.57, 144n.79, 148n.116, 169, 187n.105, 192
Saint-Berthe of Blagny 134, 144n.66
Saint-Etienne in Caen 86
Saint-Evroult 66, 72n.60, 155
Saint-Germer-de-Fly 67, 161
Saint-Ouen 66, 82n.182, 107n.26
Saint-Wandrille 9, 13n.19, 72n.60, 100, 114n.85, 154, 155, 159, 163, 177, 180n.8, 182n.27, 183n.33
Sant'Apollinare in Clase viii, 54, 55, 56, 73n.72, 120, 121, 130
see also novices; Romualdus of Ravenna
Scheer, Monique 15n.35, 41n.78
self-awareness *see* individual
sermons *see* homilies at Fécamp
Shenoute 92, 109n.49
Sinai 56
Smaragdus of Saint-Mihiel 46, 52, 75n.94, 76n.99, 170, 172, 188n.122, 189n.127
 Diadema monastica 58, 59, 60, 68n.2, 75n.94, 76n.99, 77n.119, 85, 169
 Expositio in regulam sancti Benedicti 75n.94, 76n.98
Song of Songs 30, 41n.72, 42n.91, 46, 161, 174, 176, 190
 see also 'dart of love'
Southern, Richard W. *see* affective piety
students of John of Fécamp *see* Anselm of Bec; Durandus of Troarn; Gerbert of Saint-Wandrille; Herbert Losinga; Maurilius of Rouen; Robert of Tomblaine
suffering *see* affective piety
Summe sacerdos (John of Fécamp) 142n.45
Symeon the New Theologian 56

tears 1, 16n.44, 23, 25, 26, 27–34, 35n.5, 41n.78, 43n.92, 48, 50–3, 55, 56, 60–4, 66, 70n.33, 73n.77, 77n.116, 78n.121, 84, 85, 87, 89, 93, 94, 106, 112n.76, 125, 127, 136, 155,

Index

159, 162, 169, 170, 172, 180n.13, 183n.40, 190, 191
see also affective piety
Theodore of Mopsuestia 59
Third Lateran Council 167
Thomas à Kempis 2, 174
tonsure 89, 98, 99, 101, 170, 171
Troyes 19, 36n.17, 128, 143n.58, 187n.105, 188n.120
Tuae Quidem letter *see* Letter, *Tuae Quidem*
Turin 96
twelfth-century Renaissance 15n.36, 194

Vanderputten, Steven 61
Vigilius Tapensis 97, 113n.81
  De Trinitate 97
Virgin Mary 31, 49, 50, 64, 73n.69, 183n.34, 189n.129
visitatio sepulchri 79n.129, 107n.26, 108n.35, 130
Vulfran of Saint-Wandrille 100, 114n.85
vulnera see wounds

Warin of Metz 96-7, 101, 113n.78, 126, 167
weeping *see* tears
White Monastery, Egypt 92
William of Volpiano 3, 4, 7, 9, 12n.13, 21, 37n.19, 46, 47, 55, 57-62, 63, 67, 71n.54, 74n.79, 75n.88, 76n.97, 78n.128, 79n.127, 81n.161, 86, 96, 105n.7, 106n.19, 107n.26, 111n.63, 115n.97, 122, 126, 140n.27, 144n.72, 150n.134, 161, 170, 181n.23, 184n.47, 188n.124, 189n.124
William the Conquerer 2, 12n.15, 103, 125, 134, 137, 146n.105, 149n.122, 151n.149
  Ship List 2, 149n.122
Wilmart, André 2, 19, 20, 191
wounding *see* wounds
wounds 1, 18, 27, 30, 31, 39n.46, 41n.72, 42n.91, 43n.92, 48, 49, 50, 60, 69n.11, 70n.28, 78n.121, 83, 84, 93, 94, 102, 125, 159, 167, 172, 175-7, 189n.125, 190n.143, 192
  ostentatio vulnerorum 176